PERSUASION, REFLECTION, JUDGMENT

STUDIES IN CONTINENTAL THOUGHT
John Sallis, editor

Consulting Editors

Robert Bernasconi
John D. Caputo
David Carr
Edward S. Casey
David Farrell Krell
Lenore Langsdorf

James Risser
Dennis J. Schmidt
Calvin O. Schrag
Charles E. Scott
Daniela Vallega-Neu
David Wood

PERSUASION, REFLECTION, JUDGMENT

Ancillae Vitae

Rodolphe Gasché

Indiana University Press
Bloomington and Indianapolis

This book is a publication of

Indiana University Press
Office of Scholarly Publishing
Herman B Wells Library 350
1320 East 10th Street
Bloomington, Indiana 47405 USA

iupress.indiana.edu

© 2017 by Rodolphe Gasché

All rights reserved
No part of this book may be reproduced or utilized in any form or by any means, electronic or mechanical, including photocopying and recording, or by any information storage and retrieval system, without permission in writing from the publisher. The Association of American University Presses' Resolution on Permissions constitutes the only exception to this prohibition.

The paper used in this publication meets the minimum requirements of the American National Standard for Information Sciences—Permanence of Paper for Printed Library Materials, ANSI Z39.48-1992.

Manufactured in the United States of America

Library of Congress Cataloging-in-Publication Data

Names: Gasché, Rodolphe, author.
Title: Persuasion, reflection, judgment : Ancillae Vitae / Rodolphe Gasché.
Description: Bloomington : Indiana University Press, 2017. | Series: Studies in Continental thought | Includes bibliographical references and index.
Identifiers: LCCN 2016055936 (print) | LCCN 2017008457 (ebook) | ISBN 9780253025531 (cl : alk. paper) | ISBN 9780253025708 (pb : alk. paper) | ISBN 9780253025852 (eb)
Subjects: LCSH: Phenomenology. | Aristotle. | Persuasion (Rhetoric) | Heidegger, Martin, 1889–1976. | Arendt, Hannah, 1906-1975. | Judgment.
Classification: LCC B829.5 .G37 2017 (print) | LCC B829.5 (ebook) | DDC 110—dc23
LC record available at https://lccn.loc.gov/2016055936

1 2 3 4 5 22 21 20 19 18 17

CONTENTS

vii Acknowledgments

1 Introduction

Part I. Persuasion (Aristotle)

13 1. A Truth Resembling Truth

26 2. Necessity or Probability

44 3. *Logos, Topos, Stoikheion*

Part II. Reflection (Heidegger)

73 4. Breaking with the Primacy of the Theoretical

88 5. The Genesis of the Theoretical

104 6. Beyond Theory: *Theoria*, or Watching Over What Is Still to Come

Part III. Judgment (Arendt)

145 7. The Space of Appearance

169 8. The Wind of Thought

184 9. A Sense of the World

223 Notes

251 Bibliography

257 Index

ACKNOWLEDGMENTS

THE FIRST THREE CHAPTERS of this book correspond to a three-day seminar on Aristotle's *Rhetoric* that I conducted in 2008 at the University of Chile in Santiago. These lectures were published in 2010 in book form in a Spanish translation under the title *Un arte muy frágil: Sobre la retórica de Aristóteles* by Metales Pesados Libros (Santiago, Chile). I thank Rogelio Gonzalez for his translation and, above all, Pablo Oyarzun for the generous *Prologue* with which he prefaced the book. The original English version of Chapter 3 has been published under the title Λόγος, Τόπος, Στοιχεῖον in *Internationales Jahrbuch für Hermeneutik*, ed. G. Figal, Tübingen; Mohr Siebeck, 2009, pp. 147–169. Chapter 4 in the section on Heidegger's conception of theory and reflection is the Andrew Schuwer Lecture that I gave in 2009 on the occasion of the Annual Conference of the Society for Phenomenology and Existential Philosophy in Arlington, Virginia. It has been published under the title "The Duplicity of the Theoretical: On Heidegger's First Freiburg Lectures" in *Research in Phenomenology*, 40, 1, 2010, pp. 3–19. I thank Koninklijke Brill NV for the permission to republish this essay. Chapter 5 is based on the paper I presented at an international conference on "TheorieTheorie" at the Interuniversity Center in Dubrownik, Croatia, in 2009. A first version of it was published in German under the title "Nur Hinsehen oder hütendes Schauen? Zu Heideggers 'lebensweltlicher' Begründung der Theorie" in *TheorieTheorie: Wider die Theoriemüdigkeit in den Geisteswissenschaften*, eds. M. Grizelj and O. Jahraus, Munich: Wilhelm Fink, 2011, pp. 417–431. Two three-day seminars on Heidegger's conception of theory, one at the Centro de Filosofia das Ciências at the University of Lisbon in 2009, the other at the University of Chile, Santiago, made it possible to finalize the texts that now make up the second section. Some of the chapters from the last section of the book, devoted to the question of judgment in Hannah Arendt, have been delivered as talks on several occasions. Versions of what has now become Chapter 8 have been presented as talks at the Graduate Center (CUNY), at the Goethe Universität in Frankfurt/Main, Germany, at Roanoke College (on the occasion of the annual meeting of The North American Society for Philosophical Hermeneutics in 2014), and at the University of Tokyo, Japan (also in 2014). Part of Chapter 9 was the subject of a talk at the Cardozo Law School, New York, on the occasion of a conference in 2012 on Kant's *Critique of Judgment*. It has been published under the title "Is a Determinant Judgment Really a Judgment?" in *Washington University Jurisprudence Review*, 6, 1, 2013, pp. 99–120.

PERSUASION, REFLECTION, JUDGMENT

INTRODUCTION

EACH OF THE THREE SECTIONS of this book—on persuasion in Aristotle, reflection (*Besinnung*) in Martin Heidegger, and judgment in Hannah Arendt—comes with its own introduction. Each section can, thus, be read on its own and without regard for the order in which it is presented. Yet, apart from the fact that the order in which these studies follow one another is chronological, the essays, though they do not explicitly build upon or derive from one another, are interrelated in many ways and, ultimately, pursue one question, one major concern. These prefatory remarks, which I keep to a minimum, are intended to explain this common concern and to sketch out, however schematically, the ways in which the essays might relate to one another.

Let me start with the subtitle of the book. *Ancillae Vitae* suggests that the topics explored in the three studies that it comprises, namely, on persuasion, reflection, and judgment, are ancillary to 'life.' They are held to be the maidservants or the handmaidens of life or, rather, of a certain understanding of life. I borrow the expression from Hannah Arendt, who, in her essay "Karl Jaspers: Citizen of the World," qualifies Jaspers's philosophy as one that "has lost both its humility before theology and its arrogance toward the common life of man. It has become *ancilla vitae*."[1] In other words, Arendt introduces the expression to distinguish the role of philosophy in Jaspers's thought from that assigned to philosophy in the Patristic and Scholastic tradition that took philosophical thought to be *ancilla theologiae*. In conformity with the Patristic tradition, which considered Christian wisdom the mistress of philosophy, Petrus Damiani coined the term *ancilla theologiae* when faced with an internal debate in Christianity in which the partisans of dialectics, or philosophy, claimed that only rational argumentation could decide questions of faith. Even though Scholasticism interprets the ancillary role of philosophy in a more positive light later on—holding philosophy's autonomy to be the inevitable condition for it to be able to provide theological thought with the required universal and formal principles—philosophy remains dependent on theology inasmuch as the ultimate ground of the conditions of cognition is considered to lie with revelation.[2]

Jaspers himself does not resort to the term in question to characterize his own thought, but Arendt justifies her use of it as a way to interpret his conception, not of a life of thought or of a life dedicated exclusively to thinking, but of a "thinkingly (lived) life [*denkerisches Leben*]," a life lived in a constant interchange with thought.[3] Arendt points out that thinking is understood here as "a kind of practice between men, not a performance of one individual in his self-chosen solitude."[4] It is thus a thinking that is not aloof with respect to common life but, rather, immanent to it. If this is so, furthermore, it is because what Jaspers considers to be the common life of man is itself not void of all forms of thinking. In any event, a thinkingly lived life is not 'practical' simply in a pragmatic sense, as if it were the application of some theory; rather, it is practical insofar as it is intrinsically tied to the historical and political furtherance of what Jaspers calls "limitless communication" between the living (but between the living and the dead, as well). As is clear from Arendt's essay, the context for both her and Jaspers's conception of thinking and philosophy insofar as it is at the service of life is Kant's *The Conflict of the Faculties*. Kant, in that work, is still somewhat willing to concede an ancillary relation of philosophy to the higher faculty of theology—as long as it can keep its autonomy and its commitment to truth—and observes that the question remains of whether philosophy "carries the torch in front of her lady [rather] than her train behind."[5] Arendt, however, leaves no doubt that philosophy can become *ancilla vitae* only on the condition that it is she who carries the torch and that the torch is that of thought.[6] Indeed, the expression *ancilla vitae* signifies a radical turn away from all theological and religious concerns and an emphasis on life here and now, not an otherworldly life but an exclusively worldly life. Furthermore, the life that philosophy serves is ordinary life—"the common life of man"—a life from which thought is not absent, as a certain philosophy holds. To refer to philosophy as *ancilla vitae* is, thus, not only to emphasize that it is at the service of common life, and of what within this life itself is a thinking concern with life, but also to advocate a kind of philosophy different from the one that is primarily concerned with universal principles and rules for rational argumentation. The philosophy ancillary to life in the sense of thoroughly worldly life is one that reaches back to Aristotle's conception of practical–ethical and political–philosophy where, as we will see in the three chapters devoted to Aristotle's *Rhetoric*, the concern is no longer with the absolute Good but with the only good for which humans can hope in the sublunar world and where the criteria for truth and precision are not as rigorous as they are in the exact science of metaphysics. To call philosophy the handmaiden of life is, therefore, also to advocate a different status for her. Whereas the *ancilla theologiae* was an *ancilla dominae*, at the service of her mistress, the torch-bearing *ancilla vitae* is no longer under the dominion of anything or anyone in that the philosophy that she advocates is in a way life itself, if the life in question is a life that is lived in a thinking and thoughtful manner. The philosophy that she represents is not exterior to life but, rather, immanent to it, if life is life lived in a practical, ethical, and political manner.

The topics explored in this book—persuasion, reflection, and judgment—are understood as fundamental aspects of a philosophy that is at the service of worldly life, a life, more precisely, in the world constituted by the in-between of human beings. To characterize this world and the life that makes it up as worldly is not to suggest that it is secular life, that is, a life (and a life-world) that, in spite of all its down-to-earth attributes, remains a shadow of the other-world. If persuasion, reflection, and judgment are in an ancillary position to the worldly life in a world that, ultimately, is thought to be on this side of the divide between the religious and the profane—at times I will refer to it as radically secular—it is because without them there is no such thing as public or political life. They are minimal building blocks, as it were, of worldly, public, or political life. But the reference to them as *ancillae vitae* serves to make a further point; namely, these activities are not constitutive in a technical sense of the worldly realm. Even though worldly life is not imaginable without them, persuasion, reflection, and judgment are only fundamental aids in setting up and securing the public and political realm. The distinction between constituting principles and the constituted or, more generally, between the transcendental and the empirical is, perhaps, no longer pertinent in a domain that is not only irreducible to the practical realization of some prior theoretical insights but also, as we will see, characterized by extreme ontological fragility. In other words, as regards its possibility, the opening up of the political and public realm cannot simply fall back on a mode of thought that is the highlight of theoretical philosophy. Even the most political activities characteristic of the public realm are fragile to such a point that they cannot be raised to the status of constitutive principles. Notwithstanding the necessity of persuasion, reflection, and judgment in the public domain, they are, to put it bluntly, not necessary enough to become constitutive practices.[7] And yet without them there is no such thing as a public realm. The reference to their ancillary role thus also serves to remind us of their always precarious nature.

Hereafter, persuasion will be explored on the basis of Aristotle's *Rhetoric*, reflection in the sense of *Besinnung* through Heidegger's critical debate with the notion of theory, and judgment in the work of Arendt. Considering the renewed interest in Aristotle's *Rhetoric* and, in distinction from the largely negative attitude that prevailed since the Enlightenment, the definitely more open-minded contemporary approach to the discipline and practice of rhetoric, my reevaluation of persuasion as intrinsic to the public realm probably will not draw inordinate resistance. Even though I will take issue with her reading of Kant, in all likelihood there also might not be much resistance to my interpretation of Arendt's conception of judgment and her attempts to claim his developments on reflective judgment for her own understanding of the faculty in question. But some may wonder why Heidegger's reflections on theory and *theoria* loom large in a work on significant aspects of the public world. First, because a life determined by theory is antithetical to "the common life of man," to, more precisely, the life that arises from it, the *bios politikos*. Furthermore, the question is bound to arise of whether Heidegger's allegiance in matters of politics is not to Plato and his unswerving commitment to the *bios theoretikos* but rather to Aristotle and his efforts to take the realm of the public and public speech seriously. These questions will inevitably arise because of the independent nature of each section of this book. In the part on Arendt, for instance, I do not reflect on how her reevaluation of judgment relates to Heidegger's work. Nor do I, notwithstanding repeated reminders of her indebtedness to *Nicomachean Ethics*, bring to bear Aristotle's theory of public speech, as developed in the first three chapters of this book, on Arendt's interpretation of what constitutes a judgment. Hence, some explanations seem to be warranted. How, indeed, is one to think of the interface between these three investigations?

In the rather charged debates about the respective roles that Plato and Aristotle play in Heidegger's thought, his commitment to Plato's *bios theoretikos* is taken for granted and often construed in a manner that forecloses any possibility of even filing an objection.[8] All in all I do not wish to raise any doubts about Heidegger's ultimately Platonic and highly conservative agenda. The critics in question would seem to be confirmed by Heidegger's dismissal, for example in *Being and Time*, of the public realm, which resides in nothing but the idle talk or chatter of the They who make up that realm, as an inauthentic mode of being. Indeed, as Jacques Taminiaux has argued, Heidegger never even considers the possibility that the realm of opinion could have some intrinsic legitimacy.[9] Yet, besides occasional and surprising insights in his interpretations of Aristotle concerning the space of publicity and the role of rhetoric in it in the lecture courses preceding the publication of *Being and Time*—insights that triggered to some extent my reading of Aristotle's *Rhetoric* in the first part of this volume—it is, precisely, Heidegger's unrelenting, critical debate with the concept of theory, from his first Freiburg lectures until "Science and Reflection," that I wish to highlight in the section devoted to the topic of reflection. This debate, which culminates in a reconception of *theoria* as *Besinnung*, should caution against any hasty and emotional contention concerning his unwavering embrace of the *bios theoretikos*. A more nuanced view might here be advisable. It should be remembered that *theorein*, in Homer and Herodotus for example, originally designated traveling abroad.[10] *Besinnung*, as the new form that *theoria*, understood originarily, that is, as "the beholding that watches over truth," takes in times of the unraveling of the world, resonates with this early meaning of *theorein* as traveling to behold a foreign land.[11] *Besinnung*, Heidegger writes, while pointing to the resources of the German word *sinnan* or *sinnen*, is "[t]o follow a direction that is the way that something has, of itself, already taken."[12] *Besinnung*, for Heidegger, is not merely an equivalent in the German idiom for the earliest Greek understanding of *theoria* as a going to look at, or beholding of, other cultures or traditions (the inquiry into the nature of theory in "Science and Reflection" is, by the way, framed by the demand for a debate with non-Western modes of thought); it is, above all, the way, a way that is at the same time 'theoretical' *and* 'practical,' of traveling toward the unknown, that which only announces itself and is still to come, an *other* world. Indeed, if philosophy, as François Jullien observes, has repudiated the early origin of the notion of theory as a journeying in order to explore the world and "has stayed home, no longer adventuring abroad, balking at the work of informing oneself by judging such work to be impure,"[13] Heidegger's reconception of *theoria* as a reflecting journey toward a world still to come conceives of the theoretical no longer as a contemplation of the world as it is (including its founding principles) but as an at once 'theoretical' and 'practical' watching over the signs that, perhaps, announce the advent of a world to begin with. Although not practical in the classical sense, *Besinnung* is, therefore, not simply theoretical in a Platonic sense. Its concept eludes the oppositional character of the practical and the theoretical.

If I start the inquiry into some basic elements of 'world' in the sense of a public and political space with a reinterpretation of Aristotle's *Rhetoric*, it is, at first, in order to take up Arendt's claim that any attempt to recover the political must return toward the Greek experience of the political. But it is also to set the stage for the retrieval of what makes up the political through a reinterpretation of it that goes against the grain of the Platonic values on the basis of which the constituting elements of the political have been dismissed in much of Western political philosophy. As I argue in the first part of this book, Aristotle's *Rhetoric* is about speaking with one another in the public space, the way in which arguments are made in this sphere of life, and the only basis on which those arguments can be persuasive. If the elements in the practice of speaking with one another are opinions (*endoxa*), if the truths on the basis of which claims are made in the public realm are only truths that resemble truth, and if convictions are the outcome not of solitary logical reasoning but of an interactive process of persuasion that involves both speaker and auditor in the public space, it does not mean that public speech is 'illogical' but, rather, that it has a 'logic' of its own, one that is both 'reasonable' and 'practical.' In Aristotle's *Rhetoric*, this 'logic' is formalized in his theory of enthymematic reasoning, in the doctrine of the *topoi* on which such reasoning in speaking publicly with one another rests, and, more generally, in his theory of the elements (*stoikheia*) of such speech. Why, then, did I not put Arendt's conception of judgment as the political activity par excellence—a conception that on the surface is developed in a debate with Kant's theory of reflective judgment but that is also deeply indebted to Aristotle's notion of *phronesis*—in a dialogue with the technically highly refined theory of enthymematic reasoning? As is manifest from the *Denktagebücher*, in 1953 Arendt read not only Plato's *Gorgias* but also Aristotle's *Rhetoric*. One thus cannot argue that she was unfamiliar with the latter's investigation into the nature of public speech or with the cornerstone of his account of rhetoric, namely, enthymematic reasoning. As the barely four pages of notes devoted to the first book of Aristotle's treatise demonstrate, however, Arendt holds that the theory of the enthymeme makes it impossible to separate rhetoric from dialectics, that is, from truth, and that, consequently, this theory maintains the priority of the philosopher over public speech. Although Aristotle, as we will see, speaks only of the enthymeme as a *kind* of syllogism, Arendt identifies it with the syllogism *tout court* and holds it, therefore, to be unsuited to reflect the kinds of judgments and decisions that are part of the verbal interactions of human beings in the public space.[14] As we will see, for Arendt, judgment has no logical structure. Be this as it may! However, for lack of a systematic debate with the formal structures of public speech as one encounters them in Aristotle's treatise, the very notion of what Arendt construes as judgment, as the discrimination between what is right or wrong, beautiful or ugly, remains somewhat vague in spite of its novelty in many respects. Even though a systematic confrontation of Aristotle's technical analysis of persuasive argumentation with what Arendt calls 'judgment' could, perhaps, serve to work out in greater detail the formal characteristics of judgment as she understands it and, hence, to put the novelty of her concept of judgment into greater relief, my aims here are more modest. The purpose of the present study is merely to point to a problem and to prepare the frame for its future elaboration.

But what are the relations between Arendt's reflections on judgment as a political activity and Heidegger's conception of *theoria* as *Besinnung*? For a hint concerning how to respond to this question, I wish, first, to return to the claim that I made at the beginning of this foreword, namely, that one single question drives the three studies united in this volume. This guiding question concerns the 'world.' In Aristotle, 'world' is the realm of the public interactions of human beings; in Heidegger, in the more general sense, 'world' is that toward which human beings, especially in a time of its breakdown caused by the sciences and their theory, are (always only) on the way as that to which they belong; and, in Arendt, it is again the public space of human freedom that, rather than a given, has become more fragile than ever since the advent in modernity of society as a form of collective housekeeping (hence as an extension of the private sphere), as demonstrated by the examples of the American Revolution, the short life of the republic of councils, the Soviets, or the Hungarian revolution. Even though Aristotle can be considered the theoretician of an active political realm—Greek public life—his analyses of what secures this realm show, as we shall see, the extreme extent to which this realm is fragile. Heidegger's reflection on the signs that, at the point of the complete breakdown of the world, perhaps announce the advent of the rudiments of something like 'world' also concerns something tenuous, to say the least. In Arendt's attempt to rethink political thought, I hold that she starts not only from Aristotle's conception of public life but also from Heidegger's concern with the fragile enterprise of bringing about 'world.' Indeed, if 'world' occurs, according to Arendt, through the interactions of citizens rather than in view of a pre-given ideal of 'world,' then all action within the public space is necessarily structured by a relation (without relation) to a world that only announces itself. Hence, I would venture the perhaps daring suggestion that *Besinnung* as Heidegger understands it is the kind of 'theorizing' required to rethink the political, especially if the political is to be of the order of a world that takes shape only through and within political action.

By returning to the question of theory, I address one more time the question of the subtitle of this volume, *Ancillae Vitae*. The aim of these three studies on persuasion, reflection, and judgment is not to make a case for practical as opposed to theoretical reason. Nor is it an attempt to argue, as Heidegger at times does, that theory is the highest form of praxis if it is understood in both a Platonic and an Aristotelean perspective as the insight into the ultimate Good. Rather, it is to suggest that another front needs to be opened up in the weary debate between theory and praxis by acknowledging that there is a 'theoretical' dimension intrinsic to the practical, broadly speaking, to ordinary everyday life. Ordinary life is never just mere, immediate life. It is always inhabited by some form of thought and, thus, inherently 'theoretical.' It is, as Aristotle conceives it, interlaced with opinions. Furthermore, if the theoretical (in the sense of the sciences) is rooted in ordinary life's circumspective comportment in the everyday world, as Heidegger argues in *Being and Time*, it is, precisely, because such circumspection presupposes that ordinary life is lived in some thinking way. On these grounds, I would like to suggest that Heidegger's revalorization of *theoria* as *Besinnung* is, rather than an affirmation of the *bios theoretikos*, an entirely new way of thinking of circumspection in ordinary life; it shows a way into a thinking concerned with life in a world worthy of its name. By interpreting *theoria* as *Besinnung*, Heidegger would thus draw, unwittingly perhaps, on what Pierre Aubenque has characterized as Aristotle's originality, namely, the inauguration, on the basis of "a rupture within the domain of theory," of a "new conception of the relations between theory and practice" according to which a genre of knowledge other than theoretical knowledge and a "new practical intellectualism" are envisaged.[15] Arendt's commitment to life as a public activity constituted by the unique faculty of political judgment needs, of course, no lengthy demonstration. Yet, if she wanted to be considered not as a philosopher but, rather, as a political theorist, is it not also because she no longer conceives of the political in terms of practical philosophy? Indeed, the mental activity of judgment is intertwined with "the common life of man" to such a degree that it is indistinguishable from it, to such a degree, more precisely, that it is ancillary to such life in all senses of the term. Persuasion, reflection, and judgment are handmaidens of life, then, in still another sense: not only insofar as all three activities serve life as worldly life but also insofar as these activities cultivate, develop, or refine the thinking dimension of common life. They thus harbor within themselves the possibility of opening up in "the common life of man" a sphere in which life is lived freely. Persuasion, reflection, and judgment are at the service of life in that they further life's intrinsic affirmation of itself. They are thinking activities by means of which ordinary common life can attain an autonomy, albeit always incomplete and fundamentally fragile, and by the same token become the instantiation, perhaps, of something like 'world.'

PART I

PERSUASION (ARISTOTLE)

IN ARISTOTLE SCHOLARSHIP, the Stagirite's treatise on rhetoric has undergone a peculiar treatment. Not only is it one of the philosopher's most neglected works, but this neglect has also taken peculiar forms. When it is taken seriously at all, the *Rhetoric* is considered only after all the other works of the philosopher have been dealt with. Commentators' uneasiness with the work has been so great that the place usually reserved for it is, once respect has been paid to all of Aristotle's great works, at the end of their commentaries, in the shape of an acknowledgment, an endnote, as it were, that he deigned also to write this piece. Whereas Aristotle's other writings are heralded as having (together with those of Plato) incontestably laid the foundations of Western philosophical thought—in particular, through his invention of formal logic, celebrated as a creation of genius—the *Rhetoric* has been judged to be nothing more than a collection of handbook techniques for orators. According to one recent commentator's assessment of its treatment, "it has been described as a mishmash of half-baked logic, psychology, and ethics."[1] Compared to the philosopher's indispensable theoretical, or scientific works, the scope of this book, because it is about practical matters, is often seen as very limited. As regards the subjects addressed in the treatise, for example, the emotions, their treatment is usually held to lack all scientificity and to be nothing but a rehearsal of popular opinions about them. Aristotle's "psychology" in the *Rhetoric* is not even held to be quasi-scientific. Rather, it is said to lack all scientificity whatsoever. This has led Amélie Oksenberg Rorty, for one, to remark that because of such limited psychology, "instead of resembling a quasi scientific treatise on breeding the best, most fertile chickens, the *Rhetoric* is like a treatise telling farmers how to get ordinary chickens to lay good eggs."[2] Indeed, the book's concern with practical matters has been a serious obstacle to its being taken seriously, even more so since its object is rhetoric, a practical art which, since it became a school discipline in the times of Hellenism and the Middle Ages, has received the thorough contempt of the philosophical establishment. Furthermore, the work has been found to be badly constructed, muddled, obscure, and even inconsistent; its introductory chapter found to contradict all further developments, to have been carelessly assembled; Book III found to have been artificially added to it. Questions about the latter's authenticity have even been voiced. It has been argued as well that the *Rhetoric*, as it has been handed down to us, is an unsuccessful conflation of earlier and later views by Aristotle on the art in question. Another cited problem with the treatise is that it leaves the relation of the *Rhetoric* to all of Aristotle's other writings unresolved. And last, but not least, many commentators have expressed moral outrage at what they construe as Aristotle's condescending views regarding common man, who is the target of the art of persuasion, and at the philosopher's not having shied away from advocating unsavory means to achieve this goal. It is in this spirit that Sir David Ross, after having reviewed all of the philosopher's works, starting with the Logic and ending with the shortest account of the *Rhetoric* and *Poetics*, writes in his *Aristotle*: "The Rhetoric may seem at first sight to be a curious jumble of literary criticism with second-rate logic, ethics, politics, and jurisprudence, mixed by the cunning of one who knows well how the weaknesses of the human heart are to be played upon. In understanding the book it is essential to bear in mind its purely practical purpose. It is not a theoretical work on any of these subjects; it is a manual for the speaker [...] For these reasons we have dealt very briefly with this book."[3] Not only did Ross postpone any discussion of the work until the end of his book on Aristotle, but, what is more, the editors of the 1831 Berlin Academy edition of Aristotle had already put it at the end of their edition. As Heidegger muses: "They did not know what to do with it, so they put it at the end."[4] Heidegger thus explains that the philosophical tradition has long lost any understanding of the original sense of rhetoric. Holding Aristotle in such high esteem, the editors, clearly embarrassed by the fact that the great philosopher had assented to write a piece that "is the end," had thus no choice but to put his "impossible" work on rhetoric, in an edition moreover that sought to achieve completeness, at the very end of the edition. But has the very place where the *Rhetoric* thus ended up sealed its fate?

In *Being and Time*, Heidegger remarks, in passing, as it were, that "contrary to the traditional orientation, according to which rhetoric is conceived as the kind of thing we 'learn in school,'" in short as a kind of "discipline," Aristotle's *Rhetoric* "must be taken as the first systematic hermeneutics of the everydayness of Being with one another," which is also part of "publicness, as the kind of Being which belongs to the 'they.'"⁵ This reference to Aristotle's treatise as the "first systematic hermeneutics of the everydayness of Being with one another" signals a different approach, an assessment of the work in question different than the one that had until then prevailed in Aristotle scholarship. But until the recent publication of Heidegger's lectures from 1924, *Fundamental Concepts of Aristotelean Philosophy*, devoted in large part to a commentary on Aristotle's *Rhetoric*, it has been difficult, if not impossible, to gauge the sense of Heidegger's aside in *Being and Time*, and in particular the kind of new interpretation of the *Rhetoric* that it presupposes. From these lectures of 1924 it is clear that a novel interpretation of what it means for the human being to be a being endowed with speech guides Heidegger's interest in Aristotle's treatise. According to Heidegger, in the fourth century the "Greeks lived in discourse" and "were completely situated under dominion of language" to such a degree that "being-there was so burdened with babble" that it required Plato's and Aristotle's "total efforts [. . .] to be serious about the possibility of science."⁶ The reappraisal of the *Rhetoric* that the incidental remark from 1928 suggests presupposes, according to the 1924 lectures, a different conception of speaking than the one familiar to us moderns. Defining the human being as a being capable of speech presupposes a Greek's understanding of *logos*, or speaking, Heidegger contends, which is primarily a speaking-with-one-another, "a reckoning-speaking about that which is conducive" to human beings in their world.⁷ Furthermore, the specifically Greek understanding of *logos* as, first of all, a speaking with one another as Heidegger highlights in his commentary on the *Rhetoric* in the lectures in question, implies an acknowledgment of a certain originariness of publicity (*Öffentlichkeit*). Indeed, given Heidegger's usually derogatory remarks on this topic, one may also find to one's surprise a much more favorable treatment of publicity and publicness in these lectures.

Heidegger's *Fundamental Concepts of Aristotelean Philosophy* sought to wrench a new understanding of the *Rhetoric* from the then dominant Aristotle scholarship. His reinterpretation of the work in question owes, in my view, a great deal to Nietzsche's early lectures on the Greek art of oratory. However, Heidegger seems to have been unaware of Cope's 1867 *An Introduction to Aristotle's Rhetoric*, whose commentary defines the goal of rhetoric in a manner that supports Heidegger's assessment in sometimes surprising ways. Let me also point out that during the last fifty years a variety of studies have appeared in which philosophers have begun to reclaim Aristotle's *Rhetoric* for philosophy. Although unaware of Heidegger's early lectures on the subject, many of the findings in question broadly confirm Heidegger's analyses. The object of this part of the book is not to explore Heidegger's novel interpretation of the treatise. If, however, I mention Heidegger here, it is to indicate that it is his remark in *Being and Time* on the connection of the hermeneutics of *Dasein* to Aristotle's understanding of rhetoric that motivated me to take on Aristotle's treatise to begin with; it is also to acknowledge that some of the emphases I put on certain issues in my interpretation are certainly owed to my reading of Heidegger's 1924 lectures.

In the first three chapters of this book I seek to bring to light the theoretical cornerstones of Aristotle's *Rhetoric*. I do not claim that Aristotle's work is entirely without difficulties. But I hope that once the theoretical framework of the treatise is established, it will become clear that no fundamental problems haunt this work to the point of putting its unity into question. The difficulties that one may encounter in reading the *Rhetoric* are not intractable, especially if one pays careful attention to the organization of the work. Above all, however, I hope that by elaborating in a close reading of the first three chapters of Book I on the theoretical building blocks of the treatise, I have further contributed to relocating the *Rhetoric* from a place at the end—a place that is a dead end to be sure—to a place that is, philosophically speaking, much more central, one, indeed, that directly concerns us today in that it is about being together with one another. Aristotle's *Rhetoric* is the art—a very fragile art, as we will see—of how to address our most vital concerns in the most lively form of being with one another in the practice of speaking with one another.

1
A TRUTH RESEMBLING TRUTH

WHEREAS IN THE *TOPICS*, which is closely associated with the *Rhetoric*, Aristotle clearly names his addressee, namely, students of philosophy, he does not specify for whom the *Rhetoric* is intended.[1] This alone is reason enough not to call this work a technical handbook for rhetoricians, as it has been, and still is by most of the commentators. I do not deny that the *Rhetoric* also contains advice for students about public speaking; it certainly does so. But right from the beginning, Aristotle takes issue with previous compilers of "arts" of rhetoric who have, as he argues, "provided us with only a small portion of this art" in that they have elaborated only on what is accessory to an art of rhetoric. In this way, he is also putting in question the conception of rhetoric as an art that is based on what is extraneous to rhetoric. One must distinguish, then, between the handbooks for rhetoric written by the technographers, "which chiefly devote their attention to matters outside the subject," and what Aristotle will propose in terms of an art of rhetoric (5).[2] Even if we agree that Aristotle's *Rhetoric* is addressed to would-be rhetoricians, and hence is a technical handbook of sorts, this technical consideration only occupies one part of the text. Still, the distinction made between what is outside the subject of rhetoric and what is essential to it, requires Aristotle's *Rhetoric* to be twofold. He writes "that Rhetoric is composed of analytical science and of that branch of political science which is concerned with Ethics" (41); it must be composed of a part that deals with the human being's ability of logical (syllogistic) reasoning, and another part, on character, virtue, and the emotions (17–18). It is this analytical dimension of the work concerned with reasoning and rhetoric's argumentative dimension that I will seek to engage above all. If Aristotle's *Rhetoric* is an art, it is not only an art entirely different from that of his predecessors who have exclusively focused on the *pathe* "for the arousing of prejudice, compassion, anger, and similar emotions" (5) with the primary intent of influencing the jurors, but also, because it is based above all on the human's capability for logical reasoning, it is, for the first time, an art of *logos*, an art of speaking.

As also becomes clear right from the beginning of the treatise, the art of rhetoric that Aristotle will propose is not only an art distinct from all the previous so-called arts of rhetoric in that it is based on rhetorical argument, it is also the only art of the human faculty of speaking with one another that is suitable to a well-policed state. In a city, such as Athens, that is well administered, where well-enacted laws define as much as possible, and leave as little as possible to the discretion of the judges, there is nothing left for a rhetorician whose only object is to influence the jurors. Such laws require that during trials the litigant only address the subject matter and "prove that the fact in question is or is not so, that it has happened or not"; they are forbidden to speak "outside the subject," as, for instance, when seeking to arouse "prejudice, compassion, anger, and similar emotions [that have] no connexion with the matter in hand, but [are] directed only to the dicast" (5), the dicast being a citizen eligible to sit as a judge—that is, the juror. In a well-administered state, rhetoric will have to be an art in Aristotle's sense, in that, in such a state, its function is limited to providing proof of whether the subject deliberated in a court happened or did not happen, is going to happen or not, or is or is not true, leaving it to the juror to decide whether this is so or not. In a well-governed state where the legislators have defined all issues as precisely as possible, such a decision by the judge as to whether a thing has happened or not, is going to happen or not, is or is not so, is the only thing left to the judge's discretion, and rhetoric consists precisely in nothing more and nothing less than providing the judge with proof, or reasons, that speak for or against what is under consideration. To accomplish this the rhetorician needs to be "a master of rhetorical argument," that is, to excel in the art of speaking as an art of argumentation (7).

Plato, in *Gorgias*, famously compared rhetoric to cookery: "Sophistic is to legislation what beautification is to gymnastics, and rhetoric to justice what cookery is to medicine."[3] Consequently, when Aristotle opens his treatise with the claim that "Rhetoric is a counterpart of Dialectic," Dialectic being a discipline that subjects opinions on general issues to a rational examination, rhetoric is raised to a status not only well beyond cookery, but also beyond the accusation, in other Platonic dialogues, of being no art at all, or at best one for deceiving an audience (3). Let me recall here that the Greek term *antistrophos*, rendered in English as "counterpart," is a term that designates a relation of analogy.[4] To understand in a more precise manner what the analogy between dialectic and rhetoric implies, I continue to quote from the beginning of the treatise. To his initial remark that rhetoric and dialectic are counterparts, Aristotle adds: "for both have to do with matters that are in a manner within the cognizance of all men and not confined to any special science. Hence all men in a manner have a share of both; for all, up to a certain point, endeavor to criticize or uphold an argument, to defend themselves or to accuse" (3). Aristotle stresses here only what both rhetoric and dialectic have in common, what distinguishes them from the sciences, which have their own domain, and of which only the scientists are knowledgeable, but he offers very little about their difference from one another. Both dialectic and rhetoric have this in common: they deal with matters of which all men are cognizant and thus also address a knowledge and a capability that is shared by all men. In distinction from the sciences (and philosophy) they are clearly practices of everyday life. Now, these things of which all men are cognizant, are, as we will see, everything they can have an opinion about. The way all men are cognizant of these matters is hinted at when Aristotle remarks that all men "up to a certain point, endeavor to criticize or uphold an argument, [and] to defend themselves or to accuse" (3). To speak of rhetoric as being analogous to the dialogical examination of arguments, whether in front of students or in a dispute that I have with myself about an argument, asking myself questions to which I must stand answers, is to uphold, against Plato's indictment of it as being no better than cookery, rhetoric's rational and argumentative nature. It is also to suggest from the start that rhetoric is about truth, a truth that, in distinction from the special subject domains of the sciences, pertains to those things of which all men are cognizant. Finally, although Aristotle does not explicitly address the differences between rhetoric and dialectic, the truth in question, as will become clear hereafter, is one that is a function of public deliberation.

If, apart from having the before mentioned points in common, dialectic and rhetoric are also different, it is because of a difference that concerns the way in which they dispute about issues, the nature of argumentation proper to each. The arguments that are the object of dialogical dispute are mainly arguments about general issues upheld by an opponent. Furthermore, whereas dialectic regards any issue as only probable and thus open to discussion as a sort of intellectual contest with an adversary with the goal of defeating the opponent, rhetoric deals with opinions about things that are of vital concern to the citizens in the polis and are thus discussed in public speech. Whereas dialectic argumentation could even take place, as Cope puts it, "in a man's own brain and in his own study," hence in a private way of using language, rhetoric discusses opinions on vital issues to the community and is from the start a form of public speech.[5] It follows that to hold that dialectic and rhetoric are *antistrophos* is to say, I quote Brunschwig, "that the latter is to public speech (that is, to politics in a broad sense) what the former is to private speech, whether conversational or dialogical." Brunschwig adds: "The relation of antistrophy signifies precisely that rhetoric is to the spontaneous exercise of the discourse of accusation and defense what dialectics is with respect to the spontaneous discourse of examination and affirmation."⁶ In distinction from the dialogical examination (which takes place in a question and answer process), for which dialectic provides rigorous tools, the "continuous discourse" characteristic of rhetoric provides the discursive means and standards for defending oneself and accusing others, for criticizing or upholding an argument of public interest in the domain that is the polis.⁷ As opposed to the more or less private mode of speech for which dialectic proposes rules, the art of rhetoric is the art for speaking in public, the art for what I would like to call "lively speech" in the polis where, on the one hand, one has to defend oneself, account for one's words and deeds before all others, and, on the other hand, to attack others. On the basis of what all men do spontaneously in everyday life in the polis, that is, in political life in a broad sense, rhetoric provides an art, a rigorous technique for speech-related conduct within the sphere of practical life.

In his discussion of the usefulness of rhetoric, Aristotle makes one point that I would like to emphasize right from the beginning. He notes that "it would be absurd if it were considered disgraceful not to be able to defend oneself with the help of the body, but not disgraceful as far as speech is concerned, whose use is more characteristic of man than that of the body" (13). Not to be able to defend oneself by speech would mean not to be able to defend oneself by means of, and with regard to what, according to Aristotle, distinguishes the human being from the animal, namely, the fact that he is a living thing that possesses speech. Indeed, the observation about the usefulness of rhetoric is one about the vital importance of this art for the human qua human. Rhetoric is an art that concerns the very humanity of the human being; it is not only an art for this ability that the human has qua human being, namely the ability to speak, but also for the ability to defend and even secure what precisely makes him a human being. When we see that speaking, for Aristotle, is by definition speaking with others, the full thrust of this observation about the usefulness of this art becomes even more clear: it is an art for the kind of life that distinguishes human beings from all other things, namely the *bios politikos*.

If Aristotle takes issue with the technographers of rhetoric on the grounds that they have chiefly dealt with matters outside the subject, in particular, and sometimes exclusively, the ways of "arousing [. . .] prejudice, compassion, anger, and similar emotions," the ways of the *pathe*, in short, it is because they have neglected the only thing that can make rhetoric into an art (5). He writes: "proofs [*pisteis*] are the only things in [rhetoric] that come within the province of art" (3–5), and "yet [the previous compilers of "Arts" of rhetoric] say nothing about enthymemes which are the body of proof" (5). And, he adds, "they give no account of the artificial [artistic] proofs, which make a man a master of rhetorical argument" (7), skilled in enthymemes, or, as George E. Kennedy translates, "enthymematic."[8] By centering exclusively on the emotional ways to influence the dicast, the technographers have dealt with only a small slice of speech in public life, namely with forensic, or judicial, oratory alone. In addition, they have neglected the whole argumentative character of civic discourse and the only basis on which rhetoric in civic discourse can be made into an art, that is, demonstrative proof. If, at the beginning of the first chapter (of Book I), rhetoric is said to be the analogue of dialectic, which is an art for examining the logical validity of held opinions on general subjects (for instance, the nature of justice), whose proofs have the character of dialectical syllogisms, it is because, for Aristotle, the art of rhetoric is grounded specifically in rhetorical syllogisms, called enthymemes. Considering that the syllogism, as the form of a valid deductive argument in logic, is a properly Aristotelean discovery, this also means that rhetoric, rather than being similar to the art of cooking, that is, to no art at all, is in fact a rational discipline, an art insofar as it is based on a specific mode of rational argumentation that is characteristic of public speech, of speech with one another in the everyday life of the polis.

Aristotle's emphasis in the first chapter of Book I of the *Rhetoric* on proof as the only thing that matters if rhetoric is to become an art, as well as his criticism of the *pathe* as extraneous to the art of rhetoric, has led numerous Aristotle scholars, in light of the fact that the *pathe* are discussed later in the work as an integral part of rhetoric, to question the consistency of Aristotle's treatise. In response, a couple of brief remarks may be warranted. Aristotle's dismissal of his predecessors for having paid attention only to the *pathe* despite their being extrinsic to rhetoric does not necessitate that his emphasis at the beginning of the *Rhetoric* on proof, and the enthymemes as the body of proof, means that proof in lively everyday speech would have to be of an exclusively logical character, and thus that his later discussion of the *pathe* would contradict what he establishes in the first chapter of the treatise. In the same way as the dialectical syllogism to which the rhetorical syllogism is analogous, the latter is also only "a species of the 'syllogism' in general,"[9] and in no way identical with the logical syllogism, that is, the syllogism of speculative thought and of the sciences. Indeed, the enthymeme as the implement for rhetorical proof, as William M. A. Grimaldi has argued, is not an exclusively rational structure but includes, as equiprimordially as reason, the *pathe* and is indissociable, as regards its persuasiveness, from the *ethos* of the speaker. Precisely because rhetoric concerns man's life with others and his speaking with others about all sort of things that are vital to him, that is, his life not only as a seeker of absolute truth but as "the whole man," "the enthymeme [rhetorical proof] employs both reason, emotion, *ethos*, and directs itself in its argumentation to the whole man."[10] As Aristotle had noted in *Nicomachean Ethics*, the "intellect itself [. . .] moves nothing."[11]

Indeed, in the practical thought that is the domain of rhetoric, where it is always a question of making deliberate choices or decisions (*prohairesis*), more than just reason is involved. Emotions and character are also fundamentally involved in everything that leads up to action. But, if Aristotle objects to the technographers' sole concern with emotions as outside the subject of rhetoric, could it not also be because the feelings they elaborated upon are, according to Aristotle, not the proper *pathe* that can combine with reason and ethos to form the particular kind of syllogism that is the enthymeme? Could it be that the *pathe* on which they have focused exclusively are not the *pathe* for which Aristotle will make an affirmative case in the rest of his treatise?

Rather than being the art of persuasion by way of all sorts of deception outlined by Plato in *Gorgias*, rhetoric is an art of argumentation and of making proofs. However, rhetoric is not, therefore, the philosophical art of rhetoric that Plato advocated in the *Phaedrus*. Yet, even though the specific form of proof that distinguishes rhetoric is not identical to one provided by the syllogisms of philosophy and the sciences, it is no less important. The enthymeme, indeed, is instrumental to the conduct of discussions in practical life, where scientific argumentation will not convince anyone, not simply because of its efficiency, but also, as we will see, because of its relation to truth. The rhetorical syllogism is the only kind of proof that belongs properly to the domain of civic discourse, and, as a result, we will have to give it particular attention. Having said that the enthymeme is the body of proof in the art of rhetoric, Aristotle adds: "It is obvious, that a system arranged according to the rules of art is only concerned with proofs; that proof is a sort of demonstration [*apodeixis*], since we are most strongly convinced when we suppose anything to have been demonstrated; that rhetorical demonstration is an enthymeme, which, generally speaking, is the strongest of rhetorical proofs; and lastly, that the enthymeme is a kind of syllogism [*sullogismos tis*]" (9). Rather than a demagogic method for manipulating opinion, rhetoric as an art provides the rules for proving something, for making a case, for defending an opinion on a specific issue, and as such it is a rational discipline. Rhetorical proof is offered in public discussion, and if we become convinced by the proof that is offered, then it is not only because proof amounts to a sort of demonstration, but also because it has been publicly delivered. In public discourse the enthymeme provides the strongest rhetorical proof. Now, as one knows, a syllogism is the form of a valid deductive argument by which, on the basis of reasoned inference from two premises—a major and a minor premise in the atomic form of the syllogism—knowledge is produced, that is, something cognitively new is deduced. Consequently, when Aristotle states that the enthymeme is *a kind* of syllogism, he is saying that, in the same way as the logical syllogism, which concerns the way a deductive argument is conducted in the sciences, the enthymeme is connected to the production of knowledge. In the same way as the logical syllogism, the enthymeme and the demonstration that it offers starts from preexisting knowledge (the premises) and infers from them new knowledge. In short, because of its enthymematic structure, rhetoric, like speculative thought and the sciences, is inextricably connected with the demonstration of truth. What kind of truth this will be, from which kind of knowledge it will be inferred and, since the enthymeme is a kind of syllogism, how the proof will be administered, remains to be seen.

Let us first take up the issue of truth. The sort of truth the rhetorician is dealing with in public speech becomes clear from a passage in which Aristotle credits the skilled rhetorician with abilities that Plato had denied to him:

> Now, as it is the function of Dialectic as a whole, or of one of its parts, to consider every kind of syllogism in a similar manner, it is clear that he who is most capable of examining the matter and forms of a syllogism will be in the highest degree a master of rhetorical argument, if to this he adds a knowledge of the subjects with which the enthymemes deal and the differences between them and logical syllogisms. For, in fact, the true and that which resembles it come under the purview of the same faculty, and at the same time men have a sufficient natural capacity for the truth and indeed in most cases attain to it; wherefore one who divines well in regard to the truth will also be able to divine well in regard to probabilities. (9–11)

Since the art of rhetoric applies to all possible opinions that men can have, Plato, apart from finding fault with the rhetorician's reasoning, also accused him of knowing nothing in particular, that is, of having no material knowledge of what he professes to teach. But in the passage in question, Aristotle, by considering rhetoric as a part of dialectic, underscores the need for the rhetorician to be skilled in the mechanics of syllogistic demonstration. He clearly holds that in order to be a master at the art of speech the rhetorician must be knowledgeable not only about the differences between logical and enthymematic syllogism, but also about the difference between their respective subject matters. This means that we must be profoundly familiar with the materials from which persuasive arguments are to be made. In short, in order to be a true master of his art, the rhetorician must clearly understand the difference between the kind of truth involved in logical and rhetorical syllogism. According to Aristotle, this is a difference not between truth and untruth, but between truth and what resembles it (*to homoion to alethei*), that is, probabilities or commonly held opinions (*endoxa*). Unlike Plato, Aristotle has a place for something that "only" resembles truth, and rather than dismissing it altogether, he recognizes its crucial significance for the philosophical intelligibility of a whole domain of phenomena that, until then, had been considered insignificant, namely the domain of public opinion and public debate. Furthermore, what resembles truth—probable truth—originates in the same natural capacity (*dunamis*) of man for truth (*alethes*) that culminates in the apodictic truth of speculative thought and the sciences, and because of this venerable origin it is not only not to be dismissed, but needs to be recognized as the kind of truth peculiar to everyday, or practical, life. Rhetoric, insofar as it is an art of the *logos* understood as a speaking with one another about vital concerns in the polis, is rooted in the same *dunamis* from which spring forth philosophical and scientific truth. Rhetoric, like philosophy and the sciences, is in search of truth, and it finds the truth that is appropriate to its subject matter—probable truth—by way of the rhetorical syllogism, or enthymeme, which proceeds on the basis of commonly held beliefs and principles. The truth produced by enthymemes, to put it a bit differently, is a truth that is fully adequate, sufficient, and good enough to address the citizens' everyday concerns and problems encountered in the life of the polis.

At this point, let me return to Aristotle's defense of the usefulness of rhetoric. He writes: "Rhetoric is useful, because the true and the just are naturally superior to their opposites, so that, if decisions are improperly made, they must owe their defeat to their own advocates; which is reprehensible" (11). If rhetoric, as the art of speaking in public about matters of vital concern to the polis, is by nature argumentative and takes place within a horizon of truth, even though this truth only resembles truth, then it is a way to make sure not only that the true defeats its opposite, but also that the just hold the upper hand over what is unjust. Rhetoric is thus also given a clearly ethical dimension.[12] Undoubtedly, as Aristotle readily admits, like all other useful things, with the exception of virtue (*arete*), rhetoric too, can also be used for contrary purposes and be of the greatest harm, because it rests, as we will see in a moment, on the ability of speech to prove contraries—on what the French translation renders, therefore, as the "ambiguous faculty of speech [*te toiaute dunamei ton logon*]."[13] In the same way as dialectic, which, when used in conformity with the faculty of speech, serves "to discover the real and apparent syllogism," but can become sophistry when it is used deliberately to make fallacious arguments, so too, in rhetoric, one can act either "in accordance with sound argument" and "with moral purpose," or with the intention to use false arguments (13–15). As Aristotle's remark on the usefulness of rhetoric suggests, the unfair use of this useful art that can be of the greatest benefit can also produce "an equal amount of harm" (13) when the rhetorician advocates decisions that are not in tune with the human being's natural [*phusei*] propensity for truth and justice. But let us add that precisely because this art can be misused, it is also a properly human art.

Compared to what thus seem to be the stakes of rhetoric—the practical truths of everyday life in the polis, that is, to follow Aristotle in the *Nicomachean*

Ethics, of a domain of things whose very nature does not allow for the same degree of precision as is possible in the sciences, but which nonetheless is a domain involved in truth—the previous manuals on the art of rhetoric have dealt only with matters that lie outside of this subject.[14] The aim of the art of speech as defined by these handbooks consisted merely in seeking to influence the jurors by appealing to their passions and feelings. If rhetoric was primarily inclined toward the forensic or judicial branch of oratory, it was because the practice of the Athenian law courts, courts concerned with petty and private disputes between man and man, in which the jurors usually had no direct or real interest, "allows more room for the introduction of this extraneous matter, and for the use of trickery and chicanery than that of the public assembly, which is *koinoteron*, that is, in which the interests and issues which are taken into consideration are wider and more general."[15] But apart from the forensic genre of oratory, there are two other main genres: the epideictic, or ceremonial, genre of oratory in which one bestows blame or fame on somebody or something, and above all the deliberative genre associated with the public assembly, in which matters vital to the polis as a whole, such as finances, war and peace, national defense, trade and legislation, were discussed. It is this latter genre that Aristotle's *Rhetoric* privileges, but not simply because as, Glenn W. Most conjectures, he expected "that anyone who would have the intelligence, the ambition, and the moral character to study with him would not remain content with being a lawyer but would set his sights higher."[16] Considering the argumentative structure of this genre, it is more accurate to hold, with Amélie Oksenberg Rorty, that "Aristotle makes deliberative rhetoric the focus of his analysis: it most clearly reveals the primary importance of truth as it functions *within the craft of rhetoric itself.*"[17] But there are additional reasons for the importance with which Aristotle credits the deliberative genre of oratory. Deliberation concerns practical matters of vital importance to the citizens, matters, more precisely, that are within their reach, or power. Not everything needs deliberation. Aristotle writes: "when a thing is known or judged, there is no longer any need of argument" (263). More importantly, only of those things that are in one's power to change does one seek advice. Cope puts this well when he writes that all those things we seek advice for "are all such as may be referred to ourselves as authors and agents, or 'of which the origin of generation (i.e. of bringing about, or effecting) is in our power.' For in deliberating or advising we always carry back our inquiries until we have arrived at this point; until we have ascertained, namely, whether what we are consulting about be in our power to do or not."[18] If deliberation is crucial for Aristotle's understanding of the art of oratory, it is because it concerns practical matters, matters that are not only of vital importance to life in the state, but that are also within the scope of what humans are capable of, in short, that are possible from a practical point of view. Deliberation is predicated only about that which, from a practical point of view, is possible. Aristotle repeatedly stresses that deliberation is not about just anything, for instance, when he writes: "We must first ascertain about what kind of good or bad things the deliberative orator advises, since he cannot do so about everything, but only about things which may possibly happen. Everything which of necessity either is or will be, or which cannot possibly be or come to pass, is outside the scope of deliberation" (39). But not even everything that is possible is the object of public deliberation: "Indeed, even in the case of things that are possible advice is not universally appropriate; for they include certain advantages, natural or accidental, about which it is not worthwhile to offer advice. But it is clear that advice is limited to those subjects about which we take counsel; and such are all those which can naturally be referred to ourselves and the first cause of whose origination is in our own power" (39). If Aristotle privileges this particular genre of rhetoric it is because it concerns the dimension of what lies in our power and of which the inception lies with us. Deliberation, furthermore, is of the order of being with one another in that it calls for judgment. The auditor of a speech is, by definition, in the position of a judge, of one who judges and makes a decision upon having received advice. Aristotle writes: "Now the employment of persuasive speeches is directed towards a judgement; for when a thing is known and judged, there is no longer any need of argument. And there is judgement, whether a speaker addresses himself to a single individual and makes use of his speech to exhort or dissuade, as those who give advice or try to persuade, for this single individual is equally a judge, since, speaking generally, he who has to be persuaded is a judge" (263). To the extent that the deliberative way of speaking with others invites a judgment and a decision on the part of the audience that will culminate in action (or the abstention thereof), this genre is at the core of the art of rhetoric as an art of speaking with one another about pressing issues. Even though in Greek society the deliberative genre applied primarily to deliberation in the public assembly and concerned issues of national interests, as Cope remarks, "theoretically speaking however this need not to be so, though practically it is for the most part thus limited."[19] Indeed, deliberation, which is above all about advice, can take place privately. As Aristotle notes, the exhortative or dissuading nature of this kind of speech characterizes all advising whether it takes place privately or publicly (33). If deliberation, then, is a genre that is singled out, that is because it is much more extensive than the two other genres: it includes, in principle, all forms of deliberations and of seeking council in everyday life.

To say that the deliberative genre is what defines rhetoric, is, of course, to argue that rhetoric as an art rests on a very specific subject matter, and that its argumentative form is one that is determined by the subject matter of deliberation. This is, then, also the moment to begin addressing the question of the *endoxa* and the nature of the rhetorical syllogism, that is, the enthymeme, and who its addressee is. This will also be an occasion to begin exploring what exactly it is that rhetoric accomplishes, and what it does not. Let us recall again that, in the same way as dialectic, rhetoric does not belong to a single definite class of things. Unlike the sciences, both are of general application. One could thus say that, in principle, rhetoric deals with all possible subject matters, or more precisely, with the generally accepted opinions within the polis about these matters. "Opinions" means the held beliefs about various issues, not knowledge in a strict sense, of course. Opinions resemble knowledge. Now, as a matter of fact, not all the "things said" by humans are the object of civic discourse and thus worthwhile of philosophical examination. In distinction from the opinions uttered by children, the sick, the insane, and, in certain cases, even the multitude, which often goes astray, only the *endoxa* properly are the subject matter of rhetorical deliberation. As defined by the *Topics*, *endoxa* are "reputable opinions," that is, opinions that "are accepted by everyone or by the majority or by the wise—i.e. by all, or by the majority, or by the most notable and reputable of them."[20] What distinguishes the *endoxa* from all other opinions is that "the *endoxa* are likely to hit the truth."[21] In short, then, not just any opinions, but only those that resemble truth and are probably true, represent the subject matter of deliberation.

In the context of his reflections on the usefulness of rhetoric, Aristotle remarks that "the orator should be able to prove opposites, as in logical arguments; not that we should do both (for one ought not to persuade people to do what is wrong), but that the real state of the case may not escape us, and that we ourselves may be able to counteract false arguments, if another makes an unfair use of them. Rhetoric and dialectic alone of all the arts prove opposites; for both are equally concerned with them. However, it is not the same with the subject matter, but, generally speaking, that which is true and better is naturally always easier to prove and more likely to persuade" (11–13). Let me first emphasize that the distinctive character of dialectic and rhetoric, namely that, contrary to other arts, they can reason in opposite directions, is owed to the very nature of their subject matter: popular opinions, commonly held beliefs, or the probable. Opinions, which are also the distinctive subject matter of both disciplines, however much they may resemble truth, are, qua opinions, open to question. Opinions, by definition, imply that they can be other; they can even be the opposite of what they state. Second, let me underscore the difference between the way opposite trains of arguments are dealt with in dialectic and rhetoric. The subject matter of dialectic, which is dealt with through questioning in which everything is indiscriminately either this or that, necessarily concerns alternatives. As Cope has noted, dialectic is indifferent to truth and "concludes as readily the negative as the affirmative." "To it the form or method is everything, the truth of the conclusion nothing, except so far as it follows legitimately from the exact observance of the rules of the syllogism, which is its instrument."[22] Furthermore, since dialectic reasoning is dialogical, the opposite arguments are distributed between the questioner and his opponent. This is not the case with rhetoric, where the aim is to provide reasons to take specific actions. As Kennedy remarks, "in rhetoric the speaker has usually tried to think out the opposing arguments before speaking to be able to answer them if need arises."[23] And if he does so, it is precisely because of his concern with truth. Indeed, in being skilled, like the dialectician, at arguing both sides of a case, the rhetorician, who, insofar as he has as a human being a natural propensity for the true and the good, will not only advocate what is true and just. He will also refute false arguments should they arise in public discourse. Unlike dialectic, rhetoric is not indifferent to truth, and, furthermore, proceeds on the assumption that what is naturally true and by nature better is not only more easily argued, but also more persuasive.

The aim of rhetoric is thus to promote, in a public continuous argument, an opinion about some matter vital to the community that is more likely to be true and just than another. But its aim is not to persuade its audience. Toward the end of the first chapter of Book I of the *Rhetoric*, Aristotle clearly describes the limits of what rhetoric seeks to accomplish: "its function [*ergon*] is not so much to persuade, as to find out in each case the existing means of persuasion. The same holds good in respect to all the other arts" (13). Like all the other arts, such as medicine, which does not restore health itself but promotes it by helping the patient to become healthy, the art of speech does not consist in inducing persuasion but in providing its audience with ways to make up its mind. Unlike an art of persuasion, rhetoric is not aiming at successfully persuading its audience. Its aim is much more modest. As the faculty of discovering and showing the possible means of persuasion, the function of rhetoric is only to offer its audience persuasive proof, or reasons that speak for something, so that the audience itself can make a decision. Rhetoric does not decide for the audience by persuading it; instead, rhetoric provides the reasons that speak for something so that the audience can freely make the choices that are appropriate in the situation. As we have already seen, the audience of a speech is, by definition, in the position of a judge. It is the audience alone that, after hearing the speaker, makes a decision regarding the suasiveness of the rhetorician's proofs and, consequently, decides what action to take. It follows from this that it also belongs to rhetoric "to discover the real and apparent means of persuasion, just as it belongs to dialectic to discover the real and apparent syllogism" (13). Rhetoric provides the audience with the means to distinguish between a rhetorician who uses speech to elaborate argumentatively about what speaks for a given issue and one who deliberately feeds his audience with specious arguments.

Among the points that Aristotle evokes in favor of rhetoric, I left one in abeyance. It concerns its audience. He writes: "in dealing with certain persons, even if we possessed the most accurate scientific knowledge, we should not find it easy to persuade them by the employment of such knowledge. For scientific discourse is concerned with instruction, but in the case of such persons instruction is impossible; our proofs and arguments must rest on generally accepted principles, as we said in the *Topics*, when speaking of converse with the multitude" (11). Rhetoric is the means to converse with the average citizens in the polis; they are its addressee. And it is able to speak to them, to make them aware of what speaks for something, not by scientific argument to which they are deaf, but by way of proofs (*pisteis*) that rest on common beliefs, or "generally accepted principles," that is, principles that are *koinon*. Rhetoric is not only useful in that it allows one to communicate with the crowds, it is also the only appropriate means to do so. It is the art of conducting civic discourse. Rhetoric is an art for speaking to the multitude, precisely because it is not based on persuasion, but provides the audience with suasive reasons for certain issues within a horizon of a truth that resembles truth, so that the audience itself can make the necessary decisions.

2
NECESSITY OR PROBABILITY

AFTER HAVING TAKEN issue with the previous compilers of "arts" of rhetoric, and criticized them for having dealt only with things exterior to such an art, Aristotle sets out in chapter 2 of Book I of his treatise to make a new beginning and does so by offering the following definition of what constitutes rhetoric. Rhetoric as an art of *logos*, he writes, is "the faculty of discovering the possible means of persuasion [*theoresai to endechomenon pithanon*] in reference to any subject whatsoever" (15). It is, according to the more literal translation of Kennedy, the "ability, in each [particular] case [*peri hekaston*], to see the available means of persuasion."[1] As we have already seen, rhetoric does not aim at persuasion, but at showing listeners or letting them see what inherently speaks for something. Here, Aristotle adds that rhetoric is this ability not only with respect to any contingent subject matter whatsoever, making rhetoric distinct from all the other arts (except dialectic), but also that this ability is always in relation to the specific time and circumstances of this subject matter. Rhetoric is the capability to make a case that is inherently persuasive not simply once or in general, but in and for a particular situation. This distinctive ability of rhetoric to speak about every possible issue and to argue persuasively for those issues that, in a singular circumstance, are compelling, rests on its being the artful way of public speech, the art of everyday speech as a speaking with one another—a speaking that by definition is, in principle, about any subject whatsoever.

As we saw in the previous chapter, the enthymeme, that is, the rhetorical syllogism, is the body of proof on which rhetoric as an art rests. Aristotle characterized the enthymeme as a *kind* of syllogism (*sullogismos tis*). As I pointed out already, the enthymeme is not a syllogism properly speaking, that is, a logical syllogism. Nor is it the same as a dialectical syllogism. Rather, as Cope remarks, the enthymeme is a form of demonstration that "stands to the probable proofs of rhetoric in the same relation that demonstration does to science, as its principal instrument of proofs."[2] Aristotle's reference to the enthymeme as a kind of syllogism has, from early on, led to the assumption that it is a truncated logical syllogism, a syllogism in which either one of the premises or even the conclusion is missing. Aristotle's remarks about the brevity of the enthymeme have fostered this long-lasting opinion. I will not take up this debate, since I am inclined to argue along with M. F. Burnyeat that, rather than being a truncated *logical* syllogism, the enthymeme is a specific form of syllogism particular to rhetoric, that is, to the art of speech that pursues a truth that resembles truth but is not less important.[3] Let it be said that a truth that resembles truth is not a half-truth. If Aristotle grants probabilities and truths that resemble truth a place in his *Rhetoric*, it is not only because he was aware that not all knowledge worthy of its name is true in a narrow logical sense, but also because he knew that even apodictic knowledge remains human knowledge, that is, a knowledge that only resembles that of the gods. Hence, to understand the enthymeme as a merely truncated logical syllogism is to not take Aristotle's notion of a truth that resembles truth seriously in its own right.

Now, with the distinction between the inartificial and artificial proofs by which something is made suasive, Aristotle starts a process of distinctions that progressively narrows down what properly constitutes both rhetorical proof and, in the same breath, the enthymeme. In order to get a firm grasp on Aristotle's conception of rhetoric we have, of course, to follow him through these technical distinctions. While reviewing these distinctions that are part of the process that will lead to a strict definition of what constitutes the art of rhetoric, as strict as the art of rhetoric permits, we will also gain an intriguing insight into this art itself. The first distinction concerns *atechnic* and *entechnic pisteis*, or proofs. *Atechnic*, or inartificial, proofs are those that "have not been furnished by ourselves but were already in existence, such as witnesses, [testimony from] torture, contracts, and the like," whereas *entechnic*, that is, technical, or artificial, proofs are "all that can be constructed by system [by method] and by our own efforts. Thus we have only to make use of the former, whereas we must invent [*heurein*, that is, find] the latter" (15). Obviously, technical proofs are of the resort of rhetoric, and hence it comes as no surprise that the *atechnic* proofs will only get short shrift. All the additional distinctions that Aristotle makes are only concerned with the *entechnic*, that is, artful, *pisteis* that show what speaks for this or that publicly debated subject matter under discussion in a particular situation. According to Aristotle, artful speech may furnish three different kinds of *entechnic* proofs, depending on the origin of their proof character in either *ethos, pathos*, or *logos*. He writes: "The first depends upon the moral character of the speaker, the second upon putting the hearer into a certain frame of mind, the third upon the speech itself, insofar as it proves or seems to prove" (17). Let us briefly recall Aristotle's contention that the technographers of rhetoric dealt only with things exterior to rhetoric, namely, the *pathe*, and ignored the enthymeme, which, as the body of persuasion, is essential to rhetoric as an art of speech. Does he contradict himself when, in the process of making a new beginning for rhetoric, he distinguishes these three artful ways of showing what is persuasive about a given subject? Beyond enthymematic proof, does he recognize proof based on what he first had qualified as being extraneous to rhetoric, that is, on the *pathe* in particular? *Ethos*, or moral character, had not been a concern of the theoreticians of rhetoric prior to Aristotle; on the contrary, according to them, "the worth of the orator in no way contributes to his powers of persuasion" (17). By contrast, Aristotle claims that "moral character, so to say, constitutes the most effective means of proof" (17). Yet, by highlighting the fact that moral character has proof character, and, hence, is persuasive on only the condition that the credence that it brings with it is "due to the speech itself, not to any preconceived idea of the speaker's character" (17), Aristotle demonstrates that moral character, insofar as it is relevant for the art in question, is a function of artful speech. In other words, rather than being exterior to the art of rhetoric, character is intimately linked to what constitutes the body of persuasion, namely, its syllogistic, that is, argumentative, nature. Aristotle writes that "the orator persuades by moral character when his speech is delivered in such a manner as to render him worthy of confidence" (17). The way in which he conducts his argumentative speech alone can prove him to be reliable and worthy of confidence. By making himself look trustworthy and honest through the way he conducts his speech, the rhetorician further involves the audience in the making of the argument, which thus, in a way, can be said to construe his character. Where this is the case, character, as other translators write, is "almost, so to speak, the most authoritative form of persuasion."[4] Not only does Aristotle not contradict himself by bringing to bear moral character on rhetorical proof since it is the handbook-compilers who have been responsible for its exclusion from what they considered an art, but this character, rather than being distinct and exterior to the proof character of the art of speech, appears in fact to be intrinsically connected to it. Let us bear in mind that, strictly speaking, the enthymeme is neither a logical nor a dialectical syllogism. The latter moves nothing, as Aristotle notes in *Nicomachean Ethics*. For rhetorical proof to be persuasive it must be conducted in such a way that the credibility of the orator springs from it as an effect of the speech itself, an effect that not only enhances the persuasiveness of the argument made, but *almost* entirely makes up its persuasiveness. This does not mean in any way that character supplants enthymematic reason. The latter needs to be as rigorous as possible for character to put the final touch on its persuasiveness.

For an enthymeme to be fully convincing, it must also be able to put the audience into the right set of mind. This is where the *pathe* come in. With respect to this second kind of *entechnic* proof, Aristotle remarks: "The orator persuades by means of his hearers, when they are roused to emotion by his speech; for the judgments we deliver are not the same when we are influenced by joy or sorrow, love or hate" (17). In a passage (23–25) that I will discuss in detail a bit later, one that concerns the specific mode of inference of the enthymeme, Aristotle notes that, in distinction from syllogistic reasoning, the enthymeme requires at times fewer premises than even the atomic syllogism. Indeed, when Aristotle contends that, if a premise is known to the audience, the rhetorician does not have to refer explicitly to it, he does not suggest that the enthymeme is a truncated syllogism. In fact, since "the hearer can add [the presupposed premise] himself" (25), the enthymeme is not truncated at all. Not only that: by filling in what the orator has left out, the audience becomes an active participant in the case that is made. Indeed, more than one agent is involved in the enthymeme. It is precisely this participation by the audience that is necessary for the enthymeme to be complete, a completion which the rhetorician must seek to be persuasive, and he must do so by raising the audience to emotion by his speech, that is, by how he makes his argument.

Here a word about the *pathe* may be warranted. If Aristotle characterized them in chapter 1 of Book I of the *Rhetoric* as exterior to the art of speech, but now shows them to be an integral part of rhetoric, this is not because of a lack of consistency. As we have already suggested, the *pathe* in question are emotions that the orator's speech must produce in order to be persuasive, and since his speech, if it is to be artful, must be argumentative, these emotions must spring from enthymematic proof. It follows from this that the said emotions cannot be just any emotions, and that they must also differ from those that Aristotle had first qualified as accessory to the art of rhetoric. They cannot be of the order of bodily drives, such as hunger, thirst, or the sexual drives, which no argument can bring about or allay; nor can they be charms and enchantments that, according to the artificer of persuasion that is Gorgias, overcome the hearer and work upon him in the manner of a drug. In the service of all-out persuasion, the emotional appeals of the charms or enchantments are not only distinct, but also hostile to the reasoned argumentation that Aristotle expects from the art of speech. As William W. Fortenbaugh has argued, Aristotle's analyses of individual emotions in the *Rhetoric* clearly demonstrate that, for the philosopher, emotions are not blind impulses.[5] The *pathe* that Aristotle picks out in the *Rhetoric* for analysis, ones that are interconnected with persuasion by way of demonstration, are all emotions that show an intimate relationship with cognition. In the wake of Plato's *Philebos*, Aristotle, in the *Rhetoric*, "looks upon cognition as an essential element in emotion" and makes it clear that "emotions can be reasonable and that emotional appeal need not be a matter of charms and enchantments."[6] Consequently, the *pathe* that are an integral part of the enthymematic demonstration, and that the orator has to incite in his audience for his proof to be suasive, these *pathe* that are the contribution of the audience to the argument, as it were, must be emotions in which some kind of cognition is present as the efficient cause of them. They must be reasonable emotions, open to reason, and let themselves be reasoned upon.

Lastly, after proof based on *ethos* and the *pathe*, comes the proof that rests on "speech itself [*logoi*], when we establish the true or apparently true from the means of persuasion applicable to each individual subject" (17). This final kind of *entechnic* proof is based on speech and persuasive reasoning alone. For the moment, let me simply underline (since we will return to this kind of proof in greater detail) that such proof establishes the (the logically, or scientifically) true, or, above all, the apparently true (because only probable) on the basis of whatever is persuasive in each particular case.

In sum, in order to show what speaks for, or is suasive, of a particular thing under discussion in a particular context and time, no less than three species of proof are required, all of which are intimately interwoven and interdependent. More precisely, they are integral parts of the rhetorical syllogism insofar as it is argumentative and occurs in speech itself. This is further emphasized when, in listing the rhetorician's necessary skills, Aristotle names the ability of logical reasoning first. The rhetorician cannot be the charlatan as Plato characterized him; he must rather be knowledgeable in all three areas. He "must be capable of logical reasoning, of studying character and the virtues, and thirdly the emotions—the nature and character of each, its origin, and the manner in which it is produced" (17–19). Aristotle adds: "Thus it appears that Rhetoric is as it were an offshoot [*paraphues*] of Dialectic and the science of Ethics, which may be reasonably called Politics" (19). Because the rhetorician must be skilled in a logical reasoning that, in distinction from the sciences, pertains to no special class of subjects, it can be seen to spring from, or to be grafted upon, dialectic. But since the things that are deliberated upon in civic life are for the most part either human actions or things dependent on them, the rhetorician must also be knowledgeable about everything that, like character and virtue, bears on the comportment of the individual within the polis. Therefore, rhetoric can be said to be a scion of politics or practical philosophy, since ethics, which analyzes human nature in the individual, is part of the latter.[7] Rhetoric, it follows from this, is an art at the service of the individual citizen in his daily life in the state. This is then also the reason why Aristotle can say that "Rhetoric assumes the character of Politics" (19)—or, in a more literal translation, that rhetoric slips into the garb of, puts on the mask of, politics. This disguising is also indicative of the fact that this very human art, in addition to training man for his civil duties, can lend itself also to reprehensible purposes. To sum up this discussion of rhetoric's relations to the other arts, Aristotle holds that, "as we said at the outset, Rhetoric is a division or likeness of Dialectic [it is partly (*morion*) dialectic, and resembles it], since neither of them is a science that deals with the nature of any definite subject, but they are merely [*tines*] faculties [*dunameis*] of furnishing arguments" (19). In addition to what Aristotle established in the first chapter about the fact that, contrary to all the other arts, rhetoric and dialectic are not identifiable with the knowledge of a specific subject matter, the emphasis lies now on their nature of being "merely," or "only," distinct faculties of furnishing arguments: in the case of rhetoric, the faculty of what speaks for or against something that is of vital importance for the citizens within the polis.[8]

Let us recall that the third kind of *entechnic* proof consisted of proof based on speech alone. In what follows, the distinction between Dialectic and Rhetoric will serve Aristotle to refine this third mode of artificial proof. He writes: "For purposes of demonstration, real or apparent, just as Dialectic possesses two modes of argument, induction [*epagoge*] and the syllogism, real or apparent, the same is the case in Rhetoric; for the example [*paradeigma*] is induction, and the enthymeme a syllogism, and the apparent enthymeme an apparent syllogism. Accordingly I call an enthymeme a rhetorical syllogism, and an example rhetorical induction" (19). Just as in Dialectic there are two, and only two, modes of logical proof—induction and syllogism—so too in Rhetoric there are just the example and the enthymeme to serve as modes of demonstration, both of which allow for both real and apparent proofs.

At this point, a brief reflection on the parallelism of, on the one hand, induction and syllogism, and, on the other hand, example and enthymeme, may be warranted. Indeed, when Aristotle contends that all orators produce logical persuasion through either example or enthymeme and that these are identical with induction and syllogism in dialectic because, "generally speaking" (19), all proof takes place either by induction or syllogism, it sounds as if there is no significant difference between rhetoric and dialectic (or more generally, Aristotle's logic as it has been developed, in particular, in the *Prior Analytics*) as far as furnishing proofs or demonstration is concerned. Aristotle encourages this view when he calls the enthymeme a rhetorical *syllogism*. Numerous commentators have concluded therefore that, in the *Rhetoric*, Aristotle not only brings "his logical system of deductive and inductive reasoning which for him is absolutely necessary for all *apodeixis*," that is, for all demonstration by syllogism, into the rhetoric, from the outside, so to speak, but also adapts and relaxes the strict exigencies of his logical theory of the inferential method of deduction and induction developed in the *Prior Analytics* when it comes to accounting for argumentation in everyday life.⁹ As I have pointed out, the comparison of rhetoric to dialectic in the first chapter of Book I has the clearly anti-Platonic aim of raising the stakes of the art of rhetoric. However, if rhetoric were merely to import and adapt a logical theory of deductive and inductive reasoning developed elsewhere so as to fit the domain of everyday speech, then, apart from being a watered-down mode of this theory, there would also be in principle no essential difference between induction and example, and no essential difference between syllogism and enthymeme. I wonder whether this is so, and whether, in spite of some of Aristotle's formulations, the difference is not more substantial. My critical remarks about the conception of the enthymeme as a "truncated syllogism" pointed already in this direction. (If, indeed, speaking with one another about the world in everyday life is, as Heidegger argues in his lectures from 1924 on *The Fundamental Concepts of Aristotelean Philosophy*, the ground of all theory and logic as a human possibility, then logic, rather than being prior to, and serving as the standard for the evaluation of the kinds of demonstration that occur in everyday speech, must be shown to derive from the fundamental structures that constitute argumentation in everyday speech. However broad or narrow these structures may be when compared to those of the logical syllogism, they will have to be credited with a consistency and a rigor of their own, from which all talk of a relaxation of logical standards necessarily falls short).

Anyway, according to the *Rhetoric*, proof based in speech alone is double in kind, namely either by example or enthymeme. In order to establish their difference, Aristotle refers to the *Topics*,

> where in discussing syllogism and induction, it has previously been said that the proof from a number of particular cases that such is the rule, is called in Dialectic induction, in Rhetoric example; but when, certain things being posited, something different results by reason of them, alongside of them, from their being true, either universally or in most cases, such a conclusion in Dialectic is called a syllogism, in rhetoric an enthymeme. (21)

The mode of inference from examples is the same as the one by induction: from similar cases one induces something general; the mode of inference by way of enthymemes is the same as that of syllogisms: on the basis of true premises (in the case of dialectic) or premises that for the most part are true (in rhetoric), one deduces, respectively, a new general truth or one that for the most part is true. Formally speaking, induction and example, syllogism and enthymeme, thus seem to be the same. However, does not the fact that the enthymeme produces a conclusion that is only probably true, and that the example "makes its induction from particular to particular, or inference by resemblance," and thus only puts a particular case into a more favorable light, suggest a more profound difference between these modes of demonstration in rhetoric and dialectic, one that perhaps also affects the formal nature of the methods in question?[10]

Both species of rhetorical proof have their own merits. But although "arguments that depend on examples are not less calculated to persuade [...] those which depend on enthymemes meet with greater approval" (21), Aristotle contends. The latter excite a more favorable audience response. From the passage it is clear that, in the process of progressively narrowing down what constitutes rhetorical argumentation properly speaking, Aristotle prioritizes the deductive mode of rhetorical argumentation even though the example is an integral part of rhetorical proof. Indeed, although Aristotle devotes a couple of pages to it in Book II of the *Rhetoric*, the example does not enjoy any extensive development. Yet, while postponing a discussion of "their origin [that is, the sources of both the example and the enthymeme] and the way in which each should be used" (21) until later (1358a1–35), Aristotle lingers for a moment on these proofs themselves, seeking to define them more clearly. He writes: "Now, that which is persuasive is persuasive in reference to someone, and is persuasive and convincing either at once and in and by itself, or because it appears to be proved by propositions that are convincing" (21–23). In distinction from the addressee of ordinary logical argumentation, argumentation that appeals, in principle, to any recipient whatsoever, rhetorical proof is addressed to an audience, that is, by definition, to a concrete addressee, an addressee in a particular situation at a particular time. Rather than the object of demagogic manipulation, the presence of the audience, as we have already seen, is essential to rhetorical demonstration. Unlike the logical argument, the latter is neither purely formal nor transitive. A rhetorical argument requires a judgment about its very plausibility by the audience, which participates, in this way, in the making of the argument itself.[11] This is the case whether the rhetorical argument is enthymematic or paradigmatic. But, in distinction from the argument based on examples, which persuade directly, and at once, the enthymeme rests on prior accepted truths, or what resembles truths, and thus needs also much more art for its construction than does the example. This is certainly another reason why Aristotle privileges the enthymeme over the example. Let us also take note of the fact that

> no art has the particular in view, medicine for instance what is good for Socrates or Callias, but what is good for this or that class of persons (for this is a matter that

comes within the province of an art, whereas the particular is infinite and cannot be the subject of a true science); similarly, therefore, Rhetoric will not consider what seems probable in each individual case, for instance to Socrates or Hippias, but that which seems probable to this or that class or persons. (23)

Like any art, the art of rhetoric seeks general rules and thus applies only to things that appear true or are probably true, not to the opinions of this or that individual or of the madman, whom Aristotle is about to mention. The art of rhetoric applies to public opinions about some subject matter shared by a group of people. Again, the example and the enthymeme share this concern with a probability that transcends individual beliefs. However, here too one senses a difference between the two in that the proof character of the example is, in spite of its immediate evidence, perhaps more restricted than that of the enthymeme, which rests on accepted truths and gives rise to a conclusion that can lay claim to probable universality. When Aristotle writes that "it is the same with Dialectic, which does not draw conclusions from any random premises—for even madmen have some fancies—but it takes its material from subjects which demand reasoned discussion, as Rhetoric does from those which are common subjects of deliberation [*bouleuesthai*]" (23), it would seem that, although in dialectic, induction from facts leads to general (though not universal) truths, in rhetoric, on the contrary, the example only serves to enhance another particular fact and to give it some general value. But only Aristotle's recommendation in Book II that "if we have no enthymemes, we must employ examples as demonstrative proofs, for conviction is produced by these; but if we have them, examples must be used as evidence and as a kind of epilogue to the enthymemes" (279) brings out with all desirable clarity the true status of the example in the art of rhetoric. Examples are thus clearly stopgaps and subservient to the enthymeme.

Rhetoric, as we have said already, is all about deliberation. In distinction from private matters that are the objects of courts of law and to which the jurors are usually indifferent, the matters discussed in the public assembly are the audience's own affairs [*peri oikeion*], affairs in which they thus take a keen interest. As Cope notes, "accordingly all that they want is *proof* that the course proposed is for their advantage, and everything beyond and beside this is likely to be disapproved and rejected as unnecessary and out of place."[12] What Aristotle's emphasis on the primarily deliberative character of rhetoric implies, and how it shapes rhetoric, begins to come into view when he states that "the function of Rhetoric, then, is to deal with things about which we deliberate, but for which we have no systematic rules; and in the presence of such hearers as are unable to take a general view at many stages, or to follow a lengthy chain of argument [Kennedy: "as are not able to see many things all together or to reason from a distant starting point"[13]" (23). The function of rhetoric is to provide a technique for public debate, deliberation, and counseling about affairs in which the audience has a deep interest. It is a technique that takes into account the fact that the audience is not made up of scientists, but of common people, people, in short, whose intellectual skills are limited. Now, what are these things that come up in the public assembly and require deliberation? Aristotle gives us a first hint when he says that "we only deliberate about things which seem to admit of issuing in two ways; as for those things which cannot in the past, present, or future be otherwise, no one deliberates about them, if he supposes that they are such; for nothing would be gained by it" (23). Deliberation is futile in the case of things that cannot be otherwise, that are *aion*, eternally the same. Unless they are viewed not as unshakable scientific facts but as mere opinions, there is nothing to deliberate, to consider, to weigh about them in the mind. However, about things that can be otherwise, that seem to be capable of admitting two possibilities, such as are all opinions, deliberation is essential, and it is all the more essential if these opinions concern subject matters that are of crucial importance to the audience. Deliberation is essential in this situation because it is the necessary prelude to deliberate choice, decision, and action. Furthermore, the rules that rhetoric furnishes for deliberating such matters are not formal rules for mental gymnastics, but rules intended to make a case for what in a particular situation, and at a particular moment, is the right solution, one in which truth, or what resembles truth, prevails.

Aristotle writes:

> Now, it is possible to draw conclusions and inferences partly from what has been previously demonstrated syllogistically, partly from what has not, which however needs demonstration, because it is not probable. The first of these methods is necessarily difficult to follow owing to its length, for the judge is supposed to be a simple person; the second will obtain little credence, because it does not depend upon what is either admitted or probable. The necessary result then is that the enthymeme and the example are concerned with things which may, generally speaking, be other than they are, the example being a kind of induction and the enthymeme a kind of syllogism, and deduced from few premises, often from fewer than the regular syllogism; for if any one of these is well known, there is no need to mention it, for the hearer can add it himself. (23–25)

The two modes of inference that Aristotle distinguishes at the beginning of the passage serve here as a contrast to what, precisely, the enthymematic and paradigmatic proof consists of. The first mode is that of scientific reasoning in which a conclusion is drawn from propositions that themselves have been previously demonstrated according to the syllogistic method. Because it involves a chain of syllogisms, it is too complex and lengthy to be of any relevance to ordinary man. The second mode of inference starts from propositions that are not commonly admitted to be probable and that, therefore, must be reasoned out by way of syllogistic demonstration for them to be accepted. If the first mode of inference is too complicated for the ordinary citizen to follow, then the conclusion of the second is not persuasive since the validity of its premises has not been commonly agreed upon. The enthymeme and the paradigm represent a third mode of inference (somewhere in the middle between the two others). Apart from the fact that its proper chain of reasoning requires fewer premises than scientific argumentation (for reasons that we have already seen), rhetorical inferring, in distinction from the second mode in which the premises are not commonly accepted beliefs, is based on "things which may, generally speaking, be other than they are," that is, probable truths, or generally admitted opinions, which, qua opinions, can of course also be otherwise.

Let me briefly recapitulate: as a third mode of inferring, rhetorical proof is distinct from logical or scientific proof in that the truth of its premises is not the result of previous demonstrations by syllogisms; it is distinct as well from such modes of inference that rest on assumptions that are not probable, that do not correspond to generally accepted opinions. We have also seen that among the two kinds of proof that function by way of speech alone—the enthymeme and the example—Aristotle prioritizes the rhetorical syllogism, which rests on premises that are commonly believed truths. In the remaining part of chapter 2 in Book I, a discussion of the subject matter, that is, the premises on the basis of which rhetorical argumentation proceeds, will lead to additional distinctions by means of which that which is strictly enthymematic is further narrowed down. The first of these distinctions is one between enthymemes that rest on necessary premises and those whose propositions are only probable. In technical terms, this is the distinction between *eikota* and *semeia*, that is, probabilities or likelihoods, and signs. Aristotle writes:

> But since few of the propositions of the rhetorical syllogism are necessary, for most of the things which we judge and examine can be other than they are, human actions, which are the subject of our deliberation and examination, being all of such a character and, generally speaking, none of them necessary; since, further, facts which only generally happen or are merely possible can only be demonstrated by other facts of the same kind, and necessary facts by necessary propositions (and that this is so is clear from the *Analytics*), it is evident that the materials from which enthymemes are derived will be sometimes necessary, but for the most part only generally true; and these materials being probabilities [*eikota*] and signs [*semeia*], it follows that these two elements must correspond to these two kinds of propositions, each to each." (25–27)

Necessary premises are such that their material is necessarily true, and, as a result, everything that can be concluded from them also follows with necessity. Now, if, in general, only few propositions meet this criterion in rhetorical demonstration, it is because its subject matter is human actions (what should be done and what not), and none of them are, strictly speaking, necessary. All human action, Aristotle emphasizes, is of this kind. Everything that is examined and deliberated in everyday life in the polis can be other than it is. In distinction from the sciences where the question of choosing between alternative truths does not pose itself, in everyday life things are not as clear as that, and alternative opinions and actions are always real possibilities. Different solutions, that is, opposite kinds of actions, to burning issues have to be envisaged and must be debated. Now, whereas necessary actions can be deduced from necessities, things that happen only for the most part or are only possibilities, as is the case with practical life in the polis, can only be reasoned on the basis of other such things that are equally nonnecessary. It is clear, therefore, that the premises of rhetorical syllogisms, even though they do not altogether exclude necessary ones, start primarily from premises that are only for the most part true, hence, from nonnecessary premises. Everything that is necessary will only play a marginal role in deliberation (and in subsequent decision-making). Probabilities and signs are the materials for rhetorical syllogisms, or enthymemes. Yet, whereas probabilities, or likelihoods (*eikota*), are, as the name indicates, materials that are for the most part true, signs (*semeia*) can imply necessity. In principle, the latter would thus not play a decisive role in the enthymeme. In reference to probabilities, Aristotle remarks: "For that which is probable is that which generally happens, not however unreservedly, as some define it, but that which is concerned with things that may be other than they are, being so related to that in regard to which it is probable as the universal to the particular" (27). Within the domain of the practical, the probable is, as its name indicates, not what necessarily always occurs, but only what occurs for the most part. *Eikota* never lend themselves to necessity. But that does not mean at all that these premises of enthymemes are merely whimsical assumptions. On the contrary, they are reasonable assumptions regarding the real order of practical life, assumptions, moreover, that are held true by the majority of men. They have the status of truths that, in the average, are true, and Aristotle can therefore argue that, among things that can be otherwise, these premises are to truths as the universal is to the particular. As regards the other kind of premises for enthymemes, that is, the signs, Aristotle writes:

> As to signs, some are related as the particular to the universal, others as the universal to the particular. Necessary signs are called *tekmeria*; those which are not necessary have no distinguishing name. I call those necessary signs from which

a logical syllogism can be constructed, wherefore such a sign is called *tekmerion*; for when people think that their arguments are irrefutable, they think that they are bringing forward a *tekmerion*, something as it were proved and concluded. (27)

Within the real order of things, the sign, as Grimaldi remarks, "is a relationship between two realities which has its foundation in the nature of these realities and exists objectively as soon as one of the realities exists. The relationship between sign and signate leads the mind from the known to the unknown because of this one to one correspondence." In Grimaldi's words, the sign "leads of and by itself to the probable or necessary truth of the thing signified, and so possesses a peculiar force for the demonstration of this signate." Furthermore, as he observes, as premises for enthymemes, signs possess a stronger demonstrative force than the *eikota*, precisely because of their formal relation to another thing. Grimaldi adds that the "sign argues almost immediately and directly to signate."[14] Indeed, a sign, in the real order of things, is something that either necessarily, or in all likelihood, indicates the objective existence of a signate. Now, where a sign necessarily proves something, it is called *tekmerion*; where the relation to the signate is only general and nonconstant, it has no special name: it is a *semeion anonymon*. From everything we have seen so far, only *semeia anonyma*, signs that are not strictly apodictic, are truly relevant to the domain of rhetorical argumentation, whereas the *tekmeria* are already of the order of scientific proof, a domain in which there is no place for deliberation.

But what about the analogy that Aristotle established between, on the one hand, the probable and things that can be otherwise, and, on the other hand, the universal and the particular? He remarks: "Among signs, some are related as the particular to the universal; for instance, if one were to say that all wise men are just, because Socrates was both wise and just" (27). The fact that Socrates was wise and just can be taken as a sign and used as a proposition in an enthymeme. However, on the basis of this premise, which is undoubtedly true, I cannot apodictically conclude that all wise man are necessarily just. The conclusion that can be drawn from this particular truth cannot be a universal one, but only one of probability. He writes: "But if one were to say that it is a sign that a man is ill because he has fever [. . .] this is a necessary sign. This alone among signs is a *tekmerion*; for only in this case, if the fact is true, is the argument irrefutable" (27). Such truth, however, makes the argument a syllogistic one rather than an enthymematic argument, strictly speaking. Aristotle continues: "Other signs are related as the universal to the particular, for instance, if one were to say that it is a sign that this man has a fever, because he breathes hard; but even if the fact be true, this argument also can be refuted, for it is possible for a man to breathe hard without having a fever" (27–29).

Here hard breathing is in the position of a universal from which the particular fact that this man is sick is concluded. But obviously such a conclusion can only be probable, because hard breathing can be the sign of many other things as well. To sum up, the enthymemes that use signs as their propositions are enthymemes properly speaking if the conclusion, whether the sign is in a position of universality or particularity, is nonnecessary, yet probable. As soon as the relation of the sign to its signate is necessary, it is no longer enthymematic, but syllogistic.

Returning to the question of the example, which, besides the enthemyme, is the only other form of rhetorical demonstration, Aristotle broaches the ways by which this kind of induction makes its conclusions. He writes: "It is neither the relation of part to whole, nor of whole to part, nor of one whole to another whole, but of part to part, of like to like, when both come under the same genus, but one of them is better known than the other" (29). Since Cope offers an excellent commentary of these lines, I limit myself to quoting him:

> The example stands neither in the relation of part to whole (as in induction, by which the universal is gathered from the particular and individual), nor in that of whole to part (as in the opposite process of deduction or syllogism, which concludes from the universal to the particular), nor as whole to whole (the conclusion from universal to universal, likewise effected by syllogism), but in the relation of particular to particular, or like to like; when the example, and the analogous fact that is to be inferred from it, are both under (i.e. species of) the same genus, but the one is better known than the other.[15]

In distinction from the kind of inferring characteristic of the enthymeme (and of the syllogism), which is modeled on the relations between the universal and the particular or between universals, the example as a relation between parts operates *within* a same genus or universal and makes its conclusion moving from one of its better known particulars to a lesser known. The example of Dionysius's request of a bodyguard, which Aristotle provides to illustrate the mode of inference in question, operates within the general rule, or universal: "whoever asks for such a thing, has a design upon tyranny"—a rule that is demonstrated by the particulars that are Peisistratos and Theagenes of Megara. In short, the material of an example, in order to be demonstrative, has to be a well-established and well-known part of a whole, from which another part of this whole can be shown to obey the same rule.

With this discussion of, on the one hand, likelihoods and signs and, on the other hand, known facts within the same genus, "we have now stated the materials of [enthymematic and paradigmatic] proofs which are thought to be demonstrative." But, Aristotle continues, "a very great difference between enthymemes has escaped the notice of nearly everyone, although it also exists in the dialectical method of syllogisms," that is, between different syllogisms (29). The full weight of this crucial distinction will only become clear when Aristotle, a bit later in the chapter, discusses the difference between *topoi* as commonplaces and *topoi* that are specific "places," that is, particular to a specific domain. But, in anticipation of these developments, I will note that this distinction clearly derives from the fact that some enthymemes are formed in accord with the method of rhetoric (in the same way as in dialectic, syllogisms are formed in accord with dialectic) whereas others are formed in accord with the content of other arts, including arts that are not yet established. One difference concerns the formal method by which the enthymemes are formed— between some that are formed in strict observance of the rules of rhetoric and others in observance of the rules of other arts. Now, the more speakers rely on the formal methods and contents of these other arts (such as ethics, politics, or other subjects) to construct their proofs, the more they leave the domain of the probable that is peculiar to rhetoric and rely on issues that defy deliberation. Of speakers who "specialize in a subject," Aristotle holds that "they transgress the limits of Rhetoric and Dialectic" (29–31). I said at one point that Aristotle's progressive refinement of what rhetorical proof consists of, a refinement that demanded a process in which anything not specific to it, or only marginal to its concerns, is sliced away, split off from it, reveals something significant about rhetoric as the art of publicly speaking with one another about matters vital to all. As Aristotle continues this process, making distinction after distinction and thus further narrowing down what an enthymeme actually is, the peculiar status of the art of speaking begins to take shape.

In order to refine the "very great" distinction he has introduced between enthymemes, Aristotle takes up again the question of what sets rhetoric and dialectic apart from all the other arts. He writes: "I mean by dialectical and rhetorical syllogisms those that are concerned with what we call 'topics,' which may be applied to Law, Physics, Politics, and many other sciences that differ in kind" (31). "Topics" is, of course, the key term here. What sets both rhetoric and dialectic apart from all the other arts is that their forms of demonstration make use of *topoi* that can be applied indiscriminately to any sort of material. Aristotle refers to them simply as *koina*, or *koinoi topoi*, that is, common places. The question of whether it will be necessary to make in turn a distinction between *koina* and *topoi* will concern us only later, as well as the question regarding the significance of the fact that the first example of a commonplace that comes to Aristotle's mind when explaining what a *topos* is, is "the topic of the more or less [*tou mallon kai etthon topos*]" (31). Neither in the *Topics* nor in the *Rhetoric* does Aristotle offer a clear definition of what constitutes a *topos*, which can be held to mean that he could take it for granted that the audience of his afternoon lectures on rhetoric was familiar with this notion that Aristotle, by the way, did not invent, and that can be found, in particular, in Isocrates's treatise, *Encomium of Helen*. As his focus on enthymemes that are formed in accord with the method of rhetoric as opposed to those that are shaped according to methods of the various sciences demonstrates, another reason for the neglect to give a definition of the newly introduced term of topics is that he is still in the process of separating out what essentially belongs to rhetoric. Now, even if one assumes that Aristotle did not have to define the notion of topics because everyone in the Lyceum was familiar with it, a lack of definition does not necessarily imply that Aristotle's use of the notion is the same as that of his predecessors. In fact, as we will see, by distinguishing within the *topoi* between, on the one hand, *koinoi topoi*, and on the other hand, *ta idia*, or *eide*, that is, between common *topoi* and special *topoi*, he redefines, as it were, the notion by splitting off a part of it that does not essentially belong to the enthymeme, and hence not to rhetorical debate, even though in practice most of the premises of enthymemes may rest on it.

Before I continue commenting on these last paragraphs of chapter 2, let me give you Cope's definition of what a *topos* is: "A *topos* [...] is a 'place' or 'region,' *the* place where you may look for something you want with the certainty of finding it, or a store which may be drawn upon to meet an occasional requirement; and in its application to rhetoric means a 'head' (capita, Cic. de Orat. II. 34.146) or 'genus' or general conception, which includes under it a large stock of special arguments of the same kind."[16] Throughout the tradition, and Cope is no exception, many metaphors have been used to describe or define what a *topos* is. For example, it has been called a source, a mold, a matrix, an arsenal, even a pigeonhole (Ross). In the introduction to his French translation of the *Topics*, Jacques Brunschwig, while speaking about the *topos*, uses another metaphor, that of a machine. Given the role that *topos* plays in the dialectic of providing methodical solutions to problems under discussion in the debate between a questioner and a respondent, Brunschwig calls it "a machine that serves to produce premises for the conclusion at which the questioner wants to arrive, a conclusion which the dialectician has already in advance, but which he wants to reach by relying on opinions which his adversary will not be able not to assent to." He adds that "in the case of the rhetorician things may be a bit different, but the notion of the topic as a machine for producing premises is not a bad one."[17] However, once we have shed a brighter light on what *topoi* accomplish in rhetorical argumentation, we may be compelled to add another metaphor to this list, one which is more in tune with the actual performance of *topoi* in enthymemes.

Now, apart from the *topoi* that are *koinei* and are applicable to the subject matter of all arts and sciences, there are also "specific topics [...] derived from propositions which are peculiar to each species or genus of things" (31). These are the *idia*—the term deriving from *eidos*, literally, that which is specific or particular to something. Aristotle continues: "there are, for example, propositions about Physics which can furnish neither enthymemes nor syllogisms about Ethics, and there are propositions concerned with Ethics which will be useless for furnishing conclusions about Physics; and the same holds good in all cases" (31). Whereas commonplaces "will not make a man practically wise about any particular class of things, because they do not deal with any particular subject matter," specific *topoi*, by contrast, especially if they are well chosen, will lead the speaker who uses them to "unconsciously produce a science quite different from dialectic and rhetoric. For if once he hits upon first principles [*arkhai*], it will no longer be Dialectic or Rhetoric, but that science whose principle he has arrived at" (31). In other words, an orator who selects his premises from such special topics rather than from common *topoi*, that is, from *topoi* shared by all, will "insensibly be carried beyond the boundaries of his own art into an alien and special science."[18] Yet, according to Aristotle, "most enthymemes are constructed from these specific topics, which are called particular and special, fewer from those that are common or universal" (31). As will soon become clear, to rely on special topics to make one's point is, although practically inevitable, also what I would like to call the great temptation of rhetoric. If Aristotle spends so much time separating rhetoric from all sorts of things, it is not because this discourse could be rendered absolutely pure and free of contamination by enthymemes that draw their material from special topics. However, what becomes clear here is that the danger faced by rhetoric as a very human art—an art for speaking with one another about things that are more or less what they seem to be, but are of vital importance—is not only the temptation to use it for reprehensible purposes such as sophistry and demagogy, but also the temptation of becoming a science. As Aristotle remarks, "in proportion as anyone endeavours to make of Dialectic or Rhetoric, not what they are, faculties, but sciences, to that extent he will, without knowing it, destroy their real nature, in thus altering their character, by crossing over into the domain of sciences, whose subjects are certain definite things, not merely words" (41). By basing arguments on special topics, rhetoric furnishes proofs that are necessary, and that threaten what I would like to refer to as the fragile fabric of speaking with one another about issues of importance in everyday life—issues that, by their very nature, are contingent and allow for opposite responses. Since "most of the things which we judge and examine can be other than they are, [and] human actions, which are the subject of our deliberation and examination, being all of such a character and, generally speaking, none of them necessary" (25), the necessary should not play a major role in rhetorical argumentation. All necessity, as it enters into public argumentation, thwarts as well the participation of the audience in the making of the argument, without which there cannot be any deliberation worthy of the name. As the whole process of differentiation has shown, rhetoric, if is to be a method of showing in public deliberation what speaks for a course of action and what speaks against it and, consequently, of giving the citizens an opportunity to decide on the basis of the proof that has been offered, is a very fragile thing. Speaking with one another is marked by precariousness. If it is to consist in giving advice, then such advice, in order to be able to be taken, must not be based on necessity. If the counsel given is determined by necessity, then the individual or the audience to which it is given has nothing to decide. The counsel is forced upon it. Rhetoric, as the art of speaking with one another, must navigate between two extremes—the temptation of charlatanism and that of science. Only on this condition, one which makes it a very fragile enterprise, is a deliberation one between citizens.

3
LOGOS, TOPOS, STOIKHEION

AT THE END OF CHAPTER 2 of Book I of the *Rhetoric*, Aristotle makes a distinction between elements and propositions, *stoikheia* and *protaseis*. From the context it is clear that this distinction primarily concerns the genres of rhetoric—the deliberative, judicial, and epideictic kinds of oratory—which are the subject matter of the following chapter. Indeed, having just discussed the *koinoi*, or "universal topics," Aristotle, in his conclusion to chapter 2, writes that, before continuing with a discussion of the specific topics, it will be necessary to "ascertain the different kinds of Rhetoric, so that, having determined their number, we may separately ascertain their elements [*stoikheia*] and propositions [*protaseis*]" (33). The elements and premises to be taken up, then, are those that concern each one of the three genres of the art of speech. But since the distinction between universal topics and special topics, as those topics which form "the propositions peculiar to each class of things," itself frames the distinction between the elements and propositions proper to each genre of rhetoric, is it not also clear that, while the propositions characteristic of each genre may differ, their elements are always of the order of the universal? If this is correct, then a certain universality at least must be the distinguishing trait of the elements of rhetorical argumentation, no matter what genre it assumes.

In any case, the intention of chapter 3 of Book I of the *Rhetoric* is to first clarify the genres of rhetoric so that, once their number is established, this question of what are elements and what are propositions within the various genres of rhetoric may be settled. Only then will the question of the specific *topoi* be taken up again. The three different kinds of rhetoric that Aristotle distinguishes—the deliberative, forensic, and epideictic—are a function of the corresponding "three kinds of hearers," that is, of the specific hearers "to whom the end or object of the speech refers" (33). He writes:

> Now the hearer must necessarily be either a spectator [*theoros*] or a judge [*krites*], and a judge either of things past or of things to come. For instance, a member of the

general assembly is a judge of things to come; the dicast, of things past; the mere spectator, of the ability of the speaker. Therefore there are necessarily three kinds of rhetorical speeches, deliberative, forensic, and epideictic. (33)

The three genres, then, are a function of three kinds of hearers, in that all three are concerned with time, yet in different ways. Deliberative oratory in the public assembly, which as we have seen is about vital affairs of the citizens, is oriented toward action to be taken. The time referred to is, therefore, the future. Forensic discourse, on the other hand, concerns deeds that have already been committed; its time is thus the past. Finally, in the epideictic (later also called panegyric) speeches, which bestow praise or blame on something or someone, and in which the hearer watches and judges the performance of the speaker, the dominant form of time is the present.

A couple of things in Aristotle's account of the three genres need underlining. Since I am, above all, interested in the deliberative (*symbouleutikon*) genre of public speech, I would like to note first that, according to Aristotle, this genre is either protreptic (*protrope*) or apotreptic (*apotrope*), that is, either hortative or dissuasive. He further stresses the temporality peculiar to each genre, and in particular that of the deliberative, when he writes that "to each of these a special time is appropriate: to the deliberative the future; for the speaker, whether he exhorts or dissuades, always advises about things to come" (33–35). Since this genre concerns things to come and actions to take and, in this way, exhorts to do or dissuades from doing this or that, the deliberative genre is one concerned with the possible. Since any such possibility is a concern of practical life, it is necessarily a divided possible, as one that consists in alternatives between which one must choose or decide. Furthermore, each of these three kinds of public discourse has "a different special end [*telos*]" (35). For deliberative speech this end is "the expedient [*sympheron*, the advantageous] or harmful; for he who exhorts recommends a course of action as better, and he who dissuades advises against it as worse; all other considerations, such as justice and injustice, honour and disgrace, are included as accessory in reference to this" (35). In general, speaking together in everyday life, whether it concerns issues of national interest or the private well-being of citizens, is oriented toward the attainment of what is advantageous and away from that which either is not advantageous or is even harmful. What is advantageous must be the criterion that any speaker, or anyone who gives advice, must have on his mind first and foremost.

With this I circle back to the question that Aristotle left in abeyance at the end of chapter 2, that is, the question concerning the elements and propositions, or premises, of the genres of rhetoric, the clarification of which has to precede the discussion of the specific *topoi* in the remaining part of Book I. Aristotle avers:

> From what has been said it is evident that the orator must first have in readiness the propositions [*protaseis*] on these three subjects [characteristic of the three genres: the advantageous, the just, the honorable, and their opposites]. Now, necessary signs, probabilities, and signs are the propositions of the rhetorician; for the syllogism universally consists of propositions ["is wholly from propositions," Kennedy translates], and the enthymeme is a syllogism composed of the propositions above mentioned. Again, since what is impossible can neither have been done nor will be done, it is necessary for each of the three kinds of orators to have in readiness propositions dealing with the possible and the impossible, and as to whether anything has taken place or will take place, or not. (37)

The enthymeme, as a rhetorical syllogism, must thus be composed of propositions that, with respect to the three genres of oratory, are oriented toward the advantageous, the just, or the honorable. These propositions are of the order of *tekmeria*, probabilities, and anonymous signs. But considering that rhetorical argumentation is, above all, about what can also be otherwise rather than what is necessary or impossible—it is futile to deliberate about the latter—all these propositions must not simply be, in terms of content, about the possible and the impossible, but must be framed, structured, and informed in depth by these categories of the possible and the impossible. In the case of the deliberative genre, the propositions must be about possibilities that can be realized in the future, whereas in the case of the judicial genre, they must concern what has already happened. All premises of enthymemes must be instructed categorially by this question of the possible and the impossible. Aristotle continues:

> Further, since all, whether they praise or blame, exhort or dissuade, accuse or defend, not only endeavor to prove what we have stated, but also that the same things, whether good or bad, honourable or disgraceful, just or unjust, are great or small, either in themselves or when compared with each other, it is clear that it will be necessary for the orator to be ready with propositions dealing with greatness or smallness and the greater and the less, both universally and in particular; for instance, which is the greater or less good, or act of injustice or justice; and similarly with regard to all other subjects. (37–39)

In addition to propositions about the possible and the impossible, the rhetorician also needs propositions about the great and the small as well as the greater and the lesser, both generally and specifically. (In passing let me point out that these propositions regarding amplification are not to be conflated with propositions about "the more and the less" because the latter always involves some contrast, whereas propositions regarding amplification concern degrees of magnitude or the importance of something.)[1] What follows from this is that the propositions for enthymemes in all three kind of oratory must be concerned essentially with either the possible and the impossible, the greater and the lesser, or the more and the less, both *generally* and *specifically*, as Aristotle adds. By claiming that all the propositions for enthymemes must deal with these three issues both generally and specifically, Aristotle can, in my view, only mean two things. (1) The subjects of the propositions that are to furnish the premises for enthymemes have to concern specifically factual things that are possible or impossible, that are past or of the future, and that are marked by a degree of magnitude or importance. (2). The propositions themselves have to be such that they are all (generally, or universally), in-formed, that is, categorially structured, by these issues common to all genres of rhetoric. The first example of a *topos* given in the *Rhetoric* is the *topos* of "the more and the less." In the same way, then, "the past and the future," "the possible and the impossible," "the greater and the lesser" would all seem to be *topoi*, or even *koinoi topoi*. In short, all the propositions in all three genres of rhetoric would have to, formally speaking, conform to these three, or perhaps four, *topoi*. Remember that at the end of chapter 2, Aristotle claimed that he intended to take separately the elements and propositions of the different kinds of rhetoric. What, exactly, these propositions are should be clear by now, but the question of the identity of the elements, the *stoikheia*, remains.

In conformity with all the distinctions that, with the intention of circumscribing the scope of rhetoric, have been made in chapter 2, an additional distinction, now between *stoikheia* and *protaseis*, aims at further narrowing down the true essence of rhetoric. Although the kind of proposition that will serve as the premise of an enthymeme will vary according to which specific class of things is in question, that is, according to which of the different genres of rhetoric is at work, the elements of the enthymeme, as the syllogism peculiar to rhetoric, will remain the same. These elements, then, are something that is essential to rhetoric as such. Now, on two occasions at least, Aristotle remarks that "by element and topic of enthymeme [he] mean[s] the same thing" (295), and he adds that "element (or topic) is a head under which several enthymemes are included" (341–343). Elements and topics, *stoikheia* and *topoi*, are thus supposed to be identical. Several questions pose themselves right away. First, which are the *topoi* that Aristotle declares to be the same thing as the elements? For it is the case that Aristotle distinguishes between several kinds of *topoi*, a distinction that, as Cope remarks, "as far as Rhetoric is concerned is peculiar to Aristotle's system."[2] Indeed, besides the numerous special *topoi*, or *eide*, there are not only the *koinoi topoi* and their subordinate topics (discussed in Book II, chapter 19), but also the 28 *topoi enthymematon*, or *phainomenon enthymematon* listed in Book II, chapter 23. An additional difficulty arises from the fact that though one may want to identify the elements with the *koinoi topoi*, or, simply, the *koina*, the latter can also be understood in a very large sense so as to include the *koinoi pisteis* as well as the *koinoi topoi* properly speaking.³ Clarification of this additional problematic, particularly through distinguishing now, exactly, the *topoi* that coincide with the elements that are themselves universal, will complete the theoretical scaffolding of what I have, so far, called a very frail art. The second question that Aristotle's identification of the *topoi* with the *stoikheia* raises is this: What, precisely, is meant and what is gained through such identification?

Before attempting to clarify which kind of *topoi* are, strictly speaking, *stoikheia* and what it is, indeed, that Aristotle means (since he does not elaborate) when he simply remarks that, for him, *topoi* and *stoikheia* mean the same, let me first say a word about the *stoikheia* themselves. The earliest attested use of the term in a philosophical sense is to be found in Plato's *Theaetetus*, where some of its earlier prephilosophical connotations are still manifest. It is generally agreed that the word *stoikheion* derives from *stoikos*, "a row in an ascending series," and that its most basic meaning, therefore, is that of being "a member of a series." However, as a quick glance at relevant dictionaries demonstrates, the original significations of the term are held to be primarily those of "a letter of the alphabet" (either a simple sound or a writing mark), of an element into which something is ultimately divisible (as far as matter is concerned, the elements singled out in the venerable Milesian quest for the *arche* of which the world is made, and as far as the *logos* is concerned, Parmenides's *on* (Being) in whom this quest for the *arche* came to term, and which F. E. Peters characterizes as "the absolute radical *stoikheion*"), and, finally, of an element of proof such as, for example, a basic mathematical proposition or a fundamental proposition in the theory of music.⁴ Even though Hermann Diels devoted a whole book to the Greek word *stoikheion* and its Latin equivalent *elementum*, the relation of the originary meaning of the clearly attested root *steikho* or *stoikhos* to the various meanings of the term *stoikheion* remains, as Walter Burkert has pointed out, unclear. For most scholars, the meaning of *stoikheion* as element rests on understanding the root of the notion—*steikho* or *stoikhos*—in terms of the series formed by the letters of the alphabet. However, while providing additional support for a thesis already advanced by Otto Lagercrantz, Burkert has, in my view, convincingly argued that the meaning "letter" already presupposes a meaning of "element."⁵ According to Burkert, *stoikheion* has, from the start, meant "element," in advance of its manifold meanings including that of a letter of the alphabet. But before pursuing this line of thought and taking it, perhaps, a bit further, let me linger for a moment on the philosophical use of the term in antiquity. *Stoikheia* in Plato and Aristotle are predominantly associated with the notion of ultimate elements. As is especially obvious from the *Theaetetus*, Plato uses the term most often in the context of analysis and explication of complex subject matters and suggests that they can be reduced to, and derived from, a limited number of basic elements in the same way as syllables can be shown to be made up of individual letters or sounds. According to Aristotle's definition of the *stoikheion* in *Metaphysics* (V. 3.1014a), the *stoikheion* is a basic ingredient of a composite and is not divisible. Here, its earlier significations are also largely ignored, such as, for instance, its meaning as *arche*.[6] Yet, whether all the earlier references of the term have become meaningless in Aristotle's philosophical use of the term, and whether, in particular, its meaning of being an elementary ingredient of a composite is its sole philosophical meaning here, remains to be seen. When Aristotle calls the *topoi stoikheia*, it would thus seem that it is primarily in the sense of ultimate "elements." But what are elements? Are they merely irreducible elements, such as atoms of a composite, similar to letters that make up a syllable or word? Or could it be that, in addition to being elements of a composite, their overall function is to *do* something, even though they are distinct from principles?

As Cope holds in his *Introduction to Aristotle's Rhetoric*, Aristotle's reasons for calling the *koinoi topoi stoikheia* can be found in the section in Book V of the *Metaphysics* devoted to the *stoikheion*:

> *stoikheion* is an 'ultimate element,' something either altogether indivisible, or divisible only into *similar parts*. The term may be variously applied, as in language to its ultimate divisions, or letters, indivisible component parts, or atoms; in geometry to points, *stigmai*, the ultimate elements of space; in reasoning or proof, to the simplest and normal form of syllogism [...]. A *topos*, therefore, the genus or head of a multitude of *similar* and individual *topoi* of the same kind, may be called a *stoikheion* or 'element' of enthymematic reasoning, because it is only further divisible into *similar* parts, and thus corresponds with the definition of the latter.[7]

According to Cope, by calling the *topoi stoikheia*, Aristotle not only highlights their nature as basic elements for enthymematic reasoning, but also draws attention to the fact that they are such basic elements by virtue of being genres, or heads, that lend themselves to a multitude of similar *topoi*, that is, to *topoi* of the same kind. Cope notes Aristotle's contention in the *Rhetoric* that "element and topic [are] identical, since element (or topic) is a head under which several enthymemes are included" (341–342) in support of his own interpretation. In *Studies in the Philosophy of Aristotle's Rhetoric*, Grimaldi arrives at a similar conclusion when he holds that the topics are elements because they offer forms for inference within various subject matters.[8] *Stoikheia*, then, would be ultimate elements of enthymematic reasoning whose generality is of such a nature that, while it allows a *topos* to multiply by becoming divided into parts that are only variations of the same *topos*, it also prevents the parts from deviating from the genre, and thus from becoming adulterated in the slightest way. Here, one touches upon the conditions that allow the *topoi* to be illustrated by way of the metaphors of arsenal, magazine, container, stock, and even a machine. But are these conditions sufficient to explain the role that *topoi* indeed have in enthymematic reasoning? Needless to say, an answer to this question depends, first of all, on which *topoi*, exactly, serve as *stoikheia*.

Recall the statement at the end of chapter 2 in Book I that, before speaking about the specific topics, the different kinds of rhetoric have to be determined so that "we may separately ascertain their elements and propositions" (33). As I have already pointed out, the propositions are a function of the specific material (and ends) of the three species of oratory speech, whereas the elements must be what all three have in common. Let us also bear in mind that, in the same chapter, Aristotle draws attention to "a very great difference" that has escaped nearly everyone, and which concerns the materials of proof that are held to be demonstrative in rhetoric, namely, the distinction between special and general topics—between topics that belong to a specific domain and those that are common to all domains. Although Aristotle refers to the propositions that are peculiar to a specific class of things under discussion in public speech as *eide* or *idia*, it is also clear from the work that, qua sources of enthymemes, these propositions are also topics in the same way as are the *koinoi topoi*, that is, the "places" common to all classes of things.[9] When Aristotle declares that, before expanding on the specific topics, the different kinds of rhetoric have to be elucidated so that "we may separately ascertain their elements and propositions," the notion of *koinoi topoi* has already been established in at least general terms. *Koinoi topoi*, general or universal topics, are the sources of enthymemes in the sense that they provide all rhetorical argumentation with its premises or propositions. They themselves draw on opinions held by most citizens, or by reputable figures—again opinions rather than already proven truths as in the case of scientific *apodeixis*—opinions that either resemble truth, are for the most part true, or in all likelihood may be true. These *endoxa* are the *koinoi topoi* that make up the content of the premises of the rhetorical syllogism. But a subtle distinction needs to be made here: the *koinoi topoi* are not these opinions themselves, but the forms that this material assumes when it becomes part of an enthymeme. The *koinoi topoi* are *endoxa* that are shaped in such a way as to have the form of premises. Only in this sense can the *endoxa* be qualified as sources of enthymemes. But what about the special topics, or *eide*? In making the distinction between general and specific topics Aristotle had only pointed out that, while the former truly belong to rhetoric as an art of speaking that transgresses disciplines, the latter, which "derive from propositions which are peculiar to each species or genus of things" (31), tend to "transgress the limits of Rhetoric and Dialectic" since, by furnishing apodictic truths, they do not fall within the domain of what requires deliberation. Indeed, at the end of chapter 2 Aristotle's aim is to draw attention to the fact that specific topics endanger the rhetorical enterprise. But in chapters 4–15 Aristotle takes a different route and acknowledges their actual importance for rhetorical argumentation. He argues that the specific topics not only make up the overwhelming material source of rhetorical syllogisms, but also that they outnumber the *koinoi topoi*. It follows from this that, in order to be able to resort to propositions drawn from specific classes of things in order to form arguments that continue to be of the generality of rhetoric (rather than of science), the propositions in question, rather than being apodictic insights, must be considered as *opinions* about their respective subject matter. Furthermore, these propositions made up of a subject matter specific to a given domain must also assume a form that allows them to serve in a *rhetorical* syllogism. The deferral at the end of chapter 2 of Book I of a discussion of the specific topics thus comes into sharper light. In order to show the sense in which specific topics can serve at all as the material sources for rhetorical arguments, it is first necessary to distinguish between both the genres of rhetoric and the specific ends that each one pursues so that the distinct subject matter to be deliberated, judged, praised, or blamed in each respective genre can come clearly into view. The specific topics are subjects peculiar to a specific domain that allow an informed discussion in either the deliberative, judicial, or epideictic mode. As Grimaldi notes, "the purpose of the particular topics we find is to enable one to speak intelligently, but not scientifically, upon the subject under discussion."[10] However, being able to speak intelligently about the subject matter in question clearly implies that the *eide* must present the subject matter not as well-proven facts but in the form of opinions, if such discussion is not to move toward first principles and therein to become scientific. So, here too a subtle distinction needs to be observed: the specific topics that are drawn from the subject matter of a specific domain must express only opinions about this matter if they are still to be used in enthymematic reasoning. They must have the form of what can enter into a rhetorical syllogism, and yet they must remain closely related to this particular domain. Unlike the general topics, which transgress all domains, the specific topics are confined to the matter under discussion. Furthermore, their number is infinite, whereas the number of the general topics listed in Book II, chapter 23, are a finite twenty-eight. Before moving on, let us keep in mind that everything established regarding the general and specific topics after chapter 2 of Book I concerns topics no longer in general but as they work within the three species of rhetoric. This includes what is said about both the universal and specific topics. The same is true of the distinction between *stoikheia* and *protaseis* at the end of chapter 2. This distinction also only concerns the structure of enthymemes in relation to the different kinds of oratory.

What, then, is the relation between the thus defined special and general topics? As Grimaldi remarks, if the "'particular topics' (*eide*) [are] sources of information upon the subject-matter to be discussed," then the "'general topics' (*koinoi topoi*) [are] sources for modes of reasoning by enthymeme: forms of inference most suitable for the enthymeme."[11] The twenty-eight general topics that Aristotle distinguishes in Book II, chapter 23, and which Grimaldi, following Spengel's *Über das Studium der Rhetorik bei den Alten* (Munich, 1842), calls "formal topics" since they provide forms of reasoning in distinction from the special topics which are "material topics," are universal logical forms of inference that draw upon the matter from the material, or special, topics when conditioning an inference.[12] As Grimaldi has shown, these forms of reasoning, which can be classified according to the three logical patterns of cause/effect, more/less, and some other forms of relation, all amount in one way or another to the propositional form: "if one, then another."[13] These twenty-eight forms of inference, which can be applied to material that derives from special areas and which, in the enthymeme, assume the shape of *eide* (i.e., special topics) are, according to Grimaldi, the *koinoi topoi*. These topics, as their name suggests, permit rhetorical argumentation in all three kinds of rhetoric.

Now, when Aristotle remarks that once the different kinds of rhetoric are established, it should be possible to "separately ascertain their elements and propositions," it would seem to follow that the elements in question correspond to the thus understood *koinoi topoi*. *Topoi*, whether universal or particular, are, as we have seen, always "places" from which rhetorical argumentation derives. If these "places" apply indiscriminately to all kinds of subject matter and are required by all three genres of the art of speaking, then they must have an elementary character. While citing this statement of Aristotle in the transition to chapter 23 of Book II: "let us now speak of the elements of enthymemes (by element and topic of enthymeme I mean the same thing)" (295), Grimaldi forcefully makes this point in his *Studies in the Philosophy of Aristotle's Rhetoric*. Basing himself on a passage from the concluding chapter 26 of Book II, wherein Aristotle "regard[s] element and topic as identical, since element (or topic) is a head under which several enthymemes are included" (341–343), Grimaldi seeks to answer the question of "what is meant by calling [the *koinoi topoi*] *stoikheia*." The application of the term *stoikheia* to the *koinoi topoi* tells us, he argues, that these topics are "a larger category which contains many enthymemes" in the sense that they offer "a form for inference on various objects."[14] *Koinoi topoi* are universal elements to the extent that their forms of inference are general enough to allow them to be applied, in various enthymemes, to all possible subject matter (to the extent that the latter has been shaped into *eide*, that, like opinions, are the only things that rhetoric argues about). Their qualification as elements would suggest that, although they represent a larger category or genus, they themselves are no longer divisible into heterogeneous components. Rather, they simply let themselves be divided into similar parts, namely, into the particular enthymemes to which they give rise by being applied to a specific subject matter. But, I ask, can that be all a *stoikheion* performs, or even the most important of its functions? Is it not the case that the *koinoi topoi*, which serve to intelligently debate about various subject matters, must have been formed, shaped, or structured in advance in a way to be able to perform this task? But if this is so, is it not also those very elements that accomplish such structuring of the *topoi* for this task, rather than the twenty-eight *topoi enthymematon*, which would truly merit being called *koinon*, and, by extension, *stoikheia*?

At this juncture, it may be appropriate to briefly look at Aristotle's own definition of the term in *Metaphysics*. In Book III (3.998 a20–b3), Aristotle asks, "with regard to the first principles [*archai*], whether it is the general [*gene*] that should be taken as elements and principles [*stoikheia*], or rather the primary constituents of a thing: e.g. it is the primary parts of which all articulate sounds consist that are thought to be elements and principles of articulate sound, not the common genus—articulate sound." In this passage, Aristotle seeks to distinguish the first principles from the elements as ultimate parts of a whole. Yet, as suggested by Liddell and Scott, who, in a clearly phonocentric bias, add that "*stoikheia*, therefore, strictly, were different from letters [*grammata*]," the reference to the elements of articulate sound does not amount to establishing the original meaning of the term *stoikheion* as relating primarily to *phones* (*stoikeia*), since obviously the reference in question is only an example (although the first) in a series of other examples.[15] Indeed, Aristotle immediately follows up on this example by saying: "and we give the name of 'elements' to those geometrical propositions, the proofs of which are implied in the proofs of the others, either of all or of most." So to conclude the list of his examples, he gives two more examples of *stoikheia*: Empedocles's four elements, as well as the parts of which a thing such as a bed is made, and which help to explain the nature of a thing.[16] As is evident as well from section 3 of Book V (1014a26–b15) which is devoted to the term *stoikheion*, where he calls "an element that which is the primary component immanent in a thing, and indivisible in kind into other kinds," the reference to the elements of speech is only an example that serves to illustrate, rather than saturate, what is meant by the term. In short, what these discussions of the term demonstrate is that it has a generality of its own and is not to be thought of in light of one particular kind of element such as, for instance, letters of the alphabet. As Burkert has convincingly argued, if *stoikheion* is taken to mean primarily "letter" (whether in the sense of sound or written letter), then it is difficult to see how the meaning that the term has in geometry, namely of elements in the sense of fundamental propositions, presuppositions, and axioms, could be derived from it. As I have already pointed out, in Plato and Aristotle the term is always invoked in the context of rational analysis. In the fifth century the term clearly possesses, as Burkert writes, "an aura of rational analysis."[17] Since the model for such analysis is Greek mathematics, Burkert not only highlights the fact, rarely acknowledged at least philologically, that the term has been coined by Greek mathematics, but he also makes the argument that the general meaning of the term *stoikheia* as element, a meaning that subtends all its different meanings, is located precisely in its mathematical sense of element as foundation. He writes, "The mathematical propositions, which complement each other so as to form a system, and are logically oriented toward one another, these are *stoikheia*."[18] And he adds that although the image of the series of letters may have contributed to explaining the spread of this "fashionable word [*Modewort*] from mathematics" to other enterprises, such as the Sophists' attempt to bring Greek metrics into a system *more geometrico*, what ultimately explains the recourse to this term is the scientific claim to exact analysis that is associated with it.[19] In other words, if Burkert's derivation is correct, and if "*stoikheion* means from the start something else than 'letter,'" then this is further evidence of the need to understand *stoikheia* in the general sense of fundamental propositions from which scientific analysis has to proceed, rather than primarily in the sense of an ultimate ingredient of a composite as are the letters in syllables or words.[20] Let me also add that, qua fundamental proposition, "element" has, from the outset, a meaning that concerns the conditions from which propositions are derived, in other words, one that concerns the very syllogistic character for which it provides the foundation. To emphasize the "general" sense of the term is also to highlight its meaning of element in rational analysis without prejudging its nature, and also the fact that the number of elements is indeed limited to only a few.[21] We may do well to keep this generality of the term in mind for what I will try to say in the following about the *stoikheia* in Aristotle's *Rhetoric*.

So far I have followed Grimaldi's rationale for identifying the *stoikheia* with the *koinoi topoi* that Aristotle distinguishes toward the end of Book II of the *Rhetoric*. However, before I attempt to identify another, and in my view a more fundamental, candidate as a referent for the term *stoikheia*—more fundamental because more general and fewer in number—I wish to linger briefly on the additional reasons that Grimaldi has offered for his identification of the *stoikheia* with the *koinoi topoi*, here understood as *topoi enthymematon*. I turn, therefore, to his *Aristotle, Rhetoric I: A Commentary*, where he comments in some detail on the term *stoikheion* as it appears in Aristotle's statement that he wishes to separately ascertain the elements and propositions of the different kinds of rhetoric. Grimaldi draws our attention again to the fact that Aristotle identifies the elements and the topics only after a discussion of "the particular topics for *reason, ethos, pathos*, which provide the material for statements, i.e. *protaseis*," which is then followed by "a study of the general topics (i.e., our *stoikheia*) which allow one to put the statements in the forms of simple inferences." In my examination of Grimaldi's account of the difference between *eide* and *koinoi topoi*, the latter had been characterized as offering forms of inference on various topics. When Grimaldi writes: "The topics are the method which Aristotle devised (a) to supply one with the content for an intelligent examination of the subject of discourse, and, (b) to present one with ways in which to express this content by forms of deductive reasoning," he is speaking of the topics in a general way. The topical method serves to furnish on the one hand the material necessary to discuss a particular subject matter in public discourse: these are the *eide*, or special topics, and on the other hand common places that are forms of inferential reasoning, whose function consists in providing "the forms of inference in which to present this material." Let me try to understand this function of the *koinoi topoi* as clearly as possible. In the process of speaking with people about a subject matter, and in order to provide them with reasons that speak for or against it, the orator must rely on special topics that, as we know from the *Rhetoric*, must not only concern the subject matter at issue, but also the audience (*pathos*) and the speaker (*ethos*); furthermore, the orator must shape this material by way of publicly recognized forms of inference if the discussion with one another about this material is to be convincing, in other words, if it is to be argumentative, that is, syllogistic in the specifically rhetorical way of enthymematic reasoning, and thus have the character of proof. These generally accepted forms of inference are the *topoi enthymematon*, that is, the twenty-eight forms of logical patterns distinguished in chapter 23 of Book II, which Grimaldi holds to be *koinoi topoi*. The special topics, Grimaldi adds, provide "the material element for discourse" with one another, whereas the general topics "offer the speaker the formal element for discourse, the ways in which to express the material in forms of inference." Therefore, "the work of the general topics, which give inferential forms for structuring the material" allows, I hold, for the convincing presentation in public discourse of a subject matter that is vital to the community precisely by shaping this material according to argumentative forms accepted by the audience that are perceived as persuasive. On this condition alone can the advice sought and given in public deliberation about issues of vital importance to the citizens of the *polis* be heard. If Grimaldi concludes his commentary by pointing out that, although Aristotle's *Rhetoric* must draw on both kinds of topics characteristic of the art of speech as an art of speaking with one another, but that nonetheless "the general topics are *more* proper to it as an art which, like dialectic, transcends all the specific disciplines and may be used in all of them," then it follows that it is the latter that also merit the status of elements.[22]

Here, then, is the point at which we must remind ourselves again that in the *Rhetoric* the term *topos* is a general term that, according Cope's account, is divided into three kinds. Apart from the specific *topoi* (even though the *eide* are never explicitly designated as *topoi*) and the general, or *koinoi, topoi*, there are also the *topoi enthymematon* mentioned in Book II, 23.1. These are, in fact, the topics that Grimaldi singled out in discussing the *koinoi topoi*, the only *topoi* that, according to him, truly deserve the title "elements." Yet, in *An Introduction to Aristotle's Rhetoric*, Cope had set these *topoi*, that is, the *topoi enthymematon* from which enthymemes may be derived (or that are about enthymemes), apart from the *koinoi topoi* properly speaking. But then, what are the latter?

Let me start by recalling that, after having determined in Book II the specific topics whence speakers derive proofs in the three kinds of oratory (and from which it is possible to make speeches ethical), and prior to passing on to a discussion in chapter 23 of the *topoi* from which enthymemes may be constructed, Aristotle remarks in chapter 18 that "it only remains to discuss the topics common [*koinon*] to the three genres of rhetoric" (265). Aristotle does not speak of topics here but of *koina*, thus omitting the noun to which they apply. Grimaldi goes so far as to contend that the *koina* do not even refer to the topics as defined in the *Rhetoric*, namely as "always that from which rhetorical argumentation is derived: *tous topous hex on*."[23] *Koina* cannot mean *topoi* or *koinoi topoi*, Grimaldi holds. So, before further pursuing this issue, let me first establish what the *koina* are that all orators must resort to whether they are engaged in deliberative, judicial, or epideictic speeches. Aristotle writes: "For all orators are obliged, in their speeches, also to make use of the topic of the possible and impossible, and to endeavor to show, some of them that a thing will happen, others that it has happened. Further the topic of magnitude is common to all kinds of Rhetoric, for all men employ extenuation or amplification whether deliberating, praising or blaming, accusing or defending" (265). Of these *koina* which, in the Greek original, are referred to not as topics, as the translation suggests, but as premises and common features (that is, precisely as *koina*), there are only three or, perhaps, four: the possible and the impossible (*dynaton kai adynaton*), past and future (*to gegonos kai to mellon*), the more or the less (*to mallon kai etton*), and possibly, if one follows Cope and Kennedy, amplification and depreciation (*to auxein kai meioun*), which, as a distinction that involves a degree of magnitude or importance, could be distinct from the topic of the "more or less," which refers to a contrast.[24] Aristotle continues by saying that once all these *koina* "have been determined, we will endeavour to say what we can in general about enthymemes and examples, in order that, when we have added what remains, we may carry out what we proposed at the outset" (265).

These three or, perhaps, four *koina*—I leave this undecided—are common to all three species of rhetoric, although, as Aristotle remarks at the end of chapter 18, "of the commonplaces [*koinon*] amplification is most appropriate to epideictic rhetoric, as has been stated; the past to forensic, since things past are subject of judgement; and the possible and future to deliberative" (265). They are thus, as underlined by Grimaldi—for whom they do not represent topics, as we have seen—intimately connected with the three ends, or *idia tele*, of the three kinds of rhetoric—that is, the expedient, the just, and the honorable—and are necessary to the orator for achieving the goal particular to each kind of speech. According to this author, the *koina* concern exclusively the ends of the rhetorical genres in the sense that each special end of rhetoric can be achieved only through utilizing one or all three of these common aspects. Whereas topics, for Grimaldi, "are always that *from which* rhetorical argumentation is derived," the *koina* "are those aspects of a subject *with which* rhetorical argumentation is concerned."[25] As I have already indicated in the discussion about the possible and the impossible, deliberative speech is, from the start, about things that are possible, whereas everything that manifestly is impossible is not an object of deliberation to begin with. But what became clear as well is that such material importance of the possible, as well as of the future, in deliberative oratory is not limited to being only that *with which* rhetorical argumentation is concerned. Furthermore, let us bear in mind that although, in practice, the three or four *koina* correspond, as their name "*koina*" indicates, most properly to the respective *tele* of the three genres of oratory, they constitute at the same time all three genres. None of the three genres is thinkable without these three or four *koina*.

It thus seems necessary to try to draw sharp lines around these *koina*, sharper lines than even Grimaldi has drawn, who saw himself forced to acknowledge the "particular character and the place which they occupy in Aristotle's rhetorical analysis."[26] As we have seen, for Grimaldi, they cannot mean topics, and especially not *koinoi topoi*, whereas for Cope, the *koina* "are *the* topics, *topoi*, or *koinoi topoi*, 'universal' topics [. . .] alike applicable to all the materials of the several sciences from which the *eide* are derived, and are thus 'common' to all."²⁷ Will it be necessary, then, to choose between one interpretation or another? While postponing a decision for the moment, I will begin by trying to figure out what is at stake here.

I recall again Aristotle's words toward the end of chapter 18 that, once the *koina* have been determined, he will speak about the two properly rhetorical types of proof—that is, the enthymemes as well as the examples—"in order that, when we have added what remains, we may carry out what we proposed at the outset" (265). In other words, now that the *koina* have been defined, Aristotle can move from what, until now, had only been established in a general fashion about rhetorical proof, to a more concrete rendering of it by examining how proof is actually furnished in all three genres of rhetoric, thus completing the program as it originally had been laid out. This program had been announced at the end of chapter 2 of Book I after all the major distinctions regarding rhetoric had been put into place, namely to ascertain the respective elements and propositions of the three kinds of rhetoric once these genres have been established. Aristotle makes good on this program in the last chapters of Book II, first, in Cope's words, by providing in chapter 19 an "analysis of the[se] four *koinoi topoi* into their subordinate topics" and by listing all the "modes of their application."²⁸ Secondly—following a return to the enthymeme and the paradigm as the only two *koinoi pisteis* of rhetoric (chapter 20) as well as a discussion of the *gnomai* (i.e., judgments), which are presented as a subspecies of the enthymeme (chapter 21), and finally an elaboration on the distinction between demonstrative and refutative, or destructive, enthymemes (chapter 22)—Aristotle furnishes, in chapter 23, an analysis and classification of the main specimens of the two kinds of enthymemes and an illustration, in detail, by the twenty-eight topics listed thereafter. However important these twenty-eight topics are for the formation of enthymemes in all three genres of rhetoric, they are merely subordinate in nature if one compares them to the three or four *koina* (or *koina topoi*, according to Cope), whose definitions Aristotle regards as a major part of the theoretical framework of the *Rhetoric*.

I have already briefly alluded to the first evocation of the term *topos* in the *Rhetoric*. It occurs in Book I, chapter 2, where Aristotle writes: "I mean by dialectical and rhetorical syllogisms those which are concerned with what we call 'topics' [*topous*], which may be applied alike [*eisin oi koinoi*] to Law, Physics, Politics, and many other sciences that differ in kind, such as the topic [*topos*] of the more or less, which will furnish syllogisms and enthymemes equally well for Law, Physics, or any science whatever, although these subjects differ in kind" (31). The first example given of a *topos* that is common, in that it can be applied to all sciences, is the topic of the more or less, which, as we have seen, is one of the three or four *koina* whose limited number Aristotle underscores right away. Thus it does not seem correct to hold, as does Grimaldi, that Aristotle denies the title of topics to the *koina*. Let us also take note of the fact that, in introducing the concept of topic, meaning in fact *koinon*, Aristotle is not yet concerned with the differences between genres of rhetoric, but only with that, indeed, *from which* enthymemes are constructed for any subject whatsoever.

In his assessment of the *koina*, which is entirely oriented by what Aristotle says about the three genres and their respective ends, Grimaldi submits that once it is established that there are three genres, each with its particular end and each calling for deliberation and judgment, Aristotle

> goes on to make one final determination with respect to the general nature of rhetoric. This last determination sets forth those elements which are ultimately demanded before the whole process can begin. These elements are the *koina*, which, in short, represent the common and basic requisites postulated with respect to any subject in order that it may become an object of the rhetorical *techne*. They represent categories within which a subject must fall before it can be used by the orator. Prior to the attempt to demonstrate any one of the three particular ends for any subject the orator must know and be able to show for that subject its possibility (or impossibility), its actuality (present–past) or potential actuality (future), and its general significance (great–small). This is clearly set forth [...] in the *Rhetoric* before Aristotle moves on to his discussion of the *koinoi topoi*.[29]

Unmistakably, Grimaldi recognizes the fundamental function of the *koina* for rhetoric as an art of speaking in public about issues that are of vital importance to the audience. It is a function that concerns the very nature of the subject matter to be deliberated, to be given advice on, and to be judged in public discourse. The subject must fall within the categories that are the *koina* as the categories of the possible and impossible, past and future, the more or less, and the great and the small, before it can at all be considered within the ends that determine a particular genre of rhetoric. For Grimaldi, the *koina* are fundamental categories for rhetoric insofar as they must have formed beforehand all the issues that can be the object of oratory speech. Yet, in contrast to the *koinoi topoi* from which rhetorical syllogisms are constructed, the *koina* would thus only refer to that *with which* rhetorical argumentation is concerned. The deep reason why Grimaldi reserves the designation *stoikheia* for what he considers to be the *koinoi topoi*, namely, the twenty-eight *topoi enthymematon*, is that they must be elements of rhetorical proof. However, if the term *stoikheia* refers, as Burkert has shown, to fundamental propositions thus anterior to elements of proof, the *koina* are *stoikheia* in a quintessential fashion. As I have already suggested, the three or four *koina* do not only concern the subject matter of all three kinds of oratory, but rather the propositions themselves that each orator must have at his disposition independently of the ends pursued by each kind of rhetoric.

Let me recapitulate: after having shown that the orator must have in readiness the propositions on the expedient, the just, the honorable (and their contraries) that correspond to the three ends of oratory art, and that these propositions are either necessary signs, probabilities, or anonymous signs (*tekmeria*, *eikota*, or *semeia anonyma*), Aristotle, turning again to the distinction between what is and what is not an object of rhetoric, writes in Book I, chapter 3, that "since what is impossible can neither have been done nor will be done, but only what is possible, and since what has not taken place nor will take place can neither have been done nor will be done, it is necessary for each of the three kinds of orators to have in readiness propositions dealing with the possible and the impossible, and as to whether anything has taken place or will take place, or not." (37). He continues that line of thought by saying that the orator must "be ready with propositions dealing with greatness and smallness and the greater and the less, both universally and in particular" (39). Does what Aristotle advances here not clearly indicate that *all* of the orator's propositions, whether *tekmeria*, *eikota*, or *semeia anonyma*, must deal with the possible and the impossible, the past and the future, the more or the less, and so forth, not merely in the sense of being about them, but in the sense of being formed by them? Thus understood, the three or four *koina* in question would be truly fundamental in that they would determine that with which rhetorical argumentation is concerned as well as instruct the very way in which rhetorical art speaks about its issues, independently of the particular end pursued by each particular kind of oratory.

If my interpretation is correct, would I not have to agree, then, with Cope who argues that only the *koina* are, in truth, *koinoi topoi*, and, in the same breath, the *stoikheia*? No doubt, but a caveat may be warranted as well. I recall Cope's definition of a *topos*, one that, by the way, he shares with many other commentators, Grimaldi included, namely that a *topos* is a genus or head of a multitude of similar and individual *topoi* of the same kind. The traditional metaphor for this conception of the *topos* is that of a container, an arsenal, a stock, and even a machine. Yet if the *koina* are the *koinoi topoi*, and if, indeed, they do not concern only the subject matter debated in public oratory, but the very way the argumentation takes place, then, perhaps, another term is more appropriate for referring to them as ultimate elements. Perhaps it is no longer a question of replacing one metaphor with another. Needless to say, all the metaphors that so far have been proposed to explain what a *topos* is are not simply makeshift solutions. But the term that I will propose to circumscribe the meaning and function of topics, if it still is a metaphor, is one that perhaps permits one to *think* what a *topos* accomplishes in view of enthymematic reasoning. If it is the case that the three or four *koina* must shape all of the orator's propositions about the subject matter at issue in public deliberation, could one then not speak of them, as Grimaldi already did, though in passing, as "categories"? Are they not the basic forms that allow the speaker to structure the endoxic material that is the source for propositions about things in deliberation in such a way that it can become a proposition of an enthymeme to begin with? Are the *koina* not *schema*, in the sense of shapes, that form endoxic subject material, giving it the form required for propositions about things that are discussed in the continuous discourse of rhetoric, which must concern things that are possible or impossible, great or small, that belong to the past or the future, and are to be qualified in terms of the distinction "more or less"? Let us remind ourselves about the scope of Aristotelean rhetoric: in distinction from dialectic, which takes place between a questioner and a respondent, rhetoric is a continuous discourse in which people in public speak with one another about pressing issues, deliberating and seeking advice about what next to do. Such speech is lively speech, a speech that concerns issues vital to the community and that, as Aristotle does not tire to recall, is about things that must be possible or impossible, of the past or the future, great or small, more or less. Things that have this quality are all of the sublunar domain of what humans are capable of: the possible and the impossible concerns exclusively possibilities that are of the order of what can be done or not, while the relative values of great or small, or more or less, are values that make sense only in the domain of finite quantity and proper to the relative mode of being, which is that of being with one another, and past or future is solely about things in the practical domain that have already occurred or that still need to be undertaken. In contrast to the things with which rhetoric is concerned, the *koina* are the forms that allow one to speak in lively interchange about these issues in an argumentative way, in the only argumentative way that is appropriate in this case, namely, in reasoning about the probable and that which resembles truth by way of enthymemes that present the audience with evidence on the basis of which it can make its decisions.

The *koina*, then, are *the* elements, the *stoikheia* of lively speech with one another about practical issues within the *koinonia* of the *polis*. This is not in the sense, however, that they would be the basic indivisible ingredients of a composite speech. Nor is it to be understood in the sense of *grammata*, or letters (vocal or written). Without rehearsing here, in detail, the history of the distinction between *stoikheia* and *grammata*, which Burkert has provided in exemplary fashion in his essay "STOIKHEION," I limit myself to a quote from Lagercrantz that guides Burkert's analysis. Lagercrantz writes: "Letters are *stoikheia* insofar as they are fundamental or alphabetical forms; the letters are *grammata* insofar as they are actual forms of interconnected pieces of writing."[30] As a result, *grammata* are *stoikheia* only insofar as they are fundamental forms, or elements, distinct from the letters of which an actual piece of writing is made up. Phenomenologically speaking, one could say that the *stoikheia* are, with respect to the *grammata*, the being-letter, or the being-written of the letter, and that *grammata* can be called *stoikheia* only when they mean elements in the sense of fundamental forms of actual writing marks. If the *koina*, then, are the *stoikheia* of lively speech with one another in practical life about issues of concern to all, then this can only mean that they are the forms that make it possible for such speech to be a reasoned speech, a speech that provides proof in the only manner that is appropriate in this domain, that is, by way of enthymemes structured according to commonplaces. The *koina*, as *stoikheia* of the *logos*, here understood as a speaking with one another about the practical world, are the elemental shapes or schema that, rather than stifling discourse, which philosophy has accused rhetorical topics of doing since the Enlightenment, and which, consequently, would represent a deadening obstacle within speech, preventing it from being present to itself, are the "writing" marks that make speaking with one another into lively speech to begin with, that is, a speech capable of showing the truth that resembles truth, the only truth that matters to those who, in everyday life, must decide.

As elements, the *koina* that shape speaking with one another in such a manner that this speaking becomes deliberative, and this in a way that the enthymeme becomes the core of the proof that such speaking furnishes, are elements in the sense of fundamental presuppositions. They are universal structures or schemas for rhetoric as the art of speech. They thus have an unmistakable generality or ideality. But Aristotle does not speak of the *koina* as *eide* (paradoxically, in the *Rhetoric* this term is reserved for the special topics, which are anything but ideal structures). Let us recall here Lucretius's non-authentic statement that, although immortal, the elemental and indivisible bodies that make up everything in the universe are by nature very fragile.[31] How much more fragile must the ideal and formal elements be that constitute the fragile art of speaking with one another! Undoubtedly, in the same way as the *eide* of philosophical discourse, the *koina* are *eide* of some sort. But theirs is an ideality that is determined by the particular situation in which lively speech comes about, the particular audience to which it is directed, and the particular issues that are being deliberated. The *koina* are not purely ideal structures, but, although general forms, they are at the same time contingent formal structures of the relation of the always contingent *logos* with the world. Just as the objects that are discussed in public speech are only objects that, from a practical point of view, are possible or impossible, belong to the past or the future, are great or small, or more or less, so too the *koina* are the translation into propositional structures of these finite qualities of practical life. Their universality and ideality is thus of such a kind that it fits the fragile art of speaking with one another, which, as we have seen, must navigate the discourse of the imposter and the man of science.

Since antiquity, with the exception of Aristotle, philosophy has characterized rhetoric as no art, or at best, a base art. Rhetoric has been consistently associated by the philosophic establishment with imposture and more generally with a fall from some high ground. What may be the ultimate reasons for which rhetoric has owned such a reputation? Could it be because rhetoric rests on *koina* that are ultimate elements, on *stoikheia*? It is well known that *stoikheia*, understood as ultimate particles at least, are intimately linked to a downward movement. According to the atomists, they fall in a vertical line through the void of the universe before they deviate from their straight route to form worlds. Downward movement and deviation, hence also aberration, are part and parcel of the ultimate elements. As based on *koina*, that is, commonplaces that are ultimate elements, the art of *logos* is thus the difficult task of a practice of deliberation that is by nature caught in a downward movement in which it must seek to avoid the temptations characteristic of rhetoric: charlatanism and science. But this downward movement may also be its ultimate chance.[32]

PART II

REFLECTION (HEIDEGGER)

IF SOMETHING LIKE thought were possible, that is, if thought would indeed come to pass in philosophical reflection (*Besinnung*), in an inquiry that is entirely directed toward making thought occur, then for such thought, Heidegger submits in *Besinnung*, "it would not be essential whether it succeeds in making an observation about something hitherto unknown, [and] whether something conducive to 'life' can be determined."[1] By contrast, what is essential to thought, as Heidegger understands it, is exclusively whether within it Being itself has come properly into its own (*sich er-eignet*) and, in the same stroke, has thus abysmally unsettled metaphysical, that is, philosophical, thought as we know it. For a thinking in which Being would occur, it would thus be inessential whether such thought would be conducive to, useful, or helpful for 'life.' Undoubtedly, the claim in question is somewhat provocative. However, as the single quotation marks indicate, Heidegger is not alluding to just any concept of life, or to life in general, but to a very specific conception of 'life.' Within the context of this reflection on the conditions required for thought to get under way, the concept of 'life' is indebted to a certain 'philosophy of life.' Indeed, some pages later in *Besinnung*, Heidegger remarks that even "that kind of metaphysics which pretends to have overcome Descartes and the prehistory of modernity up until the 19th century by way of a recourse to 'life' ['*das Leben*']" has in no way escaped the forgetfulness of Being but, on the contrary, has made such forgetfulness into the unavowed principle of its philosophizing.[2] Heidegger, no doubt, refers here to Henri Bergson and, above all, to

Wilhelm Dilthey as the main representatives of this philosophical movement at the end of the nineteenth and the beginning of the twentieth century, which sought to overcome the rationalist subject/object divide through recourse to the phenomena of inner life and its psychic and historico-cultural expressions. Furthermore, not only is 'life' inessential to thought; for the thinking of Being, as is manifest from the quoted passage, it is equally inessential whether or not such thinking contributes to our knowledge. This claim is no less provocative. But Heidegger has here again a very determined notion of knowledge in mind, namely, the one according to which philosophical knowledge is in essence epistemological and logical. Resisting any identification of philosophical and scientific thought, and, ultimately, the reduction of philosophy to a mere mimicry of the sciences—a maid, at best, at their service—Heidegger makes a case for philosophical thinking's autonomy by recalling its origin in the concern with Being. The uncoupling of thought from 'life' as understood in the 'philosophy of life,' that is, from a conception of life for which psychology as a pilot science provided guidance both to Bergson's biologism and Dilthey's historicism, pursues the same objective.

In the Freiburg lectures from 1919 on "The Idea of Philosophy and the Problem of *Weltanschauung*," to which the first chapter of this part of the book is devoted, the young Heidegger takes head-on the then dominating form of philosophy—neo-Kantianism—and its goal to establish a scientific philosophy, that is, philosophy as a science not of any particular domain but of what is shared by all the particular sciences, characterizing it as the epitome of an epistemological understanding of philosophical thought. Since knowledge and the theory of knowledge are in essence theoretical, philosophy thus conceived is in essence a theoretical enterprise. In the case of neo-Kantianism, furthermore, the theoretical, in the form of theoreticism, has in Heidegger's judgment become the foundation of a *Weltanschauung*. This pervasive theoreticism, which drives the thought, in particular, of Heinrich Rickert and Paul Natorp, is the main target of Heidegger's first lectures in Freiburg. However, in distinction from what obtains in the case of the later Heidegger, his critique in the early lectures of philosophy's emulation of scientific methodologism and theoreticism is conducted not only in a phenomenological perspective and in the name of lived experience but also in the name of a concept of life that, admittedly, is still indebted to the philosophy of life. Indeed, neo-Kantianism's theoreticism becomes construed as the very obstacle to accomplishing an *Ur-wissenschaft*, whose main theme would be the phenomena of life and that would itself be a form, or, rather, *the* form, of life, as well. With its emphasis on the atheoretical nature of philosophy as an *Ur-wissenschaft*, whose prime object is life as lived life, Heidegger's lectures demonstrate a clear bias against theory, theory being understood here primarily in terms of the theoretical sciences and of a philosophy such as neo-Kantianism that, afraid of losing its traditional standing as the queen of the sciences, competes with the sciences in a struggle for theoretical rigor. Even though Heidegger does not question the legitimacy of the theoretical sciences' existence or their actual servitude to a certain form of life reduced to biological or culturally mediated needs, his aversion to the theoretical sciences remains a consistent feature of his thought that takes on several forms in his work, such as the assessment of the sciences' derivative nature (which we will look at in some detail in the second chapter of this part of the book), the primarily technical nature of the modern sciences, or their inability to inquire into their own essence. Overall, this critique of the sciences is a fundamental critique of theory.

In order to gather what is at stake in such a critique, I focus for a moment on the following remarkable passage from Heidegger's first seminar, mentioned above, in Freiburg from 1919:

> Let us transpose ourselves into the comportment of the astronomer, who in astrophysics inquires into the phenomenon of the rising sun simply as a natural process, and who, remaining indifferent to this event, simply lets it take place before himself, and juxtapose to it the experience of the chorus of the Theban elders. Which on the first friendly morning after the successful defensive battle, looks, in Sophocles' 'Antigone,' at the rising sun: 'Glory—great beam of the sun, brightest of all that ever rose on the seven gates of Thebes, you burn through night at last!'[3]

Even though I cannot try here to give this juxtaposition of the scientist's attitude to that of the Theban elders the full attention it deserves, let me at least emphasize that in the juxtaposition the scientist's comportment is opposed to an experience that is expressed in Greek tragedy. It is, indeed, the first reference to Sophocles's *Antigone* by Heidegger, who, beginning with his *Introduction to Metaphysics* (1935), engages this particular tragedy in various attempts at interpretation. Despite their diversity, however, all these interpretations seek to show that the world as it existed for and was experienced or lived by the Greeks is articulated, if not inaugurated, by the poet through, precisely, the tragic genre.[4]

What does this juxtaposition of the scientific and theoretical attitude regarding the rising sun to that of the Theban elders beholding it in Sophocles's tragedy bring to light? For the indifferent astronomer who merely lets it happen in front of him as an abstract 'I,' the rising sun is just a natural event that takes its course and that can eventually be measured, calculated, and made predictable; by contrast, on this morning after the retreat of the Argive army, which under the leadership of the "Seven against Thebes" had sought to seize the city by power, the Theban elders greet the rise of the sun as the beginning of a new morning, something that was far from being assured given the threat to which Thebes had found itself exposed. The elders experience this sunrise as a singular event, not as merely another day in the continuous history of Thebes but, rather, as the unhoped for and unanticipatable beginning of a new day. The sun on this friendly morning is felt to be brighter than ever for having, indeed, burnt through the darkness of night against all odds. It is the experience of the daybreak as the beginning of an*other* morning.

Although made only in passing, the observation in the Freiburg lectures that the neo-Kantians are totally "clueless" with respect to "the phenomenon of *Fremderfahrung*"—the phenomenon of the experience of the other and what is the foreign—is telling inasmuch as this cluenessness is squarely attributed to their extreme theoreticism.[5] It is a theme, moreover, that reverberates throughout all of Heidegger's later discussions of the theoretical sciences, including the essay on "Science and Reflection" from 1953, which I will take up in some detail in the third chapter of this section. In spite of their expansion around the globe, the theoretical sciences are, as Heidegger intimates, incapable of encountering other cultures and other worlds. If this is so, it is essentially because of the sciences' representational, calculating, and measuring approach. In Ute Guzzoni's words: "Distance, being-foreign, otherness, remoteness, secret, all this is excluded if, on the one hand, constant availability and *Bestellbarkeit*, and on the other hand, universal calculability, and, therefore, also comparability of everything with everything is to be guaranteed."[6] To return, then, to the juxtaposition of the astronomer and the Theban elders, it should be clear by now that the theoretical sciences and the theoreticism of a philosophy that, at the forefront of the sciences, has abandoned walking a path of its own are unable to accommodate what is specific about the elders' experience of the rising sun. For the sciences, all sunrises, all daybreaks are the same. They are unable to account for any day in the particular way it is lived, unable, that is, to make sense not only of the experience of one day in its very newness—the todayness of today—but, indeed, also of a day that in all its unexpectedness is an*other* day, a day incomparable to any other day before. Only the atheoretical attitude of phenomenology is judged capable of responding to this experience of the miracle of the day insofar as it itself is a form of life and, as such, as we will see, attuned to the to-come, to what is not yet, to what ultimately is not foreseeable—in short, to other worlds to be lived.

Now, once Heidegger abandons the topic of life and turns toward Dasein's concern with Being and, after the *Kehre*, toward the question of Being itself, everything aimed at from the early Freiburg lectures to *Being and Time*, which could be achieved only through an atheoretical attitude attuned to lived experience, becomes the subject matter not of theory, of course, but, curiously enough, of *theoria*. However, let us not hastily conclude that Heidegger has reversed his opposition to theory, nor simply that he has now rediscovered a more originary, Greek meaning of the notion. Undoubtedly, the reevaluation of *theoria* by the later Heidegger is not at all of one piece. In the "Letter on Humanism," for example, it is still said that the characterization of thinking as *theoria*, that is, as an activity that takes place for its own sake and that therefore is not 'practical,' "occur[s] *already* within the 'technical' interpretation of thinking."[7] In other words, *theoria* is the index of a misconception of the nature of thinking that started with the inception of philosophical thought in early Greece. By contrast, thinking as the thinking of Being "exceeds all contemplation because it cares for the light in which a seeing, as *theoria*, can first live and move."[8] *Theoria*, as opposed to thinking, is, then, in essence not very different from the theory to which the sciences lay claim. *Theoria* is just the Greek name for and the etymological origin of theory. Yet if, in "Science and Reflection," thinking and *theoria* enter into a surprising relation of nearness, it is, as we will see, because the very concept of *theoria* in which modern theory has its roots undergoes, paradoxically, a radical mutation when thought takes on what is called 'theory' in the sciences.

Theoria, then, is here no longer to be understood in terms of Platonic contemplation distinct from and, in fact, in opposition to the practical concerns of life in the polis but, rather, in a more Aristotelian manner, as the highest form of the practical. More precisely, since the notions of theory and praxis mutually imply one another and, as such, rest on a metaphysical understanding of what is, *theoria* as a form of life is, as Heidegger repeatedly stresses, to be situated beyond the traditional theory/praxis divide. Rather than the highest form of a praxis understood as the correlate of a theory that in a disinterested manner inquires into things as they are understood in traditional ontology, *theoria* is now seen by Heidegger as a form of 'praxis' of the highest order in the sense that it corresponds and responds to (*Entsprechen*) what in it is beheld, that is, Being itself, and, at the same time, actively participates in what it is involved in and makes it happen by bringing it into its own. *Theoria*, consequently, is a kind of thought that is 'performative,' a kind of thinking that at the same is a kind of acting. *Theoria* is an acting-thinking more originary than the classical theory/praxis divide. It should thus be clear from the outset that the introduction of the notion of *theoria* by the later Heidegger does not simply consist of falling back on a given meaning of the concept in early Greek thought. Indeed, in spite of the evocation of the originary meaning of *theoria* in his writings, in "Science and Reflection" Heidegger literally produces a novel conception of *theoria* by way of an elaborate passage through the theory at the core of the theoretical sciences. Undoubtedly, in spite of their thorough difference from what the Greeks meant by *theoria*, the theoretical sciences have to be traced back to this origin, even though they are not only involved in a mastery of nature inconceivable to the Greeks but also, through this mastery, responsible for the current breakdown of the world. But the early Greek notion of *theoria* is a concept that remained unthought by the Greeks, and it is precisely as such an unthought concept that *theoria* became the foundation of the modern sciences. Resultantly, the concept of *theoria* that Heidegger 'returns' to in his later writings is an unheard-of concept differing from its Greek original inasmuch as what in this conception remained hidden to the Greeks has been rendered transparent. It follows that the reevaluated concept of *theoria* in Heidegger's later works is an altogether novel, in fact, an*other* concept of *theoria*. Its task is not to account for life as lived life, which, according to the early Heidegger, only an atheoretical approach could hope to achieve; nor is its aim to comprehend in a more originary gaze the structures of *Dasein*'s Being-in-the-world. Rather, in the current situation of the planetary domination of the theoretical sciences and the breakdown of the world that they have brought about, *theoria* is a last-ditch effort to prepare actively a new, an*other* relation to what is, an*other* relation to one's most proper origins, as well as an*other* relation to what Heidegger in "Hölderlin's Earth and Heaven" calls the few other great beginnings.[9] In short, *theoria* is a mode of thought beyond the traditional theory/praxis divide, a thinking that, as stated in *Besinnung*, has the character of action and is actively involved in making a however fragile contribution to restoring or, rather, to bringing about 'world,' that is, an*other* world.[10]

At this juncture, a brief remark on how to translate into English Heidegger's rendering of the Greek notion of *theoria* as '*Besinnung*' is certainly warranted. Heidegger chooses this term in order to avoid the subjectivist, metaphysical connotations of the Latin term '*reflectio*.' Even though the medieval notion of '*contemplatio*' still seems to resonate with some of the early meanings of *theoria* as a beholding, Heidegger sets these meanings aside in order to reserve its German equivalent, *Betrachtung*, which points in a completely different direction than the one that connotes meditative-monastic life, for his characterization of the gaze particular to the modern theoretical sciences. But *theorein* can also be translated, as Alfred Ernout and Antoine Meillet note in *Dictionnaire étymologique de la langue latine* (a work consulted by Heidegger), as '*consideratio*,' that is, as "a careful and respectful" or "thorough [*mûrement*] reflection."[11] With the term referring to *sidus*, "the stars forming a figure, or constellation," 'consideration' could, no doubt, serve to translate the gaze associated with *theorein*.[12] But 'consideration' and similar terms such as 'seeing' or 'discerning' are used to render the action of *theorein* associated with the new interpretation of the theory-praxis divide that emerges with Aristotle when,[13] for instance, he says in *Nicomachean Ethics* that the practical wisdom of the *phronimos* (the prudent man) makes him *dunantei theorein*, that is, capable of seeing, discerning, or considering "what is good for themselves and what is good for men in general."[14] By contrast, Heidegger's notion of *Besinnung*, admittedly much poorer than what the Greeks meant by *theoria* since it is a beholding limited to a world that barely announces itself, cannot be identified with political reflection in an already constituted public realm. For all these reasons, I will have to refer to *Besinnung*, a form of *theoria* in a world that, as Heidegger holds, is no longer strictly speaking a world, as 'reflection' even though this term is fraught with difficulties.

For what follows, it is, indeed, of utmost importance to be attentive to the fact that to say *theoria*—in Heidegger's sense—is, in the same breath, to say 'world.' 'World,' in turn, implies 'the other,' not only in the sense that a world is genuinely one only if it is the place for all others but also in the sense that it is this open place only if it welcomes more than one opening of the world. 'World' is not to be a place in which a relation to the other is to replace the relation to selfsameness. It is not a question of replacing sameness with otherness. Rather, to say 'world' is to recognize the constitutive function of the other (be it the other within the self) in the becoming of selfsameness. It is to acknowledge a responsibility toward the other without whom no selfsameness is conceivable. Yet, such acknowledgment is the active realization of 'world' in a genuine sense. *Theoria* as a correspondence and responsible response to the other is a name for this concern with 'world.' As a life-form, it is, perhaps, also a name for accomplishing that for which philosophy from the beginning has striven, namely, 'good life.'

4
BREAKING WITH THE PRIMACY OF THE THEORETICAL

NOTWITHSTANDING HEIDEGGER'S regular references to theory and the theoretical, both his criticism of the theoretical attitude in *Being and Time* and his rehabilitation of *theoria* in some of his later work do not, at first sight, seem to be a sign that the issue of theory and the theoretical are a major concern in Heidegger's work. This impression, however, is deceptive. Indeed, even a cursory glance at his first lecture course from the *Kriegsnotsemester* 1919 in Freiburg—a lecture course entitled "Die Idee der Philosophie und das Weltanschauungsproblem" in which the question of the theoretical is the central theme—shows that the debate with theory and the theoretical is intrinsically linked to Heidegger's elaboration of his own thought, and its demarcation from the dominant philosophies of time, that is, neo-Kantianism in all its variations.[1] Furthermore, the debate with the theoretical is tied to Heidegger's development of a phenomenological method that in significant ways breaks with Husserlian phenomenology as it had been outlined in *Philosophy as Rigorous Science* (1911) and *Ideas I* (1913). But Heidegger's lecture course from 1919 is of crucial importance for still another reason. Indeed, if *Being and Time*, in particular, considers the theoretical to be a derivative problematic, it is rather difficult to understand how in later writings—for example, in the *Parmenides* lectures, or in an essay such as "Science and Reflection"—the theoretical suddenly makes a comeback, and is valorized as the highest form of thought. The only way of accounting for this reevaluation of the theoretical is, indeed, the suggestion in these Freiburg lectures of "a fundamental distinction" according to which there may be "two fundamentally different kinds of the theoretical" (BP, 112–114).[2] Although to my knowledge Heidegger never returns to this distinction, I think that it explains why in his later work a rehabilitation of *theoria* becomes possible.

The immediate context of the debate with the theoretical in the 1919 lectures is the determination of philosophy as an "*Urwissenschaft*" (BP, 4). Husserl's *Logos* essay may be somehow behind this notion, but the difference with the Husserlian conception of philosophy as a rigorous science is evident right from the beginning. Indeed, the criterion for philosophy to be truly an *Urwissenschaft* is that its idea erupt into "the interconnectedness of natural consciousness of life" in "an original, radical sense," that is, in the shape of a "transforming intervention" (BP, 4). Heidegger speaks of an *Einbruch* and *Eingriff* that uproots the immediacy of the natural consciousness of life. Rather than merely a discursive (or, for that matter, merely cerebral) enterprise, philosophy as *Urwissenschaft* becomes construed as a "genuine, archontic form of life" (BP, 5). For philosophy to become a life-form, the theoretical must be kept distinct from it. Yet, if in order to be a life-form philosophy must in essence be atheoretical, in no way does this mean that it would have to be irrational, the latter being, as Heidegger is quick to point out, "theory in the worst sense imaginable" (BP, 88). Heidegger's attempt to develop the idea of philosophy as an *Urwissenschaft* takes place in a tight debate with neo-Kantianism, more precisely, the contemporary trends of critical realism and objective idealism— a debate that, in spite of its sharply critical tone and the charge that because of the inveterate theoreticism, these trends are incapable of even fancying the problem that a philosophy as *Urwissenschaft* represents, also reveals a genuine respect for their exclusively theoretical enterprise. But Heidegger's rejection of the theoretical does not imply that the idea of philosophy as an *Urwissenschaft* would be the idea of a practical philosophy, the practical being only the reverse side of the theoretical. The problem to be addressed, according to Heidegger, which calls for philosophy to become an *Urwissenschaft* in the sense of a life-form, is lived experience (*Er-lebnis*) of the surrounding world (*Umwelt*) in particular, and its intrinsic character as an event (*Er-eignischarakter*). As an atheoretical science, philosophy is a life-form precisely because of this, its "object." In what sense this is to be understood will become clear later on. But even though such a determination of the nature and task of philosophy is unmistakably indebted to Husserl's phenomenological method, one senses here also that Heidegger's emphasis on life as lived life and philosophy as a life-form will lead, at least implicitly, to a questioning of the dominance of the theoretical in Husserl's own thoughts at that time.

Even though Heidegger credits the neo-Kantians for pursuing the idea of philosophy as an *Urwissenschaft*, it is precisely the "privilege accorded to theoretization" (BP, 59) that prevents them from accomplishing this goal. This theoretical bias is manifest in the limitation of their quest for the *Ur-sprünge*, that is, the founding axioms of the theoretical sciences, and in their subordination of the realms of the ethical and the aesthetic to the theoretical (BP 59). Furthermore, by conceiving of the axioms that provide the ultimate foundation of theoretical cognition for all sciences in terms of the psychic, that is, in terms of a very specific realm of beings, and their objectification in the particular science of psychology, their theoretical approach prevents them from coming up with something truly universal. The privilege of the theoretical is manifest here in the form of the founding priority accorded to one particular domain of things, and their objectifying science. But it is, in particular, in a lengthy discussion of Heinrich Rickert's teleological–critical method that Heidegger shows why the theoretical is a fundamental obstacle to the formation of philosophy as an *Urwissenschaft*. According to Heidegger, Rickert's teleological-critical method, which seeks to provide theoretical cognition with a guiding norm, that is, the idea of truth, as well as with the material to which this norm is to be applied, remains entirely within the domain of psychology, that is to say, within always only hypothetical, never apodictic, insights. The ultimate limit of theoretization is that it only knows *Sachen*, *Sachsphären*, and *Sachzusammenhänge*, things, spheres of things, and interconnections between things, which themselves are things. It is with this *Sachlichkeit* of theoretization that Heidegger will take issue.

In order to break open this "absolute dominion of the realm of things" (BP, 62), in which strictly speaking there are not even things anymore, Heidegger asks what he qualifies as a *kümmerliche Frage*, a pathetic question, more precisely a weak, poor, miserable question, one, moreover, that in light of all the big questions asked by philosophy is barely a question. But to ask this question, however miserable it may be, is of the order of an event in that it interrupts the inconspicuous *Sachzusammenhang* at the center of neo-Kantian thought. However weak, this question opens up a difference within the leveling night in which things have sunk into nothingness. Before I get to the question itself, let us bear in mind that this question challenges the very *Sachlichkeit* in which, as Heidegger notes, not only no thing remains, but in which there is not even a "there is" anymore. So, first, Heidegger asks, "*Gibt es das 'es gibt'?*"—in other words, is there the "is there?" at all, can the "is there" be of the order of a thing that exists? (BP, 62) But by setting out to question "Is there ... ?," something is assumed to be there (*Schon in dem Frage-ansatz 'Gibt es ... ?' gibt es etwas*) (BP, 63). Since the linguistic nature of the question, "Is there ... ?"—chosen "in order to prejudge a minimum in assertions" (BP, 65)—all by itself inevitably suggests, presumes, or stipulates that there is something (*etwas*), the question is reformulated as "Is there something? [*Gibt es etwas?*]" (BP, 63). Notwithstanding the poorness of the question, a decisive problematic has come into view, and it will thus be necessary, Heidegger holds, to seek to understand this poorness in its all its purity, bracketing all the concerns that have provoked the question. This is to be accomplished through a focus on this question as an event that drives a rift into the assumption that all there is are things, in other words, by considering the question a lived experience (*Erlebnis*). Put another way, the question concerns the very "experience of the question: Is there something?" (BP, 63). In the face of the exclusive *Sachzusammenhang* posited by the neo-Kantians, the analysis of the question as a lived experience will open onto the minimal conditions at the core of theoretism. Indeed, since this question concerns things and the interconnection of things, everything worldly is already eliminated from it. Paradoxically, the experience of this question, then, is the minimal experience of un-living that constitutes the theoretical as an experientially privative attitude toward what is.

The aim of Heidegger's structural analysis of the question addressed to neo-Kantianism's *Neue Sachlichkeit*, as it were, seeks to achieve several things. Since the question "Is there something"? is, indeed, the most minimal theoretical question, the aim is first of all to show that as a lived experience not only does this question bring to light a series of constitutive features of the theoretical as an attitude, but that, as a lived experience, it itself is irreducible to the theoretical. Furthermore, the aim is to open up within the seemingly unavoidable presupposition of the theoretical that there is something, which culminates with the neo-Kantians in the question of realism, the space for a conception of the "something" that is not objective, that is other. And, finally, the aim is to determine, on the basis of the event-character of this question, the structure of lived experience in the "fullness of its being lived [*in voller Lebendigkeit*]," which itself is irreducible to any thing, object, or matter-of-factness. I highlight only the major articulations of the structural analysis of the lived question "Is there something?" Focusing on the "motivations," that is, aspects or levels of the experience of this question that show themselves when simply looked at, Heidegger contends that nothing comparable to an "I" can be found in it. Looked at the way it is experienced, the question reveals a relating toward something in the questioning mode, but it is not me as this concrete historical being that resonates in it. Even though it is "I" "who is standing here at this lectern [*Katheder*], with this name and this age," there is no meaningful reference to me in the experience of this question, which, therefore, "is separated from me, absolutely distant from me [*Ich-fern*]" (BP, 68–69). In short, "I am not present" in the experience of this question (BP, 73). Instead of me the experience reveals only an "it lives" of a general ego (BP, 66). The second aspect that springs into view when describing the experience in question is that in it I relate in a mode of positing, more precisely, of positing something as being questionable in general. And finally, the lived experience of the question "Is there something?" inquires into *etwas überhaupt*, not whether this or that concrete thing is, but whether there is something in general.

Heidegger follows up his discussion of the example of a lived experience, one that was motivated by the neo-Kantian assumption of a unique and exclusive existing interconnectedness of things, with another example regarding the lived experience of the surrounding world (as opposed to a *Sachzusammenhang*), and which I will refer to as "the experience of the seeing of the lectern [*das Kathedererlebnis*, in short]" (BP, 72). But first a remark: In describing "the lived experience: Is there something?" with its "I" in general, its mode of relating in a questioning mode in general, and in which an absolute minimum is stated about the object when it is said that it is something (BP, 68), something has been described that is not of the order of an interconnectedness of things (*Sachzusammenhang*). The described experience is "not merely an existing happening [*seiendes Geschehen*]." Rather than "an object of contemplation, it is the question whether there is an object in general. Lived experiencing is no thing that is there in brute fashion, and that begins and ends like a happening [*Vor-gang*]. The 'relating to' is not a piece of a thing to which another thing, the 'something,' is appended. Experiencing and what is experienced are not pieced together like existing objects" (BP, 69–70). In addition, the description of all the basic moments of the lived experience of the question as they offer themselves in their simple meaning, rather than being the result of an objectifying relation, rests on what Heidegger calls a *schauendes Verständnis*, that is, not only an intuiting comprehension, but an intuiting that is in sync, as it were, with what it contemplates. Methodologically speaking, to describe the structure of lived experience is itself of the order of a living relation to the "something" of the description.

With this we proceed to the lectern experience. Rather than seeing an ensemble of brown intersecting surfaces, upon entering this lecture room, and construing it subsequently as a box, a desk, and finally as an academic lectern, I, or you the students, "see it [Heidegger remarks] all at once, in one blow, as it were; I see it not only distinctly [*isoliert*], I see the lectern immediately as too high for me, and the book lying on it as bothering me [. . .], I see the lectern in an orientation, in an illumination, against a background," and so forth (BP, 71). But what would happen if we brought a Black Forest peasant into the classroom; what would he see, Heidegger asks, a lectern, a box, or simply a partition of wooden boards? The Black Forest peasant, according to Heidegger, would "see 'the place for the teacher,' [in other words] he would see the object as having a meaning attached to it," and not as a worldless thing (BP, 71). After all, even though the peasant came from the back country of the "*hohen Schwarzwald*," he belongs to the same culture as the Freiburg teacher and his students.

By contrast, what would happen, Heidegger continues, if a "Senegalese were suddenly transposed from his hut into the classroom?" What would he see? Would he, "perhaps, see something that has to do with magic, or behind which one can take cover from arrows or stones, or, would he, what is most likely, see something of which he cannot make sense, that is, would he see only color formations and surfaces, a mere thing that is simply there?" (BP, 71–72). But Heidegger will argue that the experience of the lectern by the Herr Professor and his students, the Black Forest Peasant, and the Senegalese, who, as he points out in parentheses, may be lacking science, but who is not therefore without culture, are, as far as "their essential kernel is concerned, absolutely identical" (BP, 72). Indeed, the Senegalese would not see the lectern as a mere something, as an *etwas* in general, that simply is there, that is, as the worldless object of the theoretical or scientific gaze, but as something of which he cannot make sense, and which consequently "would have for him a meaning, a meaningful moment" (BP, 72). Not only does the lectern offer itself to the Senegalese just like to the Herr Professor and the Black Forest peasant as concrete individual "I's," it does so from within an immediately surrounding world, with respect to which it is from the start immediately endowed with some meaning. What the lectern experience demonstrates is that in the experience of the surrounding world, "the meaningful is what is primary; it is present to me in an immediate way without any intellectual detour by way of a comprehension of the thing. Living in a surrounding world, everything is everywhere and at all times meaningful, everything is worldly, and 'it worlds' [*es weltet*]" (BP, 72–73).

In comparing these examples of lived experiences, Heidegger highlights the presence of the concrete I in living toward something like the lectern within a surrounding world in which, because this concrete environmental thing worlds, I fully take part (BP, 73). By contrast, in the questioning experience: "Is there something?" I am not present as a concrete I. Furthermore, "the something in general, which is questioned with respect to its 'being there,' does not world. Everything worldly has here been eliminated in that we take everything possible from the surrounding world as a something in general. This comprehending, this fixing as an object in general lives at the price of pushing back my own I. Part of the meaning of the something in general implies that *I* do *not* co-vibrate in its fixation as such [*Fest-stellung*]; this co-vibrating, this co-existing of myself has been cut off here. Being an object as such does not affect *me*. The I that fixes is not at all *me*" (BP, 73). As we have seen, the example of the questioning-experience is the prototypic experience of the theoretical way of relating (*Ver-halten*) within the world to what is. Yet, as Heidegger points out, "as a lived experience, fixing is only a rudiment of ex-periencing (*Er-leben*); it is an un-living [*Ent-leben*]. The objective, the cognized, is as such re-moved [*ent-fernt*] from experience properly speaking" (BP, 73–74). As an attitude, as a way of being and relating to the world and what is in the world, the theoretical is by no means no experience at all. It is rooted in lived experience, derivative from it, but by un-living and un-worlding both subject and object, and removing them from experience, it is itself a degree zero of experience, the barest minimum of lived experience, that is. As the example of the lectern experience has demonstrated, to live is to live toward, that is, to experience (*er-leben*) what offers itself in an always meaningful way in the surrounding world—and which as the example of the Senegalese has shown can be something unexpected, and foreign, something so other that one cannot make sense of it. Although it is still experiential in a rudimentary way, theoretical relating is of the order of a *Vor-gang*, that is, an objective happening, in which the concrete I has no part, a happening that itself concerns only things and objective happenings (*Vorgänge*). By contrast, if lived experience, as Heidegger remarks, is of the order of an event—*Er-eignis*—an event in which something is allowed to occur and at the same time to affect what is proper to a concrete I, it also follows that there is barely anything event-like in the theoretical relation to things in general. Nothing other, and in particular, no other human other, will ever be encountered in the theoretical attitude. Heidegger speaks of "the total cluelessness" of neo-Kantianism regarding "the phenomenon of *Fremdwahrnehmung*," that is, of the perception of the unfamiliar (BP, 87).

Even though most of the time we experience circumspectively, the theoretical attitude is so deeply seated that it prevents us from getting a genuine view of our experience of the surrounding world. But if the dominion of the theoretical must be broken for this experience to become thematic, it is especially because rather than being of the order of the accidental, the lived experience in question "rests on the essence of life itself; by contrast, we engage in a theoretical attitude only in exceptional cases" (BP, 88). Let me recall at this point that the watershed for philosophy to become an *Urwissenschaft* consisted of its intrinsic formal interconnection with life. We have seen as well that methodologically such a philosophy, because it is grounded in a *schauenden Verständnis*, had to be close to phenomenology. In a critical debate with Paul Natorp's objections against phenomenology, Heidegger emphasizes that the fundamental problem of phenomenology is the "scientific exploration of the sphere of lived experience," and that this exploration has to take place according to what Husserl, in *Ideas I*, called the "principle of principles," namely, that "everything that offers itself in intuition in an originary way [. . .] is to be taken simply [. . .] as that as which it gives itself" (BP, 109). After having suggested that such a principle, because it refers to something anterior to principles (or axioms), which are neo-Kantianism's turf, is no longer theoretical, Heidegger qualifies the fundamental attitude expressed by this principle for the investigation of lived experience as follows: "It is the Ur-intention of true life, the Ur-attitude of lived experience and of life as such, the absolute sympathy of life that is identical with lived experience [*mit dem Erleben selbst identische Lebenssympathie*]" (BP, 110). The fundamental attitude expressed by the methodic principle of principles for the exploration of lived experience, which so far has, according to Heidegger, guided him in progressively gaining freedom from the theoretical, "becomes absolute only if we ourselves live in it—something that no conceptual system however complex can achieve, except phenomenological life by its own growing intensification" (BP, 110). Such intensification of phenomenological life occurs when philosophy guided by the principle in question becomes a life-form. Indeed, understood as the *Urwissenschaft* of lived experience, phenomenological philosophy is not merely an expression of life, but one of its highest forms in that it is in tune, in a sympathetic relation with the essence of life itself, which is always lived life. For philosophy as an *Urwissenschaft*, life is not an object but a way of being that consists in living (*er-leben*) what gives itself, and living it in a way in which what gives itself is *er-eignet*, that is, permitted to be event-like, and to affect me in what is most proper to me.

Since I will take up the question of the genesis of the theoretical at great length in Chapter 5, I skip here the details of Heidegger's programmatic outline of such a genesis in the Freiburg lectures in which it is shown how the theoretical emerges through a progressive depriving, reducing, de-historizing of lived experience, and taking the meaningful, the lived, the historical out of it, with the result that the theoretical appears as the degree zero of a remainder. However, for what I still have to address, it is important to underline that this genesis proceeds through distinct "motivations" or "levels of *Lebendigkeit* of experiencing," such as, to briefly return to the lectern experience, through the levels of "lectern, box, the color brown, wood, [and finally] thing," (BP, 89). As Heidegger remarks: "In the pursuance of these levels, or motivations, of the process of un-living one arrives at the essence of the theoretical form [. . .] of objectivity" (BP, 90). By contrast, what I need to draw attention to is a question that Heidegger raises throughout the lectures, but especially toward their end, one which most likely was triggered by Natorp's criticism of phenomenology. It is the question of whether the phenomenological approach, and for that matter, the project of a philosophy as an *Urwissenschaft*, is truly free of the theoretical attitude. Does phenomenological seeing and description not presuppose that what is seen and described stands over against, and in a distance from such seeing and description, in the same way as is the case for the theoretical glance? Is theory not hidden in such a presupposition? Heidegger first answers this question with another one: "Are we not subject here to a linguistic deception [*einer Täuschung durch die Sprache*], an illusion produced by language, that is, by language that has been theorized?" (BP, 112). In short, what he suggests is that the suspicion that phenomenological seeing and description is theoretical and involved in objectification, and is the inevitable result of an ambiguity in language that concerns all talk about "relating to." Prevailing language, in particular, language that has been theorized, theoretical language, inevitably seems to produce such an effect.

Faced with this objection to the phenomenological attitude and, by the same token, to the idea of an atheoretical science, Heidegger claims that a "fundamental distinction [*Scheidung*]" has to be made. To spell out what this distinction, or separation, consists in, Heidegger recalls what he had established about the process of theoretization, and its progressive phases of un-living, which peak "in the wholly empty character of the something which only contains objectivity as such in a formal way" (BP, 112). From this something as the summit of this process, "all reference to a world-content however radically theorized" has been eradicated, and it is thus "the absolutely worldless, foreign to the world." This something constitutes a world in which one can no longer breathe or live (BP, 112). Now, Heidegger asks: Does this analysis of the levels of un-living, and the characterization of the process in question as culminating in the mere something in general, truly correspond to the phenomena? In order to respond to this question, he turns one more time to the example of the lectern. Although all the judgments that lead to the final one that the lectern is a mere something that is simply there can be made in a state of confusion, each one seems to have its motivation in a preceding judgment. But Heidegger asks whether phenomenologically speaking all these motivating steps must in fact be traversed in a successive way for the judgment "It is something" to be able to occur. Rather than the concluding result of a process of successive stages of un-living, is the judgment that the thing is a mere something in general not a conclusion that can be reached on each particular theoretical level of reality, though always, of course, in conformity with the latter's specificity? In that case, however, rather than being the ultimate outcome of the process of un-living, "the conclusive theoretical characterization of the mere something as such" falls entirely outside the phased order, though in such a way that the conclusion can be motivated by any particular phase (BP, 113–114). The fundamental difference that Heidegger pointed at thus begins to come in view: it concerns the mere something in general as the result of a process of un-living and the mere something in general as separate, that is, free, from this process but, at the same time, motivating judgments that "there is something" on each possible level of theoretical reality in conformity with the specifics of that sphere. If it can be made phenomenologically evident that each stage of theoretical reality contains the possibility of being theoretically intended [*meinbar*] as a mere something, then one must, indeed, distinguish between the specific *Stufengebundenheit* of each step in the process of un-living, which ultimately culminates in the fixation of something in general as something entirely worldless, and the formal theoretization of something that is free from this process. Heidegger writes: "That which hitherto was considered to be the eminently theoretical now shows itself as belonging not at all to the process of un-living" (BP, 114). Formal theoretization not only does not belong to the phased order of specific levels of un-living, and is not the culminating point of a process of un-living; its very motivation is also "a *qualitatively* different one." And Heidegger concludes that "consequently, there must be two fundamentally different kinds of the theoretical" (BP, 114). The fundamental difference alluded to is thus a difference between two kinds of the theoretical, a difference within the theoretical itself, a difference within what is named "theoretical"— a duplicity, in short of the theoretical and the "theoretical." "The essential connection" between these notions of the theoretical is "a big problem," Heidegger adds (BP, 114). What makes the relation between these two kinds of the theoretical a difficult one is that it requires a reflection on language and its inherent deceptions, more precisely, on the fold in the word "theoretical" itself, along which these two meanings, or kinds, of the theoretical, unfold, both remaining interconnected by this very linguistic fold itself.

When, after having made the argument for two fundamentally different kinds of the theoretical, Heidegger remarks that "the possibility exists that what is formally objective has, at first, no relation whatsoever to the theoretical process, and that its motivational origin in life is a qualitatively different one" than that of the theoretical process of un-living, which peaks in the wholly empty something that is simply there, this difference between the two concepts of the theoretical becomes a bit more precise. It is a difference within the theoretical between the "formally objective," whose origin in life differs from the wholly empty objectivity that crowns the process of un-living; the formally objective as opposed to this entirely empty theoretical objectivity has a characteristically deeper relation to life than the latter. Furthermore, it is a difference between an understanding of the theoretical that is not processual at all, and one which (paradoxically!) rests on a process of un-living. Indeed, the difference is qualitatively so fundamental that "to simply speak of kinds, and differences in kind, of processes of possible theoretization" is misleading (BP, 114). All talk of kinds would imply that there is one common genre to both. On the contrary, the duplicity of the theoretical that Heidegger alludes to is one between unequal and heterogeneous sides of the fold within the word "theoretical," one of which, furthermore, covers up the meaning of the other. The fold in the word not only divides it; as folded upon itself, the word itself covers over one of its sides. It effects a covering over that concerns a meaning of *theorein* that theory, in the theoretical sense, presupposes as more fundamental than its own manner of seeing.

As should be clear from what we have seen so far, this difference between two ways in which to conceive of the theoretical is one between two ways of understanding the "something," the *Etwas*. Formal objectification, the "something" as a form, is, as seen, free from all connection to levels, in that it does not require a specific motivation within a determined level in the process of theoretization. "*Each* individual level contains in itself the possibility of being seen in a formal way [*formaliter*]" (BP, 114–115). Now what is absolutely crucial for what is to follow is that formal objectification is not limited to the theoretical sphere, and its realm of objects. The scope of possible formal-objective characterization not only extends to all the spheres excluded by theoretization, or that are subordinated to it as in neo-Kantianism, that is, to the ethical and aesthetic spheres as well, but to everything that can be experienced. Heidegger writes: "Everything experienceable in general is a possible something independently of its genuine world-character. The sense of 'something' is precisely: '*the experienceable in general*'" (BP, 115). It follows from this that distinct from "radical theoretization," which is grounded in a process of un-living (BP, 116), formal objectification allows for two kinds of objectification—a theoretical objectification (that is free from all *Stufengebundenheit*) and an atheoretical objectification. As we will see in a moment, the sharp distinction that Heidegger draws is, indeed, a triple one. In any event, since the scope of what can be formally objectified as "something" extends well beyond the sphere of theoretical objectivity, formal objectification is also the index for a theoretical relating that is not theoretical in the common sense, hence atheoretical. Furthermore, since the "something" that can be predicated of just anything is that of an experienceable something, formal objectification is the eminent form of objectification that characterizes the livable, the experienceable in lived experience. The "theoretical" attitude that characterizes its object first in the formal sense of a something, looks at it in a sense of *theorein* that lets what is looked at give itself so that it can be lived [*er-lebt*], and, by being lived, experienced. It is thus a way of looking that not only is attuned to the something, but in which the something is not already prejudged as a mere thing in general. The formal theoretization of such an atheoretical approach to something lets this something simply show itself as it is in itself. Such formal theoretization must be kept separate from the formal objectivity that characterizes the realm of theory properly speaking, that is, the realm of objectivity. If it is true that the formal has a relation to life, then theoretical formal objectivity still entertains a relation to the order of life, though it is a derivative formation of it, as opposed to radical theoretization, which is based on the systematic un-living of lived experience.

Following his contention that the meaning of "something" is "the experienceable in general," Heidegger continues as follows: "The indifference with respect to all genuine worldhood that lies in the something in general, as well as the indifference with respect to all determined objecthood, is in no way identical to the un-livedness, and especially not to the latter's highest level, that of the most sublime theoretization. The 'something' does not imply the absolute interruption of the relation to life [. . .], no theoretical fixation, and no putting-out-of-the-way of something that has been experienced. Quite the opposite is the case: it is the index [*Index*] for the highest potentiality of life" (BP, 115). That the atheoretical relating to the "something" as the experienceable as such is part and parcel of life as lived life should be clear by now. But how are we to understand this rather surprising linkage between the formal objectification of the "something" and life in its highest potentiality? Between the conception of a something indifferent to all genuine worldhood and all determined objectivity, and "full life itself" (BP, 115)? Prior to clarifying this relation, it is certainly not inappropriate to recall one more time what Heidegger is up to in his early Freiburg lectures, namely, the project of philosophy as an *Urwissenschaft* that, at the same time, is a life-form, and which can only be such a life-form on the condition that it be the science of what is lived—life as lived life, the experienceable as such. "Something," that is, the formal objectivity of the atheoretical gaze of philosophy as *Urwissenschaft*, must thus be the experienceable in general. It must be attuned to life as lived life, but in what sense? And in particular in what sense of life, indeed, if the formal something is to point at life in its highest potentiality? But, then, how are we to understand here "potentiality," and moreover potentiality at its highest?

According to the Freiburg lectures in question, "the meaning of the 'something' rests in full life itself, and it signifies precisely that it [full life itself] has not yet developed any genuine and worldly characterization, but yet that such a characterization as such lives in a motivating fashion in life. It [that is, this something] is the '*Not yet* [*Noch-nicht*],' that is, that which has not yet erupted [*Herausgebrochene*] into a genuine life. It is the essentially *pre-worldly* [*Vorweltliche*]. Yet, the meaning of the something as the experienceable contains the moment of 'towardness,' 'in the direction of,' '*into* a (determined) world'—and this in its unimpaired 'life-vitality'" (BP, 115). Although I cannot give this crucial passage, which, I note in passing, introduces the category of the 'not-yet' well before Ernst Bloch did so, the attention it deserves, I will underscore those aspects of it that are of immediate importance for the questions pursued so far.³ In spite of lacking all genuine worldhood, the formal 'something' is not an abstraction. Rather it is the experienced objectification of that which has not yet been formed in a worldly fashion. It is pre-worldly in the sense that it has not yet erupted into genuine life, but stretches toward a determined realization in it. Its fundamental characteristics are those of tending toward, in the direction of, into a (determined) world, and it is such bearing toward becoming genuine life with full élan vital (*Lebensschwungkraft*). It is potentiality of life at its highest because it is not yet genuine (i.e., determined) life, it is the very swing of life extending toward such a realization. The formal something as the experienceable objectivity of whatever is encountered is *all* potentiality, as it were. Compared to the "formally objective *something of cognizability*," that is, "the something of formal theoretization," and in particular to the empty object of radical theoretization which is arrived at by dint of a process of unliving, the "pre-worldly lived-something [*Lebens-etwas*]" of the phenomenological gaze, is rich with all the potentiality of life. But, we ask, what are these potential riches? What is it that has *not yet* become genuine, determined life? What is the sense of potentiality here?

After a warning against conceiving of the "something" as that which is pre-worldly in theoretical fashion, Heidegger provides some examples of it as a "fundamental phenomenon that can be experienced in a mode of understanding [*verstehend erlebt werden kann*]" (BP, 115). From these examples a hint at how to answer the questions that I raised can be gleaned. Examples of the experience of "something" in a mode of intuiting understanding, that is, in "hermeneutical intuition" (BP, 117), are significantly enough "the experiential situation in which one slides from one world of experience into one that is genuinely other, or in moments of especially intensive life" (BP, 115). In spite of the scarcity of the situations named here, and their seeming poorness, their *Kümmerlichkeit*, if I may say so, these examples illustrate what should be the rule in the phenomenological gaze.⁴ As the examples suggest, the groundphenomenon of the lived experience of "something" is the experience not of thingness, but of something other—"other" referring to other worlds, as worlds of the other, but also of myself as when I make intensified life-experiences— that is, experiences of life that are other, and that open up a different world, or worlds. The something as the experienceable in general is indicative of potentialities for worlding that have not yet burst into genuine life, and whose full potentiality for other worlds to come, and for othering the world, has not yet been actualized. Apart from implying a definite privilege of *Fremderfahrung*, that is, of the other human being, the lived experience of "something" extends to whatever can be encountered, even things prior to their being embedded within a determined world. But one more aspect of the "something" needs to be highlighted here. Insofar as the "something" is the experienceable other in general, the something is by definition something whose full potentiality for other worlds, and for othering the world, has not yet been actualized. But precisely because of its otherness, such potentiality, rather than one of the possible, remains essentially undetermined, unpredicatable. If the "something" as the experienceable in general, rather than that of radically un-lived thingness, is, according to Heidegger, "an essential moment of life, which stands in a close connection with the event-character of the lived experiences as such," it is precisely because the "something" is of the order of the other, other worlds, othered worlds, and is thus unforeseeable as concerns the genuine worlds with which it is pregnant. To experience "something" in lived experience is to experience a potentiality of unpredictable other worlds, of worlds that lie in wait of becoming genuinely worldly.[5] And as such the experience of the "something" is an "essential moment of life," in fact of life in its highest potentiality, life as always lived life is itself intertwined with otherness, a relentless vital stretching forward toward other worlds to come.[6]

I briefly return to the issue of the fundamental distinction regarding the theoretical, a distinction that needed to be made in order to ward off the claim that even the atheoretical phenomenological gaze is incapable of escaping the theoretical. Now, "the formally objective something of cognizability," that is, "the something of formal theoretization," is, as Heidegger points out, grounded (or "motivated") in the "pre-worldly lived-something [*Lebens-etwas*]" that characterizes an entirely different kind of seeing, of theorization, as it occurs in the phenomenological gaze. How radically different the "pre-worldly lived-something," and hence the kind of theoretization involved in seeing it, is from the "something of cognizability," and its respective kind of theoretization, can be gleaned from Heidegger's omission at the end of his lectures of the term "formal" to characterize the beholding of the pre-worldly lived-something. Formality now appears associated with the derivative kind of theoretization. And as a result, rather than a mere duplicity of the theoretical, a tripartite distinction is made with respect to it (unless, of course, the theoretical has been *entirely* relegated to the sphere of the derivative). Heidegger writes: "One must thus sharply distinguish between the pre-worldly something of life in itself; the formally objective that grows from it (only from it?); and, finally the objectively [*objektartig*] theoretical. The first sphere is as one of life absolute, the two others are only relative, and contingent" (BP, 116). Yet, if the latter two, whose possibility is rooted in the possibility of theoretically preventing the tending toward a world (*Die Tendenz in eine Welt kann vor ihrer Ausprägung theoretisch abgebogen warden*), and thus interfering with life, still can claim universality it is because both kinds of theory "originate in the streaming lived experience of life" to begin with (BP, 116). The pre-worldly something of lived experience, which is the correlate of a philosophical gaze that is a life-form itself, is neither a formal nor an objective something in a strict theoretical sense. If it is the correlate of a theoretization, it is such a correlate only in the sense that the theorized is essentially not different from the act of theorization, in other words, in the unheard-of sense of *theoria* to be found only in the later Heidegger, unheard of because in spite of all references to the Greek original meaning of the term, the Greeks may factually never have thought of *theoria* in such a way. Indeed, as we will show in Chapter 6, this unheard-of concept of *theoria* will require nothing less than a reflective traversal of the theoretical sciences, intent on showing that the original Greek conception of *theoria* in which they are rooted was itself marred by something that remained hidden in it, in short, unthought.

To conclude, one more remark about language, and the duplicity of the word "theoretical." Toward the very end of his lectures, Heidegger returns to the issue and notes, "that which is of the order of meaning, that is to say, linguistic expression, does not necessarily have to be theoretical, or even objectively intentional; on the contrary, it is originarily of the order of lived experience, *pre-worldly, respectively, worldly*" (BP, 116–117). In other words, the theoretical does not necessarily have to be understood in a theoretical sense. Understood from "the founding stratum of life itself [*Grundschicht des Lebens an und für sich*]," it designates an atheoretical way of looking, one in which the lived experience of theoretization has also event-character, in that as a living toward the other, it allows other worlds to shape the concrete and historical I of the experience.

5
THE GENESIS OF THE THEORETICAL

Translated from German by David B. Collins

IN HEIDEGGER'S EARLY Freiburg lecture series from the summer semester of 1923, *Ontology: The Hermeneutics of Facticity*, there is the following parenthetical remark: "(The genesis of the theoretical, what is prior here: 'curiosity.')"[1] This problem of the genesis of the theoretical will be investigated in the following with special consideration of the role that it plays in *Being and Time* (1927). First of all, however, it may be appropriate to pose again the question of the importance of the subject of "theory" to Heidegger's thinking in general. At first glance it might appear as if his critical encounter with the theoretical is only of secondary significance. Yet, as I propose to demonstrate, a more precise consideration of the context in which these admittedly rather sparsely explicit references to the concept of theory are found weakens this impression. The assessment that the "theory problem" is not central to Heidegger's thinking can be maintained even less if, as we have seen, one takes into account his first Freiburg lecture from the War Emergency Semester of 1919 on "The Idea of Philosophy and the Problem of Worldview." There it becomes clear to what extent Heidegger's own development of a phenomenological philosophy depends upon an overcoming of the primacy of the theoretical that, according to him, dominated the most influential schools of the time such as the South-West German and Marburg schools of neo-Kantianism. However, the target of these lectures is not only the theorism of neo-Kantianism, but also, if not so explicitly, the epistemology (*Erkenntnistheorie*) at the very core of Husserl's phenomenology, which, according to Heidegger, prevents it from being a real *Urwissenschaft*. The "preference" for and "primacy of the theoretical must be broken" if phenomenology is to gain access at all to the phenomena that are specifically its own, and be able to disclose what they properly are.[2]

The phenomena correlated in accordance with the essence of phenomenological "sighting" are part of the domain of lived experience, which, according to this early lecture, means at the same time that they belong to the sphere of events. The sphere comprised of what is lived through (*Er-lebens*) and experienced (*Erlebnisse*) precedes all theorizing because within this sphere all comportment (*Verhalten*) toward worldly things still remains determined circumspectively and every worldly encounter is immediately experienced as being meaningful. Now, in order to do justice to these phenomena in all their liveliness, instead of fixing them in a reifying manner as objects, philosophy must methodically endeavor to "*look on [zuschauend] understandingly* and to understand in a mode of looking on," that is, itself be atheoretical.[3] In being, in a sense, identical with its object, that is, lived experience, it is undoubtedly a science, yet of such a kind that it also constitutes a "genuine archontic form of life."[4] To understand phenomenology in this way entails viewing it as a pretheoretical *Urwissenschaft* with the structure of lived experience, particularly the phenomenon of the lived experience of the surrounding world, as its primary object. This form of phenomenology thereby also promotes a critical confrontation with the theoretical insofar as it has governed all of philosophy up to now, not least in order to escape the temptation to let the theoretical secretly intrude upon phenomenological research.

In this context it is essential to remind us again of the fundamental distinction between "two fundamentally different kinds of the theoretical" that Heidegger makes toward the end of his lecture.[5] In an attempt to ward off the objection that phenomenological intuition is a seeing that stands in an external relation to what is seen in order to turn what stands over against it into an object of description and cognition, and thus secretly still be a form of theory, Heidegger poses the question whether all comportment to something is necessarily objectifying, and whether this 'something' is therefore a mere something, that is, one that had all of its content removed from it. Without going into too much technical detail here, Heidegger's answer may, as we have seen, be briefly summarized as follows: even if the 'something' in general from the theoretical sighting seems, as "absolutely worldless, or world-foreign," to represent the peak of a directed process of levels of un-living, there is however, phenomenologically speaking, the possibility of bringing any aspect of reality, independently of the process of un-living and free of its hierarchies, into the look as a formally objective, mere 'something.'[6] Thus formal theoretization, "previously counted as eminently theoretical, proves not at all to belong to the process of un-living," which, according to the theory, produces the motivation of the something in general.[7] Furthermore, as Heidegger notes, formal theoretization is not at all restricted to that of the theoretical sphere: "*Anything that can be experienced at all is a possible something, irrespective of its genuine world-character.*"[8] A "something" means here "anything that can be experienced at all," and the indifference toward the genuine world-character of this "something" is in no way to be identified with the un-lived and worldless quality of the hierarchical process of theoretization. Rather, a "something," in the sense belonging to formal theoretization, "is the index for the highest potentiality of life" provided that it—this "something"—is still clearly pre-worldly (Heidegger defines it as the "*not-yet*"), and as such open for the different possible worlds that are potentially laid out before it.[9] As the "object" of formal theoretization, this "lived-something" (*Lebens-etwas*) is no longer in the position of a counterpart to cognizability.[10] All comportment toward this 'something,' as vitally experienced (*er-lebt*) "out toward, or in the direction of," other worlds, is itself part of the "unabated vitality of life" that is alive in it.[11] The formally theoretical 'something' as the experienceable as such is likewise to be sharply differentiated from the formally objective 'something' of cognizability, both of which differ again from the sense of the theoretical 'something' that is to be obtained from a continuous process of un-living as its highest peak. But with this dismissal of the theoretization that dominates neo-Kantianism, principally by the differentiation of a formally theoretical something of experienceability, Heidegger has, in a way, also defined his own phenomenological approach as a particular form of the 'theoretical.' This form of the 'theoretical' admittedly does not consist of an objectifying comportment to an un-lived 'something'; in short, it is a theorizing that is no longer theoretical and in which the 'something' is experienced in an intuitive understanding as "worlding (*weltend*)."[12] Understood in this way, the 'theoretical' is thus identified with what Heidegger envisioned phenomenological science to be in the aftermath of Husserl's formulation of it in *Ideas I* as following the "principle of principles": phenomenology was to embody the sought-after *Ur-wissenschaft*, which, instead of seeking epistemologically meaningful unities and structures of essences, was to disclose the sphere of lived experience in general to science. Yet, this fundamental distinction between the two kinds of the theoretical found in this first Freiburg lecture is not alluded to in the years that follow. These early distinctions are not discernible again until Heidegger's later attempts to rehabilitate the Greek understanding of the concept of *theoria*.

I return to Heidegger's parenthetical remark in the lectures on *Ontology: The Hermeneutics of Facticity* that announces in programmatic fashion, as it were, the genesis of theory. Now, if the genesis of theory first of all requires a clarification of the phenomenon of curiosity, then this indicates that what is involved here is clearly not the genesis of *theoria*, but rather of the modern concept of theory. In the course of the lectures, curiosity is defined in the context of an outline of Dasein in its everydayness as a "*how of caring,*" in the carrying out of which "the care of curiosity constantly covers itself up," in other words, the way in which curiosity covers over nothing less than its very character as a form of care and with that its grounding in the being of human existence itself.[13] As a modification of the "*fundamental phenomenon of the being-there of Dasein*"—of care—curiosity is "the care of mere seeing and mere questioning."[14] According to Heidegger, such a mere seeing presupposes that, instead of being something whose significance is disclosed to Dasein, it "has forfeited the authentic character of its there and now holds itself in and lingers in the indifference of something we are merely able to ascertain." Nevertheless, a "there" modified into a merely "occurring object we simply take note of, observe, and ascertain" is still an everyday being, or more precisely, it exists "only as a being-there in everydayness."[15] Admittedly curiosity is, in its connection to the everydayness of Dasein, a mode of the fundamental ways of being of human existence, but it is such that this mode precisely consists in concealing its own care-character. In other words, as prior to the explicitly theoretical, curiosity remains a phenomenon grounded in the everydayness of Dasein despite its constitutive privation. It precedes the theoretical precisely because it remains embedded in the everyday despite its demarcation from the everydayness of concern for the surrounding world. In sum, then, curiosity entails a mode of seeing that, as a mere seeing, is directed at a "there" modified in turn so that the significance of the entity in its everydayness has been stripped from it and is no longer perceived in its being, but rather only according to its potential objectivity. Understood in this way, curiosity precedes the theoretical and points to the still-to-be-established genesis of the latter. What must also become clear from the preceding is how such a genesis, which presupposes care as a fundamental phenomenon of Dasein, is in a strong sense only thinkable if Dasein is fundamentally understood as being-with-others within a world. As a result of these lectures unearthed from 1923, one may—in connection to Heidegger's early application of the concept first coined by Simmel—designate this outline of the elementary features of such a derivation of the theoretical from the basis of an analysis of Dasein in its average everydayness as "life-worldly."

Here we should bear in mind that what Heidegger identified as Dasein in 1923 was before simply called life. In the first of the Freiburg lectures, where the need for an account of the genesis of the theoretical is already indicated, the attempt "to broach the problem of the essence and meaningful genesis of the theoretical even in its base lines" is also declared to be a "presumption," since, at first, it can only be a question of "*making the problem manifest.*"[16]

Notwithstanding all of the issues surrounding such a genesis, Heidegger has nonetheless already put forward the basic elements of such a genesis even if still in a very rudimentary way. To this end, before the derivation of the theoretical may be considered at all, no less than the phenomenon of lived experience itself must be brought forth in the look, especially the surrounding world and the lived experience of it that the dominant philosophy of neo-Kantianism could no longer even see "because of all its theory."[17] If the surrounding world and its lived experience are represented as *given*, then they have "already been theoretically infringed."[18] For Heidegger, "'given' is already a subtle, though still inconspicuous, yet genuine theoretical reflection."[19] The presupposition that the surrounding world is given, however inconspicuous it may be, is the first "theoretical form" of the objectification where "what is fundamentally foreign to theory" is forced "into a theoretical form" and is thereby lost sight of as such.[20] Yet, according to Heidegger, this "initial objectifying infringement of the surrounding world, its first and mere placement" before a knowing "I," is not a process that occurs outside of everydayness or befalls Dasein from outside of itself.[21] The abstraction from "the proper meaning of the surrounding world, its signifying character," through which that which is given becomes a mere thing, still takes place within the everyday surrounding world and for a "*still* historical 'I.'"[22] Before any further meaningful conception and explanation of the genesis of the theoretical is to be had, it must be made clear that the blindness of the theoretical to the problem of lived experience, as well as the general prevalence of the theoretical as such, is not of the order of coincidental phenomena. On the contrary, there is an internal relation between the theoretical and what it conceals that makes the former possible. The conditions of possibility of the theoretical are grounded in the phenomenon itself, which it covers over from the beginning by objectifying it. It has its origin in life itself within which it manifests itself in an intensifying process of objectification as a process of un-living.

With his observation that the initial objectification of the surrounding world and the lived experience of it is something that happens within the meaningfully lived and experienced surrounding world of a still historical "I"—which is to say, a concretely living "I"—Heidegger has already also outlined the basic principles of an eventual development and derivation of the theoretical. Once the surrounding world is understood as "given," it has been turned into a thing, and it is at that moment that the very first destruction of the experience of the surrounding world as lived occurs from within it, even if it is a mere thing for a still historical "I." This destruction does not so much consequently follow from thingliness having been "distilled out of the surrounding world" as from the fact that "the 'it worlds' has already been extinguished" within it.[23] Heidegger writes, "[t]he thing is merely there as such, i.e., it is real, it exists [. . .]. The meaningful has been deprived of its meaning leaving only this residue: being real. The experience of the surrounding world has been un-lived leaving only the residue: recognizing something as real. The historical 'I' has been de-historicized leaving only the remainder of a specific 'I-hood' as the correlate of thingliness; and only in following up the theoretical does it have its 'who,' i.e., merely in a 'deductive' way?!"[24] Within the everyday lived experience of the surrounding world, the three above-mentioned operations—the de-interpretation of the surrounding world as meaningful in itself, the progressively un-lived character of the lived experience of the surrounding world, and the de-historicization of the historical "I" (which, as Heidegger stresses, are in fact "inconspicuous, yet genuine theoretical reflection[s]")—already prepare for the explicitly theoretical. If the outcome of these three operations is considered to be a residue, a leftover, once the surrounding world has become a given thing for an "I" that is itself only a correlate for this thing, then it is clear that although the emergence of the theoretical in the everyday circumspective comportment of human beings is nothing but a pale shadow of the latter's original vitality, it nevertheless still depends upon this vitality. Now, the "quite original sphere distilled out of the surrounding world," which is brought into being with the residue in question, contains within itself moments for the intensification of the—at this point still limited—degree of theoretization and its progressive detachment from thingliness, in which a residue of the lived experience of the latter still resonates. With respect to the highly complex levels of objectification in the natural sciences, Heidegger speaks of the mass constants in physics as "rudiments from the reality of thingliness."[25] This intensification of the theoretical happens in a series of discrete steps of increasing un-living. The genesis of the theoretical thus consists precisely in pursuing this "process of progressively destructive theoretical infection of the surrounding world" at the phenomenal level.[26]

In the analytic of Dasein in *Being and Time*, where Dasein in its average everydayness and circumspective concern is analyzed in great detail, one finds a somewhat expanded and technically refined development of this problematic, even if the now central problem of Being undoubtedly sets limits upon the completeness of any explanation of the genesis of the theoretical. At the price of some redundancy, we must now follow Heidegger through the essentials of the genesis of the theoretical as outlined in the respective chapters of *Being and Time*. Indeed, the increased technical subtlety with which the project is described here will also allow us to formulate and answer some questions permitting a more precise delineation of the scope and aim of such a genesis.

As a definite possibility and potentiality for being of Dasein in *Being and Time*, the theoretical is a mode of comportment to the world, and thus presupposes above all being-in-the-world, primarily in the world of the everydayness of Dasein.[27] The genesis of the theoretical therefore requires an explication of the entirety of the modifications of Dasein's average circumspective comportment to and comprehension of both beings within-the-world and the world itself such that its comportment is able to be transformed into a mere seeing. It is precisely because Heidegger conceives of the theoretical as a comportment within the world from the outset that the categories by which its genesis must be thought show themselves to be modifications of Dasein's average comportment to beings. Only in this context does Heidegger's argument that the theoretical has "passed over" (*überspränge*) its foundation in the care-character of Dasein, or that it "concealed to itself" its own foundation, make sense. What must already be apparent from the above-cited lectures from 1919 and 1923 is the predominantly privative nature of these modifications: circumspective seeing and comprehending become a mere, disinterested seeing and conceiving. Moreover, this mere seeing on the part of the theoretical is only achieved when it has concealed from itself its own character of comportment—of care—thereby concealing from itself its foundation in circumspective comportment to the world as well. Not only does *Being and Time* explicitly confirm these early analyses, but in it the problematic of the genesis of the theoretical now includes a rather systematic and fully detailed determination of all of the different operations and their series of levels that are set in motion by this "passing-over" and "covering-over" of the founding of the theoretical in the circumspective concern of the everydayness of life. Thus it is clear that not only is the theoretical grounded in the atheoretical rather than in itself, but additionally, even the genesis of the theoretical itself is not a theoretical undertaking. If the theoretical understands itself as a presuppositionless and impartial seeing, theoretical understanding itself must conceal from itself its actual development out of the care-character of the averageness of Dasein and its surrounding world. This means that the demonstration of the genesis of the theoretical can only succeed in a critical encounter with it that also resists it. In no way then does Heidegger's derivation of the theoretical aim, as did Emil Lask's similar efforts, at a theory of theory.

However, before we turn toward the projected genesis of the theoretical in *Being and Time*, a question should be posed, which, even if no single answer to it is to be found, should nevertheless help to define the framework within which this genesis is to be discussed. If, in addition to all of the different privative operations to which circumspective comportment in the world must be subjected to be able to become a mere seeing, the theoretical must also conceal its origin in the everydayness of Dasein itself, then what does the theoretical properly consist in? What is the status of a phenomenon that must conceal its own proper genesis? And what, then, does a revealing of the founding of the theoretical in the atheoretical, in short, its deduction, actually seek to accomplish? Does the investigation of the diverse modifications that circumspective comportment to the world must incur in order to become a mere seeing only entail solving a theoretical and technical problem? Is the point to expose the non-originary character of theory as a derivative phenomenon, that is, to achieve something like a disenchantment of the theoretical? Or would the purpose perhaps be to initiate a reattachment of the theoretical (in an analogue to Husserl's late endeavors at a regression) to the circumspectively meaningful world of Dasein in its everydayness? But what is left of the theoretical residue if the constitutive self-concealment of its descent from the circumspective comportment of Dasein has been reversed? Can it, if it is freed from all of its passing-over and self-concealment, still find significance in the meaningfulness of the referential totality of the world? What would the essence of the theoretical have to consist of in order to be able to be reattached to the life-world in a generally meaningful way? If such a regression in the later Husserl, where it is a matter of overcoming the radical formalism of modern science, already appears to be somewhat enigmatic, the question I now pose is whether something similar can be envisioned in Heidegger's work at all. Is it conceivable that Heidegger explicitly intended a reattachment of theory to the life-world?[28]

If I see it rightly, the problem of theoretical knowing and its genesis is posed at the exact point where Being-in-the-world as the primary structure of being of Dasein is thematized in *Being and Time*. As may be inferred from chapter 12 and as its "compound expression" indicates, the phenomenon of Being-in-the-world becomes thematic as a "*unified* phenomenon" or a "whole phenomenon" (78).[29] For Heidegger, the analysis dedicated to this structure of being—a structure fundamentally not comprehensible by way of the handed-down ontological categories—is a matter of the methodical extraction of a *"seeing" by means of which this unified phenomenon may be made visible as such* once all of the "disguises and concealments" of the structure of the being of Being-in-the-world (a structure which, Heidegger explains, is always already somewhat familiar to Dasein in some way or another) are stripped away. Knowing the world is an existential "modality" of Being-in, that is, of Being-in-the-world. Yet, although Dasein is always already familiar with this state of being, it will fundamentally misconstrue this phenomenon at the point when, particularly in theoretical seeing, it is explicitly supposed to come to know it. Not only that, the very manner in which the world is seen makes it virtually "*invisible*," especially here, where knowing becomes explicit, that is, in theoretical cognition and its subject/object relation to the world (59). Accordingly, if a phenomenological grasp of this unified or whole phenomenon of Being-in-the-world is to be possible, then it must be shown both how the average understanding of the world is mostly mistaken in its understanding of the latter insofar as it conceives of the world in terms of intra-worldly beings, *and* how the theoretical, which is grounded in this average understanding, and which seeks to explicitly know the structure of being in question, not only is a mode of Dasein's concern with things in the surrounding world, but is also, on the basis of its inadequate ontological interpretation, a profound form of not-seeing.

In *Being and Time* the proposed investigation into "the way in which circumspective concern with the ready-to-hand changes over into an exploration of what we come across as present-at-hand with the world" proceeds with a particular directive in sight, namely, "the aim of penetrating to the temporal constitution of Being-in-the-world in general" (408–409). The result is that *Being and Time* does not investigate the entire scope of the genesis of the theoretical attitude. This is in contrast to the early lectures of 1919, where a fully sufficient deduction of the theoretical only had to be postponed because the atheoretical phenomenon of the lived experience of the surrounding world had first to be made visible so that the possibility and necessity of the genesis of the theoretical could then be recognized. In *Being and Time* the task of a complete deduction of the theoretical is no longer a priority: in 69b Heidegger retrospectively declares that the question of "how *theoretical* discovery 'arises' out of *circumspective* concern" only occurs in "the course of *existential ontological* analysis" (108). To begin with, this clarifies the fact that, in a certain contrast to the early Freiburg lectures, it is neither the "'logical' conception" of theory or science nor the problem of their emergence that is involved here (408). *Being and Time* only asks: "which of these conditions implied in Dasein's state of Being are existentially necessary for the possibility of Dasein's existing in the way of scientific research?" (408). The genesis of the theoretical attitude is thereby restricted to an *"ontological genesis,"* but that is also only within the limits required by the reflection on the question of Being. In short, the theoretical is central to *Being and Time* "only" (if one must say so) in terms of Dasein's comportment toward what is encountered as ready-to-hand within the world and its changeover into the merely present-at-hand. Instead of a logical analysis of the essential structure of theoretical constructs, in *Being and Time* it is solely a matter of the theoretical as a mode of Dasein's comportment to the world and the things found in it. As a result, the genesis of the theoretical attitude has to be explained in terms of the schemata that structure circumspective reflection. This is all the more important given that the schema of the as-structure is of particular importance in this context to the extent that it allows the theoretical attitude's understanding of being to be understood as a modification above all of Dasein's practical dealings with beings within the world (411–412). Even though *Being and Time* does not provide a full derivation of the theoretical, the greater technical sophistication of framing its relation to what is in terms of the schemata of circumspective understanding thus significantly contributes to clarifying its dependency on Dasein's average comportment to the world.

As already mentioned, the theoretical qua comportment presupposes Being-in-the-world as constitutive of the being-there of Dasein. However, as Heidegger explains in chapter 14, in theoretical cognition the world is interpreted from the perspective of intra-worldly beings, or more exactly, from "a limiting case of the Being of possible entities within-the-world," that is, the ontologico-categorical understanding of nature (93–94). Yet Dasein can discover the existence of nature only in a determinate mode of its Being-in-the-world. According to Heidegger, this kind of discovering has "the character of depriving the world of its worldhood in a definite way" (94). In the kind of being that belongs to the cognition of the world understood as nature, the phenomenon of worldliness is, as Heidegger emphatically notes, passed over (93). Chapter 15 then elucidates why this is so. There it is shown how, in contrast to the everyday circumspective comportment of Dasein in the world, where circumspection embodies the kind of seeing directed at the beings encountered nearby that are dealt with by using and manipulating them, the theoretical attitude arises from a modification of this kind of seeing proper to circumspective acting. The theoretical consists in a "bare perceptual cognition" (95) or, more precisely, in a way of "just *look[ing]* at the 'outward appearance' of Things," in "look[ing] at Things just 'theoretically'" (98). The modality of the adverb "just" indicates that the seeing that constitutes the theoretical is based upon a restriction, or, in Heidegger's words, a *deprivation* of the understanding of readiness-to-hand (99). In this "just looking ... without circumspection," the ready-to-hand is no longer to be found; there is, rather, only something merely present-at-hand or, to be more exact, a modification of the present-at-hand: namely, pure presence-at-hand, the "just present-at-hand" in its mere appearance (101). Certainly mere presence-at-hand is at first just a deficient mode of readiness-to-hand in the surrounding world of concern. As a mode of being of beings within-the-world encountered under certain conditions in the world of everyday circumspection, mere presence-at-hand is in no way already the correlate of an explicitly theoretical look. In chapter 16 Heidegger discusses how the character of presence-at-hand in everyday concern appears in certain situations where the "referential totalities [*Verweisungsganzheit*]" (106) and the "totality of involvements [*Bewandnisganzheit*]" belonging to readiness-to-hand are disrupted, particularly in the modes of the conspicuousness, obtrusiveness, and obstinacy of equipment that is experienced as unusable. In *Being and Time* the examples of encounters with presence-at-hand in everyday life involve equipment that has become unusable such as a hammer whose handle has broken. In the first Freiburg lectures, Heidegger, in order to illustrate a case of presence-at-hand in everyday circumspective relating to the word, imagines an African man from Senegal being suddenly transported from his hut into the lecture hall and the kind of lived experiences that he would have of things in it, like the lectern, that he would not know what to do with.[30] In any case, the present-at-hand being that is experienced in this fashion is still bound, for, as Heidegger remarks, "the ready-to-hand is not thereby just *observed* and stared at as something present-at-hand; the presence-at-hand which makes itself known is still bound up in the readiness-to-hand of equipment. Such equipment still does not veil itself in the guise of mere Things" (104). "Being-just-present-at-hand" (103) and its corresponding seeing therefore still require a further unbinding for the signifying and referential context of the world to have been fully eliminated from the form of the mere thing; only once that has happened are the mere observing and staring of theory adopted. It is thus that the theoretical attitude must work its way toward the merely present-at-hand "first *through* [*über*, over] what is ready-to-hand in our concern" (101; translation modified). The modifications that concern thereby undergoes are, ontologically speaking, the proof that theoretical knowing itself is only a "*founded* mode of Being-in-the-world" (101).

Here we should remember that, as per chapter 32 on "Understanding and Interpretation," the plain pre-predicative seeing of readiness-to-hand underlying all circumspective dealings with the ready-to-hand "is, in itself, something which already understands and interprets," and that in the same way as what is "*explicitly* understood [it] has the structure of *something as something*" (189). In order to render more distinctly the boundedness and the founding of both mere presence-at-hand in the still circumspectively concerned understanding of the world of everyday Dasein and the comportment of "just looking," it is necessary to show that the schema of interpretative-understanding of circumspective seeing, that is, its as-structure, however modified, contravenes to determine the experience of presence-at-hand in daily life as well as the explicitly theoretical positing of what is just present-at-hand. From the beginning, the comportment of just-looking is only a modification of the as-structure of the circumspective understanding that the everydayness of Dasein consists of and remains bound to it. However, the "grasp[ing] something *free*, as it were, *of the 'as'* [. . .] [w]hen we merely stare at something" happens "as a failure to understand it anymore," or to be more exact, it happens when Dasein is no longer able to interpret the "in order to" of what is circumspectively encountered in its everydayness, consequently rendering it no longer intelligible. However, the way that "as-free" sight turns out to be a mere staring, or an "as-free" grasping turns out to be a privation, means that such an "as-free" sight is still based on the "kind of seeing in which one *merely* understands. It is not more primordial than that kind of seeing, but is derived from it" (190). By contrast, theoretical seeing is founded upon this "as-free" seeing, which is itself still bound to everyday concern: compared to plain seeing it is constituted through a double "readjustment" (190). As a definite ideal of knowledge, theoretical understanding is still an understanding, but, as Heidegger writes, it is "itself only a subspecies of understanding [...] which has strayed into the legitimate task of grasping the present-at-hand in its essential unintelligibility" (194). The readjustment accomplished by this changeover from the seeing that is still bound but no longer understanding into theoretical seeing depends on an essential radicalizing of the unintelligibility of what is now only merely present-at-hand.

Insofar as theoretical seeing is grounded in and derived from a pre-thematic knowing of the world, it is no longer able to bring either the phenomenon of Being-in-the-world or an originary understanding of the world into the look. What Heidegger calls "the most primordial kind of knowing" is far more originary than any theoretical seeing: instead of assimilating itself to a definite ideal of knowledge, this knowing actualizes the essential conditions under which it can be performed—in other words, Dasein's existential fore-structure—as a characteristic potentiality-for-Being of Dasein (195). In terms of Heidegger's first Freiburg lectures, which represent his first attempt to break the primacy of the theoretical through an analysis of its genesis, such primordial knowing is, as we have already seen, an originary pre- or atheoretical knowing, that is, it is "prior" to the division of theory and practice. In this context von Herrmann speaks of the "true phenomenon of knowing the world. [...] This is 'truly' grasped if it is able to be revealed as an 'existential "modality" of Being-in.'"[31] If *Being and Time* undertakes a critique of theoretical knowledge and reveals the theoretical to be a derivative phenomenon because of its genesis out of the average mode of being of Dasein, then this is done in order to philosophically find an approach that would do justice to the ontology of Dasein in its full breadth—which includes the theoretical attitude—by bringing into the look as such what was called "life" in 1919 and is now called Being.

Now we certainly must also consider the fact that theoretical knowing, although it may be derivative and grounded upon a process of un-living (as it is incisively called in the first Freiburg lectures), is neither insignificant nor worthless. However devastating Heidegger's critique is to science, it does not challenge its right to exist or its accomplishments; at most it challenges its self-understanding. In the early lectures the theoretical is identified as an originary sphere. In *Being and Time* it is, as the discourse of the ontological genesis of the theoretical suggests, a potentiality-for-Being and as such is an integral possibility of Dasein in its very being. And if Heidegger also says of the theoretical attitude that it embodies a grasping of the present-at-hand which "has strayed [. . .] in its essential unintelligibility," then, as we have seen, such a grasping is nevertheless appreciated as a "legitimate task" (194). Considering this determination of the theoretical as being grounded in the everyday concern of Dasein, which it outgrows through a privative readjustment in order to constitute both an originary sphere and a legitimate task, the question may be asked: Should the destruction of the intelligibility and significance of the world as it is experienced in circumspection, a destruction that is proper to the theoretical, be reversed? Can theoretical knowing not be reconnected to the life-world, and the circumspective concern that constitutes the latter, and thus be made meaningful as a whole for the life-world? Why is this question, which is explicitly tackled by the later Husserl, not asked in *Being and Time*? Is it perhaps because the theoretical attitude has its foundation in the life-world insofar as the privation and modification of the latter by the former is constitutive of theory to such a degree that its being rescinded would bring with it the supercession of the theoretical itself? Or can it be that in the genesis of the theoretical from everyday concern outlined in *Being and Time*, the theoretical is anchored in the latter in such a way that the question of a return can no longer even arise? Or is it really that the dominance of the question of Being in *Being and Time* restricts any critical encounter with the theoretical to bringing only to light the obstacles that keep theory from bringing the phenomenon of Being-in-the-world suitably into language, thereby preventing the theoretical's move back into the domain of circumspection from being thematized?

I recall one more time that the problem of the genesis of the theoretical is tackled in *Being and Time*, right at the moment where the point is to bring Being-in-the-world as the originary structure of being into the look. In the preparatory analysis to this task in chapter 15, which initially aims at disclosing the being of beings encountered in concern for the surrounding world, Heidegger makes a passing remark about methodology that should interest us here:

> Such entities are not thereby objects for knowing the "world" theoretically; they are simply what gets used, what gets produced, and so forth. As entities so encountered, they become the preliminary theme for the purview of a "knowing" which, as phenomenological, looks primarily towards Being, and which, in thus taking Being as its theme, takes these entities as its accompanying theme. This phenomenological interpretation is accordingly not a way of knowing those characteristics of entities which themselves are; it is rather a determination of the structure of the Being which entities possess. But as an investigation of Being, it brings to

completion, autonomously and explicitly, that understanding of Being which belongs already to Dasein and which "comes alive" in any of its dealings with entities. (95–96)

It is here that what is at issue becomes more clear, namely, it is a matter of recovering a different form of knowing from the theoretical, a phenomenological knowing that thematizes the prethematic understanding of Being in everyday dealings with beings and is able to determine the structure of their being. Theory, as we have read, is not in a position to accomplish this. On the contrary, only a destruction of the theoretical and its control over philosophical thought—and "destruction" is understood here as a step back into the concealed foundation of the theoretical in circumspective concern—can allow a real knowing of the world to come into the look. This attempt to secure a real knowing of the world is the real aim of the debate over the theoretical carried on in *Being and Time*. This debate is first and foremost a detour necessary in order to ground a seeing in which Being may be thematized.

Now, if *theoria* undergoes a rehabilitation as it were in Heidegger's later work through a return of sorts to an originary Greek meaning of the term, that does not mean, however, that disinterested contemplation of the objectivity of presence in the sciences has been reconnected to its presuppositions in the life-world or that theoretical knowing would have been freed from its misunderstanding of the world. Instead of initiating a transformation of the theoretical by reattaching it to the life-world, theory is now defined in an originary way as *theoria*. It is unnecessary to quote here all of the extensive etymological reflections on the word "theory" in "Science and Reflection" or in the *Parmenides* lectures, which we will take up in some detail in the next chapter.[32] For the time being, it is enough to call attention to how theory is interpreted as "the perceptual relation of man to Being, a relation man does not produce, but rather a relation into which Being itself first posits man."[33] In the case of "Science and Reflection," Heidegger consistently calls theory, as it was thought by the Greeks, "the reverent paying heed to the unconcealment of what presences"; briefly put, it is nothing less than a "beholding that watches over truth." Heidegger characterizes such a beholding, by which we reveal the being of what exists and upon which "honor and esteem" are bestowed, as the highest relation to beings.[34] Thought in relation to its beginning, *theoria* thus becomes another name for originary philosophical thinking and a genuine knowing of the world. It is another word for what was already claimed in the aforementioned methodological remark from *Being and Time*: a phenomenological knowing and interpreting that looks primarily toward the being of beings. Thus one could make an attempt to show that Heidegger's later, more originary retrieval of theory not only has its implicit preconditions in this methodological remark, but that this understanding of theory in *Being and Time* would make all such attempts at reattaching the theoretical attitude to the life-world superfluous.[35] The claim I am strongly seeking to make here is that the absence of the problematic of reattaching the theoretical to concern for the surrounding world in *Being and Time* does not represent an omission. With the distinction in the 1919 Freiburg lectures between the two types of formally objective theorizing that Heidegger opposes to the absolutely empty and radically un-living theoretization, theoretical science is shown to be equally founded in life in the same way as a genuine phenomenological seeing in which the understanding of the being of Dasein has become thematized. In looking back one may claim that *theoria*, understood as a "beholding that watches," instead of being a product mediated by the expectations of the life-world, is a seeing that embodies the highest form of living. But the theoretical, more specifically that which creates an "as free" seeing from the various levels of readjustment away from the world of circumspective concern, opens as well an original sphere in the life-world itself and attempts a legitimate task that remains bound to the life-world in a meaningful way despite every possibility of degeneration, and therefore does not need to be collapsed back into it either. Both concepts of the theoretical are always already located in the life-world.

Nevertheless, there is perhaps in play still more in *Being and Time* when theoretical knowing, after emerging from the life-world through a double readjustment, is not explicitly reattached to the circumspective concern of worldly understanding and made meaningful because of that. As a modification of circumspective concern, in *Being and Time* the theoretical is first aligned with comportment and becomes solely thematized as theoretical comportment. In other words, as a comporting, theoretical sight is exclusively taken into the look from the perspective of Dasein and its Being-in-the-world. But when Heidegger suggests in the *Parmenides* lectures of 1942–43 that for us today "the 'theoretical' [. . .] is a product of the human representational subject," does that not mean that the manner by which it comes to language in *Being and Time*, despite all of the efforts to differentiate Dasein from the subject, is still thought according to the concept of subjectivity?[36] Or if it is, as Heidegger puts it in the "Letter on 'Humanism,'" that "the characterization of thinking as *theoria* and the determination of knowing as 'theoretical' comportment occur already within the 'technical' interpretation of thinking,"[37] is not the suspicion planted that for the later Heidegger the analysis of the circumspective concern of Dasein was not originary enough and proceeded too technically, i.e., too subjectively? If, neither in *Being and Time* nor in Heidegger's later work is the question asked as to whether the foundational estrangement of theory from the life-world must be undone, and theory can only be salvaged according to the way that it was thought in its beginning, does that not mean that for Heidegger such an undertaking would ultimately remain trapped in the metaphysics of subjectivity? It is not by way of the subject, but rather only through being, which means a "perceptual relation of man to Being, a relation man does not produce but rather a relation into which Being itself first posits man," that theory is once again able to be meaningful for Heidegger.[38]

As we turn now to a careful reading of "Science and Reflection," where, undoubtedly, a critique of modern theory motivates what seems at first to be a rehabilitation of ancient *theoria*, we may, perhaps, find some answers to the questions posed above. In a closer look at this text, it appears that Heidegger's reevaluation of *theoria* does not come without significant reservations. Not only does the shadow of *theoria*, Heidegger forcefully argues here, still steal into modern theory, however different the modern sciences may be from the Greek conception, but theory in the modern sense is also dependent on it. This dependence, as we will see, is a function of an unreflected trait within *theoria* itself, and of which the theoretical attitude characteristic of the sciences is the belated actualization. In other words, if *theoria* has been pregnant from the start with the breakdown of the world that the modern sciences have brought about, *theoria*, however originary, cannot simply be endorsed in its historical shape. Indeed, the thrust of "Science of Reflection" is to think toward another kind of attitude, one called *Besinnung*, beyond both *theoria* in the ancient sense *and* modern theory, even though *Besinnung* may also only be a template in preparation for a new concept of *theoria*. Yet what motivates such questioning of the venerable concept of *theoria* is not only the trait latent within *theoria* itself that made the modern breakdown of the world possible. It is above all the concern with the life-world itself, or, rather, with "world" itself.

6
BEYOND THEORY: *THEORIA*, OR WATCHING OVER WHAT IS STILL TO COME

AT FIRST SIGHT, THE LECTURE from 1953 on "Science and Reflection" is above all concerned with the modern sciences.[1] As "the theory of the real," they have shaped our sense of reality. But if this state of affairs requires a reflection, or rather a *Besinnung*, it is because something is already at work in the sciences, which, in spite of what I will call the "un-world" to which they have given rise, announces a new age of the world: an age that, in distinction from the sciences' planetary expansion, would be one of the "world" itself.[2] It is in this context that Heidegger sketches a more originary meaning of theory, no longer a derivative formation, whose basic features, as we have seen, are a compound of the reduction and systematic impoverishment (*Verarmung*) of Dasein's everyday circumspective and atheoretical comportment to the world. Henceforth, what is called theory is seen to draw upon a relation to what is that is more originary than that of Dasein in its everydayness and that corresponds to the ancient Greeks' relation to the real, in short, to *theoria*. Yet, significantly enough, Heidegger does not confront the theory of the modern sciences with a concept of *theoria* established in advance, which would have needed only to be revived by way of historical and philological research. On the contrary, through an analysis of the theory of the modern sciences themselves Heidegger retrospectively draws out the Greek conception of *theoria* whose shadow is still present in the sciences even though they are involved in something very different. Furthermore, what thus comes to light in the early conception of *theoria* is not only a more fundamental relation to what is, which the theory of the modern sciences presupposes in spite of its entirely different attitude toward what is, but also something unthought in the very Greek conception of *theoria* itself. Indeed, even though *theoria* is earlier, more originary, and more essential than modern theory, *theoria* is present in the sciences insofar as it contains an unthought, since precisely this unthought made its translation into modern science possible.

Simply falling back on the Greek conception of *theoria*, therefore, is not sufficient to retrieve a more originary relation to the world than the one that is effective in the theory of the sciences. Without expanding on what remains unthought within it—and that means without completely recasting its concept—*theoria* cannot be made fruitful for a new relation to what is. At no point in the essay does Heidegger lay claim to a positive and unadulterated notion of *theoria*. Nor is *theoria* simply reevaluated in relation to the theory of the sciences. Rather, Heidegger's approach is a reflection, or, rather, a *Besinnung*, upon the sciences. But such reflection is not merely of the order of an intellectual and detached musing about the state of affairs that characterizes the contemporary sciences. As the essay makes clear, it is a pro-visional and preparative engagement with the signs of a new world-age that announces itself within the sciences themselves, an age characterized by a certain poverty (*Armut*) that at the same time promises a richer relation to what is. *Besinnung* is, as Heidegger submits, an active way of thinking, or rather an action in the mode of thought (*denkende Handlung*). Yet even though reflection as *Besinnung* is characterized only as a preliminary, proactive engagement in thought of another relation to what is that would usher in an age beyond the modern sciences, the question arises whether it is not also a kind of thought that, because it inquires into the unthought of Greek *theoria* itself, corresponds in its own way to what the Greeks called *theoria*. Is reflection limited only to preparing a way of relating to what is different from that of the sciences by bringing to light what remained unthought in the Greek attitude of *theoria*, or is it itself not also already the very enactment of a new, postmodern way of *theoria*, one that is no longer Greek in a historical sense? In any case, such reflection is an action through thought that, in following up on the signs that point in the direction of a new world-age, lingers on them so as to make them linger on, thereby working toward inaugurating the age of the world in question.[3] These are among the questions that will guide my commentary on "Science and Reflection," to which we now proceed.

At the beginning of the essay, Heidegger contends that, in the same way as the arts, science is not merely a manifestation of the human being's spiritual and creative ingenuity prized for its cultural value. It is not merely "a fabrication of man [*ein menschliches Gemächte*]" that arises from a "mere wanting to know on the part of man" and whose dominance in the current age could be "demolished again by the will of man."[4] On the contrary, the ascendance of the sciences to dominion in the modern age is nothing simply of the order of the power of man. According to Heidegger, a greater destiny, "something other than a mere wanting to know," rules the sciences.[5] It is a fact, he adds, that in the sciences "[s]omething other reigns [*ein Anderes waltet*]," something other than everything of the order of human wanting, willing, or desiring.[6]

Indeed, if the sciences are not merely a fabrication of man, it is because they are above all one way—though "a decisive way"—among others (art being another) "in which all that is presents itself to us."[7] More precisely, when Heidegger remarks that "[t]he reality [*Wirklichkeit*] within which man of today moves and attempts to maintain himself is, with regard to its fundamental characteristics, determined on an increasing scale by and in conjunction [*in zunehmendem Masse durch das mitbestimmt*] with that which we call Western European science," science is construed as an "objective" happening that shapes all that is, or all that is real, to the point of determining the very reality of what is real.[8] In other words, the sciences concern the very way in which we perceive and experience the world as a whole from the beginning; that is, they concern the open interconnectedness of meaning anterior to the human being's subjective will to know and the interest that he may take in the products of such activity. When Heidegger states that "[w]hen we ponder this ongoing event [*Vorgang*], it becomes evident that, in the Western world and during the eras of its history, science has developed such a power as could never have been met with on the earth before, and that consequently this power is ultimately to be spread over the entire globe," it is clear that science, although merely one way "in which all that is presents itself to us," affects our sense of reality with a power unlike that of all previous epochal transformations of reality and threatens to exclude all alternatives or exceptions to the rule.[9] Although a relatively recent happening even in the Occident, this reality-shaping and world-forming event, which is becoming increasingly global, has all the appearance of being an absolute event that not only sidelines all other ways of conceiving the real but also forecloses the memory of the history that brought about the imperialist ascendance of the scientific view of the real and its power of world-formation. The stakes of what the modern sciences qua theoretical sciences have accomplished by spreading over the entire globe are condensed in one word that Heidegger uses: *Welterschütterung*, that is, an in-depth breakdown of the world, not an abolishment of world altogether but a seismic disturbance on a planetary scale of the foundations of "world" as such.

If something other reigns in the sciences, it thus does so insofar as the sciences play a dominant, although not altogether exclusive, role in fashioning the very way in which we experience what is real, that is, the reality of the real. Could one not say that they replace the world with the real or that, by becoming global, they substitute the earth (*Erde*) with the planet (*Erdball*)? However, this other that holds sway in all the sciences not only "conceals itself from us so long as we give ourselves up to ordinary notions about sciences"; it also "remains hidden to the sciences themselves," since, as we will see later, they are incapable of fathoming their own essence.[10] Now, Heidegger calls this other that reigns in the sciences "a state of affairs [*Sachverhalt*]," literally, a totality of significant circumstances that stand in a determined interconnection.[11] However, for this "state of affairs" to come into view in the first place, we first must have experienced that in which the essence (*Wesen*) of the sciences consists. So far, the sciences have been characterized as a major way in which what is real has become shaped for us. Yet, when Heidegger holds that the essence of the sciences can be expressed by the concise statement that "*science is the theory of the real*," it is made clear that the sciences condition the way "in which all that is presents itself to us" in the modern age qua theory of the real.[12] By thus defining the essence of science as the theory of the real, we are also put on the way toward an experience of "the state of affairs," or "the something other," that holds sway in the sciences and that subtends their essence (or that explains why their essence consists in the theoretical formation of the real). Let me also emphasize from the start that in speaking of the "essence of science" Heidegger does not refer to the Latin term *essentia* but uses the German word *Wesen*. In other words, his talk about the essence of science is predicated on a verbal understanding of essence, that is, on the way in which science is active, exists, or simply *is*. This must always be kept in mind; otherwise, his claim that a "state of affairs" holds sway in the sciences' essence does not make any sense.

This essence is the distinctive feature of modern science and sets it radically apart from the science of both the Middle Ages (*doctrina*) and antiquity (*episteme*). This very feature has made possible "the revolutionary character of the modern kind of knowing."[13] Notwithstanding this thorough otherness of modern science, however, Heidegger asserts that "the essence of modern science, which has become world-wide meanwhile as European science, is grounded in the thinking of the Greeks, which since Plato has been called philosophy."[14] This assertion, as he submits, in no way diminishes the modern theoretical sciences' radical otherness. The exact opposite is the case. Now, if this contention that modern science has its ultimate source in Greek thought enhances its revolutionary and distinctive otherness rather than weakening it, it is because modern science is seen to consist "in the decisive working out [*Herausarbeitung*] of a tendency [*eines Zuges*, a feature, a trait, a tug] that still remains concealed in the essence of knowing as the Greeks experienced it, and that precisely needs the Greek knowing in order to become, over against it, another kind of knowing."[15] Paradoxically, the very possibility of the radical otherness of the modern sciences to Greek *episteme* derives from the former's foundation in the latter. Let us linger for a moment on the complex way in which modern science remains indebted to Greek thought in all its thorough otherness. Modern science does not proceed in a continuous fashion from what the Greeks understood and developed as *episteme*. On the contrary, if modern science needs the Greek conception of knowledge to develop an entirely other form of knowledge of its own, it is in the sense that it works out and fully expands upon a trait or tendency present in the *episteme* that remained concealed to the Greeks. Modern science is radically other than Greek *episteme* in that it radically extrapolates a hidden tendency within the Greek understanding of knowledge. Even though Heidegger does not explicitly acknowledge that Greek *episteme* is thus already pregnant with modern science, and even though he is even more reluctant to admit that it also already harbors the threat of the un-world into which the modern sciences have shaped the real, it nevertheless follows that the Greek conception of science is clearly nothing that could be simply and uncritically celebrated in a wholesale fashion because of the trait in question that lies dormant in it. What this trait consists in remains to be seen. But it should already be clear that if modern science is, indeed, indebted in this manner to a feature, or tendency, in Greek thought that did not yet reveal itself to the Greeks (although that feature already pulled in an opposite direction from their understanding of knowing), then to understand anything at all about what obtains today for the modern sciences requires "strik[ing] root into the ground of our historical existence," that is, into Greek thought.[16] In other words, in order to grasp the radical transformation of the world, or rather the breakdown of the world, that the sciences have brought with them and by which the world is replaced by what is real, and, furthermore, to grasp that transformation in a way that is not merely "theoretical," "a dialogue with the Greek thinkers and their language" becomes inevitable.[17]

Unlike the revival of a dead past, or the historical inquiry into a past that is thoroughly bygone that can still serve to understand the genesis of the modern world, the reflective return to Greek thought and poetry in order to enable the dialogue with the Greeks is a return to a past that is still alive in the present, a past that is constitutive of the very historicity of the present. However, this living past of Greek thought and poetry in the present, that is, "in the rule of modern technology, which is thoroughly foreign to the ancient world," is also a past that is present in the present "in such a way that its [own] essence [...] is still hidden from itself."[18] Let us bear in mind that the radical otherness of the sciences and their theory is the result of a working out and full realization of a trait, of a *Zug*, within *episteme* that still remained concealed to the Greeks. If what the Greek thinkers have thought and their poets have sung is still alive in the modern age and, indeed, all the more present where one would not expect it, namely, in thoroughly un-Greek modern science and technology, it is, precisely, insofar as this heritage remains unreflected in its very essence. Very schematically, then, the dialogue with the Greeks also serves to clear up a blind spot in the Greek heritage and thus to break its foundational function with respect to modernity with the aim of retrieving an other, altogether other, world-founding dimension of this heritage through which to counter the breakdown of the "world" brought about by the sciences.

However, as Heidegger remarks, "[t]hat dialogue still awaits its beginning. It is scarcely prepared for at all."[19] In spite of all appearances, the reflections about the indebtedness of modern science to Greek thought that he undertakes in "Science and Reflection" are only mere preparations for such a dialogue. Venturing to think forward (*vordenken*) in the direction of a dialogue with the Greeks with the "practical" aim of working out a relation to the sciences and their subjection of the world to the real through which another correspondence (*Entsprechung*) between the earth and the human can be secured, "Science and Reflection" is limited at first only to the modest task of exploring the conditions of such a dialogue. Since the European sciences have expanded their power over the whole planet, however, Heidegger also acknowledges here that an inquiry into the grounding of the sciences in Greek thought alone is not sufficient to meet the challenge posed by the planetary extension of the power of the sciences; the inquiry must go hand in hand with a dialogue with other parts of the world and their traditions.[20] More profoundly: since the direction in which the modern sciences are pulled is already present at least in latent fashion in ancient *episteme* itself, and since, consequently, the possibility of the breakdown of the world looms in Greek thought as well, one must take into account what Heidegger, elsewhere, calls "other origins." The other parts of the world that the Western European sciences have come to dominate, such as the East Asian world, have to be brought into the picture as well. However planetary, the theoretical attitude of the sciences, for its part, precludes all dialogue with any other and with any other's world. For the sciences and the way in which they shape our experience of what is, there is no such thing as an other. Science knows nothing about encounters and dialogues. As a result, the dialogue still to be developed with the Greek thinkers in order to grasp the origin of modern science and what it does to the world also becomes for the Western Europeans ("for us," Heidegger says) "the precondition of the inevitable dialogue with the East Asian world."[21] Let us remind ourselves of the fact that something other than just the human will to know reigns in the sciences, that is, in a kind of knowing that originates in Greek *episteme* but has become something entirely foreign to the Greek conception of knowing, a thing, indeed, that also knows no otherness. In seeking to meet the challenge that the sciences pose today, reflection requires not only a return to what is the West's most own, that is, the Greek ground of the West's historical existence, but also an open dialogue with what is other to the West, as well. Yet, any encounter with the worlds of the other—in this case with the East Asian world—as a world in the first place and, furthermore, as a world that has an origin of its own is possible for the Western European exclusively by way of a return to the West's own origin in Greece, that is, to the Western world that the sciences have shaken to the point of breakdown.

In an effort to demonstrate how "what was primally thought [*früh Gedachtes*], primally destined [*früh Geschicktes*]" survives in the essence of the thoroughly un-Greek modern sciences and to prepare thus a reflection on their essence through the dialogue with Greek thought, Heidegger returns to the statement "Science is the theory of the real."[22] He does so to inquire, first, into the meaning of "real," then into the meaning of "theory," before finally exploring the relation between both, or more precisely, "how the two, the real and the theoretical, go to join one another from out of their essence [*aufeinander zugehen*]."[23] Let me immediately draw attention to the fact that what remains present in the statement, or proposition, on the essence of the theoretical sciences is not something that the Greeks had thought in the *past* but something that was thought *early on* compared to the present that comes *later*, something that, unlike the past that has revolved for the benefit of the present, still lives on in what is later. In distinction from the past, what is early carries on its life in what happens later. In order to show that what was primally thought continues to live on in the statement about the essence of the modern sciences, Heidegger turns to the words—*die Worte* as opposed to *die Wörter*—"the real" and "theory" in the statement in question. Admittedly, since the breakdown of the world caused by modern science is at stake here, Heidegger's recourse to etymology to elucidate the meaning of these words may be construed by some as an evasive luxury. However, as he remarks, everything depends on how this recourse to etymology happens. As we just noted, in seeking to elucidate the meanings of "the real" and "theory," he is not concerned with them as terms (*Wörter*), or linguistic tokens, that could be retraced to "old and often obsolete meanings of terms," but as "words" (*Worte*), as "the early meaning [of words] and its changes," needed "to catch sight of the realm pertaining to the matter in question [*Sachbereich*] into which the word speaks."[24] Heidegger writes: "Deliberately we say 'words' (*die Worte*) and not 'terms' (*die Wörter*), in order to emphasize that, each time, in the coming to presence and holding-sway of language, it is a destining that decides [*dass sich im Wesen und Walten der Sprache jedesmal ein Schicksal entscheidet*]."[25] Words, in the sense of terms, refer to linguistic tokens that designate things. Understood as a means of communication, language is exclusively made up of terms, terms to which corresponding terms in other languages can be found and that can thus be translated more or less without problems. By contrast, words as words presuppose that language is the opening of an essential realm for a people, a world opened up by a singular language in which what the word names, and thus brings into presence to begin with, moves. It is, therefore, words (and the language to which they belong) that send the specific meaning that they articulate to all those who are at home in this language and claim them to respond to what is addressed to them. If a certain "etymological" recourse is necessary to elucidate the early meaning of later terms, especially if these terms are translations, it also follows that the problematics of etymology and of translation are, as we will see hereafter, intimately intertwined. Indeed, any translation of words (rather than of terms) brings with it a radical change of their meaning and, consequently, a decisive transformation of what is destined by them. But, for the time being, let me return to Heidegger's dependence on "etymology" to establish the early meaning of what still speaks in later words, words that are translations of earlier words and that, additionally, may barely be words at all anymore. He writes: "What counts is to ponder that essential realm [into which words speak] as the one in which the matter named through the word moves. Only in this way does the word speak, and speak in the complex of meanings into which the matter that is named by it unfolds throughout the history of poetry and thought."[26] Rather than looking for old meanings of terms that no longer speak and that, hence, are no longer part of the present, living language, the "etymological" recourse consists in listening to the earlier meanings of words that still speak through them and make them words to begin with. "Etymology," here, is anything but the philological exercise known under this name, which, as a scientific discipline, is precisely at issue in "Science and Reflection." Instead, "etymology" is an attempt to ponder by listening both to the early meanings of words that are still alive in present words and to the realm into which these words speak. It is also an attempt to retrieve within terms their originary character of words. Yet, what is meant by "the realm pertaining to the matter in question," or "the essential realm" (*Sachbereich, Wesensbereich*), and "the matter named through the word" will only become apparent as we now turn to a detailed elucidation of the meaning of "the real" and "theory."

The first point of view from which Heidegger seeks to clarify the statement "Science is the theory of the real" concerns the meaning of the word "real." He writes: "The real (*das Wirkliche*) brings to fulfillment [*erfüllt*] the realm of working (*des Wirkenden*), of that which works (*wirkt*)."[27] The real is not only the outcome of what "works" but also that in which such working is fulfilled in the sense of a consummation. From the beginning, let us thus accentuate the double nature of the essence of the real. It is constituted by two moments: it is both a result (of working) and something that holds itself in such realization. First, however, we must ask, Heidegger avers, "[w]hat does it mean 'to work'?"[28] After adding that "'[t]o work' means 'to do' [*tun*]," he turns to "etymology" in order to define what of the early meaning of "to do" may still be present in the later word whose contemporary meaning is primarily one of (human) action and agency.[29] As a word, Heidegger holds that *tun* (doing) "belongs to the Indo-Germanic stem *dhe*; from this also stems the Greek *thesis*," both of which refer to a doing that, in contrast to the modern meaning of the word, is not exclusively human and that signifies, first and foremost, "the holding sway of nature (*physis*)," in other words, the bringing something "hither and forth (*her- und vor-bringen*), that is, into presencing."[30] If the modern limitation of the word *tun* to signifying human activity and agency is understood as the result of an epochal translation by which a narrowing, or contraction, of its early meaning of bringing something hither and forth into unconcealment occurs, then the early meaning of the word can be seen to survive in the later meaning. The "broader" and ontologically more primary meaning of doing that the "etymological" elucidation unearths is the semantic horizon within which the narrowing of the realm of doing has occurred, a horizon that thus also continues to live on in the word's later meaning. Now, if the early meaning of doing concerns the bringing hither and forth into presence, the originary realm that the word names and into which it speaks is the realm of Being, the realm in which "that which presences, presences."[31] Within the matter pertaining to this realm, the word "doing" originarily names "*one way* in which that which presences, presences" (emphasis mine), a way of coming into being by way of *thesis*, that is, by way of bringing something into presence in the mode of *hither and forth*.[32] Furthermore, since according to its early meaning this one way in which something comes into presence concerns either "something [that] brings itself forth hither into presencing of itself or [...] the bringing hither and forth of something [...] accomplished by man," the earlier meaning of doing is anterior to, older than the divide between *physis*, on the one hand, and *poiesis* and *techne*, on the other.[33]

After this explanation of the originary meaning of "doing" and "working," Heidegger returns to the question of the real in the statement "Science is the theory of the real," to the question of what of the early meaning of the word still lingers in it (and thus makes its contemporary meaning meaningful in the first place), concluding that "[t]he real (*Wirkliche*) is the working, the worked (*Wirkende, Gewirkte*); that which brings hither and brings forth into presencing, and that which has been brought hither and brought forth."[34] If this is so, "[r]eality (*Wirklichkeit*) means, then, when thought sufficiently broadly: that which, brought forth hither into presencing, lies before; it means the presencing, consummated in itself [*in sich vollendete*], of self-bringing-forth."³⁵ Two moments clearly constitute the broadly understood conception of reality: self-bringing-forth and holding itself in what has been brought forth. This double movement of presencing, especially the emphasis on the *consummation* of presencing in what has been brought forth, is indicative of a very specific interpretation of the Aristotelian notion of *energeia* on which this elucidation of the "real" in its early meaning rests.³⁶ Indeed, if *Wirklichkeit* (reality) originally signifies the doing that brings something not only hither into presencing but also forth into lying before in such a way that what has been brought hither holds itself in consummation and maintains itself in its presencing, then the German word *Wirklichkeit* (reality) translates the Aristotelian concept of *energeia*, understood not only as the actual presencing of what presences but also as the lasting, or enduring, in presencing (*entelecheia*) of what has been brought hither and forth.³⁷ Heidegger makes this connection between *Wirklichkeit* and *energeia* also on the basis that the German word *wirken* must be retraced to the Indo-Germanic root *uerg*, from which derive both the German word "*Werk*" and the Greek word *ergon*. For Aristotle, he explains, *ergon* means the work in which "the self-bringing-forth into full presencing" comes to a fulfillment and in which it holds itself: "*Ergon* is that which in the genuine and highest sense presences (*an-west*). For this reason and only for this reason does Aristotle name the presence of that which actually presences *energeia* and also *entelecheia*: a self-holding in consummation (i.e., consummation of presencing)."³⁸

The fundamental character of working and work that marks this early meaning of *ergon*, the work in which what has been brought forth is consummated and in which it holds itself in this accomplishment, must be kept radically distinct from what the Romans referred to as *efficere*, *effectus*, and *causa efficiens*. *Ergon* is not an effect brought about through an *operatio* as an *actus*. Even though these terms translate *ergon* and *energeia*, they are, as Heidegger notes, "totally different word[s], with a totally different realm of meaning."³⁹ In other words, a radical "change in the reality of the real" takes place by translating *ergon* and *energeia* into Latin:

> That which is brought hither and forth now appears as that which results from an *operatio*. A result is that which follows out of and follows upon an *actio*: the consequence, the out-come (*Er-folg*). The real is now that which has followed as consequence. The consequence is brought about by the circumstance (*Sache*) that precedes it, i.e., by the cause (*Ursache*) (*causa*). The real appears now in the light of the causality of the *causa efficiens*.⁴⁰

Now understood as that which has been brought about, as that which has been wrought (*das Erwirkte*), in other words, as the thing (*Sache*) resulting from a doing (*Tat*), the real has also become that which is factual (*Tatsächliche*). Henceforth, the real is that which is the case, in short, that which is real in the sense that it "stands" and is certain; as such, it is the opposite of that which does not stand as firm, that which is a mere appearance or simply believed to be so. Yet, in spite of the radical change that the meaning of reality undergoes in the Roman and post-Roman world, this new understanding of the real, Heidegger suggests, "still retains the more primordially fundamental characteristic, which comes less often and differently to the fore, of something that presences which sets itself forth from out of itself."[41] In other words, the two moments characteristic of *energeia* and *entelecheia* still linger on in it. Undoubtedly, by understanding the real as the result of a *causa efficiens*, its earlier meaning as the enduring-in-the-work of what has brought itself forth into the here has been suppressed. But if the early understanding of the real is still said to be alive in its later conception as the factual and the certain, then is this not because, in presencing, the modern real still "sets itself forth from out of itself," in other words, because it still continues to refer to *physis* in the original sense of bringing something hither and forth? Heidegger adds that "*objectness* (*Gegenständigkeit*)," understood as "a character belonging to that which presences itself," is "the kind of presence *belonging* to that which presences that appears in the modern age as object."[42] While this is undoubtedly a conception of the reality of the real that is thoroughly different from medieval and Greek thinking, the suppressed earlier meaning of presencing and enduring in presencing still comes to the fore in this later conception of what presences itself, although in a different way. Namely, the reality of the real as that which "shows itself as object, [as] that which stands over against (*Gegen-Stand*)," not only "*sets itself forth* [*sich heraus stellt*]" but also "*come*[*s*] *to a secured stand*" in the object in which it is "encounter[ed] as such a stand [*Stand*]."[43] Both this setting itself forth and this coming to a stand resonate with the earlier meanings of *energeia* and *entelecheia*.

In order to explain how, precisely, such setting itself forth of the objectivity of what presences itself occurs for it to come to a stand in an object, that is, how it is made to appear to be set-before, or to be re-presented (*Vor-stellen*), the statement "Science is the theory of the real" must be elucidated from a second point of view. If in the modern age that which presences is the real in its "objectivity," such objectivity also implies a subject for whom the real brings itself into an appearance (*Vorschein*) and for whom it becomes the object of a re-presentation (*Vor-stellung*). What is the precise relation of the subject to what thus appears to it as the real such that the real can be re-presented by it and such that its appearing can be brought to a stand in an object? Heidegger therefore asks: "What is the real in relation to theory, and thus in a certain respect also in and through theory?"[44] In order to respond to this question, it is, of course, first necessary to clarify first what is meant by "theory."

Originating in the Greek noun *theoria*, which itself derives from the verb *theorein*, "theory" remains, even in its modern sense, a Greek word, a word that is not fully understandable without listening to what of its early meanings still live on in it. However, since, according to Heidegger, "a lofty and mysterious [*hohe und geheimnisvolle*] meaning" is peculiar to the Greek words in question, their early meaning is not immediately evident.[45] What is mysterious about these words is, Heidegger notes, their ambiguity, their equivocality (*Mehrdeutigkeit*). What makes this equivocality especially mysterious is not the least that these words simply have several different meanings but, rather, the fact that the words in question interconnect these meanings in a very specific way. Their mysterious character is owed not only to the fact that they bind together (in a seemingly violent knot) two entirely different root verbs but also the fact that these verbs seem to call upon one another to be interlaced. Heidegger writes: "The verb *theorein* grew out of the coalescing [*zusammengewachsen*] of two root words, *thea* and *horao*," that is, out of two meanings that at first sight are unrelated to one another.[46] In spite of this unrelatedness, the two root words have grown together in the verb *theorein* and have become knitted into an organic whole, as it were. Let us underline the fact that, by highlighting the role that the *verb theorein* plays with respect to the originary meaning of *theoria*, Heidegger stresses from the start a certain active quality of *theoria* that becomes lost when it is translated into contemplation. In any case, "*thea*," the first root verb that enters into the tight knit in question, "is the outward look, the aspect, in which something shows itself, the outward appearance in which it offers itself. Plato names this aspect [*Aussehen*] in which what presences shows what it is, *eidos* [in *Theathetus*]. To have seen this aspect, *eidenai*, is to know [*Wissen*]."[47] In short, the first root verb stresses the movement of coming forth into an appearance and of presencing an aspect in which something offers itself to view. By contrast, *horao*, the second root verb in *theorein*, concerns the gaze by which something appears, the gaze that, turned toward that which shows itself, responds to the coming into appearance by "look[ing] at [it] attentively,[. . .] look[ing] it over, [. . .] view[ing] it closely."[48] Coalescing the two diametrically opposed but complementary movements, *theorein* is thus "*thean horan*, to look attentively on the outward appearance wherein what presences becomes visible and, through such sight—seeing—to linger with it."[49] Originally, then, *theorein* has to be understood as a looking at the way in which something gives itself to be seen.[50] It is concentrated not so much on what the something that shows itself is in itself as on this something offering itself to view. Furthermore, *theorein* lingers on the very presencing itself of something in an appearance. *Theorein*, therefore, is not only a looking that cor-responds (*entsprechen*) to the self-showing of something and what, in such cor-respondence, actively participates in the process of presencing; it is also a looking in which the appearing of what appears is consummated, in which this appearing can linger on and survive, as it were. The "etymological" explication of the Greek verb *theorein*, which attempted to bring to light what of the early meaning of the verb still lives on in the modern concept of theory, has thus zoomed in on the lofty and mysterious correspondence at work within theory. The correspondence between what shows itself and the gaze that responds to this self-showing not only actively participates in the disclosure in question but also, by lingering on the showing itself, allows that showing to be consummated in itself and thus to live on in the gaze that corresponds to it.

If, indeed, as Heidegger reminds us, *theorein* also names in ancient Greece a "particular way of life (*bios*)" that receives its determination from such attentive looking at and preserving by lingering on what presences, it is precisely because this life is devoted to the active participation in the process of appearing and its consummated survival.[51] Furthermore, if this particular way of life, the *bios theoretikos* as "the life of beholding" distinct from the *bios praktikos* that is dedicated to action and productivity (*Handeln und Herstellen*), "is, especially in its purest form as thinking, the highest doing," the highest form of praxis, it is not only because such life consists in looking "upon the pure shining-forth of that which presences" but also because, precisely, it allows such shining-forth to persist, to linger on or survive.[52] The highest form of life is the *bios theoretikos* first and foremost because, cor-responding to the shining forth in all its purity, this life allows what shines forth to persist in shining forth, to linger on, in short, to survive. As the "pure relationship to the outward appearances belonging to whatever presences, to those appearances that, in their radiance, concern man in that they bring the presence of the gods to shine forth [*indem sie die Gegenwart der Götter be-scheinen*]," the highest form of life—in fact, life itself—is theoretical life as a relation of correspondence to and preservation of the happening of appearing.[53] It has not only a practical (and ethical) dimension (such as in Plato); by being a praxis devoted to the survival of the disclosure of what shows itself, *theorein* is, in fact, the highest accomplishment of praxis (as in Aristotle's *Nicomachean Ethics*).

What Heidegger, so far, has developed with respect to the two remarkably different words—*thea* and *horao*, both of which express actions and which have become interconnected in the verb *theorein*, that is, in *theoria* understood as a doing, as a praxis—explains the term's mysterious meaning. With respect to the word's lofty [*hohe*] meaning, he avers that "bound up with the supremacy accorded to *theoria* in Greek *bios* is the fact that the Greeks, who in a unique way thought out of their language, i.e., received from it their human existence [*Dasein*], were also able to hear something else in the word *theoria*."⁵⁴ Listening to the kind of *bios* their language had destined for them, the Greeks, apart from the demand to correspond in responding to the shining forth of the aspects in which things are disclosed, heard in the word *theoria* still something else, something other. The word *theoria* resonated for them in still another way. Indeed, "[w]hen differently stressed, the two root words *thea* and *horao* can read *thea* and *ora* [with an omega, rather than an o]. *Thea* is goddess. It is as a goddess that *Aletheia*, the unconcealment from out of which and in which that which presences, presences, appears to the early thinker Parmenides. We translate *aletheia* by the Latin word *veritas* and by our German word *Wahrheit* (truth)."⁵⁵ Philologically speaking, to derive *thea* in *theoria* from *theos* is highly problematic. However, the ancients themselves made the connection, and this Greek inclination to hear in the word a reference to the divine in complete disregard for philological accuracy authorizes Heidegger's interpretation.⁵⁶ Even though the actual Greek experience of a reference to a divinity in *theoria* is contrary to etymological evidence, for Heidegger such an experience overrides all "scientific" considerations. Let us remind ourselves of Heidegger's statement that the Greeks "in a unique way thought out of their language, i.e., received from it their human existence."⁵⁷ The Greeks made the connection between *thea* and *theos* against all odds and, by way of that connection, determined what they considered the highest form of life precisely insofar as the similar sound of the two words made them think.⁵⁸ Whereas *thea* (in distinction from *theá*, that is, goddess) referred to the outlook in which something is disclosed and brought into unconcealment, that is, into *a-leithea*, and to which the action of *horao* responds with a lingering on this coming forth into the open of truth, *theá*, differently stressed, invokes the goddess *Aletheia*, as the personification of unconcealment and presencing, and hence her lofty and divine nature. The goddess *Aletheia* demands a specific way of responding from the mortals who behold her, one named by the Greek word *ora* (as opposed to *horao*). *Ora* is a word that also expresses an active relation to its object. Heidegger writes: "The Greek word *ora* signifies the respect we have [*die Rücksicht, die wir nehmen*], the honor and esteem we bestow."⁵⁹ Paying respect is the active relation that a deity such as the goddess of Truth requires from the mortals. Heidegger thus concludes: "If we now think the word *theoria* in the context of the meanings of the words just cited [that is, *theá* and *ora*], then *theoria* is the reverent paying heed to the unconcealment of what presences. Theory in the old, and that means the early but by no means the obsolete, sense is the *beholding that watches over truth [das hütende Schauen der Wahrheit].*"⁶⁰ With this second layer of the meaning of the word *theoria*, a reference of theory to truth is made in the sense of unconcealment, or *aletheia*. By linking this meaning in turn to theory as the beholding of the outward look in which something presences, the showing itself of something comes to signify a happening of truth. Further, by connecting the attentive gaze that welcomes and preserves something that shows itself to the reverence that mortals owe to the goddess *Aletheia*, this gaze in turn is understood as one that is actively involved in watching over truth, taking care of it, and protecting it so that it may persevere in its happening. The cor-respondence of the attentive gaze to the self-showing of something in its outlook is also a concern for maintaining and furthering the continuous occurring, or survival, of truth itself.

Undoubtedly, this early meaning of *theoria* as a beholding that watches over truth has been replaced by modern theory. Yet, as Heidegger remarks, this "ambiguous [*mehrdeutige*] and from every perspective high and lofty" meaning of *theoria* is by no means obsolete, even though it "remains buried" when, today, we speak of theory.⁶¹ As the term "buried" suggests, the early meaning of *theoria* remains encrypted within the later sense of theory. Indeed, "within 'theory,' understood in the modern way, there yet steals the shadow of the early *theoria*. The former lives out of the latter, and indeed not only in the outwardly identifiable sense of historical dependency."⁶² If the early meaning of *theoria* continues to determine from within the modern sense of theory, it is not so much because theory still can be historically retraced to *theoria* in spite of all its remarkable difference from the Greek notion, but, rather, because the specter of the originary ambiguity of *theoria*, that is, the interconnectedness of distinct but also complementary movements or actions, still pervades it. All differences considered, modern theory is also verbal in character, similarly combining, as we will see hereafter, two distinct vectorial movements that mutually call upon one another. As a further consequence, if the early meaning of *theoria* continues to live on in modern theory, even though only a spectral life of sorts, then modern theory, despite its radical otherness, is not entirely alienated from it. As we have seen, however, the opposite is true as well if, indeed, the modern sciences arose from a feature in *episteme* about which, though present from the start, the Greeks did not reflect. Let me recall at this point what Heidegger suggests about the organic interlinking of two different words in the compound "*theoria*." If *theoria*, interlacing a look at the movement of showing in which something presences itself and the movement of preserving this self-showing in what comes into presence, could nonetheless give rise to the modern sciences, it follows that what Heidegger hereafter expounds as the compartmentalizing, entrapping, and securing activity of the modern sciences, in short, their technological and artificial nature, must have inhabited the organic compound of *theoria*, and *episteme*, from the very beginning. In any case, the task of reflecting on the relation between *theoria* and the modern sciences does not consist in simply linking the modern theoretical sciences back to the ancient meaning of *theoria* from which they would have become estranged in order to make them meaningful again for the needs of men within the life-world, as Husserl had proposed (in fact, they are now more "meaningful" than ever before). Rather, this task of reflection also consists in showing how, all transformations notwithstanding, the modern theoretical sciences continue to develop in their own way, but without knowing it, a praxis, first of all, of cor-responding to what shows itself and of preserving it as such, one similar to the praxis that originally opened the historical world of the Greeks. Now, even though the sciences cannot be defined in their essence without the awareness that a shadow of *theoria* still haunts them, have they permanently replaced *theoria* in its Greek sense? Besides the necessity to reactualize the Greek understanding of *theoria* in order to show that a ghostly remainder of it lives on in modern theory, which is also to define the horizon within which modern theory's future fate may be decided, is there a possibility for *theoria* itself to reemerge in modernity in, perhaps, a new form? If, in spite of all its organicity, ancient *theoria* contained the very trait from which modern science arose and brought about the breakdown of the world, it is certainly not in this ancient and unreflected form that *theoria* would be expected to return. In any event, as we will see, the task of reflection (*Besinnung*) that Heidegger has set for himself in "Science and Reflection" is to show that a shadow of the historical world of the Greeks steals within the modern, seemingly worldless world and to show that this un-world is both a threat and a chance. Before assessing what this threat and, especially, this chance consist of, however, it is first necessary to ask the question: "In distinction from the early *theoria*, what is 'the theory' that is named in the statement 'Modern science is the theory of the real'?"[63]

To answer this question as economically as possible, Heidegger proceeds in a way that by all appearances is exterior to the subject matter, namely, a discussion of the way the words (rather than the terms) *theorein* and *theoria* have been translated into Latin and German. However, if this in fact is not at all an exterior way to go about explaining the modern sense of theory, it is because, as we have seen, translations are indicative of new and decisive, that is, epochal, shifts in what is destined through language to be the world for a people. Indeed, as Heidegger holds, these translations directly provide us with the meaning of theory in the modern sense. According to Heidegger, the Greek meaning of the words in question "vanish[es] at a stroke" when they are rendered as *contemplari* and *contemplatio* in "the spirit of the Roman language," that is, in the spirit of the Roman existence [*Dasein*].⁶⁴ Indeed, "an entirely different experience from that out of which *theorein* originates" subtends the meaning of the verb *contemplari*, namely, the experience of cutting, dividing, or "partition[ing] something off into a separate sector and enclos[ing] it therein" until one has reached "[t]he uncuttable," the atom.⁶⁵ Now, although this translation makes the early meaning of the Greek word *theorein* vanish at one stroke, it is in no way an arbitrary transposition. It is important to remark that the way this translation comes about and what it is now meant to name are not altogether foreign to Greek thought. First, there is the linguistic origin of the verb *contemplari*. The Latin *templum* in *contemplari* corresponds to the Greek *temenos*, which means to cut, to divide. Here, when Heidegger writes that "[i]n *theoria* transformed into *contemplatio* there comes to the fore the impulse, already prepared in Greek thinking, of a looking-at that sunders and compartmentalizes," it finally becomes clear what, specifically, Heidegger has in mind with the contention that the modern theoretical sciences are based on "the decisive working out of a tendency that still remains concealed in the essence of knowing as the Greeks experienced it."⁶⁶ Indeed, the trait, tendency, or disposition that was already present in Greek thought from the beginning but now gains preeminence over all other features of *theoria* is the "type of encroaching advance by successive interrelated steps toward that which is to be grasped by the eye."⁶⁷ Through the translation of *theorein* into *contemplatio*, this trait, still concealed in Greek thought, now "makes itself normative in knowing."⁶⁸ As opposed to the knowing (*Wissen*) that arises from the seeing of the aspect in which something presences and shows itself, knowing now becomes knowledge (*Erkennen*) and acquires the character of a "looking-at that sunders and compartmentalizes [. . .] that which is to be grasped by the eye [*eingeteilten, eingreifenden Vorgehens gegen das, was ins Auge gefasst werden soll*]."⁶⁹ Knowledge thus takes on the character of a procedure that actively intervenes in, and encroaches on, what it looks at by dividing and classifying it. Yet, as Heidegger notes, notwithstanding the active intervention in the object that is to be grasped by the eye, the Roman notion of *contemplatio* still remains distinct from the *vita activa*. This is a conception of *contemplatio* thoroughly distinct from its later medieval conception that reflects the religious meditations of the monastic orders. In spite of its thorough difference from *theorein*, it still resonates with *theorein* not only in that it is distinct from the life of action and production but also in that the object of *contemplatio*, as we will see, is thought in such a way as to demand such active intervention, that is, the highest form of praxis.

Yet, the process of translation of *theoria* does not come to an end with the Latin *contemplation;* the latter is translated, in turn, into German as *Betrachtung* (view, or observation), as a result of which "the Greek *theorein,* to look attentively upon the aspect of what presences, appears now as to observe or consider *(Betrachten).*"[70] Twice remote from the Greek meaning of *theorein,* this translation of *contemplatio* into German as *Betrachten* and *Betrachtung,* if only one "take[s] seriously what the German *Betrachtung* means," puts one on the way to really "recogniz[ing] what is new in the essence of modern science as the theory of the real."[71] In order to show that modern theory is "something essentially different from the Greek *theoria,*" Heidegger sets aside all the common meanings of the word *Betrachtung* (some of which still seem to echo the early meaning of the Greek word) and gives it "a different meaning, not an arbitrary invented one, but rather the one from which it is originally descended."[72] By retracing the verbal form of *trachten* (to strive) in *Betrachtung* to "the Latin *tractare,* to manipulate, to work over or refine," recalling also that in German *nach etwas trachten* (to strive after something) means "to work one's way *toward* something, to pursue it, to entrap it in order to secure it," theory as *Betrachtung* (observation) is shown to signify a way of relating to the real by which the latter becomes entrapped and worked over until it is secured *(das nachstellende und sicherstellende Bearbeiten des Wirklichen).*[73] With this detour through the Latin roots of *Betrachtung,* which itself is a translation of *contemplatio,* that is, of the "looking-at that sunders and compartmentalizes," back to the German word, the meaning of theory appears to have undergone a radical mutation. Understood in terms of an activity that seeks to entrap and secure the real, theory, as an active intervention in the real, is no longer contemplative and seems to have become part of the *vita activa.* The definitive novelty of the modern sciences, notwithstanding their indebtedness to Greek *theoria,* is that "theory" now has shed its theoretical character. According to its new sense, theory has become a belaboring of the real that in the most uncanny fashion intervenes in it *(eine unheimlich eingreifende Bearbeitung des Wirklichen).* Theory, in other words, has become practical in the sense of action and production, technical, in short.[74]

If the modern sciences, which have caused the breakdown of the world in modernity, have their roots in an impulse already prepared in Greek *episteme,* actualized first by the Latin word *contemplatio* as the active sundering and compartmentalizing intervention in the object and subsequently by the German word *Betrachtung* as the entrapping pursuit of the object that it seeks to secure in this manner, then, unmistakably, the thoroughly un-Greek modern sciences are not only already anticipated by Greek thought but, further, their un-worlding of the world has its origin in Greek thought. As will become evident, the modern sciences' approach, their active production of the real, is indebted to Greek *theoria* not only because their approach is the radical extrapolation of an unreflected trait in Greek thought itself but also because, in all its artificiality and technological essence, it continues in its own way the Greek demand of a cor-respondence between what presences and the preserving response to it. However, with this a question arises: Does this demand for cor-respondence—and thus for a certain organicity—not also have a dark side? Is the possibility of un-worlding not a danger rooted in the very cor-respondence that is accomplished by *theoria* at its origin in Greece, a danger all the more so since this threat also remained concealed to Greek thought?

Yet, if the modern theoretical sciences' encroachment upon the real is uncanny, as Heidegger contends, it is not simply because of the boundless and monstrous magnitude of the intervention in question. It is uncanny in a rigorous sense because it does not violently intervene in the real from outside but is called upon by the latter. It is an encroachment that is both made possible and asked for by the real itself, precisely, insofar as the real is the real of which science is the theory. Theory, as a kind of observing that strives after the real and is intent on securing it, does not impose itself on the real; it is, on the contrary, its true correlate. The observing that strives after the real in an attempt to secure it is pulled into such striving and securing by the real itself. Heidegger submits: "Precisely through this refining it [that is, theoretical observation] corresponds [*entspricht*] to a fundamental characteristic [*Grundzug*] of the real itself."[75] Answering to the pull of the real, modern theory, in the shape of the modern sciences, cor-responds to it. If its intervention in the real is uncanny, it is primarily because, in all its radical difference from the Greek *theorein*, the *cor*respondence between modern theory and the real is still an echo—a far echo, it is true, but an echo nonetheless—of the *cor*respondence at the heart of *theoria* as an active way of addressing and responding to what shows itself. In spite of its thorough otherness, modern theory continues to be haunted by an uncanny shadow of the early meaning of *theoria*. Of course, the spectral presence of *theoria* in the theoretical sciences, even where they have shed their purely theoretical character, makes it possible and necessary to return to, as Heidegger requests, the West's Greek origins in order to render intelligible the very essence of the sciences. But Heidegger does not consider, at least not explicitly, whether it is precisely this indebtedness of the sciences to *theoria* with all its unreflected traits that has also fostered the breakdown of the world in the current world-age.

Having thus explained how the real and theory are to be understood in the statement "Science is the theory of the real," and, furthermore, having explained what it is about the real itself in the modern age that calls upon the theoretical sciences to belabor and secure it so as to foster a *cor*respondence between the real and its theory, Heidegger has already provided an answer to the question concerning the relation between the real and the theoretical, more precisely, to the question "how the two [...] go to join one another from out of their essence." The real, which Heidegger has defined as "what presences as self-exhibiting," or, rather, as that which sets itself forth (*das sich heraustellende Anwesen*), "shows itself in the modern age in such a way as to bring its presencing to stand in objectness."[76] In objectness as the real of the modern age, presencing in the shape of setting itself forth thus comes to a stand. As such, the real calls upon the theory of the sciences to be belabored and refined, with the aim of being firmly secured and able to endure in this objective stand. This process, in which the real sets itself forth in such a manner that the theoretical sciences can work it over so as to arrest its presencing in a secured object, is one by which the real and its theory are joined together. It is the form that *cor*respondence takes in the modern age. Heidegger writes:

> Science corresponds to this holding-sway of presencing in terms of objects, inasmuch as it for its part, as theory, challenges forth the real specifically through aiming its objectness [*auf seine Gegenständigkeit hin herausfordert*]. Science sets upon the real [*Die Wissenschaft stellt das Wirkliche*, in other words, in its pursuit of the real, science arrests the real]. It orders it into place to the end that at any given time the real will exhibit itself as an interacting network [*Gewirk*], i.e., in surveyable series of designated causes. The real thus becomes surveyable and capable of being followed out [*übersehbar*] in its consequences. The real becomes secured in its objectness.[77]

Science as the theory of the real secures the latter, that is, the science makes the real last in its objectness by establishing it as the totality of working causes, making it thus assessable and comprehensible at any given time and capable of being surveyed in all its consequences.

As the theory of the real, modern science is "not anything self-evident."[78] Indeed, as Heidegger submits, the idea that "what presences [...] sets itself forth as the real in its objectness," a conception of the real that in turn calls upon science as theory to entrap and secure it in its objectness, is something altogether foreign to medieval thought and something that Greek thought would have considered with dismay.[79] He adds that such a change in the way in which what presences occurs, in response to which science as theory becomes necessary (*benötigt*) as its appropriate complement, cannot simply be the result of man's doings. Such epochal change in the way Being shines forth is not something of the order of a construct or fabrication (*Gemächte*) of man, nor is the new way of corresponding to it that it calls for—modern theory—something that the real would simply have imposed on man. Such change, Heidegger intimates, is mysterious (*geheimnisvoll*) and happens in the most inconspicuous manner.

Yet, however foreign this way of the presencing of what presences and of corresponding to it may be to previous epochs, modern theory shares with previous epochs, as we have seen, the fundamental characteristic of correspondence between the movement of a coming forth into presence and the movement of responding to and preserving what shines forth, notwithstanding Heidegger's characterization of the sciences as a striving after and entrapping of the real. To bring home this point one would have to take up one after another the seemingly increasingly violent formulations through which Heidegger characterizes modern theory's relation to the real in order to bring into view the inconspicuous state of affairs (*Sachverhalt*) that, as something other than all human fabrication, reigns in them.[80]

After concluding his elucidation of the essence of the modern sciences in general with a discussion of the inevitable departmentalization of the sciences that the very notion of the objectness of what presences brings with it, Heidegger turns again to the question of what it is that in fact and in truth reigns in the sciences.[81] This is now called the question of the "inconspicuous state of affairs [that] conceals itself in the essence of science."[82] The question itself is testimony to another parallelism between Greek *episteme* and modern scientific knowledge. Indeed, in the same way as ancient *episteme* and *theoria* contain an unreflected trait, the modern sciences, which are the radical unfolding of that very trait, not only contain in turn a state of affairs that is inconspicuous, but, as we will see, they are also incapable of bringing this state of affairs into view. In any case, in order to establish what the something altogether other is that holds sway in the theoretical sciences, something other than all human fabrication, Heidegger takes his point of departure in the area-character of the individual sciences, along with their departmentalization and specialization, and—reversing the order of his elaborations hitherto—circles back to his earlier determination of science as an entrapping observation of the real. He writes: "We shall notice this state of affairs the moment that, taking particular sciences as examples, we attend specifically to whatever is the case regarding the ordering [*wie es jeweils . . . bestellt ist*]—in any given instance—of the objectness belonging to the object-area of those sciences."[83] The first example of a particular science, the only one I will take up here, is contemporary physics (the other examples are psychiatry, history, and philology). Even though the objectness of material nature in nuclear physics shows entirely different fundamental characteristics than those found in classical physics, nuclear physics, Heidegger tells us, "still remains physics, i.e., science, i.e., theory, which entraps objects belonging to the real, in their objectness."[84] In support of his claim that "[f]or modern physics too it is a question of making secure those elementary objects of which all other objects in its entire area consist," he quotes Werner Heisenberg, who holds that the aim of modern physics is to develop "'one single fundamental equation from which the properties of all elementary particles, and therewith the behavior of all matter whatever, follow.'"[85] In spite of all the changes from classical physics to nuclear and field physics concerning "the experience and determination of the objectness wherein nature sets itself forth," what has not changed is, according to Heidegger, "the fact that nature has in advance to set itself in place for the entrapping securing that science, as theory, accomplishes."[86] Despite Heidegger's increasingly violent characterizations of theory's relation to its object, one must not lose sight of the correlate of this characterization, namely the fact that in modernity the real, or nature, sets itself forth in a position so as to be able to be encroached upon by the sciences. From classical physics to nuclear physics, including its most recent phase in which even "the *object vanishes*," the same paradigm prevails, namely, the assumption (or expectation) that nature itself calls upon theory to entrap it and to bring it to a lasting stand in objectness.[87] This, then, is also the point at which Heidegger brings up the question of the inconspicuous state of affairs that pervades the holding sway of objectness, that is, the question of the "something other [that] reigns" in the theoretical sciences. He zooms in on this inconspicuous state and characterizes it according to three distinct, but interrelated, characteristics.

Undoubtedly, "[t]heory identifies the real—in the case of physics, inanimate nature—and fixes it into *one* object-area. However, nature is always already presencing of itself. Objectification, for its part, remains dependent on nature as thus presencing."[88] In other words, for theory to entrap and arrest the real in its objectness, the real must have disclosed itself in advance, as it were, and of itself, that is, must have shown forth into presence (whether in the shape of objectness or not). Theory in the modern sense is entirely dependent on this disclosure prior to it: "Theory never outstrips nature—nature that is already presencing—and in this sense theory never makes its way around nature."[89] Let us also emphasize that what physics represents as nature—its universal and pervasive lawfulness—is nature itself only to the extent that nature has set itself forth as an object-area, *one*, more precisely, whose objectness is defined through the belaboring characteristics of physics. Not only is theory, then, dependent on a prior disclosure of nature in the shape of objectness, but such showing also implies that there is more than one way in which nature presences and that the nature addressed by physics is just one of them. Heidegger writes: "Nature, in its objectness for modern physical science, is only *one* way in which what presences—which from of old has been named *physis*—reveals itself and sets itself in position for the refining characteristic of science."[90] Nature as the object-area of the theoretical science of physics, in which it offers itself to the latter's theoretical gaze and in which it becomes belabored and secured, is only one way of nature's presencing understood as *physis*, that is, as the shining forth of all that is. It follows from this that objectness falls short of ever being able to "embrace [*einkreisen*] the fullness of the coming to presence of nature" and, further, that "[s]cientific representation is never able to encompass the coming to presence of nature [*umstellen*, that is, surround it, and round it up]."[91] Theory is constitutionally incapable of embracing and encompassing nature not only because the shining forth of nature precedes it, but also because nature always shines forth only in single ways. It follows from this that for modern theory, in this case the theoretical science of physics, nature is "that which cannot be gotten around [*das Unumgängliche*]."[92] The phrase is twofold. It means, on the one hand, that modern theory remains dependent on the prior presencing of presence in whatever form such presence presents itself, and it also means, on the other hand, that the very form the presence of what presences takes prevents the kind of representation that cor-responds to it from ever being able to surround and round up the full plenitude of nature. In the objectness of nature of which theoretical physics is the correlate, this twofold *Unumgängliche* (that which cannot be gotten around) holds sway. But all sciences have their respective *Unumgängliche*: in the case of psychiatry, it is *Dasein*; in history, "the destining resident in happening"; and in philology, language.[93] As theory, science has always already restricted itself to areas circumscribed by the limits of objectness. Because the "objects" of theory show themselves in their objectness, they represent always "only *one* kind of presencing, in which indeed that which presences can appear, but never absolutely must appear."[94] But let me also point out that to be able to see what modern theory does not see and to ask the questions that it cannot ask—the question whether nature, of which Heraclitus said that it likes to hide, in fact withdraws within modern theory rather than revealing itself—already presupposes another way of relating, another form of *theorein*, that is, another form of corresponding to its address that is possibly also different from that of Greek *theoria*. That is to say, to see what modern theory cannot see and to ask the questions that it cannot pose itself are possible only by way of a reflection, a *Besinnung* that prepares the way toward an another approach to nature.

That which cannot be gotten around, the *Unumgängliche*, thus unmistakably belongs to the sought-for state of affairs, but all by itself the *Unumgängliche* does not yet constitute it. By qualifying this state of affairs as inconspicuous, saying near the beginning of the essay that, notwithstanding its all-pervasiveness in the sciences, it "remains hidden to the sciences themselves,"

Heidegger points to additional characterizations of it that first need to be worked out, before the state of affairs itself will have been fully determined.[95] And, indeed, a further essential characteristic of the state of affairs is precisely this inconspicuousness, that is, the fact that "the something other that reigns" in the theoretical sciences does not manifest itself, particularly not to the sciences themselves. Now, if this state of affairs remains inconspicuous, it is because "it is essentially impossible" that the sciences could ever find it present within themselves, or define it as such.[96] For this to be possible, the sciences would first of all have "to conceive and represent [*vorstellen*] their own essence," something, however, that their own essence prevents them from accomplishing.[97] More precisely, proceeding by way of representation, they could only approach their own essence in the same way as they approach the objects that make up their own object-area. Among the examples of how the sciences are structurally (or for essential reasons) unable to represent their own essence, I retain only the one of physics. If "[a]ll the assertions of physics speak after the manner of physics," as Heidegger holds, physics can never become physics' own object.[98] In representing physics in the mode in which physics goes about the objectness that is proper to it, setting itself before itself (*vor-zustellen*) so that physics could come into a relation to itself, physics would strip its essence of its essence, and, rather than a way of entrapping-securing the objectness of the objects of nature, it would make itself into another natural object within its own object-area. Heidegger therefore concludes: "If it is entirely denied to science scientifically to arrive at its own essence, then the sciences are utterly incapable of gaining access to that which is not to be gotten around holding sway in their essence."[99] And he adds: "Here something exciting [*etwas Erregendes*, that is, something marvelous or fascinating] manifests itself. That which in the sciences is not at any time to be gotten around [...] is, *as* that which is not to be gotten around [*Unumgängliche*], intractable and inaccessible [*unzugänglich*] for the sciences and through the sciences."[100] That which cannot be gotten around is not only a precondition of the sciences but also one which they themselves are structurally unable to access as such. It is, literally, their blind spot. Yet, if this blind spot, which is constitutive of the state of affairs that holds sway within theory in the modern sense, is so exciting, it is because there is also something wondrous about it. However inconspicuous, unspectacular, and inapparent to the point of even being plain and ordinary, this blind spot provokes thinking. In a world dominated by theory, it is, perhaps, that which triggers thinking in an emphatic sense. But before I continue this line of thought, let me first follow Heidegger through his determination of the state of affairs in question.

As Heidegger submits, "[o]nly when we also pay heed to this inaccessibility of that which is not to be gotten around does that state of affairs come into view which holds complete sway throughout the essence of science."[101] In fact, only by further delving into the nature of the inconspicuousness of the state of affairs in question does a third characteristic of it come to the fore that allows a full description of this state. If this state of affairs has not become known, it is not for lack of attention to it. Numerous efforts have been undertaken in the past by philosophy and the sciences themselves to delimit and define the sciences' essence. But in distinction from the "strange restiveness" found throughout all the sciences today and, in particular, in distinction from the contemporary talk of "'the crisis at the foundations' of the sciences," the inconspicuous state of affairs that reigns in the sciences is of an altogether other order.[102] According to Heidegger, "[t]hat which is inaccessible and not to be gotten around, which holds sway throughout the sciences and in that way renders their essence enigmatic [*rätselhaft*], is [. . .] something essentially other [. . .] than a mere unsureness in the providing of fundamental concepts by means of which at any given time an area is placed in association with the sciences."[103] In distinction from such unsureness with regard to its concepts, the inconspicuous state of affairs that holds sway in the sciences is, as we have seen already, constitutionally inaccessible to the sciences. If that which cannot be gotten around remains inconspicuous, it is not because no attention is devoted to it but because, rather than shining forth, the state of affairs in question withholds itself. It does not of itself come into an appearance. Indeed, "[t]he fact that that which is inaccessible and not to be gotten around is continually passed over depends on it itself as such."[104] Here we touch upon the third characteristic of the state of affairs in question previously alluded to: because the inconspicuousness of what cannot be gotten around is owed to the withdrawal of this state of affairs itself, it is inevitably and constantly passed over. In other words, it is not for lack of effort but for essential reasons that what cannot be gotten around remains inconspicuous.

At this point the state of affairs that reigns in the sciences has been circumscribed in all its essential traits. In the sciences, that on which they depend as far as their object-area is concerned—nature, the human being, history, language, to name only a few—remains not only something that they cannot get around but also something that remains structurally inaccessible to them because it itself withdraws and hides from their grasp. Heidegger sums up his analysis of the something other that reigns in the sciences as follows: "The state of affairs that holds sway throughout the essence of science, i.e., throughout the theory of the real, is that which is inaccessible and not to be gotten around, which is constantly passed over [*das stets übergangene unzugängliche Unumgängliche*]."[105] This state of affairs lies hidden in the sciences, which in turn lie, or, rather, rest [*ruhen*], in this "inconspicuous state of affairs as the river lies in its source."¹⁰⁶

Now, Heidegger acknowledges that, rather than an attempt to establish what this inconspicuous state of affairs "is in itself [*in sich selber ist*]"—an undertaking that would require a renewed questioning—his aim is a more modest one, namely, merely to point to [*hinweisen*] the inconspicuous state of affairs in question "in order that it itself might gesture toward [*winke*, that is, hint at] the region [*Gegend*] from out of which stems the essence of science."¹⁰⁷ This region has been shown to be that of objectness. In it, the reality of the real as well as the theory of the real, that is, the entire essence of the modern sciences, swing (*schwingt*). Yet, while pointing toward the inconspicuous state of affairs that rules in the theoretical sciences so as to receive from it a hint about the essence of science, something additional has occurred: we have, Heidegger says, been directed upon "a way that brings us before that which is worthy of questioning."¹⁰⁸ It is essential to remind ourselves again of the claim that the seemingly worldless world brought about by the sciences is both a threat and a chance. After having expanded on the way the sciences have provoked the breakdown of the world, the new direction into which thought is shown by the analysis of the inconspicuous state of affairs that reigns as the essence of science is one that will concern the chance that arises with that breakdown. But something else is at stake at this juncture. Indeed, let us also recall that while inquiring into the inconspicuous state of affairs that pervades the sciences, namely, the sciences' constitutional inability to gain access to that which they cannot get around, Heidegger argues that something exciting manifests itself—something, I add, that gives food for thought. Is this, then, not also an occasion for us to return to the question left in abeyance regarding the conditions under which today a new way to *theoria* could, perhaps, become possible again? For, in fact, this constitutional inability of theory to bring into view what makes it possible is what causes thinking to happen in the first place. Thinking, it would thus seem, originates in the unspectacular, in the inapparent, in that which for theoretical thought remains inaccessible. Now, in "Science and Reflection," such thinking provoked by the blind spot in the sciences takes the form of a reflection about the essence of the sciences, or, rather, it triggers a *Besinnung*, a kind of thinking, which in a preparatory fashion paves the way for a happening of philosophical thought and possibly for a renewal (and reconfiguration) of *theoria* under the conditions of modernity.¹⁰⁹

But what is *Besinnung* to begin with? The question is all the more urgent since Heidegger's statements regarding the notion remain rather elliptic in the essay, and thus an outline of the meaning of the term, however succinct, is warranted. First, however, let me point out that apart from Johann Gottfried Herder, who created the neologism *Besonnenheit* for '*Reflexion*,' and who uses the term '*Besinnung*' to refer to that kind of attention that gives rise to language, *Besinnung*, to my knowledge, is raised to the status of a technical term in philosophy first with Heidegger.[110] In order to elucidate the way he understands the term, I turn briefly to some of his rather elusive remarks on the notion in question in the manuscript from 1938–39 entitled *Besinnung*. Here, as well as in "Science and Reflection," it is clear from the start that the German word "*Besinnung*" is *not* a translation of the Latin "reflection." The recourse to the German word is unmistakably an attempt to ward off the anthropo-ontological connotations of the Latin concept, and therefore I will, hereafter, leave the word in the original. Unlike reflection and its dependence on subjectivity and consciousness, *Besinnung* is not an additional and belated turn upon something that is already finished; it is not such a turn, in particular, of philosophy upon itself in order to develop a "philosophy of philosophy."[111] Nor does *Besinnung* serve to judge, assess, or justify—as does reflection—what it belatedly turns upon in order, for instance, to secure the certitude of concepts. *Besinnung*, Heidegger writes, "is the overcoming of 'reason,' either as the mere perceiving (*Vernehmung*) of what is pre-given (*nous*), as calculation and explanation (*ratio*), or as planning and securing."[112] In a further contrast to reflection, *Besinnung* "is not a delay, or an obscuring of the impotence to act."[113] On the contrary, a thinking *Besinnung* (*denkerische Besinnung*), that is, a thinking that thinks (*denkerisches Denken*), has "the character of an action [*Handlungscharakter*]."[114] It "is *one*, perhaps, the very action of thinking (*denkerische Handlung*) that thinks forward (*vor-denken*) the farthest."[115] Indeed, as a thinking that thinks forward, it thinks forward toward what is most question-worthy but also most resistant to *Besinnung*, namely, Being—the truth of Being, the Being of truth.[116] Rather than a reflective return upon a thinking that has been arrested, such thinking has, as Heidegger suggests, a performative character. In the *Besinnung* of thinking about itself as the thinking of Being, thinking performs its own beginning.[117]

Here we should recall once more Heidegger's statement in "Science and Reflection" that the aim of elaborating on the inconspicuous state of affairs that reigns in the sciences is to get a hint concerning the region from which the sciences arise. According to Heidegger, "[t]hrough this pointing to the inconspicuous state of affairs we are [. . .] directed onto a way [*in eine Wegrichtung gewiesen*] that brings us before that which is worthy of questioning."[118] By pointing to (*hinweisen*) the inconspicuous, we have been directed, or ordered (*gewiesen*), onto another direction of thought, one directed toward the question-worthy. Although Heidegger does not say so explicitly, the question-worthy, which "affords, from out of itself, the clear impetus [*klaren Anlass*] and untrammeled pause [*freien Anhalt*] through which we are able to call toward us and call near that which addresses itself to our essence," is ultimately the question of Being.[119] Now, this other direction in which one finds oneself shown by pointing to the inconspicuous state of affairs in question is the direction of *Besinnung*. Like "sinnen," which, as Dirk Westerkamp points out, "in Heidegger's conception of *Nachsinnen* and *Besinnung* not only implies the meaning of 'sense,' but relates back to the [Gothic] root *sinþa*, 'journey' or 'way,'" *Besinnung* is an entering upon a way.[120] Now, to take the way toward that which is worthy of questioning, Heidegger avers, is to get under way in a kind of traveling that in truth is a "homecoming."[121] As we have seen, in seeking to elucidate the essence of the modern sciences, the question-worthy is that which shows us the way toward our own essence on the basis of which this elucidation has happened in the first place. For, indeed, the question-worthy, toward which the elaboration on the inconspicuous state of affairs that rules within the sciences shows the way, brings us on the way back toward our own essence, as an essence dependent on something that speaks to it and to which it responds, that is, Being.

Yet, if one is directed onto a way to the question-worthy by pointing at the something other that reigns in the sciences, then has "Science and Reflection" not from the start already been involved in a *Besinnung*? If pondering (*nachsinnen*) the kind of essence (*Wesen*) that marks the sciences' activity of shaping all reality has been the essay's agenda from the beginning, the essay has been on the route toward the question-worthy from the outset. But only at this juncture, that is, toward the very end of the journey through the sciences, does Heidegger introduce the notion of *Besinnung* itself and define it in a way that sets it clearly apart from reflection. Unlike reflection, *Besinnung* is not simply a spontaneous activity by which something is made conscious belatedly through a turn upon itself, a turn through which it comes to know itself. *Besinnung* is, first of all, to be understood in terms of a way one travels, a way onto which one has been directed while pointing, within the context of the essay, to the something other that holds sway in the sciences. In recourse to the Old High German meaning of *"sinnan, sinnen,"* Heidegger conceives *Besinnung* as "follow[ing] a direction that is the way something has, of itself, already taken."[122] The essence of *Besinnung*, then, is to venture onto the way that something has of itself already taken, and this direction, moreover, is one toward the question-worthy in that it concerns the way in which something *is*. Rather than a sovereign act of spontaneity like reflection, *Besinnung*, then, is the *Gelassenheit*, the "calm, self-possessed surrender to that which is worthy of questioning," in our case, to the state of affairs that constitutes the essence, that is, the way of being, of the modern sciences, the specific essence of their holding sway.[123] *Besinnung* is, as Heidegger explicitly states, a way of actively co-responding and corresponding to something by becoming involved (*sich auf den Sinn einlassen*, or *sich auf den Weg einlassen*) in, for example, the meaning of the sciences and the way it has taken.[124] But is this simply a passive surrender to what takes place in the sciences? Or is it a beholding that actively watches over what it beholds comparable to that of *theoria*, intent on letting the essence of the sciences endure? Or could it be that the question-worthy before which one is brought by inquiring into the inconspicuous state of affairs that pervades the theoretical sciences is an invitation to change the way of relating to what is that characterizes the theoretical sciences? But if, with regard to the sciences, *Besinnung* is a preform of *theoria*, as it were, it is certainly one of a very different kind of *theoria* than the one in which the sciences are rooted in spite of their thorough difference from it.

Heidegger writes: "Through reflection [*Besinnung*] so understood [that is, as a direction toward the question-worthy] we actually arrive at the place where, without having experienced it and without having seen penetratingly into it, we have long been sojourning. In reflection we gain access to a place [*Ort*] from out of which there first opens the space [*Raum*] traversed at any time by all our doing and leaving undone [*Tun und Lassen*]."[125] If to travel in the direction of the way something has already taken by pointing at what reigns in it—that is, in the direction of the question-worthy—is a homecoming, it is one first of all, I venture to say, in the sense that it is a way toward the epochal place (relative to the history of Being) that itself opens the space for all our concrete active doing and passive letting-be. Homecoming here has no nostalgic connotations. If *Besinnung* brings us back to the place of our sojourning as that which is question-worthy, it is, at first, to a concrete space of our historical doings and omissions. Sojourning, Heidegger observes, "is constantly [*stets*, always] a historical sojourning—i.e., one allotted to us."[126] The historical home to which *Besinnung* brings us back is the non-home in which a breakdown of the world has taken place and of which the planetary expansion of the theoretical sciences are the symptom. In this time and space of a world in which the world has been shaken in its foundations (not abolished, of course) we are at home and have for a long time been sojourning. Through this *Besinnung* we arrive explicitly there where we properly are (*eigens*) and have been (in terms of the history of Being) for a long time without having been subjectively and consciously aware of it. But such homecoming cannot be the end of the story, for, if *Besinnung* makes us aware of what the space in which we are historically at home is in relation to the history of Being—that is, the space of a world in which a breakdown of the world has occurred—it also brings us onto a journey to Being itself in which we, as beings that are, are at home without ever having known it.

As Heidegger avers, "[r]eflection [*Besinnung*] is of a different essence from the making conscious and the knowing that belong to science; it is of a different essence also from intellectual cultivation (*Bildung*)."[127] Heidegger points out that *Bildung* presupposes a secured, guiding image of man according to which his predispositions are to be formed. *Bildung* also presupposes "a situation and bearing of man that is not in question and that is secured in every direction," which, for its part, "must be based on a belief in the invincible power of an immutable reason and its principles."[128] Now, if the age [*Zeitalter*] of *Bildung* is coming to its end, as Heidegger contends, it is not because of a rise of the uncultured. In the face of what reigns in the dominion of the planet by the sciences, the classical model of *Bildung* is simply powerless. Furthermore, if this age of *Bildung* comes to an end, it is "because the signs are appearing of a world-age [*Weltalter*] in which that which is worthy of questioning will someday [*erst wieder*] again open the door that leads to what is essential in all things and in all destinings."[129] What the signs of this world-age, or epoch, consist in is not made explicit, although one can presume that the emerging *Besinnung* on that which is worthy of questioning is itself already such a sign. Indeed, if that which is worthy of questioning is *first and foremost* a condition of opening *again* the doors to what is essential in all things and destinings, *Besinnung* announces an eventual, new epoch (of relating to what is). Distinct from a *Zeitalter*, it is an age that concerns the world, or rather "world" itself, at a moment when the planetary breakdown of "world" is taking place. Heidegger writes: "We will respond [*entsprechen*, that is, also correspond] to the address [*Anspruch*] of the scope [*Weite*] and the reserve [*Verhalten*, restraint] of this world-age when we begin to reflect [*besinnen*] by venturing onto [*einlassen*] the way already taken by the state of affairs (*Sachverhalt*) which shows itself to us in the essence of science—though not only there."[130] Even though the sciences are not the only place where the state of affairs in question shows itself, they have nonetheless been a privileged place because of their theoretical nature. By reflecting and getting involved in the way the state of affairs in the theoretical sciences has already taken, the possibility of a response and correspondence emerges to what is addressing and claiming us again beyond the place where we have been sojourning for a long time. More precisely, through the *Besinnung* on what is the case in the theoretical sciences, a new kind of *theoria* seems to announce itself, in other words, a new way of beholding that, rather than watching over the presencing of what presences, watches only over what is coming, namely, the new world-age, and that corresponds in responding to the signs of such an age that show themselves, lingering on them, and preserving what in all its restraint [*Verhaltenheit*] merely announces itself. By letting itself become involved in the way that the inconspicuous state of affairs in the theoretical sciences holds sway, *Besinnung*, in a beholding that allows for the survival and the continuous shining forth not of a new world-age already in place but of the signs of its arrival, begins to correspond to what thus announces itself. This is the form that *theoria*, and that also means philosophical thought, takes in the modern world. It is a very modest form of *theoria*, it is true, for, in the face of the sciences and the breakdown of the world that they have brought with them, *theoria* is revived only in the mode of a correspondence to what does not yet presence, to what only shows signs of coming, a world beyond the shaken world in which we have been sojourning for a long time, that is, "world" in the first place. Yet, however modest, *theoria* is ancillary to life, at the service of (a) "world" in which it would be worth living, but one that so far only announces itself.

In contrast to classical *Bildung*, Heidegger goes on to say, *Besinnung* "remains more provisional, more forbearing and poorer in relation to its age than is the intellectual cultivation that was fostered earlier. Still, the poverty of reflection is the promise of a wealth whose treasures glow in the resplendence of that uselessness which can never be included in any reckoning."[131] What Heidegger advances here about the provisional (*vorläufiger*), more forbearing (*langmütiger*), and poorer character of *Besinnung* with regard to the current age is even more compelling when *Besinnung* is compared to *theoria* in the ancient sense of a guarding and preserving correspondence to what it is that, rather than merely announcing itself, fully presences in coming into presence. As we have already seen, *Besinnung*, or *theoria* in the present age, arises from the inconspicuous. As we now see, it is also linked to the provisional in all the senses of the word, that is, also linked in particular to that which in thinking forward is only temporary but at the same time also the farthest ahead. Yet, in spite of all its poverty, by being involved in what it pursues, by actively partaking in what announces itself in the signs of a coming age of the world that are becoming visible, *Besinnung* promises—and such promising is already performing an actualization of what is promised—a richer world in that it is a "world" to begin with. Being engaged in a correspondence to the signs of a coming world, *Besinnung*, by guarding these signs and what promises itself through them, has already committed itself to working toward the realization of the riches promised.

As we have seen, the theoretical sciences themselves can never press forward to their essence. So, even if "every researcher and teacher of the sciences [...] can move, as a thinking being, on various levels of reflection and can keep reflection [*Besinnung*] vigilant [*wachhalten*]," that is, alive, *Besinnung* itself, whose "ways [...] constantly change, ever according to the place on the way at which a path begins, ever according to the portion of the way that it traverses, ever according to the distant view that opens along the way into that which is worthy of questioning," is always only a way of preparing the co-respondence that is required by what announces itself.[132] Heidegger writes: "even there where once, through a special favor, the highest level of reflection might be attained, reflection would have to be content only with preparing a readiness for being addressed [Zuspruch] that our human race today needs."[133] Even at its highest as philosophical thought, or rather as the shape that such thought takes today, *Besinnung* can only prepare a readiness to let oneself be challenged by the question-worthy and its way of directing us toward another world to come. Even at its highest, *Besinnung* is only a preparation for the "readiness to respond, and correspond" to what is worthy of questioning.[134]

While reflecting on the way the shadow of early *theoria* steals within "theory," it becomes clear that even in the sciences, whose essence is thoroughly foreign to the ancient world, the demand for correspondence and co-responding is still alive. Henceforth, the question arises whether, in addition to Heidegger's contention that the radical unfolding of a trait still hidden in the early conception of *theoria* and *episteme* led to the breakdown of the world brought about by the modern sciences, an equally unthought aspect of the demand for correspondence could not be shown to be responsible for the modern phenomenon of the un-worlding of the world. Needless to say, a satisfactory answer to this question would require a lengthy and patient analysis of the idea of correspondence itself. In lieu of such an analysis, therefore, let me only highlight the different kinds of correspondence and co-responding accomplished by *Besinnung*. By responding and corresponding to what only announces itself through signs—a new "world-age in which that which is worthy of questioning will someday again open the door that leads to what is essential in all things and in all destining"—in a manner, furthermore, that can only be provisional, forbearing, and poor, correspondence, rather than taking place between what presences and a preserving beholding, becomes one with respect to what is not yet, what is still to come, which as such remains undetermined. Such a way of corresponding to the signs of the to-come, which, notwithstanding its thorough undeterminedness, Heidegger thinks within the horizon of what he defines as the question-worthy, that is, within the horizon of Being, is the appropriate way of responding and corresponding to a world-age that promises to be an age of the "world"—of a world not only distinct from the un-world of modernity but distinct from the ancient world, as well. Finally, if such a *Besinnung* is not only a responding and corresponding to "the profundity [Tiefgang] of the world shock that we experience every hour" but also one that is "questioningly, reflectingly, and [. . .] in this way already [. . .] actively involved," does it not also follow that *Besinnung* is an acting form of thought of a different kind than the *theoria* that the Greeks considered the highest form of life?[135] Merely responding to what only announces itself, a corresponding that in addition is always only provisional, *Besinnung* is a way of thought that is no doubt active but, in thus relating to the signs of what announces itself, "only" an active way of preparation without assurance of any sort that what the signs promise will eventually come.

Even at its highest, *Besinnung* is, as we have seen, only a preparation for the "readiness to respond, and correspond, one that in the clarity of ceaseless questioning lets itself be taken in by the inexhaustibleness of that which is worthy of questioning, and from out of which, in the moment properly its own, responding and corresponding loses the character of questioning and becomes simply saying."[136] I conclude with just this remark: simply saying (*einfaches Sagen*) is another word for *logos*, *logos* understood, as it is by Heidegger, as anterior to the logos/mythos divide. Simply saying is the saying that occurs in Greek tragic poetry and in the thinking of the early philosophers, who, by their thoughtful poetizing and poetizing thought, set forth the originary world for Greek *Dasein*, according to Heidegger. *Besinnung*, as a questioning of the question-worthy, is on the way only toward preparing the possibility of making such saying possible—a possibility that could be realized only when the new world-age, whose signs *Besinnung* as a new kind of *theoria* in the making watches over, could, indeed, be beheld in a beholding that watches over what still has to come into existence.

PART III

JUDGMENT (ARENDT)

IN A LETTER from 1955, Hannah Arendt confides to Karl Jaspers that she intends to call a planned "book on political theories, 'Amor Mundi.'"[1] Several scholars, among them Elisabeth Young-Bruehl, have held that this book is none other than *The Human Condition*.[2] Indeed, it was the first book to be published in the aftermath of the letter to Jaspers.[3] As Ursula Ludz has convincingly pointed out, however, when Arendt spoke to Jaspers about the title in question, neither *The Human Condition* nor her *Introduction into Politics* were in progress at the time. Ludz, therefore, writes: "With 'the book on political theories,' Arendt referred to a complex of studies that gave rise, first, to the publication of *The Human Condition* (1958), followed by *Between Past and Future* (1961), and finally *On Revolution* (1963), and to which also the non-written 'Introduction *into* Politics' belongs."[4] This assessment not only seems to make sense historically; it also takes into consideration Arendt's mounting interest in the political during that period. This interest and the emerging project of developing a new theory of politics coincide with the aftermath of the devastating events and extreme conditions that marked the first half of the twentieth century. As Arendt admits in the letter to Jaspers, she chose the title 'Amor Mundi' out of thankfulness for having finally, however belatedly, "begun to love the world."[5] Undoubtedly, the atrocities that characterize the first half of the twentieth century explain Arendt's reservations regarding the world. But the reference to the love of the world in the context of her projected work on politics also shows that this love is inherently interconnected with the political or, more precisely, with her rediscovery of the political. The world to which she refers is primarily the public world, the world as the space of the political. The world is the space within which the political unfolds, and it is also the very objective of the political, that is, what the political intends to realize. Indeed, the world that the political presupposes might not yet be something fully established and might never even be a positive and certain reality. For it to become real, love might have to complete it. The world might require love of the world in order to be able to maintain itself as world. But Arendt's love of the world might also be a love for something whose realization has not yet occurred. If the world is both the condition and the telic end of politics, then love for the world is a love for something that must be produced in the first place. To love the world, then, is a commitment to bringing it about and to securing the life that it alone makes possible.

But why 'love'? As Young-Bruehl observes, Arendt wanted to call her projected book on political theory *Amor Mundi* because she rejected the philosophical tradition of *contemptus mundi*.[6] Love of the world thus implies, from the start, a turn away from the philosophical tradition and a rehabilitation of the political as, not a part of philosophy, but a kind of alternative discourse distinct from it. Since respect, rather than love, is the antonym of contempt, however, to speak of love of the world suggests that the stakes with regard to the world are of a special nature. Someone like Arendt, who has devoted a whole book to the question of love, does not oppose love to philosophical contempt for or disdain of the world without premeditation. So, what does *love* of the world mean? It is love of the world but not of the earth, which is the habitat of not only humans but also all other animal beings. Nor is it love of the cosmos of which the earth is a part. Could it be that the world is not something that one can take for granted, as one does in the case of the earth? But, then, what is the world such that it can become the object of love rather than of respect? Is it because the world, rather than being given as the natural milieu in which living beings exist, is something of which only human beings are capable and because human beings are therefore not just one animal species among others? Is it precisely because of the love of something that only human beings are capable of creating by interacting with one another as free beings in the public arena? Love thus replaces the contempt that philosophy has expressed from early on with a specifically human liberation from the fetters of nature and with the space that it both presupposes and creates.

Although the world is not the earth, it is not therefore something abstract. Nor is it, as an interconnected horizon of sense, a whole of fixed and familiar elements of intelligibility. Rather, as the worldly space of the *res publica*, the world is a space that appears directly to our bodily senses. As the space of human interaction, it is also a space of appearing; that is to say, it is not only a space that possesses (like the polis) concrete and sensible contours and thus takes on appearance but also one into which human beings enter in order to be seen and heard. As Aristotle remarks, "one city will be in one place [*topos*]."[7] In other words, by virtue of the single site that it occupies, the world as a public space is a place that is experienced in all its empirical and sensory appearance. Arendt's forceful valorization of the sensible throughout her work is a challenge to classical philosophy. Clearly, her consistent references to the world as a sensible place suggest that, rather than a bloodless idea, rather than something constitutive or regulative, the world—if such a thing ever existed—is a place that speaks to the senses. This, perhaps, is another reason why it invites an affect such as love.

On a couple of occasions Arendt highlights Kant's reflection in *Reflexionen zur Logik* that the existence of beautiful things in the world by which one is affected shows that the human being is fitted for the world.[8] Regardless of whether Kant is thinking about natural beauty, artificial beauty, or both, beauty for Arendt pertains above all to artificial things in the in-between that is the human world. If Kant's reflection is significant for Arendt, it is because the recognition that there are beautiful things is not possible without a judgment of taste. However, such a judgment presupposes the presence of others. In short, a world in which there are things that can be judged to be beautiful is a world of human beings, a world fit for them to interact with one another through judgments. Love of the world is thus the love of a space in which there can be beautiful things and in which such recognition is a testimony to active human interaction without which no such judgment could be made. It is the love for a space fitted for human beings to exercise what Arendt calls the most political of all the human mental activities, namely, judgment.

But the question still remains concerning what about love itself, which "by its very nature is unworldly," allows it to be love of the world?[9] I stress the double genitive: *Amor Mundi* as love *of* the world is not only a love whose object is the world but also the love that only the world engenders, in short, worldly love. Worldly love is a love within the world that cares for the world as a thoroughly worldly place. If, however, this worldly world invites or demands love, is it, perhaps, because the public world, in spite of its concrete and sensible nature, is not simply something given and self-evident? As Arendt remarks, "[b]y desiring what it has not, love establishes a relationship with what is not present" or whose presence is something rather precarious, such as, for example, the world.[10] Is loving it in the very precariousness of its presence not a devotion without reserve by the human being as a sensible being committed to preventing the world from vanishing in all its sensible nature, rather than primarily as an intellectual being capable of conceiving of the world only as a horizon of sense or as an idea?

The world that Arendt has in mind when she speaks of her love for it is not the earth or the planet as the natural habitat of the human being. Rather, it is the realm of human interaction, that is, the public and political realm of action. In distinction from the realm of labor in which all human activity is characterized by futility insofar as all its products are immediately consumed and hence destroyed, as well as from the realm of work in which human artifacts provide the world with durability, the action that constitutes the realm of human affairs is, for Arendt, something profoundly and radically fragile. As Paul Ricœur remarks in his analysis of the specific temporality of the realms in question, the fragility of the world of action is "a fragility that is much more formidable than all futility."[11] Because the public and political world lasts only as long as its actors maintain it through their actions, this realm produces in the beholder the unworldly affect of love. But is it not the vulnerability of the very activity—action—that makes up the world that invites the passion and affectionate concern that is the love for the world? This love of the world of action as something radically fragile is also what motivates Arendt to elaborate a political theory, rather than a philosophy, of *this* world.[12] Instead of taking her standpoint from on high, Arendt's theory takes its starting point within this world and remains within the concrete outlines of it as a space of appearance. As such, this immanent theory of the world is just as fragile as what it theorizes, not least of all because it seeks support from and bases its efforts to sustain the world and its action in the very fragility of its object.

In the first part of this book we saw the extent to which the practice of discursive persuasive engagement with one another in the public space is a fragile art in that it can always relapse into scientific discourse and the latter's invocation of necessary reasons for agreeing to a proposition. In the second part, it became clear that, if the world has been imperiled by the modern sciences to a degree that allows Heidegger to speak of its breakdown, the world is something to be watched over by a certain theoretical glance. As such, it can also only be something that is essentially precarious. In the following and concluding part of this book, I intend to show that judgment, understood by Arendt as an intrinsically political activity that represents the correlate of the action constitutive of world, is located on a thin line between cognition and practical reason. As the events of the twentieth century have shown, judgment is not a faculty to be taken for granted. Arendt's discussions of mental faculties often sound as if she is making an anachronistic case for innate psychological powers. Yet, at least in the case of judgment, the faculty in question is not a firm power of the mind. Judgment is not only a faculty that presupposes the world, a faculty whose power can manifest itself only within a world and in relation to the actions of men; it can become virtually extinct, thus threatening the existence of the faculties of understanding and thinking. A misleading assurance regarding the existence of this faculty is perhaps projected by the fact that Arendt likens her conception of judgment to Kant's notion of the judgment of taste. But even a judgment of taste is not in one's deliberate power to effectuate. It happens to the subject in an unpredictable way. Notwithstanding Arendt's claim in *The Life of the Mind* that it is an autonomous faculty, judgment's autonomy as a distinct power is anything but obvious. Furthermore, as we will see, the judgment of taste is only the starting point for Arendt's development of her notion of judgment in a strict, political sense. Despite Arendt's own terminology, it is something so precarious that great caution is warranted before simply considering it to be a faculty, or a power of the mind, in the traditional sense. Judgment, perhaps, is something other than a faculty. Indeed, what I will establish with respect to judgment in Arendt should be read with an eye to the possibility that her conception of judgment might involve a fundamental revision of the philosophical doctrine of the faculties not only as distinct psychological powers but also as functions of the mind.

The love of the world is a love for a life that is possible only within this world. It is a life that has not been particularly valued within philosophy. As Arendt observes, there is a persistent "affinity between death and philosophy."[13] Rather than loving the world, the philosopher is in love with death. Furthermore, philosophy has shown persistent contempt for the life of the multitude in which opinion, rather than truth, dominates. When the devotee of the *bios theoretikos* ventures to take on the world of the political, as Plato does in *Republic*, he does so from a position from above and in the name of immortal truth. By contrast, Arendt rejects the quasi-totality of political philosophy from antiquity to the present and demonstrates a love for the world that is rather uncommon from a philosophical perspective. This love is already manifest in the fact that her starting point is a reflection on the political from the immanent experience and praxis of political agents, that is, in the phenomena themselves that from the perspective of the agents make up the realm in question. This is obvious from the central role that her theory accords in a thematic fashion to plurality, the in-between of the public space, appearances, opinions, deliberation, persuasion, and so forth.[14] Rather than approaching the public and political space from outside or from above, that is, from a higher philosophical position intent on seeking to provide a legitimate or transcendental reason for such a volatile and futile realm and its praxis (for example, by way of laws like those that Plato establishes for the ideal city), Arendt's phenomenological description of the constitutive elements of political interaction in the space of appearance makes them the elements *sine qua non* of 'world.' So, what Arendt advances with respect to the conditions of possibility of the political (that which all political theories presuppose in a way) is not of the order of a transcendental condition. Nor is it simply the factual ground of politics, which would only establish what is already the case. Rather, I would characterize it as an 'empirical minimum' that needs to be realized first of all before something like the political becomes possible. However, this condition endows the minimum in question with an extremely fragile mode of being. Although it resembles a condition of possibility for a political world, its very contingency, due to the necessity of realizing it first, prevents it from ever becoming a secure ground.[15]

It is possible to argue that Arendt's theory of politics leaves many questions unresolved. As far as the modern age is concerned, it falls short of its goal because it does not provide any concrete or substantial content with respect to political action and debate. But does Arendt's fascination with fragile and short-lived political events—such as the American town hall meetings, the *sociétés populaires* during the French Revolution, the Soviets in Russia, or the revolutionary councils in Germany—not demonstrate a primary concern with phenomena in the modern world that appear to her as proof that a 'world' is a real possibility in modernity? One can, of course, lament the absence in her work of any sustained developments concerning such issues as the formation of political institutions, the emancipation from domination, the role of strategic competition for power in the realm of politics, and so forth. Indeed, what about Habermas's criticism that, by "styliz[ing] the image she has painted of the Greek polis into the essence of the political," by considering "communicative knowledge [. . .] as the single political category," and by understanding praxis in light of Aristotle's theory of action, Arendt undertakes a "basic conceptual narrowing of the political to the practical"?[16] Habermas acknowledges that Arendt has "an ambitious concept of the political sphere [*Öffentlichkeit*]."[17] But could we not conclude that the political sphere, which Habermas recognizes to be "highly unstable and in need of protection" because of its "innovative potential,"[18] is what Arendt refers to as 'the world' without which no such thing as the political is conceivable and that political action alone can actualize? If Habermas, in a discussion of Arendt's interpretation of the American Revolution, can assert that she "turns everything upside down," is it not because, by conceiving of the political primarily as an instituting of the world, Arendt focuses on something whose existence Habermas takes for granted, as demonstrated by his complaints regarding the lack of concrete content with respect to political action or of attention to other aspects of politics?[19] In the sense of classical political philosophy, that is, the philosophy of politics that she decries for having given short shrift to the political, Arendt puts, of course, all political matters on their head.

Needless to say, one can also argue, as Habermas does, that the Aristotelian concept of politics is not applicable to the modern world or, more generally, that "[p]olitics cannot, as with Arendt, be identical with the praxis of those who discourse together in order to act communally."[20] Yet, if Habermas's theory of communicative action does not describe what Arendt calls action or free speech in the public realm, it is because the world, within which something like communicative action in Habermas's sense could (in the best of all imaginable worlds) become a possibility and thus allow the agents eventually to regulate their discursive interaction by way of rational criteria, arises through such action in the first place. Habermas contends that, in her Greek stylization of the concept of politics, Arendt falls victim to a concept of politics that cannot be applied to modern conditions. But this approach to the concept of politics is for her the unavoidable starting point for the reflection on the minimal conditions of possibility of politics today. Does Arendt's prime focus in her theoretical writings on the circumstances under which alone there can be something like a public and political world (as opposed to all the essays in which she takes issue with concrete historical events) not provide the initial framework within which a more complex theory of politics could subsequently be developed? Is a love of the world not the very precondition for such an enterprise?

In advance of my commentary on and interpretation of the conception of politics that underlies Arendt's theory of judgment, let me briefly recall one significant aspect of Aristotle's concept of praxis. According to the philosopher, action, as opposed to *poiesis* and *techne*, is an activity that has an end in itself. Political action is not at the service of something other than itself, as is the case with making or fabricating. If action happens for its own sake, it is precisely because it itself is the desideratum since political action is the happening of human freedom. One can therefore argue that political life, thus understood, is something short of a utopian project. To conceive of political action as an end in itself would be to confuse the means to attain the end with the end itself. In reality, the task of the political would have to consist of producing, by way of an action understood in terms of *poiesis* or *techne*, the concrete conditions under which a free world could come into being. In other words, the demand would be to include in the political such tasks as drafting the political constitution for the polis. For the Greeks, these were nonpolitical activities, which were often relegated to invited foreigners. Yet, if Arendt subscribes to Aristotle's understanding of the political as an end in itself, rather than as a 'making' by which political activity itself is deferred in order, first, to lay the groundwork and the framework for it, it is because for her human interaction in the public space is from the start involved in the institutionalization of the power that human beings have as politically acting agents. In other words, political action engenders from within itself the conditions, that is, power and the institutions in which power crystallizes, necessary for it to reproduce itself. As an end in itself, political performance, whether in the form of the living deed or the spoken word, must be able to maintain itself as this end. As is manifest from *The Human Condition*, the Aristotelian concepts of *energeia* and *entelecheia*—the activity in the process of completion and the activity through which the end holds itself in the state of completion—are indispensable for understanding the way in which Arendt conceives of action as an end in itself and the power that holds it alive.[21]

To return to the question of the world as the public sphere for human interaction and the love of it that Arendt expresses, it needs to be pointed out that, for the world to have actuality, it must have the capability of maintaining itself in actuality. In other words, if action is an activity, that is, a "being active for its own sake," in Aristotle's words, it implies the demand for power, which permits the life-activity that is action to last and to endure as such.[22] The world, then, has a decidedly temporal character in that it comes into being solely as an event. As such, it is the most fragile thing and, thus, can only stay in being what it is if action translates into power. After it has been given the chance to happen, is it not true, then, that love of the world is a yearning for the world to last? Is it not the ardent wish that this fragile event should continue to be able to remain and to remain what it is?

7
THE SPACE OF APPEARANCE

HANNAH ARENDT'S REFLECTIONS on judgment, which she qualifies as the most political of all of the human being's faculties, are intimately tied to a debate over Kant's philosophy that spans almost two decades. Central to this debate is the Kantian distinction between determinant (i.e., cognitive) judgment and reflective (i.e., aesthetic or teleological) judgment. Arendt's own conception of judgment originates largely from her interest in and her commentaries on Kant's elaboration of the judgment of taste in the *Critique of the Power of Judgment*.

As the entries of August 1957 in *Denktagebuch* demonstrate, Arendt construes the difference between the two types of judgment by grounding determining judgment in the solitary self's "experience of the 'I think' and in the (a priori) principles that are thus given within it" and reflective judgment in the "experience of the world in its particularity" and, since this world is made up of particular human beings, in the self's relation to others.[1] "The presence of the universal" accomplishes for determining judgment what "the presence of the other" accomplishes for reflective judgment.[2] Whereas in determining judgment the judging self stays within itself, reflective judgment not only presupposes the existence of others; it is a judgment in which "the plural is in me," in the self itself from the start.[3] In order to bring out the difference between the two forms of judgment, Arendt consistently submits them to further distinctions between a priori and a posteriori, legislation and agreement with others, private and public, private feeling and common sense (*Gemeinsinn*), interest in life (*Lebensinteresse*) and interest in the world (*Welt-Interesse, Welt-Sinn*), and so on and so forth. By thus connecting it to the subject's relation to others and by describing it as indicative of a common sense and a sense of the world (as opposed to mere life), reflective judgment becomes indissociable from "the realm that is properly that of the human being."[4] In other words, it becomes inseparable from the realm of political life. Since there is only "one 'reflective power of judgment,'" as Arendt remarks, it also follows that judgment properly speaking is judgment only on the condition that it is reflective. This power of reflective judgment "weighs exclusively on the human world," the world that we have in common with others and that is constituted by particularities.[5] Before any further exploration of Arendt's interpretation of reflective judgment and, more generally, of judgment as such, we must first turn to what calls for such activity to begin with. If judgment is the intimate correlate of the 'world,' and if that world is the realm that human beings share insofar as they are human, then a clarification of the meaning of 'world' is certainly warranted.

In what way does Arendt refer to the 'world'? First of all, it is in the sense of 'the world of appearances.' Since 'appearances' contrast with the 'true reality' from which they supposedly originate, whether such reality is understood empirically or transcendentally, the world of appearances is generally understood as the deceptive counterpart of a truly real or, at best, a noumenal world. For Arendt, notwithstanding this inevitable relation of the concept of appearance to its opposite, there is only the world of appearances. In a way similar to Nietzsche, it is the only world, the true world itself. The world of appearances refers to *this* world as opposed to an essential world (e.g., a world of Platonic ideas) or to the true 'world' beyond the world according to Christian faith. When Arendt speaks of the world as the world of appearances, the reference is always to this and only this world, which has to be understood on the basis of itself in an immanent fashion, even though the very notion of appearance suggests that this world is only the deceiving afterimage of a more essential and truer world. Yet, if this world is a world of appearances, it is also, in yet another sense of the term, a world in which appearances have been freed from their standard opposition to the idea of a world as it really is.

In *The Human Condition*, Arendt defines 'world' as the artificial and unnatural in-between for human action brought about through work (*Herstellen*) as opposed to labor (*Arbeit*), the latter of which is inseparable from the biological process of the human body. "Work provides an 'artificial' world of things, distinctly different from all natural surroundings."[6] The world, then, "is not identical with the earth or with nature."[7] As Arendt remarks in "The Crisis in Culture," the "earthly home [*irdische Heimat*] becomes a world in the proper sense of the word only when the totality of fabricated things is so organized that it can resist the consuming life process of the people dwelling in it, and thus outlast them."[8] The world requires a certain durability, and it is precisely work that secures such permanence through its products. In distinction from nature, or the earth, the worldly home of the human being is related

> to the human artifact, the fabrication of human hands, as well as to affairs which go on among those who inhabit the man-made world together. To live together in

the world means essentially that a world of things is between those who have it in common [...]; the world, like every in-between, relates and separates men at the same time.⁹

If "[t]he human condition of work is worldliness," human beings that inhabit the artificial realm of the world created by work are necessarily worldly (rather than just biological) beings.¹⁰ Indeed, within the world as the public realm of the more or less durable in-between created by human artifacts, human beings acquire a distinctness by being separated from one another. Based on that distinctness, they can thus also relate to one another in a way that differs from that of the private sphere, which is dominated by the exigencies of the life process in which human beings are not separated on the basis of their singularity but are, rather, prosthetic extensions of one another. Only through worldly beings, that is, no longer private beings, can there be "[h]uman plurality," in short, "the basic condition of both action and speech," the activities constitutive of the public realm.¹¹ Human plurality, or what Aristotle in *Politics* called *plethos*, is the condition of public life in the *politike koinonia* insofar as it refers not only to its individual members numerically but also to their essential diversity.¹²

Arendt develops her theory of "natality,"¹³ which subtends the plurality in question, with recourse to Augustine's discovery of the miracle that each human being born into the world is the creation of a new beginning.¹⁴ In *The Human Condition*, Arendt suggests, though rather obliquely, that natality is not a category of Greek political thought. She writes: "Only the full experience of this capacity [of each individual born into the world as representing a new beginning] can bestow upon human affairs faith and hope, those two essential characteristics of human existence which Greek antiquity ignored altogether [...] faith in and hope for the world."¹⁵ The fact of natality, "in which the faculty of action is ontologically rooted," might have been recognized for the first time by the Gospels (and Arendt points this out), but that does not make it simply a religious or theological motive.¹⁶ On the contrary, on an ontological-existential level, this category is Arendt's most decisive contribution to rethinking the Greek model of political life lived through deeds and actions in a worldly space, a contribution made not merely in view of a reconception of politics in response to the exigencies of modern times but from a universal perspective.

Natality refers to the new beginning that each human being makes by virtue of being born into the world. In the same breath, this theory undergirds the claim of human beings' irreducible distinctness from one another. Rather than a specimen, each human being is a singular being—one among plural human beings who in their (impossible) totality are not to be confounded with the members of a species called Man. Made up of singular beings, the plural whole of humanity from the start defies the Eleatic, but also Platonic, demand of Oneness, whether in terms of Being or the Idea of the polis.[17] With the notion of natality, Arendt rejects in particular the generic unity of Man as species. Since natality is also a political concept linked to publicness and world, which aims at a fundamental recasting of the political since the Greeks, it follows that this concept dislodges the whole sphere of the biological from the political and the political life of the human being. Instead of biological connotations, the category of natality denotes the appearance of the human being (male or female) in the world rather than in the sphere of the biological family or in nature in general. The world is the public space for human interaction into which he or she is born always as a newcomer or stranger, male or female, distinct from all others and with the capacity of making a new beginning. Yet, this category of natality does not name a psychological power or faculty to make a new beginning. As already suggested, it is an ontological category linked to the human being's existence, that is, his or her existence based on appearing within the world.[18]

As a worldly category from the start, 'natality' does not refer to the human being's delivery into the world through childbirth but names an insertion into the world that is, as Arendt remarks, "like a second birth," which consists in the human being's appearance in the world through his words and deeds.[19] The sphere of labor, even labor in the sense of giving birth to another human being as an instance of the cyclical life process and the perpetuation of the species, precedes 'natality' as a political distinction.[20] Indeed, being born and appearing in the world are two different things. This does not exclude labor and work from also being (retrospectively) "rooted in natality in so far as they have the task to provide and preserve the world for, to foresee and reckon with, the constant influx of newcomers who are born into the world as strangers."[21] Yet, if both labor (which "assures not only individual survival, but the life of the species") and work (which through its products bestows "a measure of permanence and durability upon the futility of mortal life and the fleeting character of human time," which is not yet, however, a public and political activity) are in teleological retrospect also said to be rooted in natality, it is of course because there would be no such a thing as a world of action without them.[22] Yet, Arendt emphasizes the dominating priority of action over labor and work. She writes: "However, of the three, action has the closest connection with the human condition of natality."[23] The focus is on an ascendance that frees labor from its inherent service to the biological and on work's equally important function of sustaining life (though work also already creates the condition for the world as a space in-between for interacting human beings).

The mere fact that, from a biological point of view, every human being is delivered into the world by a woman is of no significance to the human being as always a new beginning in the public and political domain. Indeed, being delivered by a woman in labor does not endow the newborn with the condition of natality per se, that is, of being a newcomer capable of another beginning in the world. He or she has this characteristic only upon entering the public and political space as a fully autonomous and free being—free of all ties to the human species as a biological species. Similarly, it is not because the work of art is made by an artisan through work (*poiesis* or *Herstellen*) that it shows itself forth as an appearance par excellence?[24] And is not the actor in the political realm only the author of his or her words and deeds and the receiver of the public fame bestowed upon him or her to the extent that the actor is entirely freed of his or her condition as a natural being, both biological and psychological?

In any event, Arendt holds in *The Human Condition* that natality "may be the central category of the political" precisely because it concerns the possibility of action and speech understood as the activities par excellence that characterize solely the public and political realm.[25] The primary political significance of natality is further highlighted by Arendt's reference to the human being's being born into the world in terms of an appearing or appearance. The world into which the newcomer is born is a world in which he or she does not simply exist; it is a world in which he or she appears (and from which ultimately he or she will disappear again). Indeed, as Arendt points out, the birth and death ("as we understand them") of human beings presuppose a world, which is durable and enjoys relative permanence, as opposed to nature with its cyclical movements. Birth and death, therefore, are above all political in nature.[26] In appearing, the individual already makes a difference. It is as if it were the newcomer's first action through which he or she engages with others. Appearing is a first form of action that shows him or her to be a potential actor in the thoroughly unnatural arena that is the world inhabited by the many. Appearance constitutes the uniqueness of a being in the world characterized by plurality. More precisely, as Arendt argues in the first chapter of *The Life of the Mind* entitled "Appearance" (which is her most extensive discussion of the subject), for beings who, like the human being, appear, "*Being and Appearance*" coincide.[27] The ontological and existential status of the human being is to exist as appearance, in other words, in a public world, first as a new beginner and then through his or her words and deeds. Appearance, then, is also intrinsically pluralistic and invites discrimination. It is in this sense that it also invites judgment.

But what kind of notion of 'appearance' does natality as a political category put to work? In the context of an inquiry into Arendt's theory of judgment, one cannot but think of Kant's notion of appearance. Indeed, as Arendt acknowledges in *The Life of the Mind*, "[i]n the work of no other philosopher has the concept of appearance, and hence of semblance (of *Erscheinung* and *Schein*), played so decisive and central a role as in Kant."[28] But Kant's concept of appearance concerns all possible objects, that is, everything that is experienced and capable of being known. It is true that, in the context of the strongly anthropological (if not even biologistic) account of appearing in *The Life of Mind*, Arendt speaks of appearing in a way that somewhat resonates with Kant's understanding of the concept when she writes that "[t]he world men are born into contains many things, natural and artificial, living and dead, transient and sempiternal, all of which have in common that they *appear* and hence are meant to be seen, heard, touched, tasted, and smelled, to be perceived by sentient creatures endowed with the appropriate sense organs."[29] But even here some caution is warranted. Arendt's concept of appearance cannot simply be attributed to Kant given that, in the passage quoted, her emphasis lies on the spectators to whom things appear but who are, qua living things, themselves appearances. Indeed, when Arendt refers to appearing and appearances, she does not speak from a cognitive perspective, as Kant does in the *Critique of Pure Reason*. Appearance in Arendt is not the precondition of objectivity and cognitive understanding. Her concept of appearance is admittedly political; that is, it is a function of a public world. In addition, what deserves to be called an appearance, according to Arendt, is not the totality of everything objectifiable but rather (notwithstanding the statement from *The Life of the Mind*) exclusively a distinct segment of what Kant characterizes as phenomena, that is, apart from the human newcomers in the world, his or her words and deeds and works of art. Furthermore, appearing and appearance in Arendt always connote novelty. Rather than a universal characteristic of everything that manifests itself to an experiencing subject, an appearance is inseparable from the singularity, individuality, and newness (either of the actor's deed or speech) that it represents. Yet, one wonders whether Arendt's conception of appearances, which occur in the *spatial* context of the public place and, because of the human being's condition of natality, always have a *temporal* dimension, is not also deeply indebted to Kant's transcendental aesthetics?

But if one hesitates to attribute Arendt's understanding of appearance to Kant unambiguously, would it, then, be more appropriate to look for the origin of her concept of appearance in Husserlian phenomenology? For Husserl, in a phenomenon something shows itself from itself as what it is to an intuiting subject. For Arendt, as we will see, appearing is the manifestation to others through word or deed of a human being's singularity, of the difference he or she makes insofar as he or she has been born into the world. Although in appearing the individual does not show him- or herself so much in what he or she is in essence as in relation to the new beginning that he or she represents, in short, with respect to the difference that he or she makes by appearing in the world and, in the same breath, by soliciting a response from the beholding subject, we should keep the Husserlian (and also certain aspects of the Heideggerian) notion of phenomenality in mind as we further explore Arendt's reliance on the concept in question.[30]

From what we have shown so far regarding the concept of appearance—appearance as the happening of a new beginning in the world, as from the start a showing to others of what is unique in such an appearance, and, hence, also as the invitation to others to respond to the singular newness in question—it follows that appearance presupposes a specific milieu for it to occur. This milieu is the open space of a world. Appearances are addressed to others and call upon them to solicit a response. In that respect, the world is the public world. In *The Human Condition*, Arendt avers: "the term 'public' signifies the world itself, in so far as it is common to all of us and distinguished from our privately owned place in it."[31] Notwithstanding certain claims in *The Life of the Mind* where appearance is linked with a biologically grounded notion of display, Arendt's notion of appearance refers primarily to the realm of publicness, which is the open space of the realm of *Öffentlichkeit*, that is, the realm of "what lies before the eyes," of what has been exposed or made public (in a political sense).[32] The world for appearances is not only the public world but also the realm of the political interaction of human beings. Appearance thus presupposes "the visible arena of public affairs."[33] Strictly speaking, there are no appearances "in privacy and in the family, in the security of one's own four walls"; appearance requires at all times "the light that can be generated only in a public space, that is, in the presence of others."[34] The public space, as "the world one has in common with others," is "the place for appearance [*Erscheinungsort*], par excellence—as opposed to the private, which is the place of concealment and being sheltered."[35] Arendt also speaks of the world as a public space on occasion as an *Erscheinungsraum*—a space for appearance or display. In "Introduction *into* Politics," she argues that the "space for assembly [*Versammlungsraum*]" as it developed in the Middle Ages might well have been a public space or, more precisely, the public space of believers, but it was not yet a political space.[36] The space of assembly "is deceptive as long as it is merely public but not political," that is, as long as it is not constituted by the light in which appearing becomes possible.[37] To be a political space, the public space must be not only a thoroughly *worldly* space but also a *physical* space. By "being bound to the world, which is part and parcel of any physical space," the public space has the capacity to appear itself and to shine forth in the first place.[38] In sum, then, in order to be political, the public space must first be both a space that appears and a space for appearance. In short, a thoroughly worldly space.³⁹

By intimately linking the occurrence of appearance to the public and political realm, Arendt proceeds to a remarkable rehabilitation of the problematic of appearance and appearing, of *Erscheinung* and *Scheinen* (seeming), and of *Schein*—seeming, semblance, shining, (mere) appearance, and so forth. Undoubtedly, it is not of minor importance in this context to point out that the notion of appearance often connotes a certain luster, a gleaming brilliance. In any event, Arendt's rehabilitation of appearance consists in a revalorization of everything that, from the perspective of eternal truths, lacks immutability and is deceptive because it constantly changes and, hence, resists all precise fixity as regards its truth. Appearance, for Arendt, is the specificity of the public and political realm, as opposed to the concealment and secludedness of the private sphere, and thus denotes the self-manifestation and self-display of the human being to others in the open milieu of the world. From Parmenides on, philosophy has consistently sought to wring itself free from the whole sphere of seeming and to vie with the gods for a knowledge of truth unfettered by the appearances and opinions that characterize the fleeting realm of human affairs.⁴⁰ Philosophy has relentlessly questioned that which merely shines forward. In its endeavor to raise human knowledge to divine knowledge, all mere seeming is mere opinion for philosophy. By explicitly construing the domain of publicness and politics as a space for appearance, Arendt restores the luster of appearance and, thus, also confirms philosophy's reasons for its general hostility to the public realm as mere appearance and as a domain of mere opinion. Before taking up this problematic of opinion in a bit more detail, however, we need to distinguish the two main aspects of the public and political realm in which appearing occurs.

In *The Human Condition*, works of art are shown to have a very special status within the realm of artifacts. Indeed, among all the works that endow the in-between of the world with durability, works of art stand out because

> their durability is of a higher order than that which all things need in order to exist at all; it can attain permanence throughout the ages. In this permanence, the very stability of the human artifice, which, being inhabited and used by mortals, can never be absolute, achieves a representation of its own. Nowhere else does the sheer durability of the world of things appear in such purity and clarity, nowhere else therefore does this thing-world reveal itself so spectacularly as the non-mortal home for mortal beings. It is as though worldly stability had become transparent in the permanence of art, so that a premonition of immortality [. . .] has become tangibly present, to shine and to be seen, to sound and to be heard, to speak and to be read.⁴¹

Of all the things produced through work, works of art thus enjoy a certain ontological privilege. As Arendt says in the German translation of the passage above in *Vita Activa*, their permanence is not only quantitatively but also qualitatively different from that of the use-objects that make up the in-between of the world.[42] Their outstanding permanence not only consists in the fact that, by attaining "permanence throughout the ages," they secure the durability of the world; in artworks' "permanence, the very stability of the human artifice, which, being inhabited and used by mortals, can never be absolute, achieves a representation of its own."[43] In other words, the very permanence of the world itself is allowed to shine forth in works of art. In *Vita Activa*, Arendt makes this point even more pointedly. She speaks of "the worldliness of the world itself [...] which [in the artwork's durability] comes into appearance, into a shining forth, that is, into a glowing in whose brilliance change and process come into light [*selbst in Erscheinung, ja in ein Leuchten, in dessen Glanz auch der Wandel und Gang aufleuchtet*]."[44] For all these reasons, artworks are, Arendt remarks, "the most intensely worldly of all tangible things."[45] Before any further elaboration on artworks' representation and disclosure of the world itself, however, let us linger on the worldliness par excellence that artworks enjoy insofar as they have no use value.

The work of art's privilege consists in bringing to light the fact that "there is in fact no thing that does not in some way transcend its functional use."[46] Through the durability that artworks achieve by transcending the sphere of instrumentality, not only does "a premonition of immortality [...] become tangibly present, to shine and to be seen"; such transcendence, Arendt claims, "is identical with appearing publicly and being seen."[47] The essay "The Crisis in Culture: Its Social and Its Political Significance," written the same year as *The Human Condition*, forcefully makes this point.

If artworks are the worldliest things, it is because they are not fabricated for man insofar as he is involved in the life process but, rather, "for the world which is meant to outlast the life-span of mortal, the coming and going of the generations."[48] They are the worldliest things since, being created for the world, they are primarily of the order of appearances. Without any functionality, works of art are all appearance and, moreover, a lasting one. What Arendt establishes with respect to the phenomenal nature of artworks provides further clarification concerning how to understand 'appearance.' If 'appearing' constitutes the mode of being particular to artworks, the implication is that works of art cannot be what they are in the domain of seclusion or concealment of some private collection. There, they cannot "attain their own inherent validity."[49] Works of art do not realize their essence in private possession.

Rather, "they are in need of some public space where they can appear and be seen; they can fulfill their own being, which is appearance, only in a world which is common to all."[50] The works of art are what they are only insofar as they actively shine forth into a world that is public and common to all and that calls for an equally active response by those to whom the works appear. Works of art are appearances precisely because they offer themselves to the senses in order to be heard and seen for what they inherently are: useless things that do nothing whatsoever for the survival of the human being as a natural being. They only seek intercourse with the world and the plurality of human beings that interact with one another within it. Precisely their uselessness and their restriction to being ontologically nothing but appearances solicit a response from their viewers and auditors. Works of art show themselves in order to be seen and interacted with. However, all this is possible only in the in-between of the world as a space common to the many—a public space.

If artworks are the worldliest of all things, it is because, apart from showing themselves in their uniqueness, they also disclose the world itself, as we have seen. As such, they are paradigmatic of the world that human life as such requires, not because it would be part and parcel of the 'nature' of the human being—in fact, Arendt, acknowledges "the existence of worldless people"—but because he or she, due to the human condition of natality, needs a world into which to be born as a newcomer.[51] If human life as such requires a world distinct from the earth, and if artworks as the worldliest of all things disclose the world through their worldliness, it follows that the world that humans need only "insofar as [human life] needs a home on earth for the duration of its stay here" is an unnatural or artificial world constituted by appearance and appearances.[52] As a consequence, the phenomenal character of that which makes up what Arendt refers to as 'world' also necessarily shapes the nature of the activities specific to this domain, that is, the different forms of action. One major form such action takes is the activity of judgment. It is in this context that Arendt falls back on Kant's analysis of the judgment of taste in the Third Critique. In order to understand the phenomenal nature of what Arendt construes as 'world,' it is not insignificant that Arendt's interest in the Third Critique is largely limited to Kant's discussion of artificial beauty rather than of natural beauty. Even though Arendt quotes on several occasions Kant's statement from the posthumously published "Reflexionen zur Logik" that the fact "'that man is affected by the sheer beauty of nature proves that he is made for and fits into this world,'" the world as she understands it is made up and disclosed by artificial things, including works of art.[53] As a consequence, in her interpretation of the judgment of taste and, in particular, its intersubjective character, she also privileges works of art over beautiful objects of nature.

However, before taking up the question of how this choice bears upon Arendt's understanding of judgment, we must get a better grasp of the phenomenal nature of the world itself and, to do so, must delve further into Arendt's understanding of art.

In a remark in "Crisis in Culture," Arendt points out that "[e]very thing, whether it is a use object, a consumer good, or a work of art, possesses a shape through which it appears, and only to the extent that something has a shape can we say that it is a thing at all."[54] Yet, "[w]hile the thingness of all things by which we surround ourselves lies in their having a shape through which they appear, only works of art are made for the sole purpose of appearance."[55] Appearing, particularly in the case of manmade things and works of art, is thus linked to the shape of things. It is through their shape that they come into an appearance. Yet, if artworks as worldly things par excellence are paradigmatic of the world, it is precisely because they are in a way reified shapes, that is, things that offer their shape to be seen. In other words, they are things that consist primarily in their shining forth or appearing. It is in this that they are the worldliest things, things that show something about the world because they appear for the sake of appearing. In this capacity of beautiful semblance, works of art reveal what the world is—a space or place into which human beings can be born and in which they can, in resistance to the life process, show themselves in their particularity. As we will see, shapes are to worldly objects par excellence, that is, works of art, what deeds and words are to human beings insofar as they, too, are worldly beings. Undoubtedly in reference to Aristotle, Arendt claims that their appearance in the public and political world takes place through their actions and speeches. Now, Arendt also contends that "[t]he proper criterion by which to judge appearances is beauty."[56] The appearances that she has in mind are certainly not those of natural things but, rather, unmistakably those of artificial things. She adds: "if we wanted to judge objects, even ordinary use-objects, by their use-value alone and not also by their appearance—that is, by whether they are beautiful or ugly or something in between—we would have to pluck out our eyes."[57] Even though she agrees that judgments could also address the use-value of objects, judgments concern first and foremost, for Arendt, objects as they show themselves to us. It follows not only that objects, in their quality of objects that appear to us, are judged aesthetically but also that, more generally, appearance and appearing call for judgments. Judgment is the proper way of relating to what appears, and our task here will ultimately be to understand why this is so. Yet, for a judgment of appearances to be possible, it is first necessary to have a distance from the objects' eventual use-value, particularly in relation to the needs of our living organism. Arendt observes that

> in order to become aware of appearances we first must be free to establish a certain distance between ourselves and the object, and the more important the sheer appearance of a thing is, the more distance it requires for its proper appreciation. This distance cannot arise unless we are in a position to forget ourselves, the cares and interests and urges of our lives, so that we will not seize what we admire but let it be as it is, in its appearance.[58]

As far as objects are concerned, an aesthetic judgment or judgment of taste is possible only on the condition of our attentiveness to their phenomenality, that is, on the condition that one is able to abstract from their functionality in relation to the needs of our organism. Yet, when Arendt argues that this distance, created by the release from life's necessity and required for judging objects with regard to their mere appearance, lets human beings "be free for the world"—that is, for the world as the open space for objects to appear and endure in their appearance such that they can be seen and judged by a spectator—it becomes clear that judgments concern not only the beauty of things as appearing things but also their worldliness itself.[59] At the moment an appearance is judged with respect to its beauty, the judgment says something about the worldliness manifest in what is judged. Judgments about what appears are judgments about the world itself. In addition, they are also judgments about what the world as world should look like. Arendt writes: "The activity of taste decides how this world, independent of its utility and our vital interests in it, is to look and sound, what men will see and hear in it. Taste judges the world in its appearance and in its worldliness. [. . .] For judgments of taste, the world is the primary thing, not man, neither man's life nor his self."[60] When Arendt, furthermore, contends that beauty is a "public quality," she refers to the fact that for Kant aesthetic judgments "'woo the consent of everyone else' in the hope of coming to an agreement with him eventually."[61] Aesthetic judgments, thus, involve the sharing of a world. As Arendt's retranslation of "wooing" back into the Greek term *peithein* (to convince or persuade) demonstrates, the world she is thinking about is primarily a discursive world in which one judges not only publicly but also in a mode of intersubjective deliberation regarding "the sphere of public life and the common world, [. . .] what manner of action is to be taken in it, as well as to how it is to look henceforth, what kind of things are to appear in it."[62] In "The Crisis in Culture," Arendt states that taste judges "the world in its appearance and in its worldliness." In her translation of the essay into German she adds that a judgment of taste decides upon how "the world qua world" is to look.[63] Thus, taste judges not only the worldly character of what shines forth in the artwork as an appearance. The judgment of taste also concerns the world itself as the public realm in which both beautiful things and human beings make their appearance, where the latter make themselves seen and heard through their words and deeds, which artworks bring into view through their very worldliness.⁶⁴ Taste decides what the world as the 'realm of appearances' should look like. It makes this realm into the object of a judicious exchange of opinion between plural men and women.

As already indicated, objects of art are not the only appearances that shine forth into the 'realm of appearances.' The second major form of appearing in the world takes place through the words and deeds performed by human beings, that is, through *lexis* and *praxis*. When Arendt remarks that the products of art, which must find their place in the world, "obviously share with political 'products,' words and deeds, the quality that they are in need of some public space where they can appear and be seen,"⁶⁵ it follows that words and deeds are in the realm of appearances and are the political equivalent of beautiful things. As is well known, Arendt's understanding of the political is predicated on the life of free men in the Greek polis. In "Introduction *into* Politics," she writes:

> the Greeks formed the polis around the Homeric agora, the place where free men assembled and conversed, and by doing so centered what was truly 'political'— that is, what belonged to the polis and was therefore denied to all barbarians and other unfree people—on this world of coming together, being together, speaking about something with one another; and they saw this entire arena under the sign of divine *Peithō*, the power to persuade and influence, which reigned among equals and determined all things without force or coercion.⁶⁶

For our purposes, it will not be necessary to elaborate on the shift that occurs in the polis away from the emphasis on the intimate interconnection of great deeds and great words in the pre-polis experience toward speech and, in particular, speech "as a means of persuasion rather than the specifically human way of answering, talking back and measuring up to whatever happened or was done."⁶⁷ All that needs to interest us here is the character of appearances that words and deeds have in the public and political realm. It is through words and deeds that free citizens show themselves in their individuality rather than in the generality that characterizes them as members of the species 'man' (whose realm is the family). They are in the space of public display, and, striving to prove themselves in the agon characteristic of life in the polis, they do great deeds and speak great words, incessantly and everywhere, showing themselves to be the best. It is only in this very space that they meet the human condition of plurality. As Arendt remarks, even in the polis and the activity of showing oneself within it through words and deeds—"an activity that makes up the whole of life" of Athenian citizens—the model is still the contest between Hector and Achilles. It is a contest that, "quite apart from who wins or loses, gives each the opportunity to show himself as he really is, that is, by appearing in reality to become fully real [*wirklich in Erscheinung treten und damit völlig wirklich zu werden*]."⁶⁸ In the same way that the war between the Greeks and the Trojans gave both the opportunity to demonstrate who they were, the contest characteristic of the polis gives both parties "the opportunity to really show themselves."⁶⁹ Without this contest, "neither Achilles nor Hector would ever have made his appearance and been able to prove who he was."⁷⁰ In other words, deeds and words are the activities not only by which human beings appear in the public realm but also through which they show all others who they are, inasmuch as they are always new beginnings in the world. Solely by thus appearing to others through actions and words, which show them in all their singularity, do human beings become real in the world and achieve existence as individual beings. Such appearance to others is also the condition for appearing to oneself as the one who one really is. This possibility of appearing to myself through appearing to others is, Arendt avers, "of the greatest relevance to politics, if we understand (as the Greeks understood) the polis as the public-political realm in which men attain their full humanity, their full reality as men, not only because they *are* (as in the privacy of the household) but also because they *appear*." Full reality, she adds, is constituted by "the reality of this appearance."⁷¹

Compared to what the Greeks understood as the immortal order of nature, however, words and deeds have a most fleeting reality. What is more fleeting and ephemeral than "human actions and deeds, which have existence solely in the speaking and acting performance"?⁷² Another sense of appearance becomes manifest here, namely, its transience and fragility, as well as, in the same breath, the fragility of the whole sphere of what Arendt calls 'action.' This is also the context in which we should remind ourselves that "politics is never for the sake of life."⁷³ In distinction from fabrication, political words and deeds do not involve a relation of a means to an end. If, for the Greeks, "[f]abrication, but not action or speech, always involves means and ends," it is because for them action and deeds, insofar as they are constitutive of the political realm, are ends in themselves.⁷⁴ They are not meant to accomplish anything useful because bringing the utilitarian mentality of *poiesis*—making, fabricating, producing—to bear upon *praxis*, or action, threatens the very existence of the political realm. In short, not unlike artworks whose uselessness makes up their worldly character, words and deeds are not a means for something other. From a utilitarian perspective they are utterly useless and, hence, equally worldly, such that their happening secures the political realm in its distinction from the sphere of life and artifacts.

As we have seen, beautiful works of art are, by way of the thingly character of the works, also worldly because they have a durability that outlasts mortal human beings. What, then, is the equivalent of the thingly character of the works of art in actions by way of words and deeds? What is it that makes their appearing last beyond their unique occurrence in speech and action, and what is it that secures the permanence of the world as a public space? For the Greeks, the criterion for judging great deeds and words is also their beauty. As Arendt points out, "[t]he fleeting greatness of word and deed can endure in the world to the extent that beauty is bestowed upon it. Without the beauty, that is, the radiant glory in which potential immortality is made manifest in the human world, all human life would be futile and no greatness could endure."[75] Beauty or glory is "the human and merely worldly immortality claimed by what is great"; the criterion here for action, even if it concerns justice within the world, is glory, "the shining out in the space of appearances."[76] Yet, for a human being's deeds and words to be immortalized this way, politics requires art. Arguing for an intimate relation and even a mutual dependence between politics, art, and culture, Arendt remarks in "The Crisis in Culture" that "the public realm, which is rendered politically secure by men of action [*von handelnden Menschen gesicherten Raumes*], offers its space of display to those things whose essence it is to appear and to be beautiful."[77] On the one hand, the public and political space in which works of art can shine forth in their beauty is brought about by the public actions of men. They secure the realm in question. On the other hand, works of art, like the Homeric epic, recollect and thus convey the immortality of glory upon human beings' words and deeds, "which, if left to themselves, come and go without leaving any trace in the world."[78] Works of art are thus also instrumental in securing the memory of the words and deeds of human beings and, therefore, contribute to the permanence of the world as a space common to all.

Let us now return to the question of the judgment that human deeds and words solicit from their beholders. In "The Crisis in Culture," where Arendt claims that the beauty of great words and deeds makes them unforgettable (glory and beauty here are undistinguishable), she places great stress on the dependence of the realm of politics on culture even though it is political action that secures the opening for the appearing of works of art to begin with. It comes as no surprise that, precisely in this context, Arendt turns to the part of the *Critique of the Power of Judgment* that deals with the notion of the judgment of taste. She claims that this part of the *Third Critique* contains "perhaps the greatest and most original aspects of Kant's political philosophy," arguing that the judgment of taste allows one to account for what political words and deeds call forth with the aim of further securing the world as a space of appearance.[79] Analyzing a line from Pericles's famous statement, reported by Thucydides, that the Greeks, in distinction from the barbarians, love the beautiful without exaggeration, that is, only if it is moderated by *euteleia*, and thus remains within the limits of the political, Arendt argues that, for the love of the beautiful to accomplish such moderation, it must be accompanied "by the faculty to take aim in judgment, discernment, and discrimination, in brief, by that curious and ill-defined capacity we commonly call taste."[80] If taste is seen to prevent aestheticist indulgence in art (which Pericles attributes to the barbarians) and to determine its legitimate place in the polis, it is precisely because taste effects a distance in the relation to beauty. Taste implies that the beautiful is a function of a discriminating spectator. And, as Arendt notes, such critical spectatorship not only pervaded the polis. For the Greeks, this political aspect in relation to the beautiful also represented a distinguishing feature between them and all others.[81]

Even though the context of the essay we are discussing can lend itself to the hurried assumption that Arendt confounds aesthetic judgment and political judgment, extreme caution is warranted here. Undoubtedly, in "The Crisis of Culture," Arendt's goal is to make a strong case for the interconnection of the realm of culture with that of politics, and a certain affinity between aesthetic and political judgment thus becomes inevitable. Yet, as we will see in Chapter 9, Arendt's linkage of both works of art and political deeds to the space of appearances is motivated by Aristotle's contention in *Nicomachean Ethics* that both *poiesis* and *praxis* are activities in a world that is contingent. In other words, they are activities that concern that which, rather than invariable, can be other than itself. This does not mean, however, that Aristotle (or Arendt, for that matter) conflates the two forms or activities and the appearances to which they give rise. Indeed, in the same way as Aristotle, Arendt acknowledges the generically different ontological status of both. Yet, both activities and their corresponding judgments share the same domain of appearances. According to Arendt, the affinity between both the aesthetic and the political kinds of judgments is explained not only by the fact that both concern appearances in the public space but also by the fact that both call for critical and discriminating spectatorship. Before I take up the relation between these two kinds of judgment in greater detail, however, let me point out that, rather than aestheticizing politics by arguing that judgments of taste have a constitutive function in the political realm, Arendt's analysis of Pericles's statement is meant to show that it is precisely the judgment of taste's discerning and discriminating character that prevents aestheticism as a barbarian temptation of inactivity.

Taste is an active interaction with appearances in the world as a public space. As the defining criterion of culture, taste is, as Arendt asserts, something that concerns the human being's active relation to the world constituted not only by the least useful and most worldly of things (works of artists, poets, musicians, and philosophers) but also, I add, by the great words and deeds of men in the public sphere. Compared to the acts of labor required by the biological process, these things are utterly useless and utterly worldly despite the fact that it is exclusively through them that an individual's reality is shaped. Through its discernment and discrimination, then, taste shapes the worldliness of the world, and it does so by separating what is estimated to contribute to the world as we would like it to look from what does not. It is this very critical activity that, whether it concerns the worldly nature of art or great words and deeds, endows the judgment of taste with a certain political weight. If Arendt repeatedly stresses that taste is a "sensitivity to beauty, not in those who fabricate beautiful things, that is, in the artists themselves, but in the spectators, in those who move among them,"[82] and if taste is also, I add, a sensitivity to greatness, not in those who perform great deeds and great speeches, that is, in the political actors themselves, but in those who as spectators observe them and who are twice removed from the life-process, it is precisely because taste judges in works of art, great speeches, and great deeds nothing other than the world itself as the space that we have in common and that appears through them. The spectatorship involved in taste or judgment is not a withdrawal into self. Indeed, the spectator is, as Kant puts it, a *Weltbetrachter*; in spite of his or her disengagement, or because of it, the spectator is in a position to relate to the world that manifests itself through the actions of the actors.[83] Spectatorship is the condition for bringing the world that is at stake in all appearance into full focus and appraising it judiciously. The judgment of taste is an eminently political activity because it concerns the worldliness brought about either by things that shine forth into the public openness or by the glory of the words and deeds that shine out in the space of appearance. Taste as a form of judgment not only gauges the worldliness of the world but also actively contributes in judging what it should look like. What Arendt here suggests with respect to judgment hints at a new, if not singular, conception of this power of the mind. Indeed, the judgment of taste understood as having a political function serves to highlight the phenomenal and worldly character of whatever makes an act of appearance in the world and, by appearing, solidifies the world in its worldliness. As a political activity, the judgment of taste critically assesses the world. It judges whether the world meets one's expectations concerning what it is supposed to look like.

Arendt relentlessly reminds us that the need to judge works of art, words, and deeds requires a certain distance and a withdrawal from the creative production of artworks and (more controversially) from words and actions in the public space. Arendt insists, especially in her commentary on Kant's elaborations on the French Revolution, that the meaning of the whole event cannot be established without the judge's withdrawal. Arendt scholarship has repeatedly taken critical issue with Arendt's separation of the actor from the spectator. Let me only point out that, defined as appearances, the actors' great verbal performances and actions in the in-between of the space of appearance that is the public world invite judgment by others. In order to perform such judgments, they must be disengaged from the action. Now, if the world as a *spatial* in-between in which newcomers can, by virtue of their natality, that is, their *temporal* characteristic, make an appearance through their particular words and deeds, it is only because, in the medium of plurality that is the world as a public place, they relate to others only inasmuch as they are spatially distant from them.[84] But this in-between, as a space of solidarity between the space and time of the human being's *inter-esse*, also contains the possibility, and necessity, of the distance required by spectatorship. Occurring in a space of appearance, that which shows itself must be able to be beheld and judged, and such beholding and judgment can only be achieved if there is a sufficient distance. Yet, if the in-between contains the possibility of the necessary distance required by spectatorship, then the spectator, in spite of his or her seemingly transcendent position, ultimately remains immanent to the world he or she judges. It is only within the world that he or she judges as whole and that he or she appears to others as being aloof.

Let us keep in mind that the main forms of appearance that make up the public and political realm are, according to Arendt, words and deeds. They are to be seen or heard; that is, both demand a judgment as a response from the spectator. Both are also the articulation of opinions, seen either in their expression in words or in their actualization through deeds. To say that both are a function of opinions is to say, as Arendt puts it in "Truth and Politics," that they rest on convictions that are the result of an intersubjective exchange between human beings in the public and political realm. Rather than a privately held view, what is called opinion here is from the start a product of human discursive interaction in the in-between of the world as a public and political world. But these public opinions, in the same way as private opinions, are not demonstrable truths. Arendt also writes: "No opinion is self-evident." Yet, as she remarks, "[i]n matters of opinion, but not in matters of truth, our thinking is truly discursive, running, as it were, from place to place, from one part of the world to another, through all kinds of conflicting views, until it finally ascends from these particularities to some impartial generality."[85] In the course of such a discursive process, "a particular issue is forced into the open that it may show itself from all sides, in every possible perspective, until it is flooded and made transparent by the full light of human comprehension."[86] Notwithstanding this discursive process, an opinion about something never acquires the self-evidence of rational truth. For this reason, philosophy holds such discursive formation of opinions, or their articulation through deeds to be seen and heard by all, to be unworthy of consideration.

Let us bear in mind that the Greek term *doxa* does not only mean 'opinion,' as it is commonly translated. Arendt writes: "The word *doxa* means not only opinion but also splendor and fame. As such, it is related to the political realm, which is the public sphere in which everybody can appear and show who he himself is."[87] In her commentary in *Lectures on Kant's Political Philosophy* on Pythagoras's purported statement that life is like a festival and, "'just as some come to the festival to compete, some to ply their trade, but the best people come as spectators [*theatai*], so in life the slavish men go hunting for fame [*doxa*] or gain, the philosophers for truth,'" Arendt notes that the spectator remains impartial in order to judge the spectacle, whereas the actor in the game "is concerned with [. . .] *doxa*, fame—that is, the opinion of others (the word *doxa* means both 'fame' and 'opinion'). Fame comes about through the opinion of others. For the actor, the decisive question is thus how he appears to others (*dokei hois allois*)," who observe and judge his performance.[88] Fame is thus constituted by the opinion that others have qua spectators about the appearance of an actor's words and deeds in the public space. As Arendt notes, "the word *doxa*, unlike our word 'opinion,' has the strong connotation of the visible."[89] Qua fame, *doxa* concerns the public eminence that the judging spectators in the public domain bestow on an actor's performance; qua opinion, *doxa* designates the way the actor's actions look to the spectators. In other words, it designates the judges' verbal expression concerning the way in which the actor's actions appear to them.

But to express opinions is also a way of showing oneself to others in the public and political space of appearance. Arendt does not tire of recalling that *doxa* is "the formulation in speech of what *dokei moi*, that is, 'of what appears to me,'" or of "the it-seems-to-me."[90] She writes that expressing an opinion is itself an instance of "the desire to seem to others."[91] For the Greeks, in particular, the "great privilege attached to public life and lacking in the privacy of the household" consisted in the ability to show oneself, to be seen and heard by others, in asserting one's own opinion.[92] For Arendt, "[s]eeming—the it-seems-to-me, *dokei moi*—is the mode, perhaps the only possible one, in which an appearing world is acknowledged and perceived."[93] One has a world only as an opinion, that is, as something that seems-to-oneself and that one expresses publicly to others. Opinions are the public expressions of how the world appears to a singular citizen of the polis. "Every man has his own *doxa*, his own opening to the world," Arendt claims.[94] On the assumption "that the world opens up differently to every man according to his position in it," the Greek citizen, by expressing in public his opinion, shows to others "the world 'as it opens itself to [him].'"[95] Such opinion is nothing private. On the contrary, it is "part and parcel of the political reality [the citizen] lives in."[96]

Let me briefly return here to the question of natality. According to Arendt, each human is a newcomer in the world by virtue of birth. It follows that "nobody is ever the same as anyone else who ever lived, lives, or will live."[97] As I pointed out already, natality is not a biological category; nor is death. In *The Human Condition*, Arendt observes that

> Nature and the cyclical movement into which she forces all living things know neither birth nor death as we understand them. The birth and death of human beings are not simple natural occurrences, but are related to a world into which single individuals, unique, unexchangeable, and unrepeatable entities, appear and from which they depart. Birth and death presuppose a world which is not in constant movement, but whose durability and relative permanence makes appearance and disappearance possible, which existed before any one individual appeared into it and will survive his eventual departure. Without a world into which men are born and from which they die, there would be nothing but changeless eternal recurrence, the deathless everlastingness of the human as of all other animal species.[98]

Natality not only makes every human being a new appearance in the world; it is also what distinguishes the human being from being just another member of the species 'human beings.' Natality also endows each human with the possibility of being a new beginning in a plural world. If birth and death, growth and decay, are for Arendt neither categories (that is, structures of objective comprehension of the human being) nor existentialia (that is, structures of the comprehension of Being in the Heideggerian sense) but rather structures that concern the event of appearance of a new stranger by virtue of his or her birth into the world, it is because natality concerns the appearance of the human being in the world. As the public space for the free interaction of human beings with one another, the world is to be distinguished from the spheres of labor and, to some extent, of work. Yet, if natality is a political category that determines life in the public domain (i.e., life as action), it is not only because the newcomer is always born into a preexisting world but also precisely because he or she comes into this world as the potential beginning of a new world. For every human being who appears in the world, the world opens up in a different way. The world seems to him or her in a way that is always essentially distinct from the world of all of his or her contemporaries. In short, each human being comes into the world with his or her specific *doxa* as the singular way that the world appears only to him or her.

As should be clear from the preceding developments, Arendt's political philosophy is based on a formidable rebuttal of what she calls "Plato's furious denunciation of *doxa*, opinion."[99] This denunciation, which "not only runs like a red thread through his political works but became one of the cornerstones of his concept of truth," is the result of Plato's understanding of truth as the very opposite of opinion.[100] It is in the name of absolute standards (the immutable ideas) beheld in the solitary and thinking dialogue, in the two-in-one, of the philosopher that Plato despised opinions as the ever-changing, articulated expressions in public talk by the many of the *dokei moi*, the it-seems-to-me. In his condemnation of opinion, Plato does not stand alone. Ever since Heraclitus and Parmenides, the opinions of the many have been characterized by philosophers as the thoughts of mortals, in fact, as mortal thoughts that do not hold up to a philosophical knowledge that vies with divine knowledge. Philosophical knowledge originates in *thaumadzein*, that is, the pathos of wonder. By contrast, opinion, as Arendt notes in her essay "Socrates," is rooted in "*doxadzein*, in forming opinions on matters about which man cannot hold opinions because the common and commonly accepted standards of common sense do not here apply."[101] Consequently, there is no compatibility between *doxa* and truth. Arendt speaks even of "[t]he abyss between truth and opinion."[102] If *doxadzein* is indeed the opposite of and incompatible with *thaumadzein*, it is because it consists in forming opinions on matters that one knows only in speechless wonder and amounts to a refusal to endure the pathos of wonder. But Plato's condemnation of *doxa* is not restricted to denouncing its incommensurability to what can only be beheld in philosophical wonder. Constituted by the discursive interactions of the many in the public and political domain, *doxa* is condemned together with this domain that, fleeting and ever-changing, allows only for passing illusions rather than for absolute standards, or truth. Truth, therefore, can also destroy *doxa*. It can, as Arendt puts it, "destroy the specific political reality of the citizens."[103] It is against this Platonic heritage, which has, with few exceptions, shaped political philosophy in the West, that Arendt proceeds to a rehabilitation of *doxa* and, in the same breath, of the public and political domain. One can gauge the radicalness of Arendt's attempt to restore the public domain on the basis of her statement that, with the exception of factual truth, truth in an emphatic sense has no place in it. She writes that "[t]o look upon politics from the perspective of truth," that is, from the perspective of the theoretical, "means to take one's stand outside the political realm."[104] Although Arendt contends that "[w]ith Aristotle the time begins when philosophers no longer feel responsible for the city," the extent to which Aristotle's writings, particularly the *Nicomachean Ethics*, have provided the model for Arendt's rediscovery and recovery of the political world as a space of appearing will also become clear in what follows.[105]

Why does this space and everything that manifests itself within it as the open (such as words and deeds) call forth not syllogistic judgment but a kind of judgment attuned to the political sphere itself, that is, political judgment? Undoubtedly, if the realm of the public and political is constituted by appearances and the opinions that express how the world seems to oneself, judgment as a discriminating action within the realm in question concerns the appearances' correspondence to the realm of the public interchange between human beings. Do they make the world look as the citizens desire it to look? Yet, since appearances are also singular openings onto the world, political judgments are also about the world itself that shines out through them. And, finally, since all appearances in the public political space of appearing are manifestations by the newcomers that are the human beings born into this world, judgment will also appraise in a discriminatory fashion whether or not appearances are indeed new beginnings, in short, actions in a strict sense. Do they show a novel look of how the world is supposed to look? Aiming through judgment to respond to these questions raised by what appears and shines forth in seeming in the public and political domain, Arendt clearly puts into place a boldly new concept of judgment. It is a concept of judgment that is predicated on appearance. Rather than seeking to discriminate against appearance, it commands respect for it. Though thoroughly different from determinate judgment, this novel concept of judgment is not, therefore, identical with what Kant calls reflective judgment. Yet, Kant's elaborations on reflective judgment, especially with regard to beautiful objects, are for Arendt the starting point for an attempt to develop a concept of judgment that alone merits that name.

Before embarking on an examination of the way in which Arendt, on the basis of a reading of Kant's *Critique of the Power of Judgment*, develops a notion of judgment that is coextensive with the domain of appearance and appearing, that is, the public and political space of human life to which Western thought since Plato has basically been oblivious, if not even outright hostile, let us remind ourselves that this is a concept of judgment required by the fact that the "expressiveness of an appearance [. . .] 'expresses' nothing but itself." For judging appearances thus understood, "our habitual standards of judgment, so firmly rooted in metaphysical assumptions and prejudices—according to which the essential lies beneath the surface, and the surface is 'superficial'"— are inadequate.[106] Furthermore, in her last unfinished work, she also notes, undoubtedly with Heidegger in mind, that she has "clearly joined the ranks of those who for some time now have been attempting to dismantle metaphysics, and philosophy with all its categories, as we have known them from their beginning in Greece until today."[107] Differently worded, Arendt's search for a concept of judgment appropriate to the sphere of appearance requires the dismantling of the whole philosophical tradition. However, Arendt is not (as in the case of Heidegger) returning to a forgotten origin of thought in order to recover a more fundamental way of thinking.[108] In dismantling philosophy as a mode of thought forgetful of the political, Arendt seeks to retrieve a forgotten sense of the political in which the latter is no longer a narrow and specialized activity within the public sphere but coextensive with it, that is, a concept of the political that largely dominated public life in ancient Greece. There is nothing nostalgic about Arendt's gesture; nor is there any misplaced hope that one could ever return to the life of the polis. Jacques Taminiaux has strongly argued that reservations regarding the Greek conceptions of the political actually lead Arendt to a more advantageous view of Rome than of Athens.[109] Paul Ricœur, for one, opposes the suspicion of an alleged nostalgia for Greece with "a thought of resistance [on Arendt's part], in the double sense of political and philosophical resistance."[110] In any event, suffice it here to mention only her extensive, critical remarks in *The Human Condition* concerning the enormous price at which the freedom of citizens was accomplished in the Greek polis: the exclusion of labor from the condition of man's life, the constriction of women to the private household, and, more generally, slavery.[111] The fact that the Greeks called upon foreign legislators, or *nomethetai*, to draft or revise the laws of the *poleis* because, for them, such activity was of the order of making, or fabrication, amounts to a rather narrow conception of political action.[112] Finally, notwithstanding the excellency of the *eu prattein*, that is, of the political activity through which the Greeks distinguished themselves from the barbarians, one must also mention the constant threat of the polis's self-destruction due to the agonal spirit of *praxis* that consisted of "an intense and uninterrupted contest of all against all, of *aei aristeuein*, ceaselessly showing oneself to be the best of all," which eventually brought the city-states to ruin.[113] Notwithstanding the shortcomings of life in the polis, the Greek polis, according to Arendt, "will continue to exist at the bottom of our political existence—that is, at the bottom of the sea—for as long as we use the word 'politics.'"[114] Indeed, the Greek conception of *politeia*, and especially its grounding conception of *isonomia*, is for her the inevitable point of departure for any reflection on the political, including judgment as the political activity par excellence, which, of course, does not imply underwriting in a wholesale fashion the concrete form that this conception took. Yet, for a short period a public space opened up there in which free citizens' actions and speeches not only concerned the well-being of the polis but also primarily secured that very public space itself. However limited and short-lived the polis was, and in spite of the historico-social conditions under which political activity became possible for the limited number of Athenian citizens, this still remains the starting point for the critical consideration of the nature of the political for Arendt. The institution of a public space that is its own end—an institution based on deliberation and judgment in the marketplace—lives on as an idea through which any elaboration on politics today, especially in extreme conditions, must be conducted.

8
THE WIND OF THOUGHT

THE CONCERN WITH the power of judgment arises in Hannah Arendt's work in response to critical events in modernity. As a result of the impotence of familiar standards and categories to provide answers and orientation, this power has become undone. It is a question not only of the impotence of the common standards regarding certain events of modernity but also of the fact that these events have been so terrifying that they have altogether destroyed all our habitual categories of thought and standards of judgment. Yet, as Arendt remarks in 1953 in "Understanding and Politics (The Difficulties of Understanding)," that is, two years after the publication of her work on totalitarianism, "[e]ven though we have lost yardsticks by which to measure, and rules under which to subsume the particular, a being whose essence is beginning may have enough of origin within himself to understand without preconceived categories and to judge without the set of customary rules which is morality."[1] The possibility of judgment is thus intrinsically rooted in the natality of the human being that appears in the world as the space of appearances and as an always-new beginning. By virtue of the "origin within himself," that is, by virtue of the human being's "essence [that] is beginning," the human being is capable of making judgments in the absence of any standard. Such judgments, above all, concern the conformity of the world and what happens within it to "the *original* character of man."[2] As a result, these judgments must also be of a rather different kind than what is usually called a judgment.

Arendt broaches the crisis of understanding and judgment in 1953, writing that "the rise of totalitarian governments is the central event of our world."[3] However, it is only as a result of her reading (or, perhaps, re-reading) of Kant's *Critique of the Power of Judgment* in 1957 that she explicitly begins to develop a political concept of judgment that would be up to the challenge of such events as defy both common sense and cognitive understanding. In a letter to Karl Jaspers from August 29, 1957, she writes:

> At the moment I'm reading the *Kritik der Urteilskraft* with increasing fascination. There, and not in the *Kritik der praktischen Vernunft*, is where Kant's real political philosophy is hidden. His praise for "common sense," which is so often scorned; the phenomenon of taste taken seriously as the basic phenomenon of judgment [...]; the "expanded mode of thought" that is part and parcel of judgment, so that one can think from someone else's point of view. The demand for communicativeness. [...] I've always loved this book most of Kant's critiques, but it has never before spoken to me as powerfully as it does now that I have read your Kant chapter.[4]

Indeed, as is evident from an entry in her *Denktagebuch* from August 1957 on her reading of the section on Kant in Jaspers's *Die grossen Philosophen*, Arendt's ensuing reading of the Third Critique is to a large extent preprogrammed by certain points highlighted in Jaspers's work. After having noted that "judging [is] the impossibility to subsume the individual" and that "[t]he individual can only be encountered [*getroffen*], or missed, in a judgment," Arendt cites Jaspers: "'We are in the possession of the experience of something particular and we conceive of it by assuming something universal that is not known to us.'" Arendt adds that such a judgment "stands in opposition to subsumption," where "we take our starting point in a known universal, or in the determining power of judgment."[5] It is from Jaspers's reading of the Third Critique that Arendt derives the fundamental difference she makes between, on the one hand, judgment *tout court* (i.e., the forming of a decision in aesthetic reflective and political judgment) and determinant judgment as the subsumption of a particular under a given universal.

Even though the problematics of judgment had imposed themselves on Arendt in an earlier attempt to come to grips with modernity, her explicit reflections on judgment and the faculty of judgment are indissociable from her interpretative appropriation of Kant's conception of judgment as a distinct faculty. In the process of measuring herself critically up against this conception, she also progressively takes issue with the elements that constitute a judgment of taste in distinction from a cognitive judgment. A case in point is Arendt's uncompleted manuscript of "Introduction into Politics" where, sometime between 1957 and 1958, she writes that in the political arena "we cannot function at all without judging in general [*Urteilen überhaupt*], because political thought is essentially based in the power of judgment [*Urteilskraft*]."[6] These posthumously published fragments of the "Introduction" do not further elaborate the assertion that political thought is "essentially based in the power of judgment." However, they show the extent to which Arendt's attempt to link political thought to the capacity of judgment presumes a debate with Kant's *Critique of Judgment*. From the mid-fifties to the time of her death, which prevented her from completing the third and concluding part of *The Life of the*

Mind on judgment, Arendt's reflections on the political are consistently involved in an effort to make Kant's understanding of reflective judgment fruitful for a theory of politics. However, I claim that it is never Arendt's intention to provide a philologically correct reading of Kant's Third Critique. From the start, she has a certain conception of political judgment, and her aim is to find elements that would help her develop this concept philosophically. After all, she characterizes Kant as the sole exception in a tradition of political philosophy that follows Plato's condemnation of the public realm and politics.

From early on, Arendt scholars have addressed her concern with judgment and have critically taken issue with her provocative assertion that the "Critique of the Aesthetic Power of Judgment" contains a political philosophy, which Kant never explicitly developed.[7] They have also argued regularly over the thesis that Arendt's understanding of judgment evolves from an earlier period of her work, in which judgment is more intimately associated with action, to the later position in *The Life of the Mind*, in which judgment is framed by the contemplative nature of the mind.[8] More often than not, these two types of commentaries have put her reading of Kant flatly in question. Furthermore, Arendt's assertion that Kant is the first genuinely political philosopher since the Greeks inevitably drew the wrath of historians of philosophy, all the more so in that she locates the political thrust of his philosophy in his elaborations on aesthetic and reflective judgment. I do not intend to challenge these interpretations in any direct fashion. However, even though an examination of her reading of Kant easily distracts from her own original contribution to the problematics of judgment, I will not be able *entirely* to avoid critically scrutinizing Arendt's interpretations of some aspects of Kant's thought that she wishes to use in support of her own interpretation of what a judgment is. Indeed, I wish to make the point that Kant only provides Arendt with a conceptual toolbox for developing a theory of judgment distinctly her own.

On several occasions, Arendt has made the claim that she is not a philosopher. In a 1964 interview with Günter Gaus, she forcefully protests against her characterization as a philosopher and declares that her "profession, if one can even speak of it at all, is political theory. I neither feel like a philosopher, nor do I believe that I have been accepted in the circle of philosophers."[9] These declarations have not always been taken as seriously as they should be. Undoubtedly, Arendt is a thinker. More precisely, she is a thinker of political theory.[10] Her denial of being a philosophical thinker is motivated not least of all by her imputation that philosophy has ignored the Greek experience of the polis and has remained blind to the preciously few insights into the political to be found within the tradition of philosophical thought itself. Indeed, if Western philosophical thought is rooted in the forgetting of the question of Being for

Heidegger, philosophical thought is constituted by its obliviousness to the political for Arendt. But her reservations regarding philosophy go further.

In "What Is Existential Philosophy?," Arendt remarks that Karl Jaspers, participating in the "revolt against philosophy with which modern philosophy began," attempted "to transform philosophy into philosophizing and to find ways by which philosophical 'results' can be communicated in such a way that they lose their character as results."[11] This remark tells us that, for Arendt, philosophical thought abides in the activity of thinking only if it resists the temptation of seeing philosophy as a means for producing results and definite answers to the grand questions of mankind. If she does not consider herself a philosopher, it is above all because what she calls "the wind of thought" does not blow in most of what is known as philosophy.[12]

Indeed, as I will argue hereafter, Arendt's accomplishment is to have intrinsically linked the problematics of judgment to the sphere of public life—a life that, with the Greeks, she understands as being political in its entirety rather than political merely in the sense of a specific and specialized activity within the sphere in question. Although Arendt's theory of judgment as a political activity was conceptually developed with the help of Kant's elaborations on the reflective aesthetic judgment, the theory is also a reactualization and further development of Aristotle's notion of *phronesis* (or prudence), that is, of a public virtue whose object is the contingent concern with the well-being of the human being as opposed to the Good in general. As Pierre Aubenque has convincingly shown, Aristotle's understanding of *phronesis* rehabilitates (against the Platonic usage of the term in reference to *episteme*) its vulgar, popular, and prephilosophical meaning. In the same breath, Aristotle revalorizes the public and political sphere of human life.[13] Arendt not only reads Kant's Third Critique alongside the insights of Aristotle's *Nicomachean Ethics*, modeling her conception of judgment as the political activity par excellence on Aristotle's conception of *phronesis*; in a way similar to Aristotle, she also associates judgment with the activity of the human being in the public sphere, grounding it in what she will call along with Kant, although in a different sense, a *sensus communis* and thus distinguishing it radically from philosophy's concern with truth.

In order to substantiate this point, I intend to focus on one Kantian distinction in particular, namely, the difference between determinant and aesthetic reflective judgment. Indeed, Arendt lingers on this distinction primarily in order to argue that solely aesthetic judgment is a genuine judgment and an instance of the power of judgment and, further, that the judgment of taste alone paves the way for a political conception of judgment. Only the judgment of taste offers, according to Arendt, a type of judgment indicative of the free judgment needed in order to set the space of appearance constitutive of the public and political domain radically apart not only from the spheres of labor and work but also from political and public spaces characterized by violence. Solely a judgment that is free from the constraints that bear on a determinate judgment has the capability of discriminating within the space of appearances between those that are right or wrong.

At this point, then, it might be appropriate to turn to the *Lectures on Kant's Political Philosophy* from 1970, where Arendt works out her political concept of judgment in the most explicit and painstaking way. First, however, I wish to consider Arendt's unfinished work *The Life of the Mind*. True, she was unable to write the third part of this work, which was supposed to deal with judgment. But, for our purposes, the first part on "Thinking" provides a number of insights and developments that are crucial to understanding some of Arendt's presuppositions concerning judgment. In addition, even though this work is more philosophical than political, the remarks on judgment in the part on "Thinking" make it possible to see the contours within which to situate her theory of judgment philosophically. These developments give us further indication of the direction that Arendt might have taken in the unwritten third part on "Judgment."

There has been a lot of speculation on what that third part, had it been completed, would have looked like. Ronald Beiner, in particular, has argued that the "Postscriptum" to the part on "Thinking" clearly indicates that Arendt's *Lectures on Kant's Political Philosophy* from 1970 "reflect the full intended structure of the section on 'Judging.'"[14] There is much to be said for Beiner's assessment. However, in addition to the fact that Arendt introduces a number of new insights concerning the activity of judgment in the section on "Thinking," Beiner is also neglecting the fact that, while setting foot outside the political, her treatment of the faculty of judgment would probably no longer have been dominated by her earlier interpretation of this activity as the most political one.[15] Indeed, according to Elisabeth Young-Bruehl, "when she began to work on *The Life of the Mind* Arendt said that she was returning to her 'first amour,' philosophy."[16] Undoubtedly, in distinction from the activities of labor, work, and action, which characterize the first mode of human plurality, that is, being with others, the three invisible faculties under investigation in this work—thinking, willing, and judging—not only concern "the second mode of human plurality, being together with one's self" in inward dialogue; these activities, which take place in what Arendt characterizes as the 'two-in-One,' also continue to entertain a certain relation to the realm of appearances.[17] Even though the invisible activities of the mind take place in a withdrawal from the world of appearances, these activities must, as Jacques Taminiaux remarks, express themselves, and be it, in silent speech. Language is what keeps the mind alive. And in this way, the mind is essentially linked to the world of appearances. Certainly, the invisibility of the life of the mind implies a withdrawal from the world of appearances, but such a retreat is in no way a rupture with appearances. Language from which the life of the mind lives is witness of the persistence of this link with the appearances.[18]

However, whereas the faculties of the mind discussed in *The Human Condition* are all active faculties, the activities at issue in *The Life of the Mind* are "human non-active [*nicht-tätigen*] activities."[19] Consequently, judging is no longer practically involved in the political process, as it was in her previous work. Even though in *The Life of the Mind* Arendt no longer construes judgment as the activity par excellence in the public and political space of appearances and appearing, characterizing it as non-active activity, some of the more philosophically oriented elaborations on judgment are nonetheless helpful in an effort to understand better the specificity and distinctness of this faculty, as well as its link to other activities of the mind.

As Arendt argues in her last work, by setting reason (*Vernunft*) apart from the intellect (*Verstand*), Kant made a distinction between "two altogether different mental faculties, thinking and knowing, and two altogether different concerns, meaning, in the first category, and cognition, in the second."[20] Yet, Kant himself, she claims, never pursued the implications of his own thought and thus remained "less than fully aware" of what he had actually accomplished by separating thinking from cognition.[21] According to Arendt, by restricting reason's reflection to the traditional subject matter of what cannot be known (i.e., to the ultimate questions about God, soul, and immortality), Kant showed that he did not realize "the extent to which he had liberated reason, the ability to think," and that, instead of having made room for faith (as he believed), "he had [in truth] made room for thought."[22] Thinking and reason are *not* concerned with what the intellect is concerned with, and the range of thought is also much broader than that of the ultimate questions.

In addition to claiming that Kant did not follow up on the radical implications of his distinction between cognition and thinking, that there is no such "clear-cut line of demarcation between these altogether different modes [to] be found" in the whole of the history of philosophy, and, hence, that Kant's understanding of thinking is something completely new—if not even in a complete rupture with philosophical thought itself—Arendt also expands Kant's characterization of thought as the thinking of what cannot be known in order to suggest that thought raises questions that are entirely unanswerable in any cognitive sense.[23] Citing Kant's statement that "concepts of reason serve us to conceive [*begreifen*, to comprehend], as concepts of the intellect serve us to apprehend [*Verstehen*, to understand] perceptions," Arendt argues that the objective of thinking is to glean the meaning, rather than the truth, of what is given.[24] Yet, whereas all the questions raised by our desire to know are in principle answerable, "the question raised by thinking and which it is in reason's very nature to raise—questions of meaning—are all unanswerable by common sense and the refinement of it we call science."[25] Arendt adds that "the quest for meaning is 'meaningless' to common sense and common-sense reasoning."[26] We will thus have to look more closely at what Arendt herself calls thinking, that is, a faculty and mental activity that has been liberated completely from the cognitive, and to probe into what necessitates such a clear-cut distinction. Withdrawal from the world of appearances (spectatorship), the 'two-in-One' in soundless dialogue with oneself, the imagination's gift of de-sensualization, and the invisibility of thought's objects are the conditions under which the invisible activity of thinking as an activity that has its end in itself can take place.[27] Let us ask: In what does this thinking consist?

For Arendt, Socrates's example above all is significant here. Neither a philosopher nor a sophist, "Socrates, gadfly, midwife, [and] electric ray," aroused people to examine their prejudgments, made them think, purging them of their 'opinions.'[28] She writes: "It is in this invisible element's nature [that is thinking] to undo, unfreeze, as it were, what language, the medium of thinking, has frozen into thought—words (concepts, sentences, definitions, doctrines)."[29] Consequently, "thinking inevitably has a destructive, undermining effect on all established criteria, values, measurements of good and evil, in short, on those customs and rules of conduct we treat of in morals and ethics."[30] Furthermore, this destructive effect of thinking is not only subversive, as the Athenians told Socrates; it also has a paralyzing effect in that, like a hurricane, it sweeps away all the established signs by which men orient themselves. It is for this reason that Arendt compares thinking to a wind—"the wind of thought"—that blows away all thought-constructions that have been arrested and turned into customary moral forms or indelible truths through language. This striking poetic expression of thought as a wind, which Arendt considers to be inevitable because of the immateriality and invisibility of the mental activity in question, points at something essential in regard to thought.[31] It is as if Arendt were saying, think of the wind, its swiftness, and destructive onslaughts, and then you will know what it means to think.

In the section on "Thinking" in *The Life of the Mind*, she writes: "Psychologically speaking, one of the outstanding characteristics of thought is its incomparable *swiftness*—'swift as a thought,' said Homer, and Kant in his early writings speaks repeatedly of the *Hurtigkeit des Gedankens*. Thought is swift, clearly, because it is immaterial."[32] Arendt invokes *The Iliad* for its metaphorical potential for expressing "the combined onslaught of winds from several directions on the waters of the sea."[33] First of all, the expression, "the wind of thought," is a metaphor that Socrates himself used to explain thinking's ability to deal with invisibles. According to Xenophon, Socrates, "aware that he was dealing with invisibles in his enterprise," said that "'[t]he winds themselves are invisible, yet what they do is manifest to us and we somehow feel their approach.'"[34] As Arendt points out, the same image of "'wind-swift thought'" is to be found in Sophocles's *Antigone* and in Heidegger, who occasionally refers to the "'storm of thought.'"[35] When, in *What Is Called Thinking?*, Heidegger speaks directly of Socrates, he emphasizes that "'[t]hroughout his life and up to his very death Socrates did nothing other than place himself in this draft, this current [of thinking], and maintain himself in it.'"[36] Indeed, this invisible wind of thought was manifest, Arendt remarks, not only "in the concepts, virtues, and 'values' with which Socrates dealt in his examinations" but also and especially in the undoing of these invisible concepts, virtues, or values at the very moment they froze into guidelines for orientation.[37] Arendt writes: "If what you were doing consisted in applying general rules of conduct to particular cases as they arise in ordinary life, you will find yourself paralyzed because no such rules can withstand the wind of thought."[38] This wind of thought, which does not let anything stand unquestioned, not even "its own previous manifestations," ultimately makes thinking an autonomous faculty whose activity is an end in itself.[39] Indeed, according to one of Aristotle's remarks in *Meteorology*, of which Arendt seems to have been unaware, certain painters represent the winds as "drawing their source from themselves," or as "self originating."[40] In the same fashion, the winds of thought unleash their destructive effects from within themselves, thus making thought into a fully autonomous activity. When thought is enacted for its own sake and when it is its own end, that is, when liberated from cognition, all the habitual standards for orientation in the world that are frozen thoughts become unfrozen and, in short, put into question again. Not unlike the movements of the wind that, according to Hegel, agitate the waters of the sea and thus prevent stagnation and putrefaction, the movements of the wind of thought also prevent thought from inertia.[41]

If Kant liberated reason and "justified this faculty and its activity even though they could not boast of any 'positive' results," the question of how the destructive wind of thought is involved in thinking's concern with meaning arises.[42] Does this wind not simply blow all possible meaning away? As Arendt remarks, "[t]he quest for meaning [. . .] relentlessly dissolves and examines anew all accepted doctrines and rules."[43] No definite answers emerge from the activity of thought, and thus the quest for meaning never comes to a term.

Yet, this thinking's quest is not only intimately linked to unfreezing thought and rekindling its critical power; it also follows that thinking's critical activity itself gives meaning to life and that such a life, which relentlessly dissolves any determined answers to the question of meaning, is the very answer to the quest for meaning (*Sinn*). As Arendt notes, Socrates's resistance to letting critical examination come to a rest in a positive result was based on his conviction that "an unexamined life is not worth living."[44]

At this juncture, let us remind ourselves that, in *The Life of the Mind*, Arendt argues not only for the autonomy of the faculty of thinking but also for the autonomy of willing and judging. Arendt insists on the full independence of all these mental faculties, and this assertion raises an additional issue: the interaction of these basic mental activities. This issue is not to be found in the same way in Arendt's lectures on Kant. If Arendt qualifies these activities as "basic," it is "because they are autonomous; each of them obeys the laws inherent in the activity itself."[45] Their autonomy is a further indication of their intrinsic plurality. In addition, "[t]he autonomy of mental activities [. . .] implies their being unconditioned; none of the conditions of either life or the world corresponds to them directly."[46] Finally, "the three basic mental activities [. . .] cannot be derived from each other and though they have certain common characteristics they cannot be reduced to a common denominator."[47]

In the following reflections, I will only be concerned with the interrelation of thinking and judging. A detailed examination of how the will is linked to the autonomous faculty of thinking must be reserved for another occasion. Furthermore, such an analysis would have to take Heidegger's critique of the will in his Nietzsche lectures on the metaphysics of subjectivity into systematic account. Let me only briefly remark here that, according to Arendt, the will, which is the only human faculty that is self-creating and by which the self becomes its own foundation independently of all other selves, is in Michael Denneny's words driven by an "ultimately murderous dialectic" that leads, politically, to totalitarianism and, morally, to an ethics in which values are the arbitrary products of the will.[48] However one conceives of the way in which the will relates to thinking, if one wishes to avoid the effects of the will thus understood, "then the faculty of taste (judgment), which attunes us to relations between men and between men and appearance," is necessarily "the only alternative to the will."[49] In any event, in spite of what Arendt asserts with regard to the autonomy of judgment, she also suggests from the start that "the ability to tell right from wrong," in short, the ability to judge, is linked to the ability to think, that is, to the destructive wind of thought, the quest for meaning or, more precisely, for a life of unrelenting critical vigilance.[50] Indeed, although it is never caught up in thinking's reflections, Arendt expressly says in a passing remark that judgment, in the same way as willing, is "*dependent* on thought's preliminary reflections on their objects."[51] But how are we to conceive of this dependence?

Even though thinking requires a withdrawal from the world, thinking is by virtue of its "purging component [. . .] political by implication."[52] Indeed, she adds that "this destruction has a liberating effect on another faculty, the faculty of judgment, which one may call with some reason the most political of man's mental abilities. It is the faculty that judges *particulars* without subsuming them under general rules which can be taught and learned until they grow into habits that can be replaced by other habits and rules."[53] The ability to say "this is wrong" or "this is beautiful" is certainly not the same as the faculty of thinking, for "[t]hinking deals with invisibles, with representations of things that are absent," whereas "judging always concerns particulars and things close at hand." But, Arendt claims, "the two are interrelated."[54] Thinking deals with invisibles, but judgment concerns appearances that shine forth in the light of the public and political space in order to be heard and seen. Thinking operates in an invisible space and undoes all the universals that have become frozen thoughts, and judging adjudicates on particulars in sense experience. However, before we offer specifics on the interrelation of the two autonomous mental activities, some remarks on Arendt's conception of judgment in *The Life of the Mind* are warranted.

As is obvious from Arendt's characterization of judgment, her theory of judgment as a power that is freed by the purging component of thinking is predicated entirely on a reading of the Third Critique. She contends that "Kant was the first, and has remained the last, of the great philosophers to deal with judgment as one of the basic mental activities."[55] Indeed, in the "Postscriptum" to *Thinking*, the first part of *The Life of the Mind*, Arendt contends that "[n]ot till Kant's *Critique of Judgment* did this faculty [of judgment] become a major topic of a major thinker."[56] In her own translation of "The Crisis of Culture" into German, she goes so far as to suggest that Kant is, in fact, the first to discover the power of judgment. She claims that Kant "discovered [the power of judgment] in all its grandeur precisely when he came upon the phenomenon of taste and the judgment of taste."[57] Even though one could argue that the concern with judgment makes up almost all of philosophy, it is also true that judgment as a faculty has not received as much attention in the philosophical tradition as other faculties, such as thinking, reason, or the will. Kant provided the most specific determination of this power of the mind. Arendt's statements are nonetheless a bit startling if one thinks of Aristotle's definition of the syllogism, the venerable Ciceronian rhetorical concepts of *inventio* and *iudicium* (which, moreover, can be seen as the model for Kant's distinction between determining and reflective judgment), or the reflections on taste that span from Baltasar Gracián (who coined the word 'taste') through the Earl of Shaftesbury and Alexander Gottfried Baumgarten to Georg Friedrich Meier. The reasons for Arendt's seemingly hyperbolic statements regarding Kant as the discoverer of the faculty of judgment begin to come into view when, in the *Lectures on Kant's Political Philosophy*, she submits that "*behind* taste, a favorite topic of the whole eighteenth century, Kant had discovered an entirely new human faculty, namely, judgment."[58] In other words, if Kant was the first to discover judgment, it is insofar as he beheld a faculty in the back of taste that is not to be confused with the faculty of taste itself. Arendt is, of course, right to suggest that the judgment of taste is not the power of judgment itself. Indeed, Kant's critical investigation into the power of judgment does not proceed in a direct way by thematizing this power itself or as such. On the contrary, he elucidates the power in question by way of examples, particularly, by the judgment of taste in all its specificity. Yet, if the judgment of taste is only one actualization of the power of judgment, however important, this power itself can, in a way, be said to be located behind it. But Arendt's point is also that Kant did not simply discover the power of judgment in general behind the faculty of taste. Rather, she claims that, by examining the judgment of taste, Kant unwittingly rediscovered behind it a faculty that philosophy had lost sight of since Aristotle's notion of *phronesis*. The ethical and political virtue in question is the ability to deliberate well about what choices or decisions (*prohairesis*) to make regarding the best means in the human being's power to accomplish a certain end in the public realm. Rather than an absolute, *prohairesis* is a relative choice that aims at the lesser evil in the realm of public affairs. In the same way in which the fundamental concept of *prohairesis*, which Aristotle developed in the context of his theory of *phronesis* by resorting to the popular usage of the term in clear distinction from the Socratic and Platonic conception of choice, remained without a follow-up in the history of philosophy, Kant's discovery of judgment as a political rather than cognitive activity also had no further consequences until, as Arendt intimates, she herself rediscovered Kant.[59] Now, it is important to note that for Arendt, who develops a theory of judgment that she qualifies as political on the basis of Kant's elaborations on aesthetic judgment without, however, confounding both or collapsing either, judgment has "nothing in common with logical operations" or the subsumption of a particular case under a given general concept.[60] As she understands it, in other words, judgment is clearly distinct from Kant's *determinant judgment*, which is opposed to what he terms 'reflective judgment' (whether of taste or of teleological judgment). Undoubtedly, the activity of judgment is characterized by the ability *to bring* together the universal and the particular, but there are two ways of accomplishing this linkage. One is a judgment in a strict sense, and the other is not. Arendt writes:

> Judgment, [...] the mysterious endowment of the mind by which the general, always a mental construction, and the particular, always given to sense experience, are *brought together*, is a "peculiar faculty" and in no way inherent in the intellect, not even in the case of "determinant judgments"—where particulars are subsumed under general rules in the form of a syllogism—because no rule is available for the *applications* of the rule.[61]

Without yet considering what the absence of a rule means for a judgment about particulars, let me only emphasize that, for Arendt, this absence is an indication of the fact that judgment is an autonomous ability, which is "more obvious in the case of 'reflective judgment,' which does not descend from the general to the particular but ascends 'from the particular [...] to the universal.'"[62] Only where there is such an ascension from the particular to a universal to be found does a decision take place "without any over-all rules" and thereby constitute a judgment that is truly one.[63] Only in this case can one also speak of a *modus operandi* that belongs specifically to judgment.

In the same way as she argues in *The Life of the Mind* that Kant liberated reason and thinking from the intellect and cognition, Arendt holds that, under the rubric of the judgment of taste, Kant accomplished a complete liberation of judgment from syllogistic logic, or determinant judgment. In fact, she holds that, by liberating thinking from cognition, Kant at the same time freed judgment from its cognitive yoke and, for the first time, recognized it as an autonomous faculty with a modus operandi of its own. To the extent that it gains its autonomy in the wake of thinking's emancipation from cognition, judging is thus "the by-product of the liberating effect of thinking."[64] More precisely, liberated in the process of thinking's own emancipation, judgment "realizes thinking, makes it manifest in the world of appearances, where I am never alone and always too busy to be able to think. The manifestation of the wind of thought is not knowledge; it is the ability to tell right from wrong, beautiful from ugly."[65] Judgment, then, is the manifestation of the wind of thought, its realization or actualization in the world of appearances. Judgment is not without the wind of thought that *pre*-cedes and *pre*-pares it (without, however, anticipating or *pre*-figuring it) by voiding all *pre*-established criteria or categories, all *pre*-judgments.

But such *pre*-ceding and *pre*-paration of judgment by thought is not of the order of a *pre*-supposition, that is, a homogeneous enabling condition put in advance of or underneath judgment. Judgment, therefore, remains an autonomous and an entirely spontaneous activity of the mind. It is not the wind of thought itself but only its manifestation, that is, its appearance in the realm of appearances. Judgment is not to be confounded with thought, whose realm, because thought moves among invisibles (universals, essences, etc.), is not the world of sensible appearances, which is also the realm of what Arendt calls action. In the same way as action, judgment always "deals with particulars, and only particular statements can be valid in the field of ethics or politics."[66] The autonomy of the mental form of action that is judgment requires that it be strictly about particulars, in other words, things for which no concepts under which to subsume them are given in advance. For Arendt, where concepts are given, the particular is no longer or not yet a particular.[67] Consequently, relating to the particular in a cognitive judgmental fashion would in Arendt's understanding not amount, strictly speaking, to making a judgment at all, if, indeed, judgment consists in finding a universal for a particular. As is the case with action, it would also be "a great mistake," Arendt avers, "to look for [. . .] universals in practical-political matters, which always concern particulars."[68]

Let me linger for a moment on this intrinsic connection of judgment to the particular. Besides its resonances with Kantian reflective judgment, this connection between judgment and the particular rests on Arendt's phenomenal understanding of the particular. As she repeatedly remarks, the particular is of the order of the sensible. It is something that offers itself to the senses (as opposed to the invisibles of thought). The particular is thus of the order of an appearance. Particularities are sensible appearances that erupt into view or make themselves heard, that arrive unexpectedly, bring a sense of novelty, and, therefore, manifest themselves as appearances par excellence. However, as appearances, particulars demand to be judged, with respect not only to whether the world they display is beautiful or ugly, good or evil, but also to whether or not they are a manifestation of a singular world in the first place. In the space of the in-between that constitutes the world for interacting human beings, such judgments of particulars require the withdrawal and disengagement of the judge as a spectator—the "definitely 'unnatural' and deliberate withdrawal from involvement and the partiality of immediate interests as they are given by [the spectator's] position in the world and the part [he or she] play[s] in it."[69] Although they evaluate the particular's actualization of a singular world, such judgments, as manifestations in the public space, are themselves appearances in the space of appearance that is the world and, as such, also always particular. As a judgment, the spectator's ultimate decision regarding the world-character of any particular deed or word, that is, regarding the extent to which it exemplarily realizes a world (a judgment that thus also concerns the world as a 'universal' itself), remains a finite judgment and infinitely calls to be critically put into question.

Thinking is a quest for meaning, a quest to find an answer to unanswerable questions, but it is also a quest that, because of the wind of thought, thinking itself makes forever unanswerable. Precisely by undoing everything that it itself has woven, the activity of thinking's critical investigation becomes a meaningful activity itself and an ultimate response to the quest for meaning. Arendt observes not only that thinking's search for meaning is "absent from and good for nothing in the ordinary course of human affairs," not only that "at the same time its results remain uncertain and unverifiable," but also that "thinking is also somehow self-destructive."[70] She adds:

> In the privacy of his posthumously published notes, Kant wrote: "I do not approve of the rule that if the use of pure reason has proved something, the result should no longer be subject to doubt, as though it were a solid axiom": and "I do not share the opinion ... that one should not doubt once one has convinced oneself of something. In pure philosophy this is impossible. *Our mind has a natural aversion to it*" (italics added). From which it follows that the business of thinking is like Penelope's web; it undoes every morning what it has finished the night before. For the need to think can never be stilled by allegedly definite insights of "wise men"; it can be satisfied only through thinking, and the thoughts I had yesterday will satisfy this need today only to the extent that I want and am able to think them anew.[71]

Let me return one more time to the relation between the wind of thought, which consists of weaving and subsequently unraveling such invisibles, and what Arendt understands by judgment. As a result of this wind, thought is liberated from cognition and loses all fixed standards, such as universals or essences. As a consequence, judgment, which achieves an autonomy of its own as a by-product of this liberation, necessarily becomes a faculty that must find a universal for the particulars upon which it is to decide. As the manifestation of the wind of thought, all "our habitual standards of judgment, so firmly rooted in metaphysical assumptions and prejudices," are dissolved, and judgment cannot fall back on them as givens.[72] It follows from this thoroughly critical and destructive accomplishment of thinking that judgment as Arendt understands it is a novel concept of judgment, which cannot be *directly* identified with anything in Kant himself. Kant might not have recognized himself in the lineaments of this conception of judgment. As we will see hereafter, reflective judgment is only the context in which she develops this new notion. Furthermore, the universal found by reflective judgment is not the same universal that a judgment in the gust of the wind of thought must find. A judgment that results from the wind of thought is not only a novel conception of judgment. A judgment that qua judgment necessarily deals with particulars, a judgment that, therefore, cannot fall back on any of the time-honored or metaphysical generalities swept away by the wind of thought, must always find, as if for the first time, the universal that allows one to bring the particular together with the universal and thus effectuate a judgment without a rule that one possesses in advance. Rather than an operation of subsuming, judgment is thus also intrinsically of the order of a finding and an activity of discriminating or deciding. If the judgment of taste stands as the model for this new conception of judgment, it is because the former is discriminatory in an immediate fashion and decisional from the start. Arendt writes that, "[p]ractically, thinking means that each time you are confronted with some difficulty in life you have to make up your mind anew."[73] Practically speaking, this means that, in judging particulars, every judgment must be performed as if it were the first and the last judgment. It is the first because the rule for it must first be found, and it is the last because, when confronted with another difficulty in life, one cannot simply fall back on this same rule.

Only by dismantling, in full exposure to the wind of thought, "our habitual standards of judging, so firmly rooted in metaphysical assumption and prejudices," can one expect to arrive at a conception of judgment that leaves the syllogistic mode entirely behind and in which the particular in its very irreducibility calls for judgment. Such a particular demands that a universal be found for its unique appearance, a universal marked by the event of its occurrence and the particular itself that calls for its discovery by a judgment tailored for it alone. Although Arendt herself does not use this term—she speaks of it as an 'exemplary' universal—I propose to call it, for the moment, a singular universal, an infinitely singular universal insofar as no pregiven universal can serve as a model for it.

9
A SENSE OF THE WORLD

FROM WHAT WE have seen so far, Arendt's theory of judgment sketches out a novel conception of a kind of mental activity that she holds Kant to have unwittingly discovered when he came across the judgment of taste. This kind of judgment, which lies behind the reflective judgment of taste and is not identical with it, concerns appearances. What Arendt calls appearances can be retraced to Kant's transcendental aesthetics, in which he elaborated on the a priori forms constitutive of phenomena of nature that are to be subsequently subsumed by the determinant judgment under the discursive conditions of cognition, that is, the categories of the understanding. Arendt suggests that, when Kant determined the two forms of intuition constitutive of appearances (namely space and time), he did not recognize that these forms are the experiential or cognitive phantom proxies of political categories, space referring to the public space of appearance and time to the spontaneity, uniqueness, or newness of each appearance within this space. It now remains to be seen how Arendt constructs a notion of judgment on the basis of Kant's elaborations on the reflective judgment of taste, whose exclusive objects, for her, are the appearances in social space and time (i.e., the particularities) that make up public and political activity and that it alone can adequately address.

In "Introduction into Politics," Arendt writes:

> In our use of language [that is, in German], the word "judgment" has two meanings that certainly ought to be differentiated but that always get confused whenever we speak. First of all, judgment means organizing and subsuming the individual and particular under the general and universal, that is, the orderly assessment [*das regelnde Messen mit Massstäben*] by applying standards to them, with respect to which the concrete has to identify itself, and which permit deciding about it. Behind all such judgments there is a prejudgment, a prejudice.[1]

There is a prejudgment since, once adopted, the standard against which particulars are to be held is no longer put into question. In spite of what Arendt says here about the standard in this first meaning of judgment, which no doubt refers to Kant's determined concepts, one can easily recognize that she is speaking of 'determined judgments.' In such judgments, because the particular is notoriously subsumed under something that is already known in advance of the act of judging, prioritizing the known over a decision, the categorizing and ordering implied in such a judgment have "more to do with thinking as deductive [*schlussfolgerndem*] reasoning than with thinking as an act of judgment."[2] Furthermore, to conflate determining judgment with the power of judgment "tacitly assume[s] that human beings can be expected to render judgments only if they possess standards, that the faculty of judgment is thus nothing more than the ability to assign individual cases to their correct and proper places within the general principles which are applicable to them and about which everyone is in agreement."[3]

But there is a second meaning of the word and the thing we call "judgment." Arendt writes:

> Judgment can, however, mean something totally different, and indeed it always does when we are confronted with something which we have never seen before and for which there are no standards at our disposal. This judgment that knows no standards [*das massstablos ist*] can appeal to nothing but the evidence of what is being judged, and its sole prerequisite is the faculty of judgment, which has far more to do with man's ability to make distinctions than with his ability to organize and subsume.[4]

In spite of what is said about the power of judgment as having more to do with the ability to make distinctions rather than with subsumption—a contention that is, undoubtedly, tributary to Kant's translation of *facultas dijudicandi* by *Urteilskraft* but that also shows that Arendt's conception of judgment, as well as her reading of Kant on this matter, is strongly guided by the Aristotelian concept of *phronesis*—there is no difficulty in recognizing Kant's notion of reflective judgment in Arendt's description of the second meaning of judgment, to which she refers as judgment without standards (*massstabloses Urteilen*), especially since Kant's concept of the judgment of taste is explicitly mentioned. This kind of judgment without standards is the only one that merits the name "judgment," since it alone is called forth when there is something to be judged or decided upon in the strict sense of the word. As we will see later, there is more to this characterization of reflective judgment as one without standards; it also anticipates the subject matter that calls for reflective judgment itself. Arendt refers to such a judgment as "original judgment," *ursprüngliches Urteilen*, which could be better translated as "authentic" or "genuine judgment."[5]

According to Arendt, "[n]ot till Kant's *Critique of Judgment* did this faculty [of judgment] become a major topic of a major thinker."[6] Additionally, if the faculty of judgment comes to enjoy an unprecedented importance in Kant, it is paradoxically because "behind taste" Kant discovered an "entirely new faculty" that is not to be confounded with the aesthetic judgment itself but that is nonetheless reflective by nature and therefore essentially distinct from logical, syllogistic, or determinate judgment.[7] Indeed, in the "Postscriptum" to the first part of *The Life of the Mind*, entitled "Thinking," Arendt makes it clear right away that what she understands by judgment as a distinct capacity of the mind has "nothing in common with logical operations—as when we say: All men are mortal, Socrates is a man, hence, Socrates is mortal."[8] It has nothing to do with the capacity of drawing logical conclusions. Logicality, she says in "Understanding and Politics," is the "substitute" one is likely to accept "wherever common sense, the political sense par excellence, fails us in our need for understanding."[9] In fact, by recalling Kant's reference in the *Anthropology from a Pragmatic Point of View* to "logical *Eigensinn*" (i.e., logical private sense, if not pigheadedness), Arendt holds that, although such *Eigensinn* would cut off all logical cognition from experience, the implication is that logical or determinant judgment can in principle "function without communication."[10] Yet, this also implies that, for Arendt, determinant judgment is not a judgment at all. As we learn from *Between Past and Future*, if a logical judgment (and a moral judgment, as well) is not a judgment to begin with, it is because in these judgments there is nothing to judge or decide (*krinein*), and thus, strictly speaking, they are not judgments at all. The capacity to judge, she repeatedly argues, is one "for making distinctions."[11] In her *Lectures on Kant's Political Philosophy*, Arendt discusses what predisposes a judgment of the entirely private and noncommunicable senses, such as a judgment concerning the agreeable, to become nonetheless the vehicle for aesthetic reflective judgment, which makes claims to universality and actually is eminently communicable. She argues that this predisposition arises because judgment by the private sense of taste, for instance, is from the start discriminatory and, moreover, arises in an immediate fashion.[12] This instantaneous discrimination of the judgment of taste as a lower sense provides the model for the reflective judgment concerning the beautiful, which is discriminatory, as well.

Arendt's insistence on the intrinsically discriminatory nature of the judgment of taste is a cornerstone of her theory of judgment and, as such, requires some critical remarks. Undoubtedly, Kant speaks repeatedly of the feeling of pleasure and displeasure associated with a judgment of taste, which suggests that such a judgment discriminates between the two. Upon a closer look, however, the very absence of an aesthetic of the ugly in the Third Critique already calls for caution. Indeed, in Kant's aesthetic of the beautiful there is no room for

> a negated or in general negative judgment of taste, one which would contain in the space of the predicate a specific feeling of displeasure. When it is a question of whether certain representations appeal to taste or not, the only decisive alternative is not that between beautiful or ugly. When these representations appeal to the judgment of taste, they occasion judgments which because of the uniqueness of the always same feeling that they contain can only be positive. By contrast, there is no negative activity of the judgment of taste of equal rank[13]

with the judgment by which something is found positively beautiful. Furthermore, from the perspective of Kant's primarily transcendental inquiry into judgments of taste in the Third Critique, the feeling of pleasure associated with a genuine judgment of taste is always a very specific feeling of pleasure, namely, one that is founded in an a priori fashion. Nevertheless, if judgments that something is ugly occur, they are not dependent on judgments on the beautiful. Where something is experienced as ugly, it gives rise only to an aesthetic judgment of the senses and not to a judgment of taste in a strict sense. "The experience of displeasure and ugliness has an exclusive empirical character."[14] Let us not lose sight of the fact, therefore, that Arendt's characterization of the discriminatory nature of judgments of taste and, more generally, of reflective judgment as such is indicative of an empirical interpretation of the Third Critique.[15]

According to Arendt, Kant assumed that the question of how to discriminate between right and wrong, beautiful and ugly, true and untrue, does not exist for Truth and the Moral Law, since these are given and accepted in advance, and particulars only need to be subsumed under them. By contrast, since Kant "defined judgment as the faculty which always comes into play when we are confronted with particulars," a decision has to be made "about the relation between a particular instance and the general."[16] With political judgment in mind, which, apart from judgments of taste, is the main example of judgment in a rigorous sense or the instantiation of the power of judgment itself, Arendt writes that judgment in a strict sense is "[t]he faculty of judging particulars (as Kant discovered it)."[17] More precisely, it "is the faculty to judge *particulars* without subsuming them under those general rules which can be taught and learned until they grow into habits that can be replaced by other habits and rules."[18] In short, only judgments that are reflective, rather than determinant, are judgments in a rigorous sense. It is this claim that I wish to investigate hereafter. On what basis can Arendt dismiss determinant judgment as a judgment to begin with? Is this simply an outrageous contention? Or are there developments and statements in the *Critique of Judgment* that could possibly support Arendt's claim (at least up to a certain point)? Indeed, let us consider Kant's observation in section 35 of the Third Critique that

> [t]he judgment of taste differs from logical judgment in that the latter subsumes a representation under concepts of the object, but the former does not subsume under a concept at all, for otherwise the necessary universal approval could be compelled by proofs. All the same, however, it is similar to the latter in that it professes a universality and necessity [. . . that] is grounded only on the subjective formal condition of a judgment in general [*eines Urteils überhaupt*]. The subjective condition of all judgments is the faculty for judging itself, or the power of judgment.[19]

Could Kant's contention that reflective judgment meets the conditions of a judgment in general not be construed in such a manner as to justify its characterization as the only judgment worthy of this name?

The "capacity to judge," Arendt contends, "is a specifically political ability."[20] Even though Kant never developed a political philosophy, Arendt asserts that the outlines of such a philosophy, and hence a theory of judgment, are to be found in the *Critique of Judgment* and, more precisely, in Kant's distinction between reflective judgment and determinant judgment. To narrow this topic even further, the outlines of Kant's political philosophy are found in the parts devoted to the judgment of the beautiful, as well as in the parts devoted to the artwork and the genius of art. Even though Kant's aesthetic is primarily an aesthetic of the beautiful of nature, Arendt pays little to no attention to it, as if solely products of human work that have no use value would seem to demand a discerning and discriminating judgment regarding their beauty or ugliness. In all fairness, it needs to be pointed out that Arendt's privileging of Kant's elaborations on genius and the beautiful arts is justified at least by the fact that the problematic of communicability and critical debate of judgments of taste is only really broached in Kant's elaboration of the reflective aesthetic judgment concerning artificial beauty as opposed to the beauty of objects of nature. Yet, Arendt's reading of Kant's elaboration on judgment has encountered reservations of all kinds, and, although it is true that her strategy in reading Kant invites close critical scrutiny, I have chosen largely to abstract from such considerations. After all, which great thinker has not misconstrued some of his or her sources for developing a novel approach to some venerable problematic?

In order to understand how Arendt can make the point that a logical judgment is not truly a judgment, let me return to the well-known but not, therefore, necessarily well-understood distinction between determinant and reflective judgments. Although the distinction in question is not exclusive to the *Critique of Judgment*—I refer, for example, to #81 of the *Logic* from 1800, which is limited to a discussion of the accomplishment of the teleological reflective judgment—it is the former that commonly serves as the source for making the distinction.[21] Its phrasing is well known: "If the universal (the rule, the principle, the law) is given, then the power of judgment, which subsumes the particular under it [. . .] is *determining*. If, however, only the particular is given, for which the universal is to be found, then the power of judgment is merely *reflecting*."[22] However, thus stated, this definition is not only formal; it also has something formulaic about it. Furthermore, because of the inverse logic of the definition process, it suggests a facile, self-evident, and very simple distinction. More often than not, it is in this form that one encounters it in the literature. This distinction loses its deceptive simplicity only when one pays particular attention to the notions of 'subsuming' the particular under the universal, of 'finding' the universal (or, as Kant also says occasionally, of 'ascending [*aufsteigen*]' from the particular to the universal), and, especially, of 'reflecting' in a reflective judgment. Indeed, reflection is not simply the opposite of determination. As Kant makes amply clear through his insistence on the fact that the power of judgment is "merely" reflecting when it is a question of finding the universal for a particular, determining judgment also involves some reflection.[23] If all the understanding has to do is apply its categories to intuitions in order to constitute an object in general, judgment is only determinant. But as soon as its task is to find an empirical concept for a given perception, the determinant judgment is necessarily reflective. The question, then, is what reflection accomplishes in a "merely" reflective judgment and what the universal is that it finds and to which it ascends, in distinction from what happens in a determining judgment.

For Arendt, only reflective judgment (whether aesthetic or political) is the unadulterated expression of the power of judgment. Before offering the distinction between the two kinds of judgment, however, let us recall that Kant maintains that "[t]he power of judgment in general is the faculty for thinking of the particular as contained under the universal."[24] Arendt also seems to make this point when she argues that there is judgment only where one confronts the particular without having in advance fixed concepts, standards, or rules to account for it subsumptively. These, as we indicated earlier, have been blasted away by the wind of thought. When faced with the particular, the power of judgment is the only way "to say what is"—*legein ta eonta*, an expression from Herodotus that Arendt frequently invokes[25]—and it does so by finding the 'general,' which, as she remarks a bit enigmatically, "must be seen as contained in the particular."[26] On another occasion, in the seminar notes on "Imagination," Arendt says that reflective judgments "'derive' the rule from the particular" in order to be able to account discriminately for the particular.[27] By contrast, when Kant submits that "[t]he power of judgment in general is the faculty of thinking the particular as contained under the universal," it is, first of all, to establish firmly that *both* determinant and reflective judgments are judgments in a rigorous sense (one of the effects of the formulaic declaration of what distinguishes them is, precisely, to emphasize their intrinsic judgmental form). Even though Arendt frequently refers to Kant's statement that the power of judgment is the faculty to think the particular in relation to the universal, her emphasis on the particular (more precisely, "the world of particular appearances" encountered when the thinking ego no longer moves among generalities) is such that solely to the reflective judgment is a judgmental quality attributed.[28] Her emphasis that "[j]udgment deals with particulars," rather than universals, aims at the same conclusion.[29] As Arendt submits, the faculty of judgment "is the faculty to judge particulars without subsuming them under those general rules which can be taught and learned until they grow into habits that can be replaced by other habits and rules."[30] According to Kant, determining reflection only subsumes the particular under a general term (*Oberbegriff*). In conformity with the meaning of "subsumption" in the eighteenth century, it "comprehends," "unites," or "combines" (*zusammenfassen*) the particular under such a general term.[31] Yet, if it is unnecessary for the determinant judgment "to think of a law for itself in order to be able to subordinate the particular in nature to the universal," it is simply because "the law is sketched out for it *a priori*," and such laws are thus "transcendental laws, given by the understanding."[32] The concepts given to determinant judgments are the concepts constitutive of objectivity in general and not empirical and historically based rules that at one time were appropriate to judge but have now become ossified. Kant writes that the judgment is determining when it yields to "the universal laws without which nature in general (as object of the senses) could not be conceived."[33] These laws are not replaceable. Anything phenomenal presupposes these laws. It follows that what Arendt calls 'concepts' are not at all Kant's pure forms of the understanding that relieve determinant judgment from finding the laws for the particulars of nature. Furthermore, they are not the concepts that the aesthetic or teleological reflective judgments must discover in order to make sense of the singular objects—beautiful things in nature, or nature's organized forms—with which they are concerned. The concepts that are lacking in these cases are determinate, or empirical, concepts as opposed to the categories for objects in general, which determinate judgments apply to what is phenomenally intuited. They are concepts that secure the specification of the manifold of nature—roses in general, as opposed to this rose. Finally, it also needs to be pointed out that the reflective judgment is not at all a judgment free of subsumption, even though this concept might undergo a modification in the judgment of taste. In section 35 of the *Critique of the Power of Judgment*, Kant makes clear that in a reflective judgment the imagination itself, as a subjective power of the mind, is subsumed under the mental power of advancing from intuitions to concepts, that is, of the understanding as a subjective faculty.[34] In this instance, subsumption refers to the "agreement" (*Zusammenstimmung*) of both faculties.[35] From Kant's statement that determinant judgment "has *nothing to do* but [to] subsume under given laws," or that it "has *nothing further to do* than to provide the condition of subsumption under the *a priori* concept of the understanding that has been laid down for it," Arendt implicitly draws the conclusion that a determinant judgment does not do very much, that it is not really involved in the activity of judging, and, consequently, that it is barely, if at all, a judgment.[36]

However, Arendt also acknowledges that, even when a judgment only "subsumes the particular under its appropriate general rule," "this apparently simple operation has its difficulties, for since there are no rules for the subsumption, this must be decided freely."[37] Thus, Arendt suggests that determining judgment is not so deficient as far as the activity of judging is concerned. Indeed, Kant also claims that the transcendental power of judgment provides the condition of subsumption, that is, the rule for "the succession of the determinations of one and the same thing."[38] Before I take up Arendt's own understanding of reflective judgment, I would like to raise the question of whether reflective judgment in Kant really involves a much greater operational activity than determinant judgment. Undoubtedly, Kant's talk of reflective judgment's need 'to find' the universal for the particular, or 'to ascend' to the universal when only particulars are given, suggests a more laborious procedure. Yet, since such finding or ascending is accomplished by way of reflection, everything depends on what 'mere reflection' in Kant's understanding precisely consists of.

Let me first point out that, after having characterized "the capacity to judge [as] a specifically political ability in exactly the sense denoted by Kant," Arendt contends in her essay, "The Crisis in Culture," that this understanding of judging is "virtually as old as articulated political experience. The Greeks," she continues, "called this ability *phronesis*, or insight, and they considered it the principal virtue or excellence of the statesman in distinction from the wisdom of the philosopher."[39] Judgment in a genuine political sense can thus be retranslated into the Greek notion of *phronesis*, which allows Arendt to expand on the meaning of the kind of "judgment" that Kant unwittingly discovered behind the judgment of taste. Arendt translates *phronesis* as "insight." In *The Promise of Politics*, she explains that such insight is "political insight" and, more precisely, "the insight of the political man (the *politikos*, not the statesman, who did not even exist in this [Greek] world). [. . .] Such insight into a political issue means nothing other than the greatest possible overview of all the possible standpoints and viewpoints from which an issue can be seen and judged."[40] However, Arendt contends that, while it is the "cardinal virtue of the political man" according to Aristotle, hardly anyone spoke of this virtue over the ensuing centuries.[41] At the same time, she adds that "[w]e do not run across it until Kant, in his discussion of common sense as a faculty of judgment. He calls it an 'enlarged mentality' and explicitly defines it as the ability 'to think from the position of every other person.'"[42] It becomes evident that, for Arendt, *phronesis* and a certain conception of judgment in Kant are the same thing. The identification of *phronesis* with *Urteilskraft* (the power of judgment) in Kant is rather startling and presupposes, as Robert J. Dostal has argued, a rather unorthodox reading of Kant (if not of Aristotle as well).[43] Yet, however surprising it might seem to link reflective judgment to Prudence, or Practical Wisdom, this association might even have its origin in Kant's "Introduction" to the *Critique of Judgment*, despite the fact that Kant speaks there of prudence as only a technical-practical rule, or as a rule educed from a determining concept. He writes: "All technically practical rules (i.e., those of art and skill in general, as well as those of prudence, as a skill in influencing human beings and their will), so far as their principles rest on concepts, must be counted only as corollaries of theoretical philosophy."[44] But what does *phronesis*, which is generally translated as prudence or practical wisdom (in opposition to the knowledge or wisdom [*sophia*] of the philosopher), mean in the first place?

Book VI of the *Nicomachean Ethics*, in which Aristotle defines *phronesis* as calculating intelligence, is the prime source of Arendt's reference to the notion in question.[45] For the present purpose, I will forgo a discussion of the history of the term, which in Plato and in Aristotle (with the sole exception of the latter's ethical writings that rehabilitate the term's prephilosophical and popular meaning of a practical disposition with respect to life in this world) denotes knowledge (*episteme*) about everything that is invariable and is thus in accordance with the Platonic ideal of science.[46] Before I turn to Book VI of the *Nicomachean Ethics* itself and what it establishes about *phronesis* in the sense of a practical disposition, let me first point out that, if for Aristotle it is necessary for the human being to be prudent rather than wise or simply virtuous in a moral sense, it is because the world in which he or she lives and in which he or she must act is a thoroughly contingent world. To say that the world in which the human being lives and acts is marked by contingence is to say that in this world everything can be different or other than it is. *Phronesis* allows the human being to move and to orient him- or herself in this world. It is "a wisdom of the human being and for the human being" as a being who must be able to cope with chance in a world that is in constant change.⁴⁷ In preparation for what follows, a succinct definition of *phronesis* might also be appropriate: Rather than an art or a science, *phronesis* is a practical disposition that incarnates the correct rule (*orthos logos*) for the choices to be made in the ever-changing reality of human affairs with the intent of realizing in every situation the only possible good, namely, the (merely) human good as opposed to the other good that is the Good in itself.

After having made a distinction in the previous books between an irrational and a rational part of the soul, in Book VI Aristotle divides the rational part of the soul into a scientific and a calculative faculty. Whereas the scientific (*epistemonikon*) faculty contemplates "those things whose first principles are invariable," the calculative or ratiocinating (*logistikton*) faculty is one "whereby we contemplate those things which admit of variation" and thus can be other than they are.⁴⁸ The things with which the calculative faculty of the soul deals, things that admit of variation, are of two different kinds. There are "things made and action done (*poieton kai prakton*)," that is, things that are produced through art (*techne*) and actions in the domain of human affairs. The two are not to be lumped together. Stressing their generic difference, Aristotle remarks: "doing is not a form of making, nor making a form of doing."⁴⁹ It is important to note that Aristotle holds calculation to be aligned with opiniation (*doxastikon*), or deliberation (*boulesthai*). Not only is there a close proximity of deliberation and opinion (*doxa*); the virtue of deliberation (*phronesis*) is also the very virtue of the opiniating, rather than the scientific, part of the rational soul. As a form of *dianoia*, deliberation concerns the means to accomplish an end, not the end itself. The artisan, for example, has to reason according to a rule about the way to bring the thing he wants to make, or produce (*poiesis*), into existence. The deliberation that concerns the other kind of variables—actions in the domain of human affairs, which belong to a realm altogether distinct from the one of making or work—is none other than the intellectual or *dianoetic* virtue of *phronesis*, practical wisdom, or prudence. It is a disposition to act (*praktike*) that is accompanied by a rule. This knowledge of prudence is distinct not only from the knowledge of the artisan but also from that of the sages, which represents "the most perfect mode of knowledge."⁵⁰ Rather than seeking "to know the things that are good for human beings," the sages concern themselves only with "the most exalted objects."⁵¹ Furthermore, the latter's knowledge is one about things that do not change and one that does not require deliberation. It is senseless to deliberate on things that amount to ontological obstacles to this activity of the mind. As Aristotle points out, one does not deliberate about that which has already happened and can no longer be changed, about things that are immutable (or eternal), or about those things that are the effect of fundamental chance, such as natural catastrophes. Prudence, by contrast, is concerned "with the affairs of men, and with things that can be the object of deliberation," that is, those things that depend entirely on the human being.[52] Such things are not only always particular things; as Aristotle emphasizes, they are also contingent in nature.[53] In Book I of the *Nicomachean Ethics*, Aristotle states that "the aim of politics, that is, of what is the highest of all the goods that action can achieve" in the realm of public affairs, is "'the good life,'" or happiness.[54] Deliberation in the ever-changing and never-finished realm of human affairs is deliberation precisely about the highest good that action can achieve, that is, about "what is advantageous as a means to the good life in general."[55] More precisely, with respect to action, which is the highest form of life possible in the public realm insofar as it aims at bringing about the welfare of the community, *phronesis* is a knowledge of the rule to follow while choosing (*prohairesis*) the most appropriate means among those available to achieve this goal. Aristotle writes: "Deliberative Excellence must be correctness of deliberation with regard to what is expedient as a means to the end, a true conception of which constitutes Prudence."[56]

Understood as deliberation in view of a decision regarding practical matters that are always particulars, then, *phronesis* is the Greek concept after which Arendt models her understanding of judgment in a public and political sense. Let us remind ourselves of the fact that, already in Book VI, Aristotle makes it clear that political science or prudence is not "the loftiest kind of knowledge, inasmuch as man is not the highest thing in the world."[57] Having argued that "even some of the lower animals are said to be prudent," he continues: "It may be argued that man is superior to other animals, but this makes no difference: since there exist other things far more divine in their nature than man, for instance, to mention the most visible, the things of which the celestial system is composed."[58] As is obvious from Book X of the *Nicomachean Ethics*, prudence remains subordinated to the contemplative ideal of science, which deals with things that are considerably more divine in nature than man.[59] Arendt does not subscribe to the subordination in question, which would imply a wholesale endorsement of Aristotle's metaphysics. Furthermore, if she is not a neo-Aristotelian, as Habermas contends, it is because, even though she understands *phronesis* as a deliberation, the latter does not, in her view, consist in the calculation of well-balanced means for prudent action.[60] It should also be pointed out that *phronesis* in Aristotle concerns the deliberation not of appearances but, rather, of the contingent as opposed to what is necessary. Even though this Greek notion of *phronesis* guides Arendt's understanding of the judgment of appearances, in other words, the acts and deeds of singular human beings as appearances par excellence, the fact that one cannot know in advance what processes their actions or words will trigger does not therefore make them contingent. But Arendt is not a neo-Aristotelian, perhaps, for yet another reason. Aristotle, as Barbara Cassin has shown, is not of one piece but "at the same time Presocratic and Platonic," and what Arendt looks for in him are the remnants of a pre-Socratic experience of the political.[61] Furthermore, the emphasis that Arendt puts on the notions of plurality, the space of appearances, and persuasion and judgment is, as Cassin poignantly argues, of sophist origin. Cassin writes: "the sophistic movement, I think, shares certain features of great significance with what Arendt thinks of as Greek political thought and ascribes to Socrates and to Aristotle."[62] In fact, one could argue that this emphasis on sophist themes and concerns in her reading of Aristotle is part and parcel of her radical recasting of the political since the Greeks.

At this point, let me take up again the problem left in abeyance regarding the exact role that reflection plays when a reflective judgment finds a universal for a particular and how "mere reflection" is to be understood in this respect. Let us remind ourselves one more time that, according to Arendt, it is "behind taste" that Kant discovered "an entirely new human faculty, namely, judgment." I hold that the reflection on universals involved in this new faculty, which Arendt links to *phronesis*, cannot be the same as "mere reflection," which constitutes the reflective judgment of taste. Reflection in reflective judgment is understood by Arendt to correspond to the calculation (*logizesthai*) and deliberation (*boulesthai*) that characterizes prudence and that, in the same way as reflective judgment, always deals with particular things. As Aubenque has pointed out,

> the word *bouleusis*, which Aristotle is the first to use in a technical sense, refers to the institution of the *boule*, which in Homer designates the Council of Elders, and, in Greek democracy, the Council of 500, whose task it was to prepare by way of a deliberation, the decision of the Assembly of the people: the Council deliberates (*bouleuetai*), the people choose, or, at least ratify.[63]

Deliberation takes place publicly, in a democratic framework, and is essentially pluralistic.[64] In view of what I will establish about Kant's understanding of the nature of reflection in reflective judgment, I note that deliberation, in contrast to the skill in conjecturing that according to Aristotle operates rapidly, "takes a long time." "Deliberative Excellence," Aristotle adds, "is not the same as Quickness of the mind."[65]

Of what, then, does reflection in reflective judgment consist and what does it accomplish? According to section 35 of the Third Critique, when faced with a particular for which it has no concept, the judgment of taste bends or folds back upon itself inasmuch as it itself is the subjective condition of all judgments. As Kant remarks, "[t]he subjective condition of all judgments is the faculty for judging itself, or the power of judgment."[66] In reflecting upon itself, thus being "itself, subjectively, both object as well as law,"[67] reflective judgment discovers within itself the law for its act, which is none other than, precisely, the "subjective formal condition of a judgment in general."[68] But what is this subjective law, which allows the judgment of taste to profess "a universality and necessity" like determinant judgments?[69] The subjective formal condition for judgment itself, which grounds the judgment when no concept for its object is available, is "the reciprocal relation of the understanding and the imagination."[70] In other words, it is their subjective agreement or consonance (*Zusammenstimmung*). When bending back upon itself in the face of an object that it cannot subsume under a given concept, the faculty of judgment discovers within itself the very purposiveness of this reciprocal relation to which it submits itself as an a priori law in reflecting and judging the particular in question. This harmonious interplay of the faculties of representation beneficial for cognition in general is the very principle or *concept* that reflective judgment must find and under which, in turn, the judgment subsumes the mere form of the representation of an object, thus performing a judgment in all its formal rigor. Because the concept to be found in a reflective judgment is that of the subjective condition of all judging, Kant can state that the judgment of taste is "a judgment in general."[71] The reflection that constitutes it consists in turning upon the faculty of judgment's subjective conditions and discovering purposiveness there as the principle, or concept, under which it can then reflect upon the object and subsume the representation of the object (rather than the object itself). If such a judgment asserts the beauty of an object, which is immediately followed by the feeling of pleasure, it is because representation and reason find themselves in agreement. In short, rather than a protracted pondering, meditating, or deliberating operation, it follows from all of this that the "operation of reflection"[72] takes place immediately when confronted with an object for which no determined concept is available but that is judged beautiful in light of the form of its representation. Even though reflective judgment appears at first much more laborious than determinant judgment, it is not. The subjective, free interplay of the faculties of representation beneficial for cognition in general, that is, the concept that reflective judgment must 'find' (or to which it must 'ascend') in order to subsume the representation of its object, occurs immediately and is thus 'found' instantaneously. In distinction from the case of political judgment concerning particulars, no complex search or lengthy deliberation and reflection is involved in aesthetic reflective judgment.[73] It happens in no time, time being understood here in an empirical sense. Of course, this does not mean that time as a transcendental form would not be implied in subsuming the particular under the concept that is found. Indeed, in the same way as in determinant judgment, the law of the subsumption of a particular under the concept to be found by a reflective judgment would also be that of the succession of the determinations of the particular.

All of this seems to suggest that Kant's elaborations on the operation of reflection in a judgment concerning particulars for which no determinate concept is available has little similarity to Arendt's understanding of judgment. In fact, as is obvious from her lectures on Kant, especially from her comments on section 39 of the Third Critique, Arendt completely ignores the fact that for Kant the reflective judgment of the beautiful is grounded on the free interplay of the powers of cognition. She proceeds immediately to a discussion of the *sensus communis* as a sense that guarantees the power of judging and that, on at least one occasion, she calls "the mother of judgment."[74] Is Arendt simply wrong in looking at reflective judgment as a model for political judgment, as a number of her critics have suggested? And what about Kant's implicit understanding that the discovery of the law for judging particulars for which no determined concept exists must be accomplished in each case all over again? If the Kantian technicality of reflective judgment bears little resemblance to what Arendt understands by judgment, could it be that Kant's insistence on the singularity of reflective judgment in fact undergirds Arendt's contention that reflective judgment alone is a genuine judgment? Even though reflective judgment is not more toilsome than determinant judgment, even though it occurs in no time, the reflection that constitutes it must be relaunched on every occasion when one finds oneself in the presence of a particular without a universal in order to secure the agreement of the singular object's representation with the powers of representation. Furthermore, the concept or principle that must be found for a particular must be a rule that reflects this particular and not another. In short, it must be a rule that is appropriate to this particular in all its singularity. In this context, it would be necessary to follow up on Kant's observation, in sections 9 and 39, that the subjective consonance of the faculties of representation in a reflective judgment is a function of their proportionality. Proportionality is another term for agreement or consonance. At the same time, the notion suggests variability in the way the consonance of the faculties is achieved. Thus, I am suggesting that it is the possibility of the differing proportionality of the faculties that allows a reflective judgment concerning a particular to provide a law that allows for its subsumption as that particular and no other. As Kant holds, a judgment of taste is also always a "singular judgment."[75]

And yet, we face another problem. If, according to Arendt, the power of judgment does not consist in finding the general in the subjective formal conditions of a judgment about the particular for which no pregiven universal is at hand, how, then, is one to understand the reflection that the power of judgment requires? Although the answer to this question is very much a function of the kind of particulars that require such reflection, one can safely assume that Arendt conceives of reflection as deliberation (by the many rather than by the lonely subject) about things that are of immediate concern in the public realm, or the space of appearance. Furthermore, the answer to how a judgment can reflectively find the universal to relate to a particular appearance in the political realm also depends on the nature of the agent of judgment. For Arendt, this agent is a human being who is plural from the start, rather than the Kantian formal subject. Indeed, the power of judgment as the political faculty par excellence is one that from the start is shared by all, even though Arendt also stresses that in each case it has to be performed by a singular subject. As she reminds us on several occasions, no one can be relieved of this burden—the burden of freedom. In this case, however, it is not so much the play of the faculties of the judging subject as such that provides the concept but, rather, the expanded mind-set itself through which one can think in the place of others. This is the way in which the judging subject comes upon the general concept under which to subsume the particular. Arendt observes that the kind of knowledge associated with an expanded mind-set, namely, "seeing the world [...] from the other fellow's point of view," is "the political kind of insight par excellence."[76] It is in this kind of knowledge, itself rooted, on Arendt's reading, in Kant's notion of a *sensus communis*, that one must look for the standards for judging particulars.

With everything I have developed in Chapter 7 on Arendt's notion of the public and political space as the space of appearance in mind, I now wish to take up Arendt's discussion, at the very end of her *Lectures on Kant's Political Philosophy*, of the two ideas on which one must reflect in order to arrive at judgments. These two ideas, she holds, are Kant's answer to the difficulty of finding the general or universal when, in distinction from determinate judgment, only the particular is given. Arendt writes: "For the standard cannot be borrowed from experience and cannot be derived from outside. I cannot judge one particular by another particular; in order to determine its worth, I need a *tertium quid* or a *tertium comparationis*, something related to the two particulars and yet distinct from both."[77] The *tertium quid* here refers to the element or medium in which both particulars relate to one another. Yet, considering the fact that a reflective judgment is always a judgment about a particular thing and, by implication, about just one singular thing, Arendt's talk of two particulars is rather confusing. If, indeed, two particulars were given to a judgment, comparing them would provide the third term, that is, the determinate concept under which to subsume them, in which case the judgment would be no longer reflective but determinate. By contrast, the very impossibility of comparing a unique, particular thing is precisely what, according to Kant, calls for a reflective judgment. However confusing Arendt's reference to two particulars is, her evocation of the two ideas that Kant offers "[a]s a real *tertium comparationis* [. . .] on which one must reflect in order to arrive at judgments" in the case of particulars for which no universal is given unmistakably shows that, in lieu of concepts, only ideas provide the solution to what she considers the crux of a reflective judgment.[78] According to Arendt, the two specific ideas that one finds in Kant and that solve the difficulty of "combining"[79] without generalizing the particular (which, for her, is always of the order of an appearance *and* the general) seem to refer to the mediating term in reflective judgment's syllogistic structure. Indeed, as we will see in now turning to those two ideas, for Arendt, this mediating term is the idea of "world."

The first of these ideas is that of "an original compact of mankind as a whole" and, intimately linked to it, "the idea of purposiveness";[80] the second, which Arendt qualifies as "far more valuable," is *"exemplary* validity."[81] I leave the discussion of the idea of purposiveness, rated as being of secondary importance, in abeyance until the end of this chapter. In support of her argument that exemplary validity is the most fruitful idea in judging particulars, she quotes Kant's statement from the *Critique of Pure Reason* that "examples are the leading-strings" or, rather, the go-cart (*Gängelwagen*) of judgment.[82] What is important here for our discussion is that Arendt characterizes the exemplar in distinction from Platonic ideas or Kantian concepts and from mere abstractions, both of which concern the cognition of things. By contrast and in a fundamental way, the exemplar, as an idea, pertains to reflective judgment about appearances in the public realm, in short, to what she construes as judgment in a strict sense. As she recalls, "'example' comes from *eximere*, 'to single out some particular.'"[83] And she adds: "This exemplar is and remains a particular that in its very particularity reveals the generality that otherwise could not be defined."[84] In other words, for Arendt, the exemplar is the general or universal that the reflecting judgment is to find in the absence of pregiven concepts for a particular. Furthermore, if exemplarity is an idea that must guide the reflection upon something general for a particular in the absence of concepts, it is also because such a general is already "contained in the particular," which itself is of the order of an appearance in the public space. If such a general is contained in the particular, it also follows that this generality as something exemplar is, paradoxically, still particular. In other words, if the Kantian idea of the exemplar is a more fruitful solution to the problem that the reflective judgment must solve, it is precisely because the reflective judgment discovers—through reflection and deliberation—a general that, since it is still particular, does not override the particularity of the object to be judged. The exemplar is, indeed, a singular universal that permits judgment of a particular appearance while preserving its uniqueness. Rather than doing violence to the particular, the exemplarity that is drawn from the particular as capable of it does not subsume but, if I may say so, empowers the particular.

If the power of judgment that Kant unwittingly discovered when he came upon the judgment of taste is not identical to the reflective judgment of taste but is, as Arendt suggests, the more fundamental power of judgment that is constitutive of the political, one cannot expect the analogy between the judgment of taste and the political judgment to be seamless.[85] From what I have shown so far about the concept that has to be found in an aesthetic reflective judgment so that the particular can be related to it, it is clear that Kant is not so much concerned with the particular itself as with securing the possibility of judgment in the absence of concepts for particulars and, hence, of being able to uphold the fundamental conformity between nature and reason. In her *Lectures on Kant's Political Philosophy* Arendt acknowledges in passing that "purposiveness is an idea by which to regulate one's reflections in one's reflective judgments."[86] Through the idea of purposiveness, Kant establishes the conformity of the form of a particular thing of nature (or of a work of art) to our mental faculties even in a situation in which no determinate concepts for it are at our disposal. For Arendt, however, this idea is not particularly fruitful. As a consequence, Robert J. Dostal is basically correct when he holds that "throughout her lectures Arendt studiously avoids the theme of purposiveness which is the single dominant and unifying theme of the *Critique of Judgment*."[87] It also follows that the judgmental accomplishment of the power of judgment as an intrinsically political faculty must be very different from that of the pure aesthetic judgment. Here one would have to return again to Arendt's identification of the power of judgment with a certain *phronesis* and to her characterization of judgment as being involved in distinguishing, discriminating, and deciding. If, for instance, one follows Maurizio Passerin d'Entrèves's remark that, in order to connect the activity of thinking to that of judgment as Arendt attempts to do in *The Life of the Mind*, one must release judgment "from ossified categories of thought and conventional standards of behavior," it follows not only that judgment has to become reflective rather than determinant but also that it must be relieved from much of what constitutes for Kant aesthetic reflective judgment itself.[88] By construing the reflection involved in judgment primarily as deliberation, that is, as a form of "calculating intelligence" or *phronesis*, and despite the fact that she appeals to Kant's *sensus communis*, Arendt cannot successfully bend this notion to fit her own needs.

Before engaging Arendt's extensive commentary in *Lectures on Kant's Political Philosophy* on section 40, "On taste as a kind of *sensus communis*," of the *Critique of the Power of Judgment*, let me first briefly draw on her earlier evocation of this notion in "The Crisis of Culture." After having linked or, rather, identified the power of judgment with *phronesis* and associated this power with the statesman as opposed to the philosopher, Arendt avers:

> The difference between this judging insight and speculative thought lies in that the former has its roots in what we usually call common sense, which the latter constantly transcends. Common sense—which the French so suggestively call the "good sense," *le bon sens*—discloses to us the nature of the world insofar as it is a common world; we owe to it the fact that our strictly private and "subjective" five senses and their sensory data can adjust themselves to a nonsubjective and "objective" world which we have in common and share with others. Judging is one, if not the most, important activity in which this sharing-the-world-with-others comes to pass.[89]

In order to distinguish this common sense from vulgar (*gemeiner*) common sense, Arendt refers to it in the same way as Kant by its Latin designation as *sensus communis*, a term that she repeatedly characterizes as a sense for the communal (*gemeinschaftlich*) or as "an extra sense—like an extra mental capability [...]—that fits us into a community."[90] Arendt justifies this interpretation of *sensus communis* on the basis of Kant's reference to it as "the idea of a *communal* sense."[91] As an idea, this sense is for Kant an idea of reason that can only be approximated, but for Arendt it is a specifically human sense, a sense with which the human qua human is actually endowed. What is most crucial here is that, for Arendt, this extra sense "discloses to us the nature of the world insofar as it is a common world."[92] In other words, in distinction from the senses' relation to inner and outer nature (that is, to the natural world), which Arendt qualifies as private and subjective, the extra sense of the *sensus communis* is a sense for the world as the 'objective' opening for the appearances that make up the public space. It is a sense for the world that fits us into the world to begin with, a world (distinct from the natural world) that represents the space for human interaction though appearances. Significantly enough, in her German translation of the essay, Arendt proposes to call this sixth sense "simply a sense of the world [*Weltsinn*]," thus not only stressing its inherent nonsubjectivity and publicness in distinction from the other senses but also offering the subjective senses another arena for an 'objective' activity, namely, the 'objective' perception of the appearances in the public world.[93] Judging, according to Arendt, has its roots in this *sensus communis*; it is also, as we have already heard, "one, if not the most, important activity through which this sharing-the-world-with-others comes to pass."

It would follow that judgment is intimately tied up with the sense of the world and the main activity through which world as a world is shared and actuated. When turning to Arendt's discussion of *sensus communis* in her *Lectures on Kant's Political Philosophy*, we should not lose sight that the stakes of this discussion concern primarily the possibility for human beings of having a world together. Furthermore, it is important to recall that, in Arendt's account of the judgment of taste, judgment is something that requires an actual presence of others. As was already the case in "The Crisis of Culture," in the *Lectures*, too, she holds not only that a judgment is a public activity, not only that it is communicable and expects others to join in, but also that it is made in such a way that it takes account of actual judgments by others. Arendt continues to understand and use *sensus communis* in a different way than Kant. Citing Kant, she acknowledges that aesthetic judgment "is based on 'that common and sound intellect [*gemeiner und gesunder Verstand*] which we have to presuppose in everyone.'"[94] But, in this instance, *sensus communis* is not understood as a transcendental condition for a singular judgment about a beautiful thing for which no determinate concept is available but which, notwithstanding this lack, makes claims to universality; rather, it is understood as the factual or empirical ground on which judgments are made. What Kant establishes as the transcendental a priori conditions of a judgment of taste, that is, the conditions for a 'cognition in general,' is immediately construed as what de facto underlies such a judgment. In order to glean what is specific about Arendt's interpretation of the *sensus communis*, one must at all moments be attentive to her remarks on the *Critique of the Power of Judgment*, in which she consistently disregards the primarily transcendental thrust of Kant's treatise. The sense of the world implied in the *sensus communis* is no exception in this respect. For Arendt, it is a sense that any actively judging participant in the public world actually possesses and enacts by judging.

In section 40 of the *Critique of the Power of Judgment*, Kant defines the *sensus communis* as "the idea of a *communal* [*gemeinschaftlichen*] sense," that is, as "a faculty for judging [*Beurteilungsvermögen*] that in its reflection takes account (*a priori*) of everyone else's way of representing in thought, in order *as it were* to hold its judgment [*Urteil*] up to human reason as a whole."[95] The *sensus communis* is a sensory capacity, but, strictly speaking, it is not a sense, that is, a lower faculty of the mind. Rather, it is within the realm of the sensory a higher faculty of sorts, a faculty not of ordinary judgment but for judging or evaluating acts of judgment themselves. Kant defines the operation of reflection constitutive of the *sensus communis* as follows:

> Now this happens by one holding his judgment up not so much to the actual as to the merely possible judgments of others, and putting himself into the position of everyone else, merely by abstracting from the limitations that contingently attach to our own judging; which is in turn accomplished by leaving out as far as is possible everything in one's representational state that is matter, i.e., sensation, and attending solely to the formal peculiarities of his representation or his representational state.[96]

In German, *Urteil* and *Beurteilung* are often used synonymously, and Kant, at first glance at least, seems to employ the two notions without distinction. Yet, if *Urteil* is the outcome of an act of judgment, Kant draws one's attention to the operation or activity of judging by speaking of *Beurteilung*. The fact that the verb *urteilen*, to judge, is an intransitive verb also means that it is a verb that indicates a complete action without being accompanied by a direct object. Only the verbal prefix *Be-* makes this intransitive verb into a transitive one. Indeed, a *Beurteilung* is an evaluative judgment as opposed to an *Urteil*, a mere judgment. This distinction may be held to be too subtle or too refined, but in this context it is crucial for understanding what the *sensus communis* in Kant is all about.

The communal sense in question is a faculty of judging judgments, and one's own judgments in particular, by holding them against possible judgments by others and, ultimately, by humanity as a whole. The aim is to secure the 'objectivity' of judgments by warding off any subjective conditions that would make them merely private 'judgments' without any legitimate claims to objectivity. Even though a judgment of taste is at once an *Urteil* and its *Beurteilung*, I wish here to distinguish between them for analytical reasons. Differently worded, the *sensus communis* is a faculty of judging distinct from the judging involved in judgments of taste—if you like, one on top of them or, better, beneath them—whose function is to minimize the latter's subjective conditions and to secure the claims that they can make in view of the possible agreement of all others.[97] According, to Kant, this reflective operation of evaluation is accomplished by "tak[ing] account (*a priori*) of everyone else's way of representing in thought." As the reference to the a priori indicates, the reflection in question does not presuppose and does not follow from any actual or empirical attendance to the judgments of others. Rather, the reflection involved in the *sensus communis* upon one's judgment of taste takes place "in thought" and evaluates one's judgment of taste as though (*gleichsam*) it compared it to the judgment of others, independently of any actual exchange with others, in view of "human reason as a whole." Rather than holding in thought one's judgment with its subjective conditions up to the actual judgments of others, the *sensus communis* in the reflective judgment of taste compares it only "to the merely possible judgments of others." This operation of reflection is, transcendentally speaking, constitutive of the judgment of taste as such and explains why Kant calls it a reflective aesthetic judgment in the first place.

At this point, let us remind ourselves again that Kant speaks of the *sensus communis* as an idea, as "the idea of a communal sense." Rather than a concept of the understanding, the communal sense is a concept of reason. Considering the fact that Kant construes the judgment of taste as grounded above all in the faculties of understanding and the imagination, the reference to the idea of a communal sense shows that reason, on top of the two former faculties, plays an equal if not even decisive role in such a judgment. Reason demands that a judgment based on the free play of the subjective faculties of the imagination and understanding be consonant with the possible judgments of others, that is, objective, if not potentially universal. As an idea of reason, the *sensus communis* plays a regulative role in a judgment of taste. In other words, it does not make such a judgment into an instance of its actual realization but only into a judgment that must woo others into agreement with it. Furthermore, the reflection by which one's judgment is put into relation to everyone else's judgment is an operation undertaken all by oneself, such as the case of the solitary beholder of a beautiful flower in nature, and does not require any actual acknowledgments of or confrontation of judgments by others.

Since Arendt rests her interpretation of the *sensus communis* largely on Kant's claim that, in the operation of reflection constitutive of a judgment of taste, one holds one's judgment up "to the merely possible judgment of others" and, especially, "put[s oneself] into the position [*in die Stelle*] of everyone else," let us linger for a moment on how Kant himself understands this claim. Arendt correctly underlines the fact that the need to put oneself into the position of others to be able to make a judgment of taste is not a question of empathy.[98] Indeed, in empathy the distinction between my own judgment and that of others would become effaced. According to the above passage from section 40 of the *Critique of the Power of Judgment*, putting oneself into the position of everyone else is accomplished "merely by abstracting from the limitations that contingently attach to our own judging." By abstracting from everything subjective tied to one's own judgment—stripping it of its "matter, i.e., sensation, and attending solely to the formal peculiarities," that is, to what by necessity one shares with everyone who makes a judgment to begin with—one puts oneself into a position that is the same as that of others. This alone allows one to presuppose the potential agreement of others with one's own judgment.[99] Kant adds: "Now perhaps this operation of reflection seems too artificial to be attributed to the faculty that we call *common* [*gemeinen*] sense; but it only appears thus if we express it in abstract formulas; in itself, nothing is more natural than to abstract from charm and emotion if one is seeking a judgment that is to serve as a universal rule."[100] But the reflection on a judgment of taste guided by the idea of communality makes this judgment comparable to possible judgments by others (that meet the same formal criteria for being judgments) by divesting it of all contingencies and thus securing its very communicability. Such a reflection on one's judgment is also the necessary corrective for the possibility that, in judging a thing for which one does not have a concept, one might not have correctly subsumed the form of its representation under the universal. In this case, the universal is the free play of the faculties of the imagination and the understanding, which is beneficial for a cognition in general. Since one can never be really sure "that the case [has been] correctly subsumed under [the] ground as the rule of approval," one cannot count on others' assent.[101] On the contrary, one has to court others into agreement with one's judgment.

For Arendt, reflection in a judgment, and especially in a judgment of taste, "always reflects upon others and their taste, [and] takes their possible judgments into account."[102] Yet, since she does not take into account what Kant establishes about the *sensus communis* (namely, that it concerns only an idea of reason necessary for securing the communicability of taste rather than an already formed community), reflection upon others in making a judgment of taste means something other than the reflection that targets the judgment itself in a judgment of taste. As is evident from Arendt's commentary on section 40 of the *Critique of the Power of Judgment*, her interpretation of the *sensus communis* rests to a large extent on the maxims of the common human understanding spelled out by Kant in the paragraph immediately following the introduction of the idea of the communal sense in question. Even though these maxims, that is, the subjective rules that follow from an idea of reason, can serve "to elucidate [*Erläuterung*]" the critique of taste's fundamental principles, such elucidation is no longer of the order of the transcendental investigation that leads to the establishment of the *sensus communis* as a fundamental principle of judgment of taste.[103] Elucidations take place by way of examples, as is evident from all the cases where Kant proposes an elucidation.[104] This is also why he makes it clear from the beginning that his invocation of the maxims in question is not a part of the critique. Furthermore, these maxims are not for the *sensus communis* itself (as Arendt holds) but, rather, for common sense as healthy human understanding (*gesunder Menschenverstand*), which itself is opposed to vulgar common sense. Kant's remarks on the maxims in question are an excursion into the practical, if not even pragmatic, consequences of the idea of a *sensus communis*. In fact, he qualifies the whole of this discussion of the maxims as a digression (*Episode*)—a mere development alongside the main thread (*epeisodion*) of his transcendental inquiry into the principles of taste—before taking up again the thematic thread that he had temporarily laid aside.

Although Kant is rather explicit as to the status of these remarks on the maxims of common human understanding, Arendt does not take the shift in levels of discourse involved here into account. As regards the three intimately interconnected maxims—"1. To think for oneself; 2. To think in the position of everyone else; 3. Always to think into accord with oneself"—Arendt singles out the second one, which is a maxim for "the *broad-minded* [*erweiterten*]" way of thinking.[105] In Kant's words, such broadmindedness characterizes the way of thinking (rather than cognition) of the man who makes a purposive use of the subjective rule in question and who "sets himself apart from the subjective private conditions of the judgment, within which so many others are as if bracketed, and reflects on his own judgment from a *universal standpoint* (which he can only determine by putting himself into the standpoint of others)."[106] Even though Kant observes, after closing his digression, that "taste can be called *sensus communis* with greater justice than can the healthy understanding, and that the aesthetic power of judgment rather than the intellectual can bear the name of a communal sense," Arendt nonetheless makes the second maxim's purposive use for healthy understanding into a crucial model for her own understanding of the *sensus communis*.[107] As already indicated, the three maxims—the first of which is a way of unprejudiced thinking, the second of taking the standpoint of others into account, the third (of which Arendt is less fond) of thinking consistently (*konsequenten Denkungsart*)—are intimately interconnected. All three make up the enlightened mode of thinking of a man of healthy common sense, that is, of a way of thinking that heeds the demands of reason. The broadmindedness of healthy common sense is not to be confused with the *sensus communis* as an idea of reason to which Kant resorts primarily to explain how a singular judgment of taste on a thing for which universal determined concepts are missing can nevertheless appeal to universal agreement.

Yet, as we have seen, Arendt qualifies the *sensus communis* as a sense that fits us into a community. This sense, she argues, "is the specifically human sense because communication, i.e., speech, depends on it."[108] It is a specifically human sense, perhaps, the human sense par excellence, because the human in distinction from all the other animals is, as Aristotle held, a being endowed with speech. It is a specifically human sense insofar as speech, or communication, is not understood primarily as a means of expression (animals also express themselves) but, rather, as one form that action takes in the plural human world. The community into which the *sensus communis* fits us is the public space of appearances in which human beings, all of them newcomers, interact by showing themselves to one another through words and deeds. More precisely, as far as verbally communicative interaction is concerned, Arendt thinks above all of judgmental activity in the public space. She is concerned with judging, in which one holds one's own judgment up against that of everyone else and thus accomplishes something that not only transgresses everything private but also contributes to the fabric of actual public life. The originality of Arendt's move is to conceive of judgment as the primarily public, linguistic action of that being which is a *zoon logon echon*. From the start, the speech with which such an animal is endowed, the speech taken to be that which makes speaking together in the public sphere possible, is political. For Arendt, the *sensus communis*, understood in terms of what Kant called "healthy common sense," fits human beings into a community through acts of judgments that tie them together inasmuch as they imply putting oneself into the place of others, in a view of what is communal, in that which is no longer private but public. Judgments are thus also intrinsically political in that they are acts that manifest the sense of the world.

As already noted, judgments are eminently political for Arendt because of their exclusive subject matter. To show that this is the case, I refer one more time to Kant's three maxims for healthy human understanding, which she construes as rules that guide the *sensus communis* itself. She writes that these maxims do not concern matters of knowledge but, rather, are needed exclusively "for matters of opinion and in judgments."[109] When she adds that "the maxims of judgment testify to one's 'turn of thought' (*Denkungsart*) in the worldly matters that are ruled by the community sense," it becomes clear that the subject matter of what Arendt calls judgments and opinions concerns those who interact in the world as the in-between of public space.[110] If the maxims for the turn of thought involved in worldly matters concern judgments and opinions about the latter and represent the rules that guide being together, then it also follows that the communal sense fits us into a community, according to Arendt, by fitting us into the world as the space of appearance for opinions and judgments. If judgments and opinions are expressions of the communal sense that fits us into the space of appearance, it is not only because this sense is, like the judgment of taste, discriminating from the beginning—a sense that distinguishes between the private and the public, the private and the communal, the *idiotikon* and the *koinon*—but also because, subject-wise, it bears exclusively on public matters that concern the well-being of the world. However, the judgment of taste, on the basis of which Arendt develops her concept of judgment, is not about worldly matters but about particular things that would put the congruence of human reason and nature radically into question if they could not be made into the objects of a judgment.

In light of what follows, I wish to return briefly to the issue regarding Arendt's interpretation of the Third Critique. From what we have seen so far, it should be clear that Arendt entirely disregards Kant as a transcendental philosopher. If, however, one judges her reading exclusively in light of Kant's inquiry into the transcendental conditions under which a judgment of taste can legitimately claim universality, one misses the exact role that the Third Critique occupies in her work. As we delve further into her discussion of the *sensus communis* and, especially, sociability and communication, it will become increasingly clear that Arendt's interpretation draws primarily on Kant's *digressions* in the Third Critique into matters that are of empirical or pragmatic interest to Kant as a philosophical anthropologist. When she argues that Kant, unwittingly, developed a theory of the political in his elaborations of the judgment of taste, it is the Kant who occasionally deals with empirical and anthropological matters that Arendt has in view. Hereafter, I will systematically put those empirical or anthropological elements that she borrows from Kant into greater relief, since the uniqueness of her own contribution to a theory of judgment rests primarily on them.

According to Arendt, without the ability to actually put oneself into the place of others, judgments could not become the building events of the public world. In distinction from Kant, for whom one does not need actual others to make a judgment that can appeal to everyone else—by stripping my judgments of everything subjective attached to them I am already in the position of others—for Arendt the presence of others is instrumental for engaging in judgmental activity. For her, no judgment worthy of its name is possible without effectively putting oneself in the position of others. Consequently, if others do not happen to be present, they have to be made present. How, then, does Arendt conceive of this operation, without which one cannot engage the opinions of others in judgmental fashion? To accomplish the enlarged mentality capable of making judgments that take others into account, Arendt falls back on the faculty of the imagination as the power to make present what is absent, such as absent others and their possible opinions on some matter. Compared to the faculty of the imagination that enters into a free relation to the faculty of understanding to make a judgment of taste with a legitimate universal appeal possible, the imagination as the power to make something absent present is the imagination as a reproductive faculty. In other words, it is a faculty derivative from what Kant calls transcendental or productive imagination.[111] According to Arendt, however, the imagination also "transforms an object into something I do not have to be directly confronted with but that I have in some sense internalized."[112] It transforms the object into a re-presentation by which the object itself is kept from affecting me in immediate fashion.

Imagination is fundamentally the faculty of re-presentation. As such, "[t]his operation of imagination prepares the object for 'the operation of reflection.' And this second operation—the operation of reflection—is the actual activity of judging something."[113] Even though judgment requires the presence of others, the operation of reflection that constitutes the actual activity of judging is not so much about the actual opinions of others on a given subject matter of communal interest as about the representations of these opinions in one's own inner sense. At first glance, Arendt's recourse to re-productive imagination to explain how the necessary openness to others in a judgment worthy of its name is to be accomplished seems to fall back on a very simple concept of the imagination. Yet, since the reflection on the thus re-presented absent judgments of others takes place within me, not between me and myself but between me and re-presented others, in order to deliberate about them and to discriminate between them in a judgmental fashion, the notion of imagination on which Arendt relies is not so much a notion that by Kant's account is only of secondary importance. Rather, because of its intimate connection to deliberation, it is, in my view, Aristotelian. Indeed, does Aristotle not distinguish, in *De Anima*, "deliberative imagination [*phantasia bouletike*]" from "[s]ensitive imagination"? While "sensitive imagination" is concerned merely with the production of images and is also found in all animals, "deliberative imagination," by contrast, is specific only to "those [animals] who are calculative [*logikois*]" and who possess "a single standard to measure by"; it is the capacity to compare with one another the various images produced by sensitive imagination by deliberating about them.[114] Indeed, in her commentary on how within oneself one makes oneself aware of the judgments of others through re-presentation, before reflectingly deliberating about them, Arendt evokes "the standards of the operation of reflection," pleasure or displeasure, which determine the deliberate choice involved in one's own judgment about the judgments by others.[115]

In order for a judgment to be rooted in the *sensus communis*, one must inevitably put oneself in the place of everyone else. In order for the choice that it expresses to be agreed upon by others, one must, in turn, 'show' or make one's judgment heard to everyone else. Let us recall that, according to Kant's transcendental inquiry into the conditions required for a judgment of taste to have the credentials necessary to make claims to universality, it must be divested of all subjective conditions. If this is the case, such a judgment is in the position of "universal communicability," that is, of having the possibility or capability of being communicated (a capability designated in German by *-keit*, in English by *-ity*).[116] More precisely, a judgment that meets the condition of communicability is in a position to demand others to agree with it. In section

19 of the *Critique of the Power of Judgment*, Kant claims that "[t]he judgment of taste ascribes [*sinnet . . . an*] assent to everyone" and that "[o]ne solicits [*wirbt um*] assent from everyone else because one has a ground for it that is common to all."[117] Unlike cognitive or scientific propositions, which are compelling but "not judgments, properly speaking," a judgment of taste cannot expect everyone to accept its validity on simply logical grounds.[118] The same is especially true for what Arendt considers the manifestations of the power of judgment that Kant unwittingly discovered behind judgments of taste. Judgments qua judgments or "judgments strictly speaking," that is, those that "are the product of reflection and imagination," are not logically compelling.[119] She avers that "one can never compel anyone to agree with one's judgments"; rather, "one can only 'woo' or 'court' the agreement of everyone else."[120] Despite the fact that Arendt uses the same terms as Kant, namely, "wooing" and "courting," in order to describe these judgments' outreach to others, they have a different meaning when the issue concerns the way judgments discovered behind judgments of taste ascertain their universal validity.[121]

To substantiate this point I need to return to Arendt's elaborations on the *sensus communis*. She writes:

> This *sensus communis* is what judgment appeals to in everyone, and it is this possible appeal that gives judgments their special validity. The it-pleases-or-displeases-me, which as a feeling seems so utterly private and noncommunicative, is actually rooted in this community sense and is therefore open to communication once it has been transformed by reflection, which takes all others and their feelings into account.[122]

The discrimination between the feeling of pleasure and displeasure uttered in a judgment of taste is "actually rooted" in the community sense, that is, the sense that makes us look for what we have in common and that transcends the private in the direction of the world. This discriminating judgment is "actually rooted" in the *sensus communis* only once the feeling in question has been transformed through the operation of reflection that reaches out to "all others and their feelings." In what precedes, I have already laid some emphasis on the fact that Arendt's conception of the *sensus communis* suggests its factual, or empirical, existence rather than an idea. Everyone actually possesses it qua being human—it is the most human sense, inasmuch as it fits us into a human community—and it is on this factual ground that judgments rooted in it are impartible (of course, on condition that they have been held against those of all others). At this point one already has the presentiment that the *sensus communis* is not merely the ground of possibility of judgments but also, and at the same time, the product of judgments that meet the latter's requirements.

Nonetheless, this does not suspend Arendt's fundamentally realist conception of the sense in question. Before I inquire into this other facet of the *sensus communis*, however, I wish to highlight the active and productive side of judgment itself. As a discriminating act, and one that is based on an operation of reflection in which the judgment is compared with the judgments of all others, a judgment is an act through which community is engendered. If such a judgment can solicit others to join in, it is only insofar as they are also interested in overcoming the private in view of something universal that brings human beings together. In this case, the communal is not merely a given but rather something to be brought about or, at least, something to be reanimated. Unlike the color of the sky, which is evident to our senses and, hence, compelling, the production of the communal, in distinction from judgments of taste made in the expectation that others will join, requires more than just what Kant called "wooing" or "courting." After having used these terms in her commentary on such judgments as "'[t]his is beautiful,'" Arendt writes that "in this persuasive activity one actually appeals to the 'community sense.'"[123] Indeed, throughout her work on Kant's reflective judgment, she consistently construes "wooing" and "courting" as acts of persuasion.[124] For example, following the exposition of Kant's conception of the judgment of taste, Arendt remarks that these judgments

> share with political opinions that they are persuasive; the judging person—as Kant says quite beautifully—can only "woo the consent of everyone else" in the hope of coming to an agreement with him eventually. This "wooing" or persuading corresponds closely to what the Greeks called *peithein*, the convincing and persuading speech which they regarded as the typically political form of people talking with one another.[125]

In short, persuasion is required for judgments themselves to be productive of community. And yet, we must ask, do not acts of persuasion presuppose that one is already in a community, even if the acts of judgment are simultaneously constitutive of such communal being? Such acts, inasmuch as they need to be persuasive, paradoxically implicate an already existing community constituted by the *sensus communis*. As opposed to the "wooing" of which Kant speaks, persuasion, as a rhetorical notion, presupposes a political community of citizens and takes place in the public place. "Wooing" is "only" a structural feature of a judgment of taste and, by having freed itself of everything subjective, is in principle in a position only to solicit assent by everyone else. In making a judgment of taste, one appeals to everybody, but in the case of the Third Critique the inclusion of all others takes place only in an ideal sense. From a transcendental point of view, there is never any assurance that a correct reflective judgment secures the actual agreement of others. Legitimately, it can only solicit assent. By contrast, when soliciting is replaced by persuasion, agreement is actually within reach, along with the empirical realization of the being together of men in the plural. Since Arendt links Kant's notions of "wooing" and "courting" to the rhetorical notion in question, it is prudent to explore what she herself has to say about the term "persuasion." In the essay "Socrates," after having evoked Plato's doubt regarding the validity of persuasion, she writes that

> [w]e have difficulty in grasping the importance of this doubt, because "persuasion" is a very weak and inadequate translation of the ancient *peithein*, the political importance of which is indicated by the fact that Peithō, the goddess of persuasion, had a temple in Athens. To persuade, *peithein*, was the specifically political form of speech, and since the Athenians were proud that they, in distinction to the barbarians, conducted their political affairs in the form of speech and without compulsion, they considered rhetoric, the art of persuasion, the highest, the truly political art.[126]

Because of today's negative connotations of forcing one's opinion upon others, the word "persuasion" is not an exact translation of the Greek word *peithein*, which names and points to the specifically political form of speech itself—the speech by deliberating, free citizens in the public space. *Peithein*, Arendt observes, designates "the convincing and persuading speech which [the Greeks] regarded as the typically political form of people talking with one another. Persuasion ruled the intercourse of the citizens of the polis because it excluded physical violence."[127] Citing Aristotle, Arendt reminds us that persuasion not only "always addresses a multitude (*peithein ta plēthē*)" but also takes place entirely in the realm of the *doxai*.[128] As opposed to the specifically philosophical form of speech, which, since Plato, proceeds in a dialectical way (*dialegesthai*) and is possible only in a dialogue between two whose aim is truth, Arendt notes that persuasion "does not come from truth, it comes from opinions."[129] Rather than a way of forcing one's opinion on others, persuasion as the mode of verbal interaction between plural men in the public space draws its power of conviction from the shared opinions of the multitude.[130]

Toward the end of her *Lectures on Kant's Political Philosophy*, Arendt highlights two ideas that guide judgments about particulars for which there are no given universals. I have dealt with the idea of exemplarity, which she rated as the most important in this respect. The other idea is purposiveness, which Arendt does not value as much. This is perhaps because Kant speaks of purposiveness primarily in the context of the natural manifold, as opposed to the condition of plurality of human beings.[131] However, intimately tied to this idea of purposiveness is "the idea of an original compact of mankind as whole," that is, the purpose of a supra-sensible destiny of mankind to be found in Kant's political writings and "occasionally" in the Third Critique.[132] In spite of her cursory treatment of this second idea, consideration of it is necessary to understand her own take on the *sensus communis* better. However, in order to explain what in Arendt's view this second idea by which one regulates one's reflections in a reflective judgment amounts to, we have to follow her thoughts in some of the commentaries of section 41 of the *Critique of the Power of Judgment* in the thirteenth and last session of her *Lectures on Kant's Political Philosophy*. In section 41, entitled "Of the Empirical Interest in the Beautiful," Kant writes:

> The beautiful interests empirically only in *society*; and if the drive to society is admitted to be natural to human beings, while the suitability and the tendency toward it, i.e., *sociability*, are admitted to be necessary for human beings as creatures destined for society, and thus as a property belonging to *humanity*, then it cannot fail that taste should also be regarded as a faculty for judging everything by means of which one can communicate even his *feeling* to everyone else, and hence as a means for promoting what is demanded by an inclination natural to everyone.[133]

In this passage, Kant no longer speaks in the voice of the transcendental philosopher but, rather, in that of a philosophical anthropologist in all its empirical concreteness. As is obvious from the final paragraph of the section where Kant states that the indirect interest in the beautiful through an inclination to society "is of no importance to us here," such interest is empirical.[134] Consequently, the section is a digression beyond the primary transcendental nature of his inquiry, which explores what belongs a priori to a judgment of taste. Even though everything that Kant advances in this section about society, sociability, communication, and the idea of an original contract is from the start empirical, we must linger on what he asserts, because these empirical observations bear heavily on Arendt's interpretation of the *sensus communis*. According to Kant, the human being is characterized by the natural property of sociability (*Geselligkeit*), that is, the capacity for socializing. He or she has this property insofar as he or she is human. Indeed, the capacity in question belongs to his or her humanity (*Humanität*). Having this capacity, he or she is a being destined to be in society (*Gesellschaft*), and this capacity manifests itself in his or her equally natural drive to be with others. This drive makes it necessary for the human being to be in society, to communicate with others, and to share with everyone just everything that is communicable. This drive is also what causes the human being's desire to extend the limit of the communicable wherever possible. Yet, there are things that are not communicable, such as feelings because they are simply private. If there is an empirical interest in the beautiful, it is because the feeling of the beautiful expressed in a judgment of taste is the sole affect that can be universally communicated. Judgments of taste not only extend the communicable to this one feeling of pleasure, qua reflective judgments; they also extend the operations of judging itself beyond those of determinant judgments, which are per se communicable. Reflective judgments of taste are thus ways of increasing and expanding the occasions of socialization.

Empirically speaking, the drive to society not only incites one to expand the communicable as far as possible. One also expects others to do the same. Kant writes that "each expects and requires of everyone else a regard to universal communication, as if from an original contract [or compact] dictated by humanity [*Menschheit*] itself."[135] He even claims that, as far as the empirical history of civilization demonstrates, the value of objects whose inherent interest might not be particularly noticeable is "almost infinitely" increased if they yield to "the idea of [their] universal communicability."[136] It is *as if* this drive to universal communication, which is manifest empirically in every human being's drive to socialization (and in the history of mankind), devolved from "an original contract dictated by humanity itself." From the beginning, a *contrat social*, as it were, binds human beings qua human beings together. From an exclusively empirical point of view, the idea of an original contract dictated by humanity (*Menschheit*) to the individual human being and to the history of the species man can only be a fiction.[137] Nonetheless, it informs the way human beings empirically relate to one another.

After referring to Kant's statement, in "Conjectural Beginning of Human History," that "'the highest end intended for man is sociability,'" Arendt remarks that sociability is considered "the very origin, not the goal, of man's humanity" in section 41 of the *Critique of the Power of Judgment*.[138] She adds that here

> we find that sociability is the very essence of men insofar as they are of this world only. This is a radical departure from all those theories that stress human interdependence as dependence on our fellow men for our *needs* and *wants*. Kant stresses that at least one of our *mental faculties*, the faculty of judgment, presupposes the presence of others. And this mental faculty is not just what we terminologically call judgment; bound up with it is the notion that "feelings and emotions [*Empfindungen*] are regarded as of worth only insofar as they can be generally communicated"; that is, bound up with judgment is our whole soul apparatus, so to speak.[139]

Since Arendt's remarks on sociability as "the very origin" of the human being's humanity are based on her reading of the section "On the Empirical Interest in the Beautiful," it follows that sociability is for her of the order of a natural and empirical drive. Furthermore, sociability as the empirical origin of humanity is construed as "the very essence of men insofar as they are of this world." In other words, everything that Kant advanced in an empirical perspective in section 41 on sociability, society, and communicability, including the originary contract or compact, is understood as a case in point of the human being as a being "of this world," a being to be thought in terms of this world rather than a world beyond this world. If sociability is an origin of the human being's humanity, then it will consist of communicating, communicating with others, and communicating whatever offers itself to such an activity. Such being-together makes up the open space of the world, that is, the public and political realm. If Arendt qualifies this understanding of sociability as the origin of the world as "radical," it is also insofar as it represents a departure from the traditional understanding that human beings form societies only under the pressure of biological needs and wants. Rather than being grounded in the human being's material needs and wants, sociability is the origin of another, 'higher' disposition of the human being, that is, his or her life with others. With her insistence on the 'thisness' of the world constituted by the human being's interaction, Arendt also points to the *reality*, rather than the *ideality*, of this world. It is neither a fiction, nor an idea, but the concrete correlate of the human being's social nature. Even if it is lacking, it is lacking as the empirical fulfillment of the human being's equally empirical essence. And, in spite of its inherent fragility, it is always tangible, even when lacking.

Arendt affirms that "Kant stresses that at least one of our *mental faculties*, the faculty of judgment, presupposes the presence of others."[140] This implies not only that qua *mental* faculties these faculties, or at least one of them, are liberated from the biological process but also that their true field of operation is the in-between of plural human beings. At least one of them, that is, the faculty of judgment, presupposes the presence of others (men in the plural), which also suggests the intrinsically worldly character of this particular power of the mind. Yet, as Arendt's talk of "at least one faculty" suggests, all the other faculties might, at the hand of sociability, perhaps, also undergo a liberation from the biological process and become accommodated to the life together of plural men in the actual space of appearance. Her understanding of sociability also implies a conception of the relation between thinking and judgment that differs significantly from the one we encountered in *The Life of the Mind*, in which judgment is no longer (or not yet) the prime manifestation of the wind of thought but, rather, that very wind itself. Let us remind ourselves that, in "Introduction *into* Politics," Arendt spoke of "thinking as an act of judgment."[141]

In her further comments on sociability, Arendt remarks that bound up with judgment (at least with judgment of taste) is the assumption that only feelings that can be generally communicated are of any worth. With this, she stresses not only the difference of the world as a public space from the private but also communicability and publicness's demand of being as inclusive as possible. When she contends, on the basis of Kant's empirical digression on sociability, that "our whole soul apparatus, so to speak," is bound up with the worldly nature of judgment, the apparatus as a whole is also determined as belonging, perhaps, even in an essential manner, to the human being's worldly, rather than natural or biological, reality.

Sociability and its inherent *sensus communis* respond to needs and wants of the human being other than those concerned with the sustenance of biological life, namely, mental needs and wants related to communication and interaction of autonomous beings. These appear in the activity of judgments concerning matters of public interest and in the communication of aesthetic feelings. Arendt writes: "By communicating one's feelings, one's pleasures and disinterested delights, one tells one's *choices* and one chooses one's company."[142] If, as Arendt submits, communication "depends on the enlarged mentality," that is, if "one can communicate only if one is able to think from the other person's standpoint," it follows that a mental faculty such as thinking becomes entirely transformed within the context of the world as a public and political space.[143] From the silent and solitary activity of the two-in-one, thinking becomes in the space of appearances the discriminating activity of judgment itself, which manifests itself in the telling of "one's *choices*" and, in the same stroke, in the choosing of one's company. What follows from all of this is that, in the public realm, judgment is not the result of the wind of thought as Arendt held in her later work; rather, it is thought itself insofar as it takes place in the public sphere, among men, and from the perspective of an enlarged mentality. Judgment as an activity that presupposes others is thinking as a mental faculty entirely mediated by the *sensus communis*, which manifests itself by way of the discriminating choices that are made and the company that such choices imply.

As Arendt's dialogue with Kant's notion of infinite communicability in advanced civilization demonstrates, linking together judgmental choice and the choice of community is a function not only of an enlarged mentality but also of what human beings wish the world to look like. While the discriminating activity of judgment is intrinsically a function of the aim of realizing the good of which human beings are capable in this worldly world that is the world of appearances, the choice regarding one's company is dictated by the aim shared by others, who also judge in light of an enlarged mentality. As Kant conjectured, the more the enlarged mentality is realized, the more one's judgments are divested of their subjective conditions, and the more sweeping communication becomes, the more it seems *as if* there existed "an original compact, dictated by mankind itself."[144] According to Arendt, by making the demands of enlarged mentality, communication, and socialization in the elemental features of an original compact between human beings into an idea, Kant extended the demands in question beyond the activity of judgment to action itself, that is, to the practical intervention in the world with the goal of securing universal communicability. Arendt remarks:

> This compact, according to Kant, would be a mere idea, regulating not just our reflections on these matters but actually inspiring our actions. It is by virtue of this idea of mankind, present in every single man, that men are human, and they can be called civilized or humane to the extent that this idea becomes the principle not only of their judgments but of their actions.[145]

If so far the *sensus communis* has been limited to ensuring the universal communicability of the activity of thinking as a discriminating activity that necessarily requires a distance to the object to be judged, the sense in question is extended to the realm of the practical itself when the *sensus communis*, as a sense of the world, is raised to the status of the idea of an original compact. In other words, if sociability in the realm of human inter-esse transforms all mental faculties, and thinking in particular, action, too, is transmuted so as to orient itself according to the *sensus communis*. As a consequence, Arendt holds that

> [i]t is at this point that actor and spectator become united; the maxim of the actor and the maxim, the "standard," according to which the spectator judges the spectacle of the world, become one. The, as it were, categorical imperative for action could read as follows: Always act on the maxim through which this original compact can be actualized into a general law.[146]

Even though we have seen that judgment, in spite of the spectatorship, is not simply passive or contemplative but also, as a critical appearance in the world, an active intervention, in her lectures Arendt has treated it as an attitude that is primarily predicated on a distanced and disinterested glance. With Kant, furthermore, she held actors in the public sphere to be oblivious to the larger picture into which their action fits. But, at the end of her *Lectures on Kant's Political Philosophy*, Kant's idea of an original compact allows her to bridge the divide between spectator and actor, impartiality and partiality, judgment and action, and thinking and praxis. No longer predicated merely on the disinterested glance of a spectator or on the perspective of an actor oblivious of the larger picture within which he or she operates, Arendt's political theory proceeds from within the world as a public space in which the actor judges and critically evaluates in immanentist fashion his or her own actions and those of others.

Let us recall that Arendt characterized the second idea on which one must reflect in order to arrive at a judgment, namely, the idea of an original compact of mankind as a whole, as less valuable than the idea of exemplary validity. Except for the fact that the concept of an original compact of humanity is a regulative idea, it is difficult to see why Arendt could have found it less fruitful than the idea of exemplarity even though it concerns the world itself. Indeed, compared to the idea of exemplarity, which Arendt interprets as meaning that the exemplar is contained in an empirical particular and only has to be extracted from it in order subsequently to relate both the particular and its (particular) exemplarity in a judgmental fashion, the idea of a compact of humanity is an idea in a strong sense. And yet, since this idea concerns the world itself, why did Arendt not make it fruitful for her understanding of the world by translating it into her empirically oriented theory of politics and political judgment?

According to Arendt, judgment presupposes actual others, but, since one judges by being guided by a communal sense, one also judges only if one has a sense of the world. Commenting on Kant's theory of hospitality in *Perpetual Peace*, Arendt submits: "One judges always as a member of a community, guided by one's community sense, one's *sensus communis*. But in the last analysis, one is a member of a world community by the sheer fact of being human; this is one's 'cosmopolitan existence.'"[147] These remarks are clearly part of a commentary on Kant, but Arendt aims for something higher or other. She seeks to bring the elements of a political conception of judgment into relief, which Kant unwittingly discovered when he took on the judgment of taste. On this basis, we can safely assume that for Arendt a political judgment, a judgment in the strict sense, is not possible without a sense of the world. While discussing Arendt's conception of the sense of the world as a sixth sense, it became clear that she understands sense as a sensible awareness in space and time of the world not as an idea but, rather, as the 'objective' opening for the public space and its constituting appearances.

At this point, let me take a different interpretive approach. Instead of following the letter of Arendt's interpretation of Kant's conception of judgment, I will interpret this interpretation in light of what I consider the ultimate stakes of her debate, namely, the world. On the basis of what has been established so far about the conclusion Arendt reaches in her *Lectures on Kant's Political Philosophy*, it should be clear that in judging particulars, whether actions or words, one judges at the same time as a world spectator—a *Weltbetrachter*—and as an intra-worldly actor, who contributes to bringing about a world in the act of making a judgment guided by the sense of the world. Judging requires being with one another, that is, being already in community with others, and within a given world, but in judging, and thus in manifesting one's choices, one also instigates another world, a new world that one offers to the world, a world as one wishes the world to look, and that competes with already existing "proposals" for worlds.

As we have seen, a world requires durability as opposed to the cyclical nature of the natural processes. Newcomers are born into a world that already exists, but, as strangers to this world and as beginners, they also bring with them a new world, which did not exist before, a world that they donate to the world and that is a correlate of their natality. Natality is the promise of a new world made from scratch, made all over again, a world created *as if* for the first time. With this newly donated world, the relative durability bestowed on the world through work is reshaped, and, in the same flourish, the world's ground in the pre-worldly activities of labor and work is both confirmed and recast. Through his or her words and deeds, judgments and actions, the newcomer brings this new world into an appearance, which in turn is judged by others. These judgments, in order to be judgments in the first place, must be guided by the idea of exemplarity, that is, by a standard of judgment that, in lieu of a given universal, allows for deciding and possibly empowering the particular world that has been donated to them. The idea of exemplarity that guides judgment is that of a world that is new and, as a result, other and singular. It is always the first appearance of a world within the world, claiming not only to be novel, as far as world is concerned, but also to be an originary or first donation of a world, of, more precisely, a this-worldly world.

In closing, let me go back to Arendt's drastic separation of reflective and determining judgment. If Arendt can claim that determinant judgment is not really a judgment at all, is it not because reflective judgment (in its aesthetic form at least) is an autonomous form of judging with an a priori principle of its own? Even though Arendt does not attend to the transcendental nature of Kant's investigation into what constitutes a pure judgment of taste, his demonstration that the aesthetic power of judgment is a particular faculty with an a priori principle of its own, which distinguishes it from determinant or logical judgment, is essential to Arendt's claim that judging is a distinct faculty of the mind. What Arendt looks for in Kant is to establish the faculty of judgment in all its independence from knowledge and truth, something Albrecht Wellmer has branded as a "mythology of judgment." For Wellmer, to put determinant judgment into question rests on a narrow conception of rationality informed by the traditional way of understanding argumentation in the sciences.[148] Be that as it may! By contrast, let us remind ourselves of Arendt's suggestion that, at the hands of sociability and the enlarged mentality, one faculty, and possibly others, is freed from the biological process. In the world as a public and political space, thinking itself even undergoes a transformation in such a way that its activity becomes judgmental through and through. Although it is only in *The Life of the Mind* that she refers explicitly to Aquinas's conception of the *sensus communis* as a sixth sense, one that is "needed to keep my five senses together and guarantee that it is the same object that I see, touch, taste, smell and hear," is it not precisely because of this unification of all our sensible faculties that her earlier conception of the *sensus communis* could be understood as a sense that fits us into a community and, ultimately, a world? For Arendt, judgment as the most political, that is, world-oriented, faculty is the faculty that unites the activity of thinking and that of the senses into one. In this way, the faculty is always able to have the space of appearances, or world, as its 'object' or, put another way, as the space for its manifestation.

By severing judgment from determinant, cognitive judgment and also from aesthetic reflective judgment, Arendt construes it as an activity whose political thrust is manifest in the choices that are made possible in the public space as a space of appearance. However, such judgment is also an activity that judges the existing world in view of a world and in terms of how one wishes it to look. In other words, at stake in her radical distinction between the two forms of judgment is, ultimately, the possibility of the political. It is a conception of the political whose primary objective is the realization of the world without which the political remains unconceivable.

Presenting it as a political faculty from the start, Arendt develops judgment in analogy to what Kant establishes about the pure judgment of taste. Indeed, in analogy to Kant's separation of the judgment of taste not only from mere judgments of the senses but also from judgments of cognition (and morality), and in analogy to Kant's claim that the aesthetic reflective judgment enjoys a law particular to itself, Arendt argues in turn that the power of judgment, as "the most political of man's mental abilities," is a distinct faculty with a 'logic' of its own.[149] This does not mean, as a number of critics hold, that she aestheticizes the political. The notion of analogy consists precisely in establishing structural resemblances between two entities or domains whose irreducible difference remains intact. Before Arendt even links judgment with the specific type of phenomena that constitute the sphere of publicness and grounds it in the *sensus communis*, Kant's transcendental inquiry into the judgment of taste serves her to secure the claim of the autonomy of judging as a faculty that—distinct from what the judgment of taste establishes when it calls a particular object beautiful (rather than ugly or, at its worst, nauseating), namely, its formal conformity (or nonconformity) to the powers of representation and, hence, the harmony of reason and nature—is all about distinction, discrimination, and decision. Yet, to seek autonomy for a faculty of judgment whose prime thrust is critical is not to construe it as a faculty of a sovereign subject that gives itself the law. Rather, it seems to imply that, notwithstanding the fact that judgment has a modus operandi that is strictly its own, judging always institutes itself anew and from scratch on each occasion that a concrete situation demands to be addressed in a judgmental fashion.

To conclude, let us keep in mind that for Arendt the political is the realm of action (as opposed to labor and work) not only between people in the plural but also between free citizens. The domain of the interactions of people in the public space is a domain that is not ruled by a utilitarian logic of ends and means. The latter belongs to the realm of work. Action, and, in particular, judgment as the most political of all actions, is not only an activity of free people; it itself is free and is its own end. One is reminded here of what Aristotle says in Book VI of *Nicomachean Ethics* about political action, to which Arendt subscribes without reserve. Arguing that "doing (*praxis*) and making (*poiesis*) are generically different, since making aims at an end distinct from the act of making," Aristotle submits that, "in doing [*prattein*, which Arendt translates as action], the end cannot be other than the act itself: doing well is indeed the end."[150] Judging as an action, which for Arendt implies the in-between dimension of the commerce of human beings qua free beings, is a doing whose discriminating nature is not only political in an emphatic sense but also, as such a doing-well, its own end. It is a doing whose meaning is immanent to it and does not lie in an end separate from or outside it.[151] It is autonomous and free. The detour through Kant's *Critique of the Power of Judgment* aims at philosophically buttressing this insight before using other elements from it—such as the *sensus communis*, the enlarged mentality, the relation between actor and spectator, and exemplary validity—to flesh out this autonomous activity's further characteristics.

Finally, let me return briefly to Arendt's characterization in "Introduction *into* Politics" of reflective judgment as "a judgment without standards [*massstabloses Urteilen*]," distinct from the determinate judgment that applies concepts or standards that are already known and accepted to the particular to be subsumed under them. In this "Introduction," she writes that

> [b]ecause by its very nature action always creates relationships and ties as it moves into the world, there is inherent in it excessiveness or boundlessness [*Masslosigkeit*]. [...] To the Greek mind, this excess did not lie in the immoderateness of the man who acts, or in his hubris, but in the fact that the relationships arising through action are and must be of the sort that keep extending without limits. By linking men of action together, each relationship established by action ends up in a web of ties and relationships in which it triggers new links, changes the constellation of existing relationships, and thus always reaches out ever further, setting much more into interconnected motion than the man who initiates action ever could have foreseen.[152]

In other contexts, Arendt says that action triggers linear processes whose end cannot be contained in advance by any concept of an end or goal. But this boundlessness and excessiveness "inherent in those free human actions that establish relationships" in unforeseeable, unpredictable, and unprogrammable ways are at the same time also a danger because they can unleash "devastating processes" that create "a wasteland between men."[153] In order to "seal off action from the danger of excessiveness always inherent in it"[154] without, however, making it subservient to utilitarian ends and means that would destroy action's political nature, Arendt calls for the free judgmental activity of a judgment without standards. Without applying in advance known concepts or standards to particular actions, judgment singularly discriminates between those actions that cement the public space, thus reanimating it, and those that put it in jeopardy. Such judgment without standards is not only the sole way to do justice to the singularity of what the many begin in the public space but also to ward off the danger that besets all free action without destroying the latter's intrinsically free nature. In Arendt's native German, a judgment without standard is called a *massstabloses Urteil*. If an 'originary judgment,' or 'judgment in a strict sense,' is a judgment that can proceed only in the absence of criteria, we must ask whether a *massstabloses Urteil* is not also *masslos*—boundless, extreme, excessive, exceeding all standards, even mad. And yet, is a judgment that is equal only to excess not also the only kind of judgment appropriate to address "the thrust toward limitlessness" inherent to political action?[155] Indeed, only such a judgment would seem to be able to discriminate between, on the one hand, actions that link human beings into a web of ties and relationships that continue to further the public and political realm and, on the other, actions in which the thrust to limitlessness becomes destructive. Is it not also in this sense that judgment is a doing well that is its own end?

NOTES

Introduction

1. Hannah Arendt, *Men in Dark Times*, New York: Harcourt Brace, 1993, p. 86.
2. Wolfgang Kluxen, "Ancilla theologiae," in *Historisches Wörterbuch der Philosophie*, Vol. 1, ed. J. Ritter, Darmstadt: Wissenschaftliche Buchgesellschaft, 1971, pp. 294–295.
3. Arendt, *Men in Dark Times*, p. 86, n. 8.
4. Ibid., p. 86.
5. Immanuel Kant, "The Conflict of the Faculties," in *Religion and Rational Theology*, trans. A. W. Wood and G. di Giovanni, Cambridge: University of Cambridge Press, 1996, p. 255 (translation modified).
6. Arendt, *Men in Dark Times*, p. 93.
7. But if the conditions of the political can, perhaps, no longer be cast in transcendental terms, this does not mean that they would, therefore, be of the order of the empirical, and would lack all necessity. Thinking about the political requires navigating between those two pitfalls.
8. Jacques Taminiaux argues that, in his lectures on the *Sophist* from 1924/25, Heidegger views ancient Greece exclusively from the perspective of the excellence of the *bios theoretikos* as it has been celebrated by Plato and interprets Aristotle's notion of *phronesis* in an ontological, that is, Platonic, way by "projecting *sophia* and *theoria* upon the axis of *phronesis/praxis*." (Jacques Taminiaux, *The Thracian Maid and the Professional Thinker: Arendt and Heidegger*, trans. M. Gendre, Albany: SUNY Press, 1997, p. 8) See also the considerably more polemical contribution to this subject by Josef Kopperschmidt, "Heideggers Umweg in Platons Höhle oder: Über einige Irritationen in Heideggers Aristoteles-Vorlesung von 1924," in *Heidegger über Rhetorik*, ed. Josef Kopperschmidt, Munich: Wilhelm Fink, 2009, pp. 301–432.
9. Taminiaux, *Thracian Maid*, p. 12.
10. Of Solon, Herodotus writes that "to see the world, [he] set out upon his travels [*theories . . . heineken*]." (*The History of Herodotus*, Vol. 1, trans. G. Rawlinson, New York: E. P. Dutton, 1936, pp. 13–14.)
11. Martin Heidegger, "Science and Reflection," in *The Question Concerning Technology and Other Essays*, trans. W. Lovitt, New York: Harper & Row, 1977, pp. 164–165.
12. Ibid. p. 180.

13. François Jullien, *De l'Universel, de l'uniforme, du commun, et du dialogue entre les cultures*, Paris: Fayard, 2008, p. 106.

14. Arendt writes: "The method [of rhetoric] is the *enthymema*, that is, a syllogism, ergo part of dialectics! [...] Rhetoric, therefore, is not *antistrophos*, but in essence part of dialectic. Dialectic has to do with truth, rhetoric with what resembles truth [...] Ergo, the priority of the philosopher is upheld." (Hannah Arendt, *Denktagebuch*, Vol. 1 (1950–1973), Munich: Piper Verlag, 2003, pp. 408–409.)

15. Pierre Aubenque, *La Prudence chez Aristote*, Paris: PUF, 1963, p. 144.

Part I

1. William M. A. Grimaldi, *Studies in the Philosophy of Aristotle's Rhetoric*, Wiesbaden: Franz Steiner Verlag, 1972, p. 15.

2. Amélie Oksenberg Rorty, "Structuring Rhetoric," in *Essays on Aristotle's Rhetoric*, ed. Amélie Oksenberg Rorty, Berkeley: University of California Press, 1996, p. 11. (In all fairness, I must add not only that Rorty's essay is an excellent piece of scholarship on the *Rhetoric*, but that she is also the editor of one of the finest collections of essays by contemporary philosophers on Aristotle's treatise.)

3. Sir David Ross, *Aristotle*, London: Methuen, 1966, pp. 275–276.

4. Martin Heidegger, *Grundbegriffe der aristotelischen Philosophie*, *Gesamtausgabe*, Vol. 18, Frankfurt/Main: Klostermann, 2002, pp. 109–110.

5. Martin Heidegger, *Being and Time*, trans. J. Macquarrie and E. Robinson, New York: Harper & Row, 1962, p. 178.

6. Heidegger, *Grundbegriffe der aristotelischen Philosophie*, pp. 108–109.

7. Heidegger, *Grundbegriffe der aristotelischen Philosophie*, p. 61.

Chapter 1

1. See also Glenn W. Most, "The Uses of *Endoxa*: Philosophy and Rhetoric in the *Rhetoric*," in *Aristotle's Rhetoric*, eds. D. J. Furley and A. Nehamas, Princeton: Princeton University Press, 1994, pp. 167–190.

2. Aristotle, *The "Art" of Rhetoric*, trans. J. H. Freese, Cambridge, MA: Harvard University Press, 2006. All page references in Chapters 1–3 text are to this edition.

3. Plato, *Collected Dialogues*, eds. E. Hamilton and H. Cairns, Princeton: University of Princeton Press, 1980, p. 247 (265 c–d).

4. Jacques Brunschwig, "*Rhétorique et Dialectique, Rhétorique et Topiques*," in *Aristotle's Rhetoric*, eds. D. J. Furley and A. Nehamas, Princeton: Princeton University Press, 1994, p. 59.

5. E. M. Cope, *An Introduction to Aristotle's Rhetoric with Analysis Notes and Appendices*, London: Macmillan, 1867, p. 88.

6. Brunschwig, "*Rhétorique et Dialectique, Rhétorique et Topiques*," pp. 59, 63.

7. Cope, *An Introduction to Aristotle's Rhetoric*, p. 68.

8. Aristotle, *On Rhetoric: A Theory of Civic Discourse*, trans. George A. Kennedy, Oxford: Oxford University Press, 2007, p. 33.

9. Jacques Brunschwig, "Introduction," Aristote, *Topiques*, Vol. 1, Paris: Les Belles Lettres, 1967, p. xxxi.

10. William M. A. Grimaldi, *Studies in the Philosophy of Aristotle's Rhetoric*, Wiesbaden: Franz Steiner Verlag, 1972, p. 144.

11. *The Complete Works of Aristotle*, Vol. 1, ed. J. Barnes, Princeton: Princeton University Press, 1984, p. 1798 (1139b 35–36).

12. In his discussion of the utility of maxims in rhetorical discourse, Aristotle explicitly stresses the fact that they make "speeches ethical. Speeches have this character, in which the moral purpose is clear. And this is the effect of all maxims" (289).

13. Aristote, *Rhétorique*, Vol. 1, trans. M. Dufour, Paris: Les Belles Lettres, 1960, p. 75.

14. *The Complete Works of Aristotle*, Vol. 1, p. 1730 (1094 b12–28).

15. Cope, *An Introduction to Aristotle's Rhetoric*, pp. 141–142.

16. Most, "The Uses of *Endoxa*," p. 183.

17. Amélie Oksenberg Rorty, "Structuring Rhetoric," in *Essays on Aristotle's Rhetoric*, ed. Amélie Oksenberg Rorty, Berkeley: University of California Press, 1966, p. 6.

18. Cope, *An Introduction to Aristotle's Rhetoric*, p. 173.

19. Ibid., p. 120.

20. *The Complete Works of Aristotle*, Vol. 1, p. 167 (100b 21–23).

21. Most, "The Uses of *Endoxa*," p. 176. Most adds: "It should be noted that the *endoxa*, so defined, include a wide spectrum of opinions, ranging from the moral intuitions in which all or most people believe, to specific (and not necessarily popular or intuitive) philosophical doctrines" (176).

22. Cope, *An Introduction to Aristotle's Rhetoric*, p. 88.

23. Aristotle, *On Rhetoric*, p. 35.

Chapter 2

1. Aristotle, *On Rhetoric: A Theory of Civic Discourse*, trans. George A. Kennedy, Oxford: Oxford University Press, 2007, p. 37.

2. E. M. Cope, *An Introduction to Aristotle's Rhetoric with Analysis Notes and Appendices*, London: Macmillan, 1867, p. 102.

3. M. F. Burnyeat, "Enthymeme: Aristotle on the Logic of Persuasion," in *Aristotle's Rhetoric. Philosophical Essays*, eds. D. J. Furley and A. Nehemas, Princeton: University of Princeton Press, 1994, pp. 3–55.

4. Aristotle, *On Rhetoric*, p. 39; Aristote, *Rhétorique*, Vol. 1, p. 77.

5. Fortenbaugh's analysis of Aristotle's definition of anger, "Let anger be a desire for revenge on account of apparent insult" (1378a 30–31), highlights the fact that the thought of outrage is essential to anger, and that it is that thought that represents its efficient cause. (William W. Fortenbaugh, "Aristotle's Rhetoric on Emotions," *Archiv für Geschichte der Philosophie*, 52, 1970, pp. 59–60.

6. Fortenbaugh, "Aristotle's Rhetoric on Emotions," p. 42.

7. Cope, *An Introduction to Aristotle's Rhetoric*, pp. 68, 123, 152–153.

8. Rhetoric and dialectic are *free* faculties, or possibilities, as Heidegger translates *dunameis*, free because not bound to any specific realm of things or knowledge thereof; they are faculties for making arguments and for judging. It is as if only such free faculties could be adequate to the specific demands that come with the very domain of human affairs as one of probabilities. One cannot but wonder whether Kant's conception of the free play of the faculties in a reflective judgment is not also indebted to Aristotle's elaboration on dialectic and rhetoric as arts that are not bound by specific subject matters.

9. William M. A. Grimaldi, *Studies in the Philosophy of Aristotle's Rhetoric*, Wiesbaden: Franz Steiner Verlag, 1972, p. 67; Burnyeat, "Enthymeme: Aristotle on the Logic of Persuasion," pp. 30–31.

10. Grimaldi, *Studies in the Philosophy of Aristotle's Rhetoric*, p. 89. About the way that example remains nonetheless "a coordinate instrument with enthymeme for rhetorical demonstration," see pp. 104–105.

11. See Mary Margaret McCabe, "Arguments in Context: Aristotle's Rhetoric," in *Aristotle's Rhetoric: Philosophical Essays*, eds. D. J. Furley and A. Nehemas, Princeton: Princeton University Press, 1994, pp. 152–158.

12. Cope, *An Introduction to Aristotle's Rhetoric*, p. 141.

13. Aristotle, *On Rhetoric*, p. 41.

14. Grimaldi, *Studies in the Philosophy of Aristotle's Rhetoric*, pp. 111–112. The almost immediate demonstrative force of signs as sources of enthymemes likens them to the example, i.e., the second type of rhetorical proof.

15. Cope, *An Introduction to Aristotle's Rhetoric*, p. 165.

16. Ibid., p. 125.

17. Jacques Brunschwig, "Introduction," Aristote, *Topiques I–IV*, Paris: Les Belles Lettres, 1967, p. xxxix.

18. Cope, *An Introduction to Aristotle's Rhetoric*, p. 93.

Chapter 3

1. See Kennedy's remarks in Aristotle, *On Rhetoric: A Theory of Civic Discourse*, trans. George A. Kennedy, Oxford: Oxford University Press, 2007, p. 50.

2. E. M. Cope, *An Introduction to Aristotle's Rhetoric with Analysis Notes and Appendices*, London: Macmillan, 1867, p. 126.

3. William M. A. Grimaldi, *Studies in the Philosophy of Aristotle's Rhetoric*, Wiesbaden: Franz Steiner Verlag, 1972, p. 35.

4. H. G. Liddell and R. Scott, *A Greek English Lexicon*, Oxford: Clarendon Press, 1968, pp. 1647–1648; J. Ritter and K. Gründer, eds., *Historisches Wörterbuch der Philosophie*, Vol. 10, Darmstadt: Wissenschaftliche Buchgesellschaft, 1998, pp. 197–198; F. E. Peters, ed., *Greek Philosophical Terms: A Historical Lexicon*, New York: New York University Press, 1967, pp. 180–182.

5. Walter Burkert, "STOIKHEION: Eine semasiologische Studie," *Philologus* 103 (1959): 169.

6. It is, indeed, the case that as an element of a composite, the *stoikheion* is from now on thoroughly distinct from an *arche*, given that the latter can also exist independently of what it engenders or explains. See in particular *Metaphysics* 1070b23, where Aristotle unmistakably distinguishes between element and principle when he writes that "not only the elements present in a thing are causes, but also something external, i.e. the moving cause, clearly while principle and element are different both are causes, and principle is divided in these two kinds." See also 1014a19–21.

7. Cope, *An Introduction to Aristotle's Rhetoric*, pp. 127–128.

8. Grimaldi, *Studies in the Philosophy of Aristotle's Rhetoric*, pp. 131–132.

9. See ibid., pp. 124–126.

10. Ibid., p. 129.

11. Ibid., p. 129.

12. Ibid., pp. 125–126.

13. Ibid., p. 131.

14. Ibid., p. 132. By contrast, in his translation of the *Rhetoric*, George A. Kennedy seems to equate *stoikheia* and *idia*. See Aristotle, *On Rhetoric*, p. 52.

15. Liddell and Scott, *A Greek English Lexicon*, p. 1647.

16. *The Complete Works of Aristotle*, p. 1577.

17. Burkert, "STOIKHEION," p. 178.
18. Ibid., p. 193.
19. Ibid., p. 196.
20. Ibid., p. 170.
21. As Plato says in *Politeia* (402a), compared to the *grammata* understood either as "letters" or "writing marks," the *stoikheia* are finite. See Burkert, "STOIKHEION," p. 172.
22. William M. A. Grimaldi, *Aristotle, Rhetoric I: A Commentary*, New York: Fordham University Press, 1980, p. 77.
23. Grimaldi, *Studies in the Philosophy of Aristotle's Rhetoric*, p. 36.
24. While admitting that one could make them five, or even six, since Aristotle's language seems to vary, Cope claims that the author "does in fact regard them as four, neither more nor less" (Cope, *An Introduction to Aristotle's Rhetoric*, pp. 252–253). But let me also point out that in Book II, 26, Aristotle remarks that amplification and depreciation is not a *stoikheion*.
25. Grimaldi, *Studies in the Philosophy of Aristotle's Rhetoric*, pp. 36–37.
26. Ibid., p. 37.
27. Cope, *An Introduction to Aristotle's Rhetoric*, p. 126.
28. Ibid., p. 253.
29. Grimaldi, *Studies in the Philosophy of Aristotle's Rhetoric*, p. 38. Grimaldi adds: "The *koina* are in many ways analogous to the concept of the *organa* in the *Topics* (I. cc. 13–18) but they are more sharply delineated and explained. The *koina* are as critical to the process of rhetorical discourse as the *organa* are to topical methodology for without each there can presumably be neither rhetorical discourse nor topical investigation. It would be satisfying to determine these *koina* more definitely by having the noun to which they apply, but Aristotle apparently felt no need for one since he never suggests one" (pp. 38–39).
30. Burkert, "STOIKHEION," p. 174.
31. Lucrèce, *De la nature*, trans. H. Clouard, Paris: Garnier Flammarion, 1964, p. 35.
32. See Jacques Derrida, "My Chances/*Mes chances*: A Rendezvous with Some Epicurean Stereophonies," in *Psyche: Inventions of the Other*, Vol. 1, eds. P. Kamuf and E. Rottenberg, Stanford: Stanford University Press, 2007, pp. 348–349.

Part 2

1. Martin Heidegger, *Besinnung, Gesamtausgabe*, Vol. 66, Frankfurt/Main: Klostermann, 1997, pp. 62–63.
2. Ibid., p. 67.
3. Martin Heidegger, *Zur Bestimmung der Philosophie, Gesamtausgabe*, Vol. 56/57, Frankfurt/Main: Klostermann, 1987, p. 74.
4. See "The Originary World of Tragedy," in my *Europe, or the Infinite Task: A Study of a Philosophical Concept*, Stanford: Stanford University Press, 2009, pp. 144–207.
5. Heidegger, *Zur Bestimmung der Philosophie*, p. 87.
6. Ute Guzzoni, *Der andere Heidegger: Überlegungen zu seinem späteren Denken*, Freiburg: Verlag Karl Alber, 2009, p. 96.
7. Martin Heidegger, *Basic Writings*, ed. D. F. Krell, New York: Harper & Row, 1977, p. 194 (emphasis mine).
8. Ibid., p. 239.
9. Martin Heidegger, *Elucidations of Hölderlin's Poetry*, trans. K. Hoeller, Amherst, NY: Prometheus Books, 2000, p. 201.

10. Heidegger, *Besinnung*, p. 47.

11. Alfred Ernout and Antoine Meillet, *Dictionnaire étymologique de la langue latine*, Paris: Klincksieck, 2001, p. 623. Heidegger consults this dictionary in "Science and Reflection" in order to lay the grounds for his translation of *contemplatio* as *Betrachtung*. (See *The Question Concerning Technology and Other Essays*, trans. W. Lovitt, New York: Harper & Row, 1977, p. 166.)

12. Ernout and Meillet, *Dictionnaire étymologique de la langue latine*, p. 623.

13. Pierre Aubenque, *La Prudence chez Aristote*, pp. 144ff.

14. Aristotle, *The Complete Works*, ed. J. Barnes, Princeton: University of Princeton Press, 1984, p. 1800.

Chapter 4

1. For the significance of this early lecture for the formation of *Being and Time*, see Theodore Kisiel, *The Genesis of Heidegger's Being & Time*, Berkeley, CA: University of California Press, 1995, pp. 15–20.

2. Martin Heidegger, *Zur Bestimmung der Philosophie*, Gesamtausgabe, Vol. 56/57, Frankfurt/Main: Klostermann, 1987. Hereafter abbreviated as BP, followed by page numbers. All the translations are mine.

3. This is not a unique occurrence of the term in Heidegger's work. He refers to the category of the not-yet in Chapters 48 and 50 of *Being and Time* as well.

4. Heidegger remarks that the phenomenon in question does "especially not or rarely occur in such types of experience that are riveted to a world, *without* attaining within these a maximally amplified intensification of life" (BP, 115).

5. In these elaborations on the "pre-worldly lived something," one touches on possibilities in his early thought that, in spite of what we will encounter in our commentary on one of his later essays on theory in Chapter 6, Heidegger may never have taken up again, and that could have opened other ways in which to proceed in thought.

6. I recall that a couple of years later, in 1924, the term "life" becomes synonymous with Dasein, before Heidegger drops the term altogether.

Chapter 5

1. Martin Heidegger, *Ontology: The Hermeneutics of Facticity*, trans. John van Buren, Bloomington: Indiana University Press, 1999, p. 73.

2. Martin Heidegger, *Zur Bestimmung der Philosophie*, Gesamtausgabe, Vol. 56/57, Frankfurt/Main: Klostermann, 1987, p. 59.

3. Ibid., p. 65.
4. Ibid., p. 5.
5. Ibid., p. 114.
6. Ibid., p. 112.
7. Ibid., p. 114.
8. Ibid., p. 115.
9. Ibid., p. 115.
10. Ibid., p. 116.
11. Ibid., p. 115.
12. See ibid., p. 89.
13. Heidegger, *Ontology*, p. 80.

14. Ibid., p. 80.
15. Ibid., p. 73.
16. Heidegger, *Zur Bestimmung der Philosophie* p. 88.
17. Ibid., p. 87.
18. Ibid., p. 88.
19. Ibid., pp. 88–89.
20. Ibid., p. 89.
21. Ibid., p. 89.
22. Ibid., p. 89.
23. Ibid., p. 89.
24. Ibid., p. 89.
25. Ibid., p. 90.
26. Ibid., p. 89.
27. Martin Heidegger, *The Basic Concepts of Aristotelian Philosophy*, trans. Robert D. Metcalf and Mark B. Tanzer, Bloomington: Indiana University Press, 2009, pp. 40–41.
28. As Ute Guzzoni has argued, even though the early Heidegger considered the possibility that philosophical thought could help the sciences accomplish a different way of proceeding and self-understanding, the later Heidegger increasingly became skeptical of such a possibility. Ute Guzzoni, *Der andere Heidegger: Überlegungen zu seinem späteren Denken*, Freiburg: Verlag Karl Alber, 2009, pp. 28–30.
29. Martin Heidegger, *Being and Time*, trans. John Macquarrie and Edward Robinson, New York: Harper & Row, 1962. All page references in this chapter text are from this translation of the text.
30. Heidegger, *Zur Bestimmung der Philosophie*, p. 71.
31. Friedrich-Wilhelm von Herrmann, *Hermeneutische Phänomenologie des Daseins: Ein Kommentar zu "Sein und Zeit,"* Vol. 2, Frankfurt/Main: Klostermann, 2005, S 83.
32. Martin Heidegger, "Science and Reflection," in *The Question Concerning Technology*, trans. William Lovitt, New York: Harper & Row, 1977, pp. 155–182, see esp. 163–167; Martin Heidegger, *Parmenides*, trans. André Schuwer and Richard Rojcewicz, Bloomington: Indiana University Press, 1998, see esp. pp. 147–148.
33. Heidegger, *Parmenides*, p. 147.
34. Heidegger, "Science and Reflection," pp. 164–165.
35. Ibid., p. 165.
36. Heidegger, *Parmenides*, p. 147.
37. Martin Heidegger, "The Letter on 'Humanism,'" in *Pathmarks*, ed. William McNeill, trans. Frank A. Capuzzi, Cambridge: Cambridge University Press, 1998, p. 240.
38. Heidegger, *Parmenides*, p. 147. But even then a new question imposes itself upon us. As imperative as all such originary questions may be, do they not also precisely imply an inevitable danger, the danger of cutting adrift what is merely derivative—in this instance, theoretical knowing—and thereby passing over the possibility of shaping it into something new and more meaningful?

Chapter 6

1. Originally, "Science and Reflection" was a lecture given to a small group of people in Munich in August of 1953 in preparation for a conference several months later that the Bavarian Academy of the Fine Arts in Munich organized on "The Arts in the Age of Technology." At this conference, Heidegger presented "The Question Concerning Technology."

2. Martin Heidegger, *The Question Concerning Technology and Other Essays*, trans. W. Lowitt, New York: Harper & Row, 1977, p. 157.

3. Martin Heidegger, *Besinnung*, Gesamtausgabe, Vol. 66, Frankfurt/Main: Klostermann, 1997, p. 24.

4. Heidegger, *The Question Concerning Technology*, p. 156.

5. Ibid.

6. Ibid.

7. Although Heidegger does not pick up the question of art again in the essay, the contrast between art and the sciences serves at the beginning to powerfully make the following point: whereas art is a way of bestowing upon man the splendor of the real, making him see it more purely and more clearly in this light, the sciences lack from the start anything similar (Heidegger, *The Question Concerning Technology*, p. 156).

8. Ibid.

9. Ibid.

10. Ibid.

11. Ibid.

12. Ibid., p. 157.

13. Ibid.

14. Ibid.

15. Ibid.

16. Ibid., p. 158.

17. Ibid.

18. Ibid.

19. Ibid.

20. Heidegger explicitly makes this point only in "Hölderlin's Earth and Heaven" (1959). See Martin Heidegger, *Elucidations of Hölderlin's Poetry*, trans. K. Hoeller, Amherst, NY: Prometheus Books, 2000, p. 201.

21. Heidegger, *The Question Concerning Technology*, p. 158.

22. Ibid.

23. Ibid. (translation modified)

24. Ibid., p. 159.

25. Ibid. p. 165. For a more detailed discussion of the distinction of words and terms as "portraying names," see "Words," in Martin Heidegger, *On the Way to Language*, trans. P. D. Hertz, San Francisco: Harper, 1971, pp. 139–156.

26. Heidegger, *The Question Concerning Technology*, p. 159.

27. Ibid., p. 159.

28. Ibid.

29. Ibid.

30. Ibid.

31. Ibid., p. 160.

32. Ibid.

33. Ibid.

34. Ibid.

35. Ibid.

36. The distinction between *dynamis*, *energeia*, and *entelecheia* is a consistent concern in many of Heidegger's seminars. See above all Martin Heidegger, *Aristotle's Metaphysics Θ 1–3. On the Essence and Actuality of Force*, trans. W. Brogan and P. Warnek, Bloomington: Indiana University Press, 1995.

37. Heidegger writes: "Aristotle's fundamental word for presencing, *energeia*, is properly translated by our word *Wirklichkeit* (reality) only if we, for our part, think the verb *wirken* (to work) as the Greeks thought it, in the sense of bringing *hither* [*her*]—into unconcealment, *forth* [*vor*]—into presencing" (*The Question Concerning Technology*, pp. 160–161). As one can gather from this passage, it is not only a question of etymologically elucidating German words by retracing them back to Greek words but also of properly translating Greek words into German words so that these can continue to speak to us. Etymology and translation mutually call upon one another. Only under the condition that "we, for our part, think the verb *wirken* (to work) as the Greeks thought it" can *Wirklichkeit* (reality) translate the Greek *energeia*. In other words, the whole etymological recourse requires us to render our German words Greek by thinking them in a Greek manner. In contemporary German, *wirken* means to bring about, to do, to effect but not, at least not explicitly, to bring hither (into unconcealment) and forth (into presencing). Yet, if the word *Wirklichkeit* is to be connected to the Greek meaning of *energeia* as the coming into and holding something within presence, the German word has first to be understood in a Greek sense.

38. Heidegger, *The Question Concerning Technology*, p. 160.

39. Ibid. To think of the *ergon* as the result of a cause, of an *Ur-Sache*, or *Ur-thing*, is to model it after the paradigm of artisanal production. (See also Hannah Arendt, *The Human Condition*, Chicago: University of Chicago Press, 1958, p. 312.)

40. Heidegger, *The Question Concerning Technology*, p. 161.

41. Ibid., p. 162.

42. Ibid., p. 163.

43. Ibid. p. 162.

44. Ibid., p. 163.

45. Ibid.

46. Ibid.

47. Ibid.

48. Ibid.

49. Ibid.

50. In a commentary on Plato's *Phaedrus*, Heidegger writes: "*thea*, 'viewing,' is also the supreme apprehending, the grasping of Being. The look reaches as far as the highest and farthest remoteness of Being; simultaneously, it penetrates the nearest and brightest proximity of fleeting appearances. The more radiantly and brightly fleeting appearances are apprehended as such, the more brightly does that of which they are the appearances come to the fore—Being." (Martin Heidegger, *Nietzsche*. Vol. 1: *The Will to Power as Art*. Vol. 2: *The Eternal Recurrence of the Same*, trans. D. F. Krell, Harper, 1991, p. 196.)

51. Heidegger, *The Question Concerning Technology*, p. 163.

52. Ibid., p. 164.

53. Ibid.

54. Ibid.

55. Ibid.

56. See my "Theatrum Theoreticum," in *The Honor of Thinking: Critique, Theory, Philosophy*, Stanford: Stanford University Press, 2007, p. 200.

57. Heidegger, *The Question Concerning Technology*, p. 164.

58. One cannot but also think here of Plato's, or Socrates's, recourse to extravagant etymologies to score points, or make an argument, which in the eyes of the modern scientifically trained reader are sheer aberrations. See, for example, G. R. F. Ferrari, *Listening to the Cicadas: A Study of Plato's "Phaedrus,"* Cambridge: Cambridge University Press, 1990, pp. 114–117, and especially p. 155.

59. Heidegger, *The Question Concerning Technology*, p. 164. According to Liddell and Scott's *Greek-English Dictionary*, the term means "care, concern."
60. Heidegger, *The Question Concerning Technology*, pp. 164–165.
61. Ibid., p. 165.
62. Ibid.
63. Ibid.
64. Ibid.
65. Ibid.
66. Ibid., pp. 166, 157.
67. Ibid. p. 166.
68. Ibid.
69. Ibid.
70. Ibid.
71. Ibid.
72. Ibid.
73. Ibid., pp. 166–167.
74. Heidegger has emphasized time and again that technology is not the practical conclusion of the theoretical sciences, since the latter are technical from the start.
75. Heidegger, *The Question Concerning Technology*, p. 167.
76. Ibid.
77. Ibid., pp. 167–168 (translation modified)
78. Ibid., p. 168.
79. Ibid.
80. As Heidegger contends, theoretical observation as a striving responds to the real that presences in the shape of objectness by entrapping it in a representation, or, more precisely, in an "entrapping representation [*nachstellende Vorstellung*]," by means of which the real in its objectness is made to stand before a subject. He avers: "Entrapping representation, which secures everything in that objectness which is thus capable of being followed out, is the fundamental characteristic of representing through which modern science corresponds to the real" (Heidegger, *The Question Concerning Technology*, p. 168). It is through representation that modern theory belabors the real and expressly works the real out into an objectness, breaking (sundering, dividing) it up in the shape of a manifold of objects that subsequently can be secured in their standing over against the representing agency, but through which objectness is also made to last, to endure, to live on. Representation accomplishes "the all-decisive work" (ibid.) through which modern theory corresponds in its own fashion to the real that offers itself to be arrested in securely standing objectivity. It is through representation and in the form of a representation that the modern real is made to linger and survive its presencing. It is as an entrapping representation that modern theory accomplishes the cor-respondence that lets the self-showing of the real as the factual and the objective stay alive in the diversity of objects arrested in representation.
81. As we have seen, in translating *theorein* into *contemplari*, the Romans brought out a feature that had already been latently present in Greek thought, namely, the feature of a looking-at that sunders and departmentalizes. As the theory of the real, modern science, as Heidegger intimates, is precisely such a bringing of what presences in objectness to a stand in distinction from other areas of objectness that are secured as well in what he calls "[e]ntrapping representation [*nachstellende Vorstellen*]" (Heidegger, *The Question Concerning Technology*, p. 168). Such departmentalization of knowledge is not accidental; it is the direct consequence of a conception of the real that rests on objectness. For reasons of time and space, I will not take up here Heidegger's elaborations on what this inevitable departmentalization of the sciences brings with it, namely, the area-character of all

objectness, specialization of research, the departmentalization of the sciences, the priority of methodology, and so forth.

82. Heidegger, *The Question Concerning Technology*, p. 171.
83. Ibid.
84. Ibid., p. 172.
85. Ibid.
86. Ibid., pp. 172–173.
87. Ibid., p. 173.
88. Ibid. (translation modified)
89. Ibid.
90. Ibid., p. 174.
91. Ibid.
92. Ibid.
93. Ibid., p. 175.
94. Ibid., p. 176.
95. Ibid., p. 156.
96. Ibid., p. 176.
97. Ibid., p. 176.
98. Ibid.
99. Ibid., p. 177.
100. Ibid. (translation modified)
101. Ibid.
102. Ibid., p. 178.
103. Ibid.
104. Ibid., p. 179.
105. Ibid.
106. Ibid.
107. Ibid. (translation modified)
108. Ibid.
109. For the concept of "Besinnung" as preparation, see also Ute Guzzoni, *Der andere Heidegger: Überlegungen zu seinem späteren Denken*, Freiburg: Karl Alber Verlag 2009, pp. 69–87.
110. See Johann Gottfried Herder, "Über den Ursprung der Sprache," in *Werke*, Vol. 2, ed. W. Pross, Darmstadt: Wissenschaftliche Buchgesellschaft, 1987, pp. 276–277.
111. Heidegger, *Besinnung*, pp. 49–50.
112. Ibid., p. 48.
113. Ibid.
114. Ibid., p. 47.
115. Ibid., p. 24.
116. In "The Age of the World Picture," a text from the same period as his reflections on *Besinnung*, Heidegger determines *Besinnung* from the start as a concern with Being: "the questioning belonging to reflection [*Besinnung*] never becomes either groundless or beyond all question, because, in anticipation, it questions concerning Being. Being is for it that which is most worthy of questioning. Reflection finds in Being its most extreme resistance, which constrains it to deal seriously with whatever is as the latter is brought into the light of its Being." (Heidegger, *The Question Concerning Technology*, p. 137)
117. Heidegger, *Besinnung*, p. 53.
118. Heidegger, *The Question Concerning Technology*, p. 179.
119. Ibid., p. 180.

120. Dirk Westerkamp, "Weg," in *Wörterbuch der philosophischen Metaphern*, ed. R. Konersmann, Darmstadt: Wissenschaftliche Buchgesellschaft, 2007, p. 541.
121. Heidegger, *The Question Concerning Technology*, p. 180.
122. Ibid.
123. Ibid.
124. Ibid., p. 182.
125. Ibid., p. 180.
126. Ibid., p. 181.
127. Ibid., p. 180.
128. Ibid.
129. Ibid., p. 181.
130. Ibid. (translation modified)
131. Ibid.
132. Ibid., pp. 181–182.
133. Ibid., p. 182 (translation modified).
134. Ibid.
135. Ibid., p. 157.
136. Ibid., p. 182 (translation modified).

Part 3

1. Hannah Arendt/Karl Jaspers, *Correspondence 1926–1969*, trans. R. and R. Kimber, New York: Harcourt Brace Jovanovich, 1992, p. 264.
2. Elisabeth Young-Bruehl, *Hannah Arendt: For Love of the World*, New Haven: Yale University Press, 1982, p. 352.
3. As Young-Bruehl recounts, after the publication of *The Origins of Totalitarianism*, Arendt began work on a study that was to be called "Totalitarian Elements of Marxism." It was conceived as a complement to the book on totalitarianism. She worked on this study between 1952 and 1956 but never completed it. Since *The Human Condition* came from the same train of thought, it is not certain that her evocation in 1955 of a book on political theories refers to that work at all. (See Young-Bruehl, *Hannah Arendt*, pp. 276–279.)
4. Ursula Ludz, "Hannah Arendts Pläne für eine 'Einführung in die Politik,'" in Hannah Arendt, *Was ist Politik?*, Munich: Piper Verlag, 2003, p. 148.
5. Arendt/Jaspers, *Correspondence 1926–1969*, p. 264.
6. Young-Bruehl, *Hannah Arendt*, p. 353.
7. Aristotle, *The Complete Works*, Vol. 2, ed. J. Barnes, Princeton: Princeton University Press, 1984, p. 2001.
8. Hannah Arendt, *Lectures on Kant's Political Philosophy*, Chicago: University of Chicago Press, 1982, p. 30.
9. Hannah Arendt, *The Human Condition*, Chicago: University of Chicago Press, 1958, p. 242. See also p. 52.
10. Hannah Arendt, *The Life of the Mind, One/Thinking*, New York: Harcourt Brace Jovanovich, 1978, p. 178.
11. Paul Ricœur, *Lectures 1: Autour du politique*, Paris: Editions du Seuil, 1991, p. 65.
12. Additional reasons for the radical fragility of *praxis* as opposed to *poiesis* are, as Jacques Taminiaux argues, its ambiguity, unpredictability, irreversibility, and individuation in plurality. (See Jacques Taminiaux, "La Réappropriation de l'*Ethique de Nicomaque*: poiesis et praxis dans l'articulation de l'ontologie fondamentale," in *Lectures de l'ontologie fondamentale: Essais sur*

Heidegger, Grenoble: Editions Jerôme Millon, 1989, p. 151.) Another reason for action's fragility is that an agent's intervention in the world is, in spite of its individuation, inevitably expropriated by all the others who are exposed to it.

13. Arendt, *The Life of the Mind, One/Thinking*, p. 79.

14. Since much of what follows concerns Arendt's attempt to develop in a debate with Kant a new conception of judgment, let me also point out that her understanding of plurality as a human condition is certainly also indebted to Kant. In his *Anthropology from a Pragmatic Point of View*, Kant writes: "The opposite of egoism can only be pluralism, that is, the way of thinking in which one is not concerned with oneself as the whole world, but rather regards and conducts oneself as a mere citizen of the world." (Immanuel Kant, *Anthropology, History, and Education*, eds. P. Guyer and A. W. Wood, Cambridge: Cambridge University Press, 2007, pp. 241–242)

15. In order to account for the *possibility* of the *bios politicos*, as understood by Arendt, and its distinction from biological life, the empirical/transcendental divide is no longer sufficient. The notion of an *empirical transcendental* could perhaps prove fruitful for exploring the specific, if not singular, mode of possibility that characterizes the political.

16. Jürgen Habermas, "Hannah Arendt: On the Concept of Power," in *Philosophical-Political Profiles*, trans. G. G. Lawrence, Cambridge, MA: MIT Press, 1988, pp. 178–179.

17. Ibid., p. 183.

18. Ibid., p. 175.

19. Jürgen Habermas, "Die Geschichte von den zwei Revolutionen," in *Philosophisch-politische Profile*, Frankfurt/Main: Suhrkamp Verlag, 1987, p. 226.

20. Habermas, "Hannah Arendt," p. 183.

21. Arendt, *The Human Condition*, p. 206.

22. Aristotle, *Nicomachean Ethics*, 1175a12.

Chapter 7

1. Hannah Arendt, *Denktagebuch*, Vol. 1 (1950–1973), eds. U. Ludz and I. Nordmann, Munich: Piper Verlag, 2003, p. 569. Arendt's characterization of determining judgment as rooted in the solitary self's experience and of reflective judgment as witness to the self's relation to others does not do justice to Kant's understanding of theoretical cognition. From "The Canon of Pure Reason" of the *Critique of Pure Reason*, it is clear that, in order to make a truth claim, a cognitive, that is, determined, judgment must also seek the assent of the whole community of scientific inquirers. See, in particular, Rudolf A. Makkreel, *Orientation & Judgment in Hermeneutics*, Chicago: Chicago University Press, 2015, pp. 84–92.

2. Ibid., p. 570.

3. Ibid., p. 578 (see also p. 583).

4. Ibid., p. 573.

5. Ibid., p. 572.

6. Hannah Arendt, *The Human Condition*, Chicago: University of Chicago Press, 1958, p. 7.

7. Arendt, *The Human Condition*, p. 52. The epithet "artificial" characterizing the world created through work is even more called for in the case of public life and the world of action. Speaking of the friendship between husband and wife, Aristotle writes, for example, that "man is by nature a pairing creature even more than he is a political creature, inasmuch as the family is an earlier and more fundamental institution than the State, and the procreation of offspring a more general characteristic of the animal creation." (Aristotle, *Nicomachean Ethics*, trans. H. Rackham, Cambridge, MA: Harvard University Press, 1934, p. 503.)

8. Hannah Arendt, *Between Past and Future. Eight Exercises in Political Thought*, Enlarged Edition, Harmondsworth, Middlesex: Penguin Books, 1968, p. 210.

9. Arendt, *The Human Condition*, p. 52.

10. Ibid., p. 7.

11. Ibid., p. 175.

12. Aristotle, *The Complete Works*, ed. J. Barnes, Princeton: Princeton University Press, 1984, p. 2001.

13. "Natality" comes from the Latin *natio*, "being born, birth," but, in her German writings, Arendt also employs the terms *Gebürtigkeit* or *Gebürtlichkeit*. In ordinary German, only the adjective *gebürtig* is in use; it means being born in a specific place and, therefore, being a native from there. *Gebürtig* in the sense of "natality" is used by Heidegger in chapter 72 of *Being and Time* when he speaks of Dasein's being toward its beginning. It follows that, rather than a critical response to Heidegger's analysis of *Dasein*, Arendt's theory of natality is indebted to *Being and Time*, where Heidegger holds that factical Dasein exists not only toward death but also in relation to its birth. In the chapter in question, Heidegger admits that the explication of Dasein in terms of its Being-towards-death has been "'one-sided'" and has to be completed by Dasein's "Being-towards-the-beginning." He writes: "*Factical* Dasein exists as born [*existiert gebürtig*]; and, as born, it is already dying [*gebürtig stirbt es*], in the sense of Being-towards-death. As long as Dasein factically exists, both 'ends' and their 'between' *are*, and they *are* in the only way which is possible on the basis of Dasein's Being as care." (Martin Heidegger, *Being and Time*, trans. J. Macquarie and E. Robinson, New York: Harper & Row, 1962, p. 426.) However, Arendt's theory of natality is distinguished from Heidegger's in that the "between" that according to Heidegger is opened up between birth and death in which Dasein's "occurrence [Geschehen]" occurs as the ontological condition of historicity is, for Arendt, decidedly the public and political realm of action (ibid., p. 427; translation modified).

14. See for instance Hannah Arendt, *The Life of the Mind*, Vol. 2, *Willing*, New York: Harcourt Brace Jovanovich, 1978, pp. 10–110, 217. For an excellent discussion of the genesis of Arendt's notion of natality, see Miguel Vatter, "Natality and Biopolitics in Hannah Arendt," in *Revista de Ciencia Politica*, 26, 2, 2006, pp. 137–143. However, Vatter emphasizes the Augustinian sources of Arendt's notion of natality in the spirit of Carl Schmitt's assertion that all political categories are secularized theological categories in order to be able to argue for a theological foundation of this concept throughout her work. As a result, the overwhelming Greek background of Arendt's understanding of the political, the public, and the worldly gets short shrift, and the difference between the *bios politicos* and *zoe*, biological animal life, is overlooked for the benefit of a conception of natality that refers to a difference within biological life itself. In this context, the human being as a biological animal is essentially a created being. Vatter thus construes natality as the difference that the politicization of *zoe* brings about within *zoe* itself. As a result, political life becomes a form of secularized creatural life. Without engaging here in a search for influences that might have shaped Arendt's understanding of natality, should one not instead explore the intersections that might exist between the concept of natality and, for instance, Edmund Husserl's conception in the *Cartesian Meditations* (1931) of the alter ego as not only another ego distinct from me but also another absolute origin of the world? Indeed, natality also refers to the fact that every human being is a new beginning not only within the world but also, as we will see, of the world. Undoubtedly, for Arendt the human being is not a new beginning in that he is a transcendental other but, rather, on the basis that his factual appearance in the world common to all is already the event of something new. Another possible work to contextualize Arendt's theory of natality could be *The Nature of Sympathy* from 1913, in which Max Scheler speaks of the life of the human being as "in every case a *new and original manifestation* of universal life itself" and of the "unfailingly new and unprecedented *miracle* of man's first beginning in birth." (Max Scheler, *The Nature of Sympathy*, trans. P. Heath, London: Routledge & Kegan Paul, 1954, pp. 120, 126.)

15. Arendt, *The Human Condition*, p. 247.

16. Ibid., p. 247. Only after the completion of this book did I come across the remarkable essay on "The Survivor" by Jean-François Lyotard, who argues that Arendt's notion of natality and beginning might still be of the order of "humanistic, salvationist thinking." Lyotard's question in this essay is "whether 'birth' (the ability to judge, the vocation to begin) makes 'administered life' just a survival in comparison with the true life of the soul. I wonder if, from this still possible miracle, we can expect any alternative to the system." (Jean-François Lyotard, "The Survivor," in *Toward the Postmodern*, eds. E. Harvey and M. S. Roberts, New Jersey: Humanities Press, 1993, pp. 152, 162.)

17. In the same way as Hegel, who writes that "[i]t is not Man that exists, but the specific individual" (Georg Wilhelm Friedrich Hegel, *Introduction to the Philosophy of History*, trans. L. Rauch, Indianapolis: Hackett, 1988, pp. 26–27), Hannah Arendt too repeatedly remarks that "men, not Man, live on the earth and inhabit the world." (Arendt, *The Human Condition*, p. 7.)

18. Natality is thus the ontological condition for beginning a new series from scratch; it is, in short, another name for the human being's freedom. In this context, it might be interesting to confront Arendt's thought on nativity with Kant's elaborations on absolute causality in his discussion of the third antinomy of reason. According to Kant, the "faculty of beginning a series of successive things or states *from itself*" is a faculty of the acting subject solely insofar as he or she is an intelligible subject. It is "a merely intelligible faculty" that, unlike the faculties of the empirical subject, has "to be declared free of all influences and determination by appearances." Kant writes that only with respect to such an intelligible or noumenal subject can one "say quite correctly that it begins its effects in the sensible world *from itself*, without its action beginning *in itself*." (Immanuel Kant, *Critique of Pure Reason*, trans. P. Guyer and A. W. Wood, Cambridge: Cambridge University Press, 1998, pp. 486, 542, 537.) However, natality, the power to begin something new, is in Arendt the result of the empirical human being's appearance in the space of appearances.

19. Arendt, *The Human Condition*, p. 176. The category of natality has nothing to do with childbearing and giving birth. The male/female distinction is just one of the infinitely plural differences that come into the world with each newcomer as a *new* beginning. In fact, to understand natality as a natural phenomenon is to uncritically subscribe to the fourth version of immortality (and mortality) on which the thought of natality is based in the modern age when the common world of the polis is gone, namely, the immortality of species life, and which, as Anne O'Byrne has shown, is clearly distinct from the three other versions that Arendt distinguishes, natality premised on political immortality in Periclean Athens, philosophical immortality (based on the soul's affinity with what is not of this world, i.e., the transcendental realm), and Christian individual immortality promised by God. (See Anne O'Byrne, *Natality and Finitude*, Bloomington: Indiana University Press, 2000, pp. 78–106.)

20. Although Julia Kristeva explicitly acknowledges the nonbiological nature of natality, she still links what Arendt calls "the miracle of birth" to motherhood whose place, for Arendt, is clearly not the agora but, rather, the private realm. Does Kristeva, then, surreptitiously reintroduce the biological into Arendt's political conception of natality? To seek to free motherhood from the private sphere against the odds of what has been and still is a politically highly charged concept might have some merit. I mention only its history in national socialism and, in recent developments, in the more moderate Islamic world in which "motherhood" (a concept that, in Recep Tayyip Erdogan's words, feminists don't understand) serves not only to put women back to the hearth where by nature they supposedly belong but also to exclude them from the public space that is by definition male centered (Ceylan Yeginsu, "Turkey's President Accuses Advocates of Birth Control of Being Traitors," *New York Times*, December 22, 2014, p. A8). But the attempt to free motherhood cannot be accomplished by legitimizing it through a recourse to Arendt's concept of natality without stripping it entirely of its fundamental political significance. When Kristeva claims "that life as Arendt understands the term, is either a feminine life or nothing at all," it is difficult to avoid the conclusion

of a naturalization and biologization of life. Even when she defines the love involved in motherhood as love "for the ordinary life" and the relation in ordinary life to the Other, such life might not be the same as the "'survival of the species,'" but it cannot therefore be identified with what Arendt terms 'life.' For Arendt, such life is not political but an extension, however important, of the private sphere—the life with friends, for examples. (See Julia Kristeva, *Hannah Arendt*, trans. R. Guberman, New York: Columbia University Press, 2001, pp. 45–48.)

21. Arendt, *The Human Condition*, p. 9.

22. Ibid., p. 8. As Arendt suggests, each form of activity requires a "redemption" (in *Vita Activa*, she abandons the religious and theological terms and speaks of *Heil* (salvation) or *Heilmittel* (remedy). Whereas biological life is redeemed by the worldliness of work, the shortcomings of worldliness are remedied by action and speech. But the sphere of action also needs redemption. Here, however, redemption is not provided by way of a higher activity. "Here, the remedy against the irreversibility and unpredictability of the process started by acting does not arise out of another and possibly higher faculty, but is one of the potentialities of action itself. The possible redemption from the predicament of irreversibility [. . .] is the faculty of forgiving. The remedy for unpredictability, for the chaotic uncertainty of the future, is contained in the faculty to make and keep promises." (Arendt, *The Human Condition*, pp. 236–237.) Significantly enough, forgiving and promising are not Greek 'values.' They are Judeo-Christian corrections of the Greek conception of action. This should be kept in mind when later in this chapter we broach the issue of Arendt's so-called Graecomania. For a fine discussion of "redemption" in Arendt, see Jacques Taminiaux, "Athens and Rome," in *The Cambridge Companion to Hannah Arendt*, ed. D. Villa, Cambridge: Cambridge University Press, 2000, pp. 165–177.

23. Arendt, *The Human Condition*, p. 9.

24. In this context, it is important to keep in mind that Arendt consistently conceives of the process of production of a work of art in terms of work (*poiesis*). It is this characteristic, rather than the notion of creation, that links the work of art to the space of appearance that is the world.

25. Arendt, *The Human Condition*, p. 9.

26. Ibid., pp. 96–97. Even though she suggests that "natality, and not mortality, may be the central category of political, as distinguished from metaphysical, thought" (ibid., p. 9), that is, thought from antiquity to Heidegger, Arendt does not, as this reference demonstrates, simply replace the Heideggerian emphasis on death with an emphasis on birth, as sometimes has been claimed. Rather, both are understood as the condition of the human being to the extent that he or she authentically assumes the nonnatural possibility of dwelling in the world as characterized by publicness.

27. Hannah Arendt, *The Life of the Mind*, Vol. 1, *Thinking*, New York: Harcourt Brace Jovanovich, 1978, p. 19. Even though this chapter, entitled "Appearance," is Arendt's most elaborate treatment of the issue, it is also in several ways very problematic. For example, by following Portmann's contention that all animal life is involved in displaying itself to be seen or heard, the connection of the problematics of appearance to the political domain, which until then motivated Arendt's interest in "appearance," is put into question. From the perspective of *The Life of the Mind*, appearance has biological roots rather than being a distinctive feature of the human world as a public and political space.

28. Arendt, *The Life of the Mind*, Vol. 1, *Thinking*, p. 40.

29. Ibid., p. 19.

30. I do not agree with Philippe Lacoue-Labarthe's contention that Arendt's conception of the world as a space of appearance is "of Heideggerian inspiration," especially because Arendt's understanding of appearance places it in the world as a public space, for which Heidegger does not manifest much sympathy. (Philippe Lacoue-Labarthe, "Talks," *Diacritics*, Fall 1984, pp. 25–27.)

31. Arendt, *The Human Condition*, p. 52.

32. For the etymology of "öffentlich," see Friedrich Kluge, *Etymologisches Wörterbuch der deutschen Sprache*, ed. E. Seebold, Berlin: de Gruyter, 2002, p. 663.

33. Hannah Arendt, *The Promise of Politics*, ed. J. Kohn, New York: Schocken Books, 2005, p. 120.

34. Ibid., p. 123.

35. This citation is from Arendt's own translation of "The Crisis in Culture" into German. (Hannah Arendt, *Übungen im politischen Denken*, Vol. 1: *Zwischen Vergangenheit und Zukunft*, ed. U. Ludz, Munich: Piper, 2000, p. 296.)

36. Arendt, *The Promise of Politics*, p. 140.

37. Ibid., p. 123.

38. Ibid., p. 140. With Homer in mind, Arendt notes that the "public space does not become political until it is secured within a city, is bound, that is, to a concrete place that itself survives" the deeds and words of its agents, until it is bound, more specifically, to the polis. (Ibid., p. 123.)

39. Arendt, *The Promise of Politics*, p. 140. A space of assembly of the faithful might already be somewhat public, but it can never become a political space. See ibid., pp. 139–140.

40. Unlike philosophy's shunning of the sphere of appearance through a complete withdrawal from the domain of human affairs, early Christianity "did not turn away from politics in order to withdraw entirely from the realm of human affairs" but, rather, in order to devote itself to managing human affairs in a personal realm between one man and another. Yet, this "retreat from the public arena and avoid[ance of] its spotlight [*sich aus dem Öffentlichen und seinem Licht fernzuhalten*]" on the grounds that "to be seen and heard [while performing good deeds] inevitably takes on the glow of appearance in which all holiness [...] instantly becomes hypocrisy" amounts, all differences considered, to a condemnation of appearance as well. (Ibid., p. 137.)

41. Arendt, *The Human Condition*, pp. 167–168.

42. Hannah Arendt, *Vita Activa, oder vom tätigen Leben*, Munich: Piper Verlag, 1981, p. 202.

43. Arendt, *The Human Condition*, pp. 166–167.

44. Arendt, *Vita Activa*, p. 202.

45. Arendt, *The Human Condition*, p. 167.

46. Ibid., p. 173.

47. Ibid., pp. 168, 173.

48. Arendt, *Between Past and Future*, p. 209.

49. Ibid., p. 218.

50. Ibid., p. 218.

51. Ibid., p. 209.

52. Ibid., p. 209. As the example of the nomad shows, to have a tent to protect oneself against the elements is not yet to have a world as a home for the human being's dwelling on earth. A world requires a certain durability; it must outlast individual human beings and be distinct from the earth and its temporality. It comes into being only in resistance to the all-consuming life process through which the individual and the species biologically survive.

53. See, for instance, Hannah Arendt, *Lectures on Kant's Political Philosophy*, Chicago: University of Chicago Press, 1982, p. 30.

54. Arendt, *Between Past and Future*, p. 209. In *The Human Condition*, she writes: "Everything that is, must appear, and nothing can appear without a shape [*Gestalt*] of its own." (Arendt, *The Human Condition*, p. 173.)

55. Arendt, *Between Past and Future*, p. 210.

56. Ibid., p. 210.

57. Ibid., p. 210.

58. Ibid., p. 210. As is clear from the context, Arendt refers here to Kant's notion of disinterest in the first chapters on the "Analytic of the Beautiful," as well as to chapter 58, where he speaks of the "favor [*Gunst*] with which we take nature in and [which is not] a favor that it shows to us." (Kant, *Critique of the Power of Judgment*, trans. P. Guyer and E. Matthews, Cambridge: Cambridge University Press, 2000, p. 224.)

59. Arendt, *Between Past and Future*, p. 210.
60. Ibid., p. 222.
61. Ibid. p. 222.
62. Ibid., p. 223.
63. Arendt, *Übungen im politischen Denken*, Vol. 1, p. 300.
64. Ibid., p. 222.
65. Arendt, *Between Past and Future*, p. 218.
66. Arendt, *The Promise of Politics*, p. 164.
67. Arendt, *The Human Condition*, p. 26.
68. Arendt, *The Promise of Politics*, p. 166.
69. Ibid.
70. Ibid., p. 171.
71. Ibid., p. 21.
72. Arendt, *Übungen im politischen Denken*, Vol. 1, p. 287.
73. Arendt, *The Human Condition*, p. 37. Considering what has happened since the twentieth century, namely, the Holocaust and other crimes against humanity, it is far from certain that one can uphold this claim in this form, especially if life is also the foundation for the political.
74. Arendt, *Between Past and Future*, p. 215.
75. Ibid., p. 218.
76. Arendt, *Übungen im politischen Denken*, Vol. 1, p. 287; Hannah Arendt, "On Hannah Arendt," in *The Recovery of the Public World*, ed. M. A. Hill, New York: St. Martin's Press, 1979, p. 311.
77. Arendt, *Between Past and Future*, p. 218.
78. Ibid.
79. Arendt, *Between Past and Future*, p. 219.
80. Arendt, *Between Past and Future*, pp. 214–215. For a fine discussion of Arendt's commentary on the Periclean epigram, and her interpretation of the term *euteleia*, which "to the Hellenist [. . .] will seem no less forced than Heidegger's," see Barbara Cassin, "Greeks and Romans: Paradigms of the Past in Arendt and Heidegger," trans. J. Barnes, in *Sophistical Practice: Towards a Consistent Relativism*, Bronx, NY: Fordham University Press, 2014, p. 185.
81. Arendt, *Between Past and Future*, p. 214.
82. Arendt, *Between Past and Future*, p. 213.
83. Arendt, *Lectures on Kant's Political Philosophy*, p. 76.
84. Since the newcomers' words and deeds can claim uniqueness only on the condition that they are made at the appropriate time, it would be important to clarify the link between natality and time as *kairos*. For a discussion of how, in the realm of ever-changing appearances, *phronesis* implies an awareness of the right time in which to act in view of the good that is possible in such circumstances, see Pierre Aubenque, *La Prudence chez Aristote*, Paris: PUF, 1963, pp. 95–105.
85. Arendt, *Between Past and Future*, p. 242.
86. Ibid., p. 242. See also Arendt, *The Life of the Mind*, Vol. 1, pp. 95–97.
87. Arendt, *The Promise of Politics*, p. 14.
88. Hannah Arendt, *Lectures on Kant's Political Philosophy*, Chicago: University of Chicago Press, 1982, p. 55.
89. Arendt, *The Promise of Politics*, p. 29.
90. Ibid., p. 14; Arendt, *Lectures*, p. 56.
91. Arendt, *Lectures*, p. 56.
92. Arendt, *The Promise of Politics*, p. 14.
93. Arendt, *The Life of the Mind*, Vol. 1, p. 21.
94. Arendt, *The Promise of Politics*, p. 15.
95. Ibid., p. 14.

96. Ibid., p. 23.
97. Arendt, *The Human Condition*, p. 8.
98. Ibid., pp. 96–97.
99. Arendt, *The Promise of Politics*, p. 7.
100. Ibid., pp. 7–8.
101. Ibid., p. 34.
102. Ibid. p. 25.
103. Ibid.
104. Arendt, *Between Past and Future*, p. 259.
105. Arendt, *The Promise of Politics*, p. 26.
106. Arendt, *The Life of the Mind*, Vol. 1, p. 30.
107. Ibid., p. 212.
108. For a distinction of Arendt's and Heidegger's relationship to antiquity, see Cassin, "Greeks and Romans: Paradigms of the Past in Arendt and Heidegger," pp. 164–188.
109. Jacques Taminiaux, "Performativité et grécomanie?," in *Sillages Phénoménologiques: Auditeurs et lecteurs de Heidegger*, Brussels: Editions Ousia, 2002, p. 101. For what follows here, see also pp. 100–107.
110. Paul Ricœur, *Lectures 1: Autour du politique*, Paris: Seuil, 1991, p. 16.
111. Arendt, *The Human Condition*, pp. 84, 119–122.
112. Ibid., pp. 194–195.
113. Arendt, *The Promise of Politics*, p. 16.
114. Hannah Arendt, *Men in Dark Times*, New York: Harcourt Brace, 1993, p. 204.

Chapter 8

1. Hannah Arendt, "Understanding and Politics (The Difficulties of Understanding)," in *Essays in Understanding 1930–1954: Formation, Exile, and Totalitarianism*, ed. J. Kohn, New York: Schocken Books, 1994, p. 321.
2. Ibid.
3. Ibid., p. 308.
4. Hannah Arendt/Karl Jaspers, *Correspondence 1926–1969*, trans. Robert and Rita Kimber, New York: Harcourt Brace Jovanovich, 1992, p. 318. The reference is to Karl Jaspers's *Die grossen Philosophen*, Vol. 1, Munich: Piper Verlag, 1957. Arendt edited the part of Jaspers's work devoted to Kant, which was translated into English by R. Manheim in 1962. However, it should be remarked that Jaspers does not elaborate extensively on reflective judgment. Moreover, in the two pages devoted to the difference between determinate and reflective judgment, he is primarily interested in reflective judgment's accomplishment with respect to nature and its manifold laws, as well as its role of accounting in the shape of a teleological judgment for particular objects of nature that, by virtue of their inner organization, are contingent from the perspective of lawfulness, which is the hallmark of knowledge. Indeed, Jaspers barely mentions the judgment of taste, which for Arendt is the paradigm of reflective judgment. (Karl Jaspers, *Kant*, ed. H. Arendt, New York: Harcourt, Brace & World, 1962, pp. 60–63.)
5. Hannah Arendt, *Denktagebuch*, Vol. 1 (1950–1973), Munich: Piper Verlag, 2003, p. 569.
6. Hannah Arendt, *The Promise of Politics*, ed. J. Kohn, New York: Schocken Books, 2005, p. 101 (trans. mod.).
7. See, for example, Robert J. Dostal, "Judging Human Action: Arendt's Appropriation of Kant," in *Review of Metaphysics*, 37, 1984, pp. 725–755.
8. See, for example, Ronald Beiner's "Interpretative Essay," in Hannah Arendt, *Lectures on Kant's Political Philosophy*, Chicago: University of Chicago Press, 1982, pp. 89–156.

9. Hannah Arendt, "'What Remains? The Language Remains': A Conversation with Günter Gaus," in *Essays in Understanding 1930–1954*, p. 1.

10. However, in *The Life of the Mind*, Arendt turns away from the political experience that until then represented the main incentive for her work and offers a more philosophically inspired study. But whether or not it is the work of what she characterized as the professional philosopher is an altogether different question.

11. Hannah Arendt, *Essays in Understanding*, pp. 182–183.

12. Hannah Arendt, *The Life of the Mind: One/Thinking*, New York: Harcourt Brace Jovanovich, 1978, pp. 174–175.

13. Pierre Aubenque, *La Prudence chez Aristote*, Paris: PUF, 1963, pp. 23–24.

14. Ronald Beiner, "Judging in a World of Appearances: A Commentary on Hannah Arendt's Unwritten Finale," *History of Political Thought*, 1, 1980, p. 128.

15. For additional insights into the nature of judgment see, in particular, Arendt, *The Life of the Mind: One/Thinking*, p. 95.

16. Elisabeth Young-Bruehl, *Hannah Arendt: For Love of the World*, New Haven: Yale University Press, 1982, p. 327.

17. Ibid., p. 327.

18. Jacques Taminiaux, "Le temps et les tensions internes de la vie de l'esprit," in *Sillages phénoménologiques: Auditeurs et lecteurs de Heidegger*, Brussels: Editions Ousia, 2002, p. 111. For a somewhat different take on the subject of judgment in Arendt's *Life of the Mind* than the one I propose here, see pp. 128–130.

19. Hannah Arendt/Martin Heidegger, *Briefe 1925–1975 und andere Zeugnisse*, Frankfurt/Main: Klostermann, 1999, p. 208.

20. Arendt, *The Life of the Mind: One/Thinking*, p. 14.

21. Ibid.

22. Ibid.

23. Ibid., p. 58.

24. Ibid., p. 57. In the texts written in her native language, Arendt speaks of *Sinn*, or sense, rather than of *Bedeutung*, or meaning, which designates the referent of propositions.

25. Ibid., pp. 58–59.

26. Ibid., p. 59.

27. Ibid., p. 129.

28. Ibid., p. 173.

29. Ibid., 174.

30. Ibid., p. 175.

31. To my knowledge, the wind, as distinct from breath (*pneuma*), has not been a subject or image that has enjoyed special interest in Western philosophical thought. In Japanese and Chinese thought, by contrast, it plays a significant role and has recently attracted the attention of the phenomenologist. See, in particular, Tadashi Ogawa, "Qui and Phenomenology of Wind," in *Continental Philosophy Review*, 31, 1998, pp. 321–335. In this context, let me also refer to Ryosuke Ohashi, "Der 'Wind' als Kulturbegriff in Japan," in *Japan im interkurellen Dialog*, Munich: Iudicium Verlag, 1999, pp. 23–39, who shows to what extent the figure of the wind is intertwined with the understanding of 'culture' in Japan, and how this figure can serve to mark an essential difference in the Japanese relation to nature as opposed to that of other cultures.

32. Arendt, *The Life of the Mind: One/Thinking*, p. 44.

33. Ibid., p. 106.

34. Ibid., p. 174. See also Xenophon, *Memorabilia*, trans. A. L. Bonnette, Ithaca: Cornell University Press, 1994, p. 127.

35. Arendt, *The Life of the Mind: One/Thinking*, p. 174.

36. Ibid. See also Martin Heidegger, *What Is Called Thinking?*, trans. J. Glenn Gray, New York: Harper & Row, 1986, p. 17.
37. Arendt, *The Life of the Mind: One/Thinking*, p. 174.
38. Ibid., p. 175.
39. Ibid., p. 174.
40. Aristotle, *The Complete Works*, Vol. 1, ed. J. Barnes, Princeton: Princeton University Press, 1984, p. 570; Aristotle, *Meteologica*, trans. H. D. P. Lee, Cambridge, MA: Harvard University Press, 1962, p. 91. A similar point is made in "Movement of Animals" when Aristotle writes that painters paint Boreas as "sending the breath out from himself" (Aristotle, *The Complete Works*, p. 1088).
41. Hegel uses the image of the wind to illustrate the invigorating powers of war that prevent a people from languishing and corruption. See Georg Wilhelm Friedrich Hegel, "Uber die wissenschaftlichen Behandlungsarten des Naturrechts . . . ," in *Werke in zwanzig Bänden*, Vol. 2 (*Jenaer Schriften*), Frankfurt/Main: Suhrkamp Verlag, 1970, p. 482.
42. Arendt, *The Life of the Mind: One/Thinking*, p. 63.
43. Ibid., p. 176.
44. Ibid.
45. Ibid., p. 70.
46. Ibid.
47. Ibid., p. 69.
48. Michael Denneny, "The Privilege of Ourselves: Hannah Arendt on Judgment," in *Hannah Arendt: The Recovery of the Public World*, ed. M. A. Hill, New York: St. Martin's Press, 1979, pp. 266 and 259.
49. Ibid., pp. 266, 260.
50. Arendt, *The Life of the Mind: One/Thinking*, p. 13.
51. Ibid., p. 92, emphasis mine.
52. Ibid., p. 192.
53. Ibid., pp. 192–193.
54. Ibid., p. 193.
55. Ibid., p. 95.
56. Ibid., p. 215.
57. Hannah Arendt, *Übungen im politischen Denken*, Vol. 1: *Zwischen Vergangenheit und Zukunft*, Munich: Piper Verlag, 2000, p. 299 (translation mine). (Hannah Arendt, *Between Past and Future: Eight Exercises in Political Thought*, Enlarged Edition, Harmondsworth, Middlesex, England: Penguin Books, 1987, p. 221.)
58. Arendt, *Lectures on Kant's Political Philosophy*, p. 10, emphasis mine.
59. Aubenque, *La Prudence chez Aristote*, p. 127.
60. Arendt, *The Life of the Mind: One/Thinking*, p. 215.
61. Ibid., p. 69 ("*brought together*" is emphasized by me). The most general expression that Kant uses for the relation between the powers involved in a judgment of taste is that of "holding together [*zusammenhalten*]." He writes that "the judgment of taste is merely contemplative, i.e., a judgment that, indifferent with regard to the existence of an object, merely connects its constitution together [*zusammenhält*] with the feeling of pleasure and displeasure." (Immanuel Kant, *Critique of the Power of Judgment*, trans. P. Guyer and E. Matthews, Cambridge: Cambridge University Press, 2000, p. 95.)
62. Arendt, *The Life of the Mind: One/Thinking*, p. 69.
63. Ibid.
64. Ibid., p. 193.
65. Ibid.
66. Ibid., p. 200.

67. Considering that particulars are conceptually linked to universals and, consequently, have always already been disincarnated by being related to, subsumed under, or, in the case of speculative logic, disincarnated by the universal that, in order to be truly universal, must in turn incarnate itself in particulars, Arendt has singulars in mind when she speaks of particulars. I thank Maud Meyzaud for having drawn my attention to a passage from *On Revolution* where, in the context of a comparison of Maximilien Robespierre with Fyodor Dostoyevsky's "The Grand Inquisitor," Arendt contrasts pity and compassion, arguing that pity knows only depersonalized sufferers, whereas compassion "can comprehend only the particular, but has no notion of the general and no capacity for generalization." Arendt, then writes: "To Dostoevski, the sign of Jesus's divinity clearly was his ability to have compassion with all men in their singularity, that is, without lumping them together into some such entity as one suffering mankind." (Hannah Arendt, *On Revolution*, Harmondsworth, England: Penguin Books, 1987, p. 85.) For a detailed discussion of the passage in question see Maud Meyzaud, *Die stumme Souveränität: Volk und Revolution bei Georg Büchner und Jules Michelet*, Munich: Fink, 2012, pp. 207–209.
68. Arendt, *The Life of the Mind: One/Thinking*, p. 200.
69. Ibid., p. 76.
70. Ibid., p. 88.
71. Ibid.
72. Ibid., p. 30.
73. Ibid., p. 177.

Chapter 9

1. Hannah Arendt, *The Promise of Politics*, ed. J. Kohn, New York: Schocken Books, 2005, p. 102 (translation modified). Since Arendt refers here to the use of the term "judgment" in (the German) language, it is a bit surprising, given that Kant's language is to a large extent based on legal terminology, that she does not point out that this term has, if not at first, a juridical sense. Although the notion of a 'determinant judgment' refers to cognitively predicative judgment, one should not lose sight of the fact that the way Arendt characterizes this meaning of judgment also has strong juridical connotations.
2. Ibid., p. 104.
3. Ibid., p. 103.
4. Ibid., p. 102.
5. Ibid., p. 104.
6. Hannah Arendt, *The Life of the Mind, One/Thinking*, New York: Harcourt Brace Jovanovich, 1978, p. 215.
7. Hannah Arendt, *Lectures on Kant's Political Philosophy*, Chicago: University of Chicago Press, 1982, p. 10.
8. Arendt, *The Life of the Mind*, p. 215.
9. Arendt, *Essays in Understanding*, p. 318.
10. Arendt, *Lectures on Kant's Political Philosophy*, p. 64.
11. Hannah Arendt, *Essays in Understanding, 1930–1954: Formation, Exile, and Totalitarianism*, ed. J. Kohn, New York: Schocken Books, 1994, p. 407.
12. Arendt, *Lectures on Kant's Political Philosophy*, pp. 66–67.
13. Wolfgang Wieland, *Urteil und Gefühl: Kants Theorie der Urteilskraft*, Göttingen: Vandenhoeck & Ruprecht, 2001, p. 218 (translation mine).
14. Ibid., p. 219.

15. Lyotard calls Arendt's reading of the Third Critique an anthropologization, and as regards her interpretation of the *sensus communis*, "an abusively sociologizing reading." (Jean-François Lyotard, "The Survivor," in *Toward the Postmodern*, eds. R. Harvey and M. S. Roberts, New Jersey: Humanities Press, 1993, p. 162.

16. Hannah Arendt, *Responsibility and Judgment*, New York: Schocken Books, 2003, p. 137.

17. Ibid., p. 189.

18. Ibid., pp. 188–189.

19. Immanuel Kant, *Critique of the Power of Judgment*, trans. P. Guyer and E. Matthews, Cambridge: Cambridge University Press, 2000, p. 167.

20. Hannah Arendt, *Between Past and Future: Eight Exercises in Political Thought*, Enlarged Edition, Harmondsworth, Middlesex: Penguin Books, 1968, p. 221.

21. The distinction in the *Critique of Pure Reason* between an '"apodictic' use of reason" in which "the universal is *in itself certain* and given, and only *judgment* is required for subsuming, and the particular is necessarily determined through it," and a merely hypothetical use in which "the universal is assumed only *problematically*, and it is a mere idea, the particular being certain," seems to prefigure the distinction between determinant and reflective judgment. (Immanuel Kant, *Critique of Pure Reason*, trans. P. Guyer and A. W. Wood, Cambridge: University of Cambridge Press, 1998, p. 592.) However, since this distinction between an apodictic and a hypothetical use of reason, which is made in the context of a discussion of the status of ideas, concerns their universality and their regulative function in bringing about systematic unity within a manifold of given particulars, i.e., particular cognitions of the understanding, this is a problematic entirely different from the one that the reflective judgment faces in the Third Critique.

22. Kant, *Critique of the Power of Judgment*, pp. 66–67.

23. Indeed, according to Kant, concepts as universal representations originate in reflection. Without reflection no discursive, i.e., conceptual, cognition, is possible. See also my *The Idea of Form: Rethinking Kant's Aesthetics*, Stanford: Stanford University Press, 2003, pp. 17–18.

24. Kant, *Critique of the Power of Judgment*, p. 66.

25. Arendt, *Between Past and Future*, p. 229. And yet, is to say *what is* not to make a cognitive judgment, which is syllogistic in nature?

26. At the end of her last lecture, however, when Arendt highlights the problematics of the exemplar, her talk about the universal as being contained within the particular not only becomes clear but also points in the direction of how to conceive of such a universal in the first place.

27. Arendt, *Lectures on Kant's Political Philosophy*, p. 83. And she continues: "In the schema, one actually 'perceives' some 'universal' in the particular" (ibid.).

28. Arendt, *The Life of the Mind*, p. 215.

29. Ibid.

30. Hannah Arendt, *Responsibility and Judgment*, New York: Schocken Books, 2003, pp. 188–189.

31. Friedrich Kluge, *Etymologisches Wörterbuch der deutschen Sprache*, ed. E. Seebold, Berlin: Walter de Gruyter, 2002, p. 896.

32. Kant, *Critique of the Power of Judgment*, p. 67.

33. Ibid., p. 70.

34. Ibid., p. 167.

35. Ibid.

36. Ibid., p. 70 (emphasis mine).

37. Arendt, *Responsibility and Judgment*, p. 137.

38. Kant, *Critique of the Power of Judgment*, p. 70.

39. Arendt, *Between Past and Future*, p. 221.

40. Arendt, *The Promise of Politics*, pp. 33, 168.

41. Ibid., p. 168.
42. Ibid.
43. Robert J. Dostal, "Judging Human Action: Arendt's Appropriation of Kant," *Review of Metaphysics*, 37, June 1984, pp. 725–755.
44. Kant, *Critique of the Power of Judgment*, p. 60.
45. See, for instance, Hannah Arendt, *The Human Condition*, Chicago: University of Chicago Press, 1958, p. 226, n. 66.
46. For the history of the term and, more generally, for a superb account of the notion of *phronesis*, I refer to Pierre Aubenque, *La Prudence chez Aristote*, Paris: PUF, 1963. By arguing that the notion of *phronesis* that Aristotle develops in his writings on ethics with recourse to its prephilosophical sense calls the finite human being back to his limits, Aubenque links this notion to the insights of Greek tragedy. Although the notion of *phronesis* as understanding and judging is, as Christian Meier has shown, already to be found in Aeschylus's *Eumenides*, Arendt does not take the meaning of the term that it has there into account, namely, according to Athena's *phronein*, assigning and guaranteeing to "everyone his proper place in the *polis*." (Christian Meier, *The Greek Discovery of Politics*, trans. D. McLintock, Cambridge, MA: Harvard University Press, 1990, pp. 115–116.)
47. Aubenque, *La Prudence chez Aristote*, p. 30. For an in-depth discussion of the cosmology and, more profoundly, the ontology of contingence and the fundamental unfinishedness of the world that, according to Aristotle, makes it possible for human beings to take initiatives at all in order to realize a bit of the Good (i.e., the human good) that the divinity was unable to introduce in it, which also subtends his conception of prudence, see pp. 64–95. Aubenque writes: "Prudence is the properly human substitute for a failing Providence" (p. 95).
48. Aristotle, *Nicomachean Ethics*, trans. H. Rackham, Cambridge, MA: Harvard University Press, 1934, p. 327.
49. Ibid., p. 335.
50. Ibid., pp. 343, 345.
51. Ibid., p. 345.
52. Ibid.
53. Aristotle writes that, if prudence is not the same thing as scientific knowledge, it is because "it apprehends ultimate particular things, since the thing to be done is an ultimate particular thing" (ibid., p. 351).
54. Ibid., p. 11.
55. Ibid., p. 337.
56. Ibid.
57. Ibid., p. 343.
58. Ibid., p. 345.
59. Aubenque writes that "for Aristotle prudence is never anything more than a last resort, the imperfect *substitute* for a wisdom more than human." But he also adds: "One cannot speak of an *ideal* of prudence in Aristotle, not even of a primacy of political life." (Aubenque, *La Prudence chez Aristote*, p. 19.)
60. See also Albrecht Wellmer, "Hannah Arendt on Judgment," in *Endspiele: Die unversöhnliche Moderne: Essays und Vorträge*, Frankfurt/Main: Suhrkamp Verlag, 1993, p. 309.
61. Barbara Cassin, "Greeks and Romans: Paradigms of the Past in Arendt and Heidegger," trans. J. Barnes, in *Sophistical Practice: Toward a Consistent Relativism*, Bronx, NY: Fordham University Press, 2014, p. 175.
62. Ibid., p. 178.
63. Aubenque, *La Prudence chez Aristote*, p. 111.
64. The very practice of deliberation emerges in Greece from the warrior class's egalitarian practice of making one's opinion or concern known regarding what kind of action to take by stepping

into the "middle" (*meson*) of the circle formed by the sitting soldiers. As Marcel Detienne notes: "Once he had withdrawn from the middle, the speaker became a private citizen again." The notion of the private, and its distinction from the public, reaches back to this practice. Detienne writes: "By distinguishing so clearly between public and private, and by opposing speech relating group interests to that of private matters, political thought expands a distinction that was fundamental to the deliberations of professional warriors." (Marcel Detienne, *The Masters of Truth in Archaic Greece*, trans. J. Lloyd, New York: Zone Books, 1996, p. 102 [translation modified].)

65. Aristotle, *Nicomachean Ethics*, p. 353.
66. Kant, *Critique of the Power of Judgment*, p. 167.
67. Ibid., p. 168.
68. Ibid., p. 167.
69. Ibid.
70. Ibid., p. 166.
71. Ibid., p. 167.
72. Ibid., p. 174.
73. Needless to say, the decision or choice (*prohairesis*) that follows deliberation also in principle takes place in no time.
74. Arendt, *Responsibility and Judgment*, p. 141.
75. Kant, *Critique of the Power of Judgment*, p. 100.
76. Arendt, *The Promise of Politics*, p. 18.
77. Arendt, *Lectures on Kant's Political Philosophy*, p. 76.
78. Ibid.
79. Ibid.
80. Ibid. Even though Arendt characterizes "purposiveness" as a less fruitful regulative idea for judging, by linking this idea in her interpretation to being at home in *this* world, judgment is implicitly shown to be the prerogative of a being that belongs to this world and no other, and the activity in question is a way of affirming it.
81. Ibid.
82. Kant, *Critique of Pure Reason*, p. 269.
83. Arendt, *Lectures on Kant's Political Philosophy*, p. 77.
84. Ibid.
85. See Irina Spiegel, *Die Urteilskraft bei Hannah Arendt*, Muenster: Lit Verlag, 2011, pp. 23–25, 148–160.
86. Arendt, *Lectures on Kant's Political Philosophy*, p. 76.
87. Dostal, "Judging Human Action," p. 740. Let me also note that Dostal rightly points out that, in her discussion of the involvement of the imagination in reflective judgment, Arendt completely ignores the relation of the imagination to the understanding and thus also, as I claim, to the concept to which, in a reflective judgment, one must ascend to be able to subsume the particular under it. (See also Frank Hermenau, *Urteilskraft als politisches Vermögen: Zu Hannah Arendts Theorie der Urteilskraft*, Lüneburg: zu Klampen Verlag, 1999, p. 57.) It is clear from her dismissive reference to this central concept of purposiveness that Arendt overlooks the para-epistemic importance of the aesthetic judgment on the beautiful of nature and mistakes purposiveness as a concept belonging to the teleological judgment. She does not recognize that in Kant the concept of purposiveness is precisely the concept to be found in the case of a particular object of nature for which the understanding cannot provide a concept.
88. Maurizio Passerin d'Entrèves, "Arendt's Theory of Judgment," in *The Cambridge Companion to Hannah Arendt*, ed. D. Villa, Cambridge: University of Cambridge Press, 2000, p. 248.
89. Arendt, *Between Past and Future*, p. 221.

90. Arendt, *Lectures on Kant's Political Philosophy*, p. 70. Let me also point out that Arendt takes no notice of Kant's hesitation when he calls the *sensus communis* a sense. See Kant, *Critique of the Power of Judgment*, pp. 173, 175.

91. Kant, *Critique of the Power of Judgment*, p. 173. See also p. 123, where Kant speaks of the *sensus communis* as "a merely ideal norm."

92. In *The Life of the Mind*, Arendt speaks with Thomas Aquinas of the *sensus communis* as a sixth sense, one that is "needed to keep my five senses together and guarantee that it is the same object that I see, touch, taste, smell, and hear." This sixth sense is no longer, as in her previous work, a sense that fits us into the world as a public and political open space but rather, since this sense's "corresponding worldly property is *realness*," one that fits us into the world as "physical appearance" (*The Life of the Mind, One/Thinking*, p. 50). Even though Arendt writes that "it is the sixth sense's function to fit us into the world of appearances and make us at home in the world given by our five senses" (p. 59), the world here is no longer to be understood primarily as the space of appearance in the sense we have discussed so far.

93. Hannah Arendt, *Übungen im politischen Denken*, Vol. 1: *Zwischen Vergangenheit und Zukunft*, Munich: Piper Verlag, 2000, p. 299 (translation mine).

94. Arendt, *Lectures on Kant's Political Philosophy*, p. 70.

95. Kant, *Critique of the Power of Judgment*, p. 173.

96. Ibid., p. 174.

97. Even in the case of the cognitive function of judgment, a supplementary reflective judgment that takes the whole of the scientific inquirers into account is necessary for it to be able to make truth claims. As shown by the distinction that Kant makes, in the "Canon of Pure Reason" of the *Critique of Pure Reason*, between cognition (*Erkenntnis*) and knowledge (*Wissen*), even theoretical cognition by way of a priori categorical understanding by an individual subject must be judged and confirmed in communication with the whole community of inquirers for it to be subjectively certain knowledge, that is, true knowledge. Rudolf A. Makkreel writes: "No matter how much objective meaning a cognitive claim may provide, it will not count as an actual truth claim until it is also supported by 'subjective causes in the mind of him who judges.' The cognitive function of judgment is to refer concepts to objects, but knowing also requires something more from the judging subject. [. . .] The final test for a truth claim will require the subject to reflect and consider the 'possibility of communicating it and finding it to be valid for every human being.' It is [only] through scientific communal agreement that we can attain the certainty that Kant assigns to knowledge." (Rudolf A. Makkreel, *Orientation & Judgment in Hermeneutics*, Chicago: University of Chicago Press, 2015, p. 87.)

98. See for instance, Arendt, *Between Past and Future*, p. 241; or Arendt, *Lectures on Kant's Political Philosophy*, p. 43.

99. Kant, *Critique of the Power of Judgment*, p. 174.

100. Ibid.

101. Ibid., p. 122.

102. Arendt, *Lectures on Kant's Political Philosophy*, p. 67.

103. Kant, *Critique of the Power of Judgment*, p. 174.

104. See, for instance, section 14 of the Third Critique.

105. Kant, *Critique of the Power of Judgment*, p. 175.

106. Ibid.

107. Ibid.

108. Arendt, *Lectures on Kant's Political Philosophy*, p. 70.

109. Ibid., p. 71. Arendt claims that, when it comes to cognition and truth, one does not need maxims. But what about the doctrine of the ideas in Kant's *Critique of Pure Reason*, which provides nothing less than maxims for cognition and cognitive truths in order to accomplish the greatest systematic unity possible?

110. Ibid.

111. It is true that Kant writes that "[i]*magination* is the faculty for representing an object even *without its presence* in intuition." (Kant, *Critique of Pure Reason*, p. 256.) However, this is imagination as a reproductive faculty, as opposed to imagination as the synthesizing faculty par excellence, which comprises productive and reproductive imagination. Productive imagination is required to prevent losing representations preceding a current representation, so that a whole representation can arise without which no cognition or experience is possible. More fundamentally, as a transcendental activity of the mind, the synthesis of reproduction is inseparable from the synthesis of all apprehension (see pp. 229–230). Let me add that Arendt's commentaries on the faculty of the imagination that take up the notion of the productive imagination involved in schematism, especially in the seminar notes that Ronald Beiner published as an appendix to the *Lectures on Kant's Political Philosophy*, are especially disappointing.

112. Arendt, *Lectures on Kant's Political Philosophy*, p. 66.

113. Ibid., p. 68.

114. Aristotle, *The Complete Works*, ed. J. Barnes, Princeton: University of Princeton Press, 1984, p. 690. See also Chiara Bottici, *Imaginal Politics: Images Beyond Imagination and the Imaginary*, New York: Columbia University Press, 2014, p. 19.

115. Arendt, *Lectures on Kant's Political Philosophy*, p. 69.

116. Kant, *Critique of the Power of Judgment*, p. 177.

117. Ibid., pp. 121–122.

118. Arendt, *Lectures on Kant's Political Philosophy*, p. 72.

119. Ibid.

120. Ibid.

121. Let me point out that the terms Arendt uses in English to convey Kant's expression of *ansinnen* and, in particular, *werben um* come from J. H. Bernard's translation of the *Critique of Judgment* (New York: Hafner, 1951).

122. Arendt, *Lectures on Kant's Political Philosophy*, p. 72.

123. Ibid., p. 72.

124. However, the Enlightenment thinker Kant would never have agreed to such an inference.

125. Arendt, *Between Past and Future*, p. 222.

126. Arendt, *The Promise of Politics*, p. 7.

127. Arendt, *Between Past and Future*, p. 222.

128. Arendt, *The Promise of Politics*, pp. 12–13.

129. Ibid., p. 13.

130. If Arendt connects the judgment of taste's solicitation of assent to the problematic of persuasion, it is on the basis of her contention of a proximity of aesthetic reflective judgment with political judgment. This contention enables her to argue that, through Kant's elaboration on the judgment of taste, one can rediscover a decisive aspect of political judgment of which political philosophy since the Greeks has lost sight.

131. Nor does Arendt give "purposiveness without purpose" much consideration.

132. Arendt, *Lectures on Kant's Political Philosophy*, p. 76.

133. Kant, *Critique of the Power of Judgment*, pp. 176–177.

134. Ibid., p. 177.

135. Ibid.

136. Ibid.

137. In section 42 of the Third Critique, "On the Intellectual Interest in the Beautiful," which Arendt does not include in her *Lectures*, Kant develops requirements that from a transcendental perspective allow one to speak of this original contract as an idea of reason.

138. Arendt, *Lectures on Kant's Political Philosophy*, pp. 73–74.

139. Ibid., p. 74.
140. Ibid.
141. Arendt, *The Promise of Politics*, p. 104.
142. Arendt, *Lectures on Kant's Political Philosophy*, p. 74.
143. Ibid.
144. Kant, *Critique of the Power of Judgment*, p. 177.
145. Arendt, *Lectures on Kant's Political Philosophy*, pp. 74–75.
146. Ibid., p. 75.
147. Ibid.
148. Wellmer, "Hannah Arendt on Judgment," pp. 314, 321.
149. Arendt, *The Life of the Mind*, p. 192.
150. Aristotle, *Nicomachean Ethics*, p. 337. See also Aristotle, *Metaphysics*, where he states: "that in which the end is present is an action. E.g. at the same time we are seeing and have seen, are understanding and have understood, are thinking and have thought." Aristotle, *The Complete Works*, Vol. 2, Princeton: Princeton University Press, 1984, p. 1656.
151. See Arendt, *The Promise of Politics*, p. 193–94.
152. Ibid., pp. 186–187 (translation modified).
153. Ibid., p. 190.
154. Ibid., p. 196 (translation modified).
155. Ibid., p. 187.

BIBLIOGRAPHY

Arendt, Hannah, *Between Past and Future: Eight Exercises in Political Thought*, Enlarged Edition, Harmondsworth, Middlesex: Penguin Books, 1968.
Arendt, Hannah, *Denktagebuch*, 2 vols., Munich: Piper Verlag, 2003.
Arendt, Hannah, *Essays in Understanding 1930–1954: Formation, Exile, and Totalitarianism*, ed. J. Kohn, New York: Schocken Books, 1994.
Arendt, Hannah, *The Human Condition*, Chicago: University of Chicago Press, 1958.
Arendt, Hannah, *Lectures on Kant's Political Philosophy*, Chicago: University of Chicago Press, 1982.
Arendt, Hannah, *The Life of the Mind, One/Thinking, Two/Willing*, New York: Harcourt Brace Jovanovich, 1978.
Arendt, Hannah, *Men in Dark Times*, New York: Harcourt Brace, 1993.
Arendt, Hannah, "On Hannah Arendt," in *The Recovery of the Public World*, ed. M. A. Hill, New York: St. Martin's Press, 1979, pp. 301–339.
Arendt, Hannah, *On Revolution*, Harmondsworth, England: Penguin Books, 1987.
Arendt, Hannah, *The Promise of Politics*, ed. J. Kohn, New York: Schocken Books, 2005.
Arendt, Hannah, *Responsibility and Judgment*, New York: Schocken Books, 2003.
Arendt, Hannah, *Übungen im politischen Denken*, Vol. 1: *Zwischen Vergangenheit und Zukunft*, ed. U. Ludz, Munich: Piper Verlag, 4, 2000.
Arendt, Hannah, *Vita Activa, oder vom tätigen Leben*, Munich: Piper Verlag, 1981.
Arendt, Hannah/Jaspers, Karl, *Correspondence 1926–1969*, trans. R. and R. Kimber, New York: Harcourt Brace Jovanovich, 1992.
Arendt, Hannah, and Martin Heidegger, *Briefe 1925–1975 und andere Zeugnisse*, Frankfurt/Main: Klostermann, 1999.
Aristotle, *The "Art" of Rhetoric*, trans. J. H. Freese, Cambridge, MA: Harvard University Press, 2006. (All page references in Chapters 1–3 text are to this edition.)
Aristotle, *The Complete Works*, ed. J. Barnes, Princeton: Princeton University Press, 1984.
Aristotle, *Meteologica*, trans. H. D. P. Lee, Cambridge, MA: Harvard University Press, 1962.
Aristotle, *Nicomachean Ethics*, trans. H. Rackham, Cambridge, MA: Harvard University Press, 1934.

Aristotle, *On Rhetoric: A Theory of Civic Discourse*, trans. George A. Kennedy, Oxford: Oxford University Press, 2007.

Aristote, *Rhétorique*, Vol. 1–3, trans. M. Dufour and A. Wartelle, Paris: Les Belles Lettres, 1960–1973.

Aubenque, Pierre, *La Prudence chez Aristote*, Paris: PUF, 1963.

Beiner, Ronald, "Interpretative Essay," in Hannah Arendt, *Lectures on Kant's Political Philosophy*, Chicago: University of Chicago Press, 1982, pp. 89–156.

Beiner, Ronald, "Judging in a World of Appearances: A Commentary on Hannah Arendt's Unwritten Finale," *History of Political Thought*, 1, 1980, pp. 117–135.

Bottici, Chiara, *Imaginal Politics: Images Beyond Imagination and the Imaginary*, New York: Columbia University Press, 2014.

Brunschwig, Jacques, "Introduction," Aristote, *Topiques I–IV*, Paris: Les Belles Lettres, 1967, pp. vii–cxlviii.

Brunschwig, Jacques, "Rhétorique et Dialectique, Rhétorique et Topiques," in *Aristotle's Rhetoric*, eds. D. J. Furley and A. Nehamas, Princeton: Princeton University Press, 1994, pp. 57–96.

Burkert, Walter, "STOIKHEION: Eine semasiologische Studie," *Philologus*, 103 (1959): 167–197.

Burnyeat, M. F., "Enthymeme: Aristotle on the Logic of Persuasion," in *Aristotle's Rhetoric: Philosophical Essays*, eds. D. J. Furley and A. Nehamas, Princeton: University of Princeton Press, 1994, pp. 3–55.

Cassin, Barbara, "Greeks and Romans: Paradigms of the Past in Arendt and Heidegger," trans. J. Barnes, in *Sophistical Practice: Towards a Consistent Relativism*, Bronx, NY: Fordham University Press, 2014, pp. 164–188.

Cope, E. M., *An Introduction to Aristotle's Rhetoric with Analysis Notes and Appendices*, London: Macmillan, 1867.

Denneny, Michael, "The Privilege of Ourselves: Hannah Arendt on Judgment," in *Hannah Arendt: The Recovery of the Public World*, ed. M. A. Hill, New York: St. Martin's Press, 1979, pp. 245–274.

Derrida, Jacques, "My Chances/*Mes chances*: A Rendezvous with Some Epicurean Stereophonies," in *Psyche: Inventions of the Other*, Vol. 1, eds. P. Kamuf and E. Rottenberg, Stanford: Stanford University Press, 2007, pp. 344–376.

Detienne, Marcel, *The Masters of Truth in Archaic Greece*, trans. J. Lloyd, New York: Zone Books, 1996.

Dostal, Robert J., "Judging Human Action: Arendt's Appropriation of Kant," *Review of Metaphysics*, 37, 1984, pp. 725–755.

Entrèves, Maurizio Passerin d', "Arendt's Theory of Judgment," in *The Cambridge Companion to Hannah Arendt*, ed. D. Villa, Cambridge: University of Cambridge Press, 2000, pp. 245–260.

Ernout, Alfred, and Antoine Meillet, *Dictionnaire étymologique de la langue latine*, Paris: Klincksieck, 2001.

Ferrari, G. R. F., *Listening to the Cicadas: A Study of Plato's "Phaedrus,"* Cambridge: Cambridge University Press, 1990.

Fortenbaugh, William W., "Aristotle's Rhetoric on Emotions," *Archiv für Geschichte der Philosophie*, 52, 1970, pp. 40–70.

Gasché, Rodolphe, *The Idea of Form: Rethinking Kant's Aesthetics*, Stanford: Stanford University Press, 2003.

Gasché, Rodolphe, "The Originary World of Tragedy," in *Europe, or the Infinite Task: A Study of a Philosophical Concept*, Stanford: Stanford University Press, 2009, pp. 144–207.
Gasché, Rodolphe, "Theatrum Theoreticum," in *The Honor of Thinking: Critique, Theory, Philosophy*, Stanford: Stanford University Press, 2007, pp. 188–208.
Grimaldi, William M. A., *Aristotle, Rhetoric I: A Commentary*, New York: Fordham University Press, 1980.
Grimaldi, William M. A., *Studies in the Philosophy of Aristotle's Rhetoric*, Wiesbaden: Franz Steiner Verlag, 1972.
Guzzoni, Ute, *Der andere Heidegger: Überlegungen zu seinem späteren Denken*, Freiburg: Verlag Karl Alber, 2009.
Habermas, Jürgen, "Hannah Arendt: On the Concept of Power," in *Philosophical-Political Profiles*, trans. G. G. Lawrence, Cambridge, MA: MIT Press, 1988, pp. 171–187.
Habermas, Jürgen, "Die Geschichte von den zwei Revolutionen," in *Philosophisch-politische Profile*, Frankfurt/Main: Suhrkamp Verlag, 1987, pp. 223–228.
Hegel, Georg Wilhelm Friedrich, *Introduction to the Philosophy of History*, trans. L. Rauch, Indianapolis: Hackett, 1988, pp. 2–27.
Hegel, Georg Wilhelm Friedrich, "Uber die wissenschaftlichen Behandlungsarten des Naturrechts, seine Stelle in der praktischen Philosophie und sein Verhältnis zu den positiven Rechtswissenschaften," in *Werke in zwanzig Bänden*, Vol. 2 (*Jenaer Schriften*), Frankfurt/Main: Suhrkamp Verlag, 1970.
Heidegger, Martin, *Aristotle's Metaphysics Θ 1–3: On the Essence and Actuality of Force*, trans. W. Brogan and P. Warnek, Bloomington: Indiana University Press, 1995.
Heidegger, Martin, *The Basic Concepts of Aristotelian Philosophy*, trans. Robert D. Metcalf and Mark B. Tanzer, Bloomington: Indiana University Press, 2009.
Heidegger, Martin, *Basic Writings*, ed. D. F. Krell, New York: Harper & Row, 1977.
Heidegger, Martin, *Being and Time*, trans. J. Macquarrie and E. Robinson, New York: Harper & Row; 1962. (All page references in Chapter 5 text are to the Harper & Row edition.)
Heidegger, Martin, *Being and Time*, trans. Joan Stambough, Albany: SUNY Press, 2010.
Heidegger, Martin, *Besinnung*, Gesamtausgabe, Vol. 66, Frankfurt/Main: Klostermann, 1997.
Heidegger, Martin, *Elucidations of Hölderlin's Poetry*, trans. K. Hoeller, Amherst, NY: Prometheus Books, 2000.
Heidegger, Martin, *Grundbegriffe der aristotelischen Philosophie*, Gesamtausgabe, Vol. 18, Frankfurt/Main: Klostermann, 2002.
Heidegger, Martin, *Nietzsche*, Vol. 1: *The Will to Power as Art*; Vol. 2: *The Eternal Recurrence of the Same*, trans. D. F. Krell, Harper, 1991.
Heidegger, Martin, *On the Way to Language*, trans. P. D. Hertz, San Francisco: Harper, 1971.
Heidegger, Martin, *Ontology: The Hermeneutics of Facticity*, trans. John van Buren, Bloomington: Indiana University Press, 1999.
Heidegger, Martin, *Parmenides*, trans. André Schuwer and Richard Rojcewicz, Bloomington: Indiana University Press, 1998.
Heidegger, Martin, *Pathmarks*, ed. William McNeill, trans. Frank A. Capuzzi. Cambridge: Cambridge University Press, 1998.
Heidegger, Martin, *The Question Concerning Technology and Other Essays*, trans. W. Lovitt, New York: Harper & Row, 1977.
Heidegger, Martin, *Towards the Definition of Philosophy*, trans. Ted Sadler, London: Althone Press, 2008.

Heidegger, Martin, *What Is Called Thinking?*, trans. J. Glenn Gray, New York: Harper & Row, 1986.

Heidegger, Martin, *Zur Bestimmung der Philosophie, Gesamtausgabe*, Vol. 56/57, Frankfurt/Main: Klostermann, 1987. (Abbreviated as BP with page references in Chapter 4 citations. All translations in Chapter 4 are mine.)

Herder, Johann Gottfried, "Über den Ursprung der Sprache," in *Werke*, Vol. 2, ed. W. Pross, Darmstadt: Wissenschaftliche Buchgesellschaft, 1987, pp. 251–399.

Hermenau, Frank, *Urteilskraft als politisches Vermögen: Zu Hannah Arendts Theorie der Urteilskraft*, Lüneburg: zu Klampen Verlag, 1999.

Herrmann, Friedrich-Wilhelm von, *Hermeneutische Phänomenologie des Daseins: Ein Kommentar zu "Sein und Zeit,"* Vol. 2, Frankfurt/Main: Klostermann, 2005.

Herodotus, *The History of Herodotus*, trans. G. Rawlinson, Vol. 1, New York: E. P. Dutton, 1936.

Jaspers, Karl, *Die grossen Philosophen*, Vol. 1, Munich: Piper Verlag, 1957.

Jaspers, Karl, *Kant*, ed. H. Arendt, New York: Harcourt, Brace & World, 1962.

Jullien, François, *De l'Universel, de l'uniforme, du commun, et du dialogue entre les cultures*, Paris: Fayard, 2008.

Kant, Immanuel, *Anthropology, History, and Education*, eds. P. Guyer and A. W. Wood, Cambridge: Cambridge University Press, 2007.

Kant, Immanuel, *Critique of Judgment*, trans. J. H. Bernard, New York: Hafner, 1951.

Kant, Immanuel, *Critique of the Power of Judgment*, trans. P. Guyer and E. Matthews, Cambridge: Cambridge University Press, 2000.

Kant, Immanuel, *Critique of Pure Reason*, trans. P. Guyer and A. W. Wood, Cambridge: Cambridge University Press, 1998.

Kant, Immanuel, *Religion and Rational Theology*, trans. A. W. Wood and G. di Giovanni, Cambridge: University of Cambridge Press, 1996.

Kisiel, Theodore, *The Genesis of Heidegger's Being & Time*, Berkeley, CA: University of California Press, 1995.

Kopperschmidt, Josef, "Heideggers Umweg in Platons Höhle oder: Über einige Irrationen in Heideggers Aristoteles-Vorlesung von 1924," in *Heidegger über Rhetorik*, ed. Josef Kopperschmidt, Munich: Wilhelm Fink, 2009, pp. 301–432.

Kluge, Friedrich, *Etymologisches Wörterbuch der deutschen Sprache*, ed. E. Seebold, Berlin: Walter de Gruyter, 2002.

Kluxen, Wolfgang, "Ancilla theologiae," in *Historisches Wörterbuch der Philosophie*, Vol. 1, ed. J. Ritter, Darmstadt: Wissenschaftliche Buchgesellschaft, 1971, pp. 294–295.

Kristeva, Julia, *Hannah Arendt*, trans. R. Guberman, New York: Columbia University Press, 2001.

Lacoue-Labarthe, Philippe, "Talks," *Diacritics* (Fall 1984), pp. 25–27.

Liddell, H. G., and R. Scott, *A Greek English Lexicon*, Oxford: Clarendon Press, 1968.

Lucrèce, *De la nature*, trans. H. Clouard, Paris: Garnier Flammarion, 1964.

Ludz, Ursula, "Hannah Arendts Pläne für eine 'Einführung in die Politik,'" in Hannah Arendt, *Was ist Politik?*, Munich: Piper Verlag, 2003, pp. 137–187.

Lyotard, Jean-François, "The Survivor," in *Toward the Postmodern*, eds. E. Harvey and M. S. Roberts, New Jersey: Humanities Press, 1993, pp. 144–163.

Makkreel, Rudolf A., *Orientation & Judgment in Hermeneutics*, Chicago: Chicago University Press, 2015.

McCabe, Mary Margaret, "Arguments in Context: Aristotle's Rhetoric," in *Aristotle's Rhetoric: Philosophical Essays*, eds. D. J. Furley and A. Nehemas, Princeton: Princeton University Press, 1994, pp. 129–165.
Meier, Christian, *The Greek Discovery of Politics*, trans. D. McLintock, Cambridge, MA: Harvard University Press, 1990.
Meyzaud, Maud, *Die stumme Souveränität: Volk und Revolution bei Georg Büchner und Jules Michelet*, Munich: Fink, 2012.
Most, Glenn W., "The Uses of *Endoxa*: Philosophy and Rhetoric in the *Rhetoric*," in *Aristotle's Rhetoric*, eds. D. J. Furley and A. Nehamas, Princeton: Princeton University Press, 1994, pp. 167–190.
O'Byrne, Anne, *Natality and Finitude*, Bloomington: Indiana University Press, 2000.
Ogawa, Tadashi, "Qui and Phenomenology of Wind," in *Continental Philosophy Review*, 31, 1998, pp. 321–335.
Ohashi, Ryosuki, "Der 'Wind' als Kulturbegriff in Japan," in *Japan im interkulturellen Dialog*, Munich: Iudicium Verlag, 1999, pp. 23–39.
Oksenberg Rorty, Amélie, "Structuring Rhetoric," in *Essays on Aristotle's Rhetoric*, ed. Amélie Oksenberg Rorty, Berkeley: University of California Press, 1996, pp. 1–33.
Peters, F. E., ed., *Greek Philosophical Terms: A Historical Lexicon*, New York: New York University Press, 1967.
Plato, *Collected Dialogues*, E. Hamilton and H. Cairns, Princeton: University of Princeton Press, 1980.
Ricœur, Paul, *Lectures 1: Autour du politique*, Paris: Editions du Seuil, 1991.
Ritter, J., and K. Gründer, eds., *Historisches Wörterbuch der Philosophie*, Vol. 1–13, Darmstadt: Wissenschaftliche Buchgesellschaft, 1998.
Ross, Sir David, *Aristotle*, London: Methuen, 1966.
Scheler, Max, *The Nature of Sympathy*, trans. P. Heath, London: Routledge & Kegan Paul, 1954.
Spiegel, Irina, *Die Urteilskraft bei Hannah Arendt*, Muenster: Lit Verlag, 2011.
Taminiaux, Jacques, "Athens and Rome," in *The Cambridge Companion to Hannah Arendt*, ed. D. Villa, Cambridge: Cambridge University Press, 2000, pp. 165–177.
Taminiaux, Jacques, "Performativité et grécomanie?," in *Sillages Phénoménologiques: Auditeurs et lecteurs de Heidegger*, Brussels: Editions Ousia, 2002, pp. 91–107.
Taminiaux, Jacques, "La Réappropriation de l'*Ethique de Nicomaque*: *poiesis* et *praxis* dans l'articulation de l'ontologie fondamentale," in *Lectures de l'ontologie fondamentale: Essais sur Heidegger*, Grenoble: Editions Jérôme Millon, 1989, pp. 147–189.
Taminiaux, Jacques, "Le temps et les tensions internes de la vie de l'esprit," in *Sillages phénoménologiques: Auditeurs et lecteurs de Heidegger*, Brussels: Editions Ousia, 2002, pp. 108–130.
Taminiaux, Jacques, *The Thracian Maid and the Professional Thinker: Arendt and Heidegger*, trans. M. Gendre, Albany, NY: SUNY Press, 1997.
Vatter, Miguel, "Natality and Biopolitics in Hannah Arendt," in *Revista de Ciencia Politica*, 26, 2, 2006, pp. 137–159.
Wellmer, Albrecht, "Hannah Arendt on Judgment," in *Endspiele: Die unversöhnliche Moderne. Essays und Vorträge*, Frankfurt/Main: Suhrkamp Verlag, 1993, pp. 309–332.
Westerkamp, Dirk, "Weg," in *Wörterbuch der philosophischen Metaphern*, ed. R. Konersmann, Darmstadt: Wissenschaftliche Buchgesellschaft, 2007, pp. 518–544.

Wieland, Wolfgang, *Urteil und Gefühl: Kants Theorie der Urteilskraft*, Göttingen: Vandenhoeck & Ruprecht, 2001.
Xenophon, *Memorabilia*, trans. A. L. Bonnette, Ithaca: Cornell University Press, 1994.
Young-Bruehl, Elisabeth, *Hannah Arendt: For Love of the World*, New Haven: Yale University Press, 1982.

INDEX

Achilles, 157–58
Aeschylus, 246n46
Aquinas, Thomas, 219, 248n92
Arendt, Hannah, 1–8, 137–222, 224n14, 234n3, 235n14–15, 235n1, 236n13–14, 237n16–20, 238n22, 238n24, 238n26–27, 239n35, 239n58, 240n80, 241n108, 241n4, 242n10, 242n18, 244n67, 244n1, 245n15, 245n26, 247n80, 247n87, 248n90, 248n92, 248n109, 249n111, 249n121, 249n130–31, 249n137
Aristotle, 1–63, 71, 113, 116, 139, 142–43, 147, 155, 160, 165, 172, 176, 178–79, 185, 192–94, 206, 209, 212, 221, 223n8, 224n2, 225n12, 225n5, 226n6, 227n24, 227n29, 231n37, 235n7, 243n40, 246n46–47, 246n53, 246n59, 248n90, 248n92, 248n109, 250n150
Athena, 246n46
Aubenque, Pierre, 8, 172, 195, 240n84, 246n46–47, 246n59
Augustine, Saint, 147, 236n14

Baumgarten, Alexander Gottfried, 179
Beiner, Ronald, 173, 249n111
Bergson, Henri, 65–66
Bloch, Ernst, 84
Brunschwig, Jacques, 15, 41
Burkert, Walter, 48, 54, 59, 61
Burnyeat, M. F., 27

Cassin, Barbara, 194, 240n80, 241n108
Cicero, 178
Cope, E. M., 11, 15, 21–22, 24, 26, 34, 39, 41, 47, 49, 56–58, 227n24

Damiani, Petrus, 1
Denneny, Michael, 177
Descartes, René, 65
Detienne, Marcel, 247n64
Diels, Hermann, 48
Dilthey, Wilhelm, 66
Dionysius of Syracuse, 39
Dostal, Robert J., 192, 200, 247n87
Dostoyevsky, Fyodor, 244n67

Empedocles, 53
Entrèves, Maurizio Passerin d', 200
Erdogan, Recep Tayyip, 237n20

Ferrari, G. R. F., 231n58
Fortenbaugh, William W., 29, 225n5

Gaus, Günter, 171
Gracián, Baltasar, 179
Grimaldi, William M. A., 17, 38, 49, 51–52, 54–57, 59–60, 227n29
Guzzoni, Ute, 68, 229n28, 233n109

Habermas, Jürgen, 142–43, 194
Hector, 157–58
Hegel, Georg Wilhelm Friedrich, 176, 237n17, 243n41
Heidegger, Martin, 1, 3–8, 10–12, 65–136, 151, 166–67, 172, 176–77, 223n8, 225n8, 228n11, 228n3–6, 229n28, 229n1, 230n7, 230n20, 230n36, 231n37, 231n50, 232n74, 232n80–81, 233n116, 236n13, 238n26, 238n30, 240n80, 241n108

257

Heraclitus, 126, 165
Herder, Johann Gottfried, 130
Herrmann, Friedrich Wilhelm von, 99
Herodotus, 5, 189, 223n10
Homer, 5, 159, 175, 195, 239n38
Husserl, Edmund, 73–74, 79, 88, 90, 100, 119, 150–51, 236n14

Isocrates, 41

Jaspers, Karl, 1–2, 137, 169–70, 172, 241n4
Jullien, François, 5

Kant, Immanuel, 1–2, 4, 139, 141, 145, 150, 154, 156, 159, 161, 169–172, 174–82, 184–92, 195–221, 225n8, 235n14, 235n1, 237n18, 239n58, 241n4, 243n61, 244n1, 245n23, 247n87, 248n90–91, 248n97, 249n111, 249n121, 249n124, 249n130, 249n137
Kennedy, George E., 16, 24, 26, 35, 46, 57, 226n14
Kisiel, Theodore, 228n1
Kopperschmidt, Josef, 223n8
Kristeva, Julia, 237n20

Lacoue-Labarthe, Philippe, 238n30
Lagercrantz, Otto, 48, 61
Lask, Emil, 94
Lucretius, 62
Ludz, Ursula, 137
Lyotard, Jean-François, 237n16, 245n15

Makkreel, Rudolf A., 235n1, 248n97
Meier, Christian, 246n46
Meier, Georg Friedrich, 179
Meyzaud, Maud, 244n67
Most, Glenn W., 21

Natorp, Paul, 66, 79–80
Nietzsche, Friedrich, 11, 146, 177

O'Byrne, Anne, 237n19
Ogawa, Tadashi, 242n31
Ohashi, Ryosuke, 242n31

Parmenides, 48, 117, 152, 165
Peisistratos, 39
Penelope, 182
Pericles, 159–60, 240n80
Peters, F. E., 48
Plato, 4–7, 9, 11, 14, 18–19, 29–30, 48–49, 54, 107, 115–16, 141, 148, 164–66, 171–72, 179, 192, 199, 212, 223n8, 227n21, 231n50, 231n58
Portmann, Adolf, 238n27
Pythagoras, 163

Rickert, Heinrich, 66, 75
Ricoeur, Paul, 140, 167
Robespierre, Maximilien, 244n67
Rorty, Amélie Oksenberg, 9, 21, 224n2
Ross, David, 10, 41

Scheler, Max, 236n14
Schmitt, Carl, 236n14
Shaftesbury, Earl of, 179
Simmel, Georg, 91
Socrates, 165, 175–77, 179, 195, 231n58
Solon, 223n10
Sophocles, 67, 176

Taminiaux, Jacques, 4, 167, 173, 223n8, 234n12, 238n22
Theagenes of Megara, 39
Thucydides, 159

Vatter, Miguel, 236n14

Wellmer, Albrecht, 219, 246n60
Westerkamp, Dirk, 131

Xenophon, 176, 242n34

Young-Bruehl, Elisabeth, 137–38, 173, 234n3

RODOLPHE GASCHÉ
studied philosophy in Munich, Berlin, and Paris. He holds an
M.A. and Ph.D. in philosophy from the Freie Universität Berlin
(Germany). His interests concern nineteenth- and twentieth-
century philosophical thought, with a specialization in German
Idealism and Romanticism, phenomenological, and post-
phenomenological thought. Rodolphe Gasché is Distinguished
Professor & Eugenio Donato Chair of Comparative Literature at
the University at Buffalo, State University of New York. Before
coming to Buffalo, he taught at the Freie Universität, Berlin and
the Johns Hopkins University.

www.ingramcontent.com/pod-product-compliance
Lightning Source LLC
Chambersburg PA
CBHW030616230426
43661CB00053B/2007